THE BEST BUSINESS S
OF THE YEAR: *2001 Editio..*

Andrew Leckey, nationally syndicated investment columnist for the Chicago Tribune Company, is also contributing editor of the Quicken.com financial Web site. He is a teaching fellow in Business Journalism at the Graduate School of Journalism of the University of California, Berkeley. Leckey was previously a financial anchor on the CNBC cable television network and TV reporter for the syndicated "Quicken.com Money Reports." He received the National Association of Investors Corporation's Distinguished Service Award in Investment Education. The latest of his six books is *The Lack of Money Is the Root of All Evil: Mark Twain's Timeless Wisdom on Money and Wealth for Today's Investor.*

Marshall Loeb, columnist and advisory board member for the CBS MarketWatch.com financial Web site, is also a commentator for the CBS Radio Network and the MarketWatch weekly television program. He previously served as the chief editor of *Money*, *Fortune*, and *Columbia Journalism Review*. He has received every major award in economic and financial journalism, including the Gerald M. Loeb Award for Lifetime Achievement and the Society of American Business Editors and Writers Achievement Award. Loeb is a former president of the American Society of Magazine Editors. The most recent of the fourteen books he has written is *52 Weeks to Financial Fitness*.

THE BEST BUSINESS STORIES OF THE YEAR

2001 Edition

Edited by *Andrew Leckey*

with guest editor *Marshall Loeb*

VINTAGE BOOKS

A DIVISION OF RANDOM HOUSE, INC.

NEW YORK

A VINTAGE ORIGINAL, MARCH 2001

Copyright © 2001 by Andrew Leckey
Introduction copyright © 2001 by Marshall Loeb

Library of Congress Cataloging-in-Publication Data
The best business stories of the year : 2001 edition / edited by Andrew Leckey, with guest editor Marshall Loeb.
p.   cm.
ISBN 0-375-72500-8 (trade paper : alk. paper)
1. Business. 2. Businesspeople. I. Leckey, Andrew. II. Loeb, Marshall.
HF1008 .B47 2001
070.4'49650—dc21   00-47707

Book design by Christopher M. Zucker

www.vintagebooks.com

Printed in the United States of America
10   9   8   7   6   5   4   3   2   1

CONTENTS

FOREWORD

THESE ARE HEADY DAYS for business journalists. "The best time in history to be a business journalist" was the description in a *Fortune* editorial by managing editor John W. Huey Jr. We are experiencing "The Great American Business Journalist Shortage," according to a cover headline in the newsletter of the Society of American Business Editors and Writers.

Journalism graduates from the Class of 2000 with just a handful of business stories in their personal clippings found themselves picking and choosing among numerous good-paying jobs, a phenomenon I observed firsthand with my own Business Journalism students at the Graduate School of Journalism at the University of California, Berkeley. For business journalists already employed, fierce talent raids by rival news organizations have become commonplace.

This explosion of coverage, ignited by the dot-com revolution and a worldwide fixation with all things stock-related, provides the backdrop for the first annual edition of *The Best Business Stories of the Year.* The new strength in business journalist numbers is impressive, as coverage grows dramatically through new publications, Web sites, and television programming. Much of this growth involves spot news coverage and the race to be first with a story, which is understandable because the success of companies, individual stocks, and the markets can literally turn on a dime (at least when a key earnings estimate is involved).

Yet the episodic nature of today's rush of coverage makes it more important than ever to take a deep breath, organize one's thoughts, and carefully craft the type of well-researched, intriguing stories that run a bit longer. They're pieces with the innovative leads and striking personalities that grab us, and the vivid word pictures that keep us reading to the very end. Stories of substance that make us stop and think are seldom the work of an enterprising reporter working alone, but are backed by solid editing and critical feedback from fellow staff members. They're articles in which an entire organization can take pride.

The goal of this anthology is to spotlight quality business stories and make them accessible to a wide range of readers, whether they're sophisticated or novices in finance. Few readers have the opportunity to regularly see all the business and general publications whose stories are included here. Besides looking through hundreds of articles in print and on Web sites, we consulted editors, writers, contest officials, and academics to seek additional recommendations. Their help was appreciated. We hope that with the publication of this first edition, more and more people will become aware of our intentions, and give us further suggestions so we can present as diverse a mix as possible each year. We also hope that many publications and Web sites that feature primarily short articles will try to expand to include more in-depth stories that could eventually find their way into our pages. We like the stories in this edition, and look forward to many more in the future.

Many thanks to Marshall Loeb, who as guest editor of the inaugural edition brought a wealth of suggestions and, of course, his sound editorial judgment. Spirited discussions leading to final selections were a delight, and this book is much richer due to the involvement of one of the most respected business journalists. Thanks also to Edward Kastenmeier, the editor of this project at Vintage Books, who immediately saw the potential in the series proposal and offered his enthusiasm and guidance on the way to publication.

The stories in *The Best Business Stories of the Year: 2001 Edition* were originally published between July 1, 1999 and June 30, 2000. Selections for each year's anthology will be made on this same "fiscal year" basis. Editors or writers who wish published or online business stories to be considered for next year's edition should send copies to Andrew Leckey, c/o *The Best Business Stories of the Year*, Vintage Books, 299 Park Avenue, New York, NY 10171.

—*Andrew Leckey*

INTRODUCTION

ONE OF THE GREAT THINGS about being an editor is that I'll never get a swelled head—because I'm constantly surrounded by people who are smarter than I.

That thought, which I've echoed to my wife and kids for years, came back to me as I read and judged the many finalists and close contenders for this enlightening and entertaining book. Time and again I found myself saying to myself, "Boy, I wish I could write like that!"

I also found myself moved or frightened or inspired or amused—or all of the above. Most important, I thought the stories held a mirror up to our times and revealed many of our hopes, visions, sins, fears, accomplishments. If this volume were buried in a time capsule and unearthed a century or two from now, I hope the readers would say, "Yes, that's how they were, way back in 2000, that's how those people lived and worked and dreamed."

In this book, you'll read about the fall of the mighty, ranging from what now seems like the inevitable crash of a young IPO jillionaire, to the ousting of one of America's most powerful bankers (John Reed), who was outflanked and outmaneuvered by his smooth partner (Sandy Weill). You'll learn of the widespread devastation caused by the decline of a celebrated corporation (Procter & Gamble) and by the accidental tainting of some lowly hot dogs.

You will be angered and aroused by the tale of how a cynical moneybags used his fatcat political contributions to alter U.S. trade policy. By contrast, you may well break out laughing, as I did, when you read about the plight of business frequent flyers, those Willy Lomans of the skyways, trapped without space enough to flip open their PCs on their airless nerd birds.

You'll be amused by the foibles and fancies (as well as some of the get-richer-and-richer tricks of the trade) of the super-wealthy, be they a falconeering Saudi prince or a bird-chasing Gotham greed king. You'll get behind closed doors and high walls to grab a voyeuristic view of the media-and-high-tech elite at work and play in a Sun Valley retreat; and to see what life is really like if you're a housemaid-for-hire (at little more than the minimum wage), cleaning up the messes left by the affluent.

You'll gain new insights into some of the earth-turning scientific advances of our time, notably cloning and unlocking the genome code. And you'll get some rare perspective on our latest upheaval—and how the information revolution relates to the industrial revolution—from Peter Drucker, who is the freshest 90-year-old you'll ever encounter.

If you are profoundly worried, as I am, about the plight of the have-nots in our society, you will have even more to be concerned about as you read of how low-wage workers are often denied the fringe benefits that many of us take for granted in our jobs; also how many people are down and out in Silicon Valley; and how hundreds of thousands of lower-income African-Americans are still paying more than other citizens for their life insurance.

But . . .

You also will come away stimulated and encouraged by the many stories here of human enterprise and bravery. These tales are told by journalists and other writers who not only burrow to the elusive bottom but also display style and grace and wit. They remind us that crusading, investigative reporting is alive and very well in business journalism. And that the whole field, for all its flaws, has never been better.

—*Marshall Loeb*

THE BEST BUSINESS STORIES OF THE YEAR: 2001 *Edition*

An entire city of confident Procter & Gamble shareholders was aghast when this supposedly defensive investment took an unexpected, dramatic tumble. Geri Willis of *SmartMoney* magazine, well-versed in how pervasive P&G is in its headquarters city, puts into human terms the financial loss and accompanying sense of betrayal felt by retirees and employees.

Gerri Willis

THE STOCK THAT ATE CINCINNATI

IF ANYTHING, DON APKING thought he might be erring on the side of caution. After all, the Procter & Gamble retiree is young—just 62—and along with his wife, a retired schoolteacher, he intends to enjoy a nice long retirement. That means he's going to need some real growth from his investments—the kind of growth that, for many investors, means tech stocks. But still, his Cisco Systems stake made him nervous. The stock had more than doubled in the past year. Its rich valuation made it vulnerable to any bad news.

His simple solution: He'd sell his shares of Cisco at $110 and put the proceeds into Procter & Gamble. True, that'd make him a little heavy in P&G stock. Its shares would represent a full 25 percent of his holdings. But the stock had been a strong performer for him over the 35 years he worked for the consumer-products giant, and better yet, it looked like a bargain, as its shares had recently slipped to $99 from an all-time high of $118. "Procter had been great," he says. "It had always been very stable."

But not this time. On the afternoon of March 7, less than two months after he dumped his Cisco stake, Apking came home from a round of golf and flipped on CNBC. What he saw nearly knocked him over. Procter & Gamble's stock had positively cratered. It had tumbled to $57, a fall of 35 percent from the previous day's close—and a decline of 52 percent from its high.

At first, says Apking, "I thought it was a typographical error." But then the reality began to sink in: It was no mistake. He was looking at a loss of seven figures. As Apking listened to the official explanation—there had been a surprise earnings warning, sparked by higher energy and material costs, inventory problems in Europe, increased competition abroad—he could feel his blood boiling. "That's B.S.," he says. "There is no way management should have been surprised. I would have fired the CFO the next day. Someone's head has to roll."

Rage against Procter & Gamble is something a lot of people are feeling right now. The stock was supposed to be a bulwark against the onslaught of crazy dot-com valuations, a defensive stock you could count on in good times and bad. Just the day before the earnings surprise, J.P. Morgan's U.S. equity strategist, Douglas Cliggott, had touted P&G shares in a report titled "Buy Some Staples, Sell Some Tech." And *Money* magazine, which had recommended P&G last year, cited a Banc of America Securities analyst and reassuringly wrote that "current shareholders can let their stomachs settle" in its March issue—just before the plunge.

In fact, P&G's stunning reversal came as a shock to even the most experienced Wall Street prognosticators. "Everyone got caught with their pants down," says First Call's Joe Cooper. Professional investors, among them Kemper Growth portfolio manager Valerie Malter, were quick to punish the stock. The earnings warning was the last straw for Malter, who sold a significant part of her fund's stake that morning. "Companies with a focused strategy, good management, and good fundamentals don't blow up," she says. "Companies shouldn't make promises they can't deliver on."

The Procter & Gamble meltdown is a stark reminder that no

stock is totally "safe," especially in a market like this one. Indeed, things are so high-strung, in the wake of the Internet correction and concerns about inflation, that even a slight earnings disappointment can translate into a massive selloff. The message for investors should be clear: diversify. Keeping a high percentage of your portfolio in any stock, or in any sector, is riskier now than ever. "We all take shortcuts in our thinking," says Ron Meier, a professor at the College for Financial Planning in Greenwood Village, Colorado, which trains certified financial advisers. "You say, 'I don't have to look at the financials, it's a big company, it pays a dividend and it's not a dot-com.' It seems safer. But there is no such thing as a safe stock."

Nowhere is the pain over Procter's misfortune being felt more severely than in Cincinnati. With a payroll of 15,000, P&G is the biggest private employer in town. (Worldwide, it employs 110,000.) Thousands more Procter retirees live in the area. And because those two groups together hold 20 percent of the company's stock, its blowup—from which it has since come back only 16.7 percent—has shaken the city's very foundations. Some even wonder if the stock's collapse might signal the start of a local recession.

When news of P&G's monumental fall first ripped through town, Cincinnati financial planner Michael Chasnoff fielded one panicked call after another: When would the stock come back? Should I sell? *Why did this happen?* For Chasnoff—who has spent much of his career advising his clients to diversify their portfolios, to not put so much into Procter stock—it didn't feel good to be right.

"Most of these people have 100 percent of their retirement money in P&G stock," he says. "The most recent decline was a reality check for a lot of employees. Now they realize that no investment is safe from a market decline."

Blame Procter's rigid retirement plan for much of the problem. That's because it requires workers to hold at least half of their money in P&G stock. There are no other stock investment options available, only a money-market fund, a bond fund, and an annuity. And the voluntary plan for retirees, Retirement Plus, has the same minimum Procter investment requirement: 50 percent. As it turned out, the retirement plan—a generous profit-sharing trust that has turned scores of workers into millionaires—became the so-called Proctoids' own worst enemy. (In typically efficient Procter style, the company reaped $46.8 million in tax savings from the plan last year.)

At the March monthly get-together of P&G retirees held at the Wigwam restaurant, no one could stop talking about the stock plunge. "People were extremely disturbed," says Robert G. Laughlin, 69, a Procter research chemist for 43 years until his retirement last October. "They were critical of [CEO Durk] Jager. These people weren't pleased with how upper management dealt with the press."

In the aftermath, shareholders from around the country have filed six separate lawsuits in U.S. District Court in Cincinnati. At stake is whether P&G broke securities laws by concealing adverse information about the company, misleading investors who bought the stock. They cite a January 26 press release from the company stating that management was "comfortable with the current range of analysts' estimates for fiscal year earnings" and upbeat comments from Procter CFO Clayton Daley at a March 1 consumer products conference hosted by Merrill Lynch.

"The CFO was saying how rosy everything looked," says John Halebian, one of the lawyers representing shareholders. "That guy should never have been that positive. You don't go out making statements that aren't true." P&G declines to comment on the lawsuits other than to say they are "without merit."

Don Apking disagrees. In fact, he's signed on to one of them. "As investors, we were misled," he says. "It was a tragedy."

When Ludmilla Tenkman's father retired from Procter & Gamble years ago, her mother took her aside and begged her never to sell the P&G stock she would someday inherit. "My mom and dad would never have dreamed of selling it," says Tenkman, 78. "Everybody said Procter stock was your lifeline." At its peak earlier this year, her stake was worth $1.6 million. She and her husband used the dividends to finance vacations or to help her children out with college fees, only occasionally selling small stakes. A few years ago, the two started giving away some of the stock to their five children and their spouses.

But when Tenkman's husband died last October, her household income took a dive. Tenkman went to see Michael Chasnoff, who told her she needed to diversify her holdings by selling off as much as 75 percent of her Procter stake. Tenkman's eldest daughter, Martha, and her husband were wary of this advice. It sounded too aggressive, too risky.

While the family was debating what to do, Procter's stock went into its nosedive, costing Tenkman more than $900,000. She swears she doesn't blame her kids for making her wait. She'll make do on Social Security and dividends, she insists. She'll cut back on her travel plans. But the one thing she really regrets, she says, is that for now, she's had to stop giving Procter stock to the kids.

Plenty of others in Cincinnati are tightening their belts. Ed Givens, a former P&G engineer who turned 55 in March and retired that month, had just bought his dream house—a $445,000, four-bedroom colonial in an upscale neighborhood—where he hoped to pursue his love of organic gardening.

By the time the stock dropped, he'd already closed on his new home. "We went out on a limb with this house," says Givens. "We've had to scale back. Some rooms won't get furnished. We'll cut back on travel. We wanted to do some significant things in terms of gifting for our children, but we'll wait. I have to lower my expectations a little bit."

As a result of the stock drop, Givens's portfolio plunged from a high of $3.5 million to $2.1 million. Lucky for him, he'd taken about a third of his nest egg out of Procter stock.

Some had it even worse. Robert Laughlin, the chemical engineer, lost several million dollars; he hadn't yet diversified any of his nest egg. "We were in the middle of that process when the bottom fell out of the stock," he explains. Laughlin, who holds a Ph.D. from Cornell and is an expert in an area called surfactants, dreamt of funding a chair at Cornell in his research specialty, but the stock's drop has "thrown a monkey wrench into that." He had planned to fund the cost—some $2.5 million—with some of his retirement money. He's still doing it, but now he'll pay over time and it'll take a larger proportion of his wealth.

For every retiree who will make do, however grudgingly, on less money, there's another who is nothing less than devastated. Roy Randall Sr. had every penny of his retirement account in Procter stock. "We thought of it as a lifetime guarantee," says the 56-year-old former pipe fitter. "I felt it was very safe."

Randall had fulfilled one of his retirement dreams with a $30,000, 19-foot, 200-horsepower Ranger bass boat to fish the lakes of Tennessee, Ohio, and Kentucky. In January he put down another $40,000 for a GMC Yukon XL to haul the boat with. He even planned a 13-day cruise in Alaska for his wife and himself with two other Procter retirees and their spouses.

But then his nearly $2 million nest egg dwindled to less than $1 million. "For all the years I've been with Procter, there were flat spots in my career, but the stock always went up," he says. "You always had faith in the stock because you'd seen other people retire and not change their lifestyle. This is a first. There is nothing you can do. It was very disappointing."

He canceled the Alaska trip and decided to take shorter and fewer trips with the boat. For now, he's stopped cashing in any of the stock to fund his living expenses and is surviving on the returns of a small amount of money he set aside in mutual funds in his wife's name. "I can't take that big of a loss," he says. "I need that stock as income for the rest of my life."

If the stock doesn't rebound by year's end, he'll have to retire from his retirement. "We're watching our pennies. I really don't want to go back to work," says Randall, who doesn't understand how the company's managers couldn't have seen trouble coming. Lifetime guarantee? Randall doesn't believe that anymore. "P&G

used to be a big family. You take care of them, they take care of you," he says. "Now it's a one-way street."

It's easy to see why the company inspired such loyalty. Ever since William Procter and James Gamble set up shop 163 years ago, using the grease and fat from Cincinnati's swine slaughterhouses to make candles and soap, P&G has been a major force in the city's growth. When the city—then known as "Porkopolis"—lost its standing as the pork-processing capital of the country, P&G was there, taking up the slack, hiring locals to make new products such as Dreft and, much later, Tide. During the Depression, its Ivorydale plant never shut down.

Yet at times the company's insular corporate culture verges on the paranoiac. When *Wall Street Journal* reporter Alecia Swasy wrote a series of stingingly critical articles on the company in 1991, P&G convinced Cincinnati police and the local prosecutor to obtain her phone records, thereby exposing all her sources for the story. *SmartMoney*'s repeated requests for interviews with senior executives, including CEO Durk Jager, were declined. In fact, analysts say the appearance of P&G's chief executive is rare at investor meetings. Employees, likewise, talk to the media only grudgingly, often out of fear for their jobs. And the company's intranet warns employees not to speak to anyone about the shareholder lawsuits.

All of which makes it even more remarkable that so many formerly loyal employees—such as Wilbur Yellin, a 67-year-old retiree—are speaking out now. Yellin lost 30 percent of his portfolio, and, like so many others, puts the blame for the stock catastrophe squarely on the CEO's shoulders. "Management screwed up," he says bluntly.

Yellin, a former chemist, also finds it hard to believe that the company didn't know earlier about its earnings shortfall. "This surprised most of us who had been in middle management," he says. "We know Procter manages costs very closely to keep budgets in line. The concern is that there are a lot of young managers who aren't watching their Ps and Qs."

But what really rattles Yellin is this: Not only did March's earnings warning come out of the blue, it also seemed to follow reassurances that the company was doing okay. Yellin remembers reading upbeat comments from the CEO on the company's Web site only weeks earlier. "It sounds like the left hand didn't know what the right hand was doing," he says.

Perhaps not. But one thing is indisputable: Both those hands belong to one man. Ever since being promoted to chief executive on January 1, 1999, the Netherlands-born Durk Jager, a 29-year veteran of the company, has been obsessed with jump-starting Procter's growth and bringing its single-digit annual revenue increases more into line with the Nasdaq's stratospheric numbers. Six months into the job, he detailed a six-year, $1.9 billion restructuring that would lighten the company's ranks by some 15,000 people and change the organizational structure from a geographic-based model to one built around products. Ultimate savings? Some $900 million. Jager described his plan, which he called Organization 2005, as "the most dramatic change to P&G's structure, work processes, and culture in the company's history."

Analysts agreed that change was overdue. Long regarded as one of the most innovative of brand developers and marketers, P&G had seen its flagship, Crest toothpaste, overtaken by Colgate; its high hopes for fat-substitute Olestra dashed; its Pampers disposable diapers losing market share. And the company has hardly been a model of innovation in recent years. (One former marketer says it took five years of testing to roll out Bounty paper napkins.) So after Jager made a series of much-criticized missteps—among them aborted attempts to acquire drugmakers American Home Products and Warner Lambert and a flirtation with buying Gillette, in addition to the surprise earnings warning—investors dumped shares like so many used Pampers. Since hitting $53.88 on March 10, a three-year low, the stock has made a modest comeback. But the consensus on the Street is that Procter stock won't be seeing its recent highs for a long time to come.

Recovering from the earnings surprise will be no mean feat,

says Andrew Shore, a consumer-products analyst at Deutsche Banc Alex Brown, who has covered Procter for 14 years. "It called into question every fundamental thing we knew about Procter. We started asking ourselves, 'How did this paradigm of excellence fail so badly?'" Shore says the problem with the consumer-products sector in general is that executives are too optimistic. It'll be tough for these companies to show the kinds of double-digit earnings gains that Wall Street is demanding. He believes that Procter can make the low end of its earnings-estimate range—growth of 11 to 13 percent a year. When asked if the stock is going to make it back to $118, he simply laughs.

What happens if P&G's stock suffers a prolonged downturn? The potential hometown impact is huge. According to a study by the University of Cincinnati, more than 40,000 jobs owe their existence to the fact that Procter makes its home there. It's responsible for total household earnings impact of $4.28 billion and total business sales of $1.3 billion.

Since the plunge, real estate sales planned by P&G executives or retired executives in Cincinnati's most expensive neighborhoods have slowed. "We've heard several stories about people at the higher end—the $1 million to $2 million home buyers—who decided to delay their plans indefinitely or wait another year," says Richard Bondie, a Fifth Third Bank senior vice president.

Charities and arts organizations were also stung. It's not just the prospect of dwindling donations: Many of these groups hold Procter stock themselves. Catholics United for the Poor, an organization that sponsors shelter and food programs, received a gift of $50,000 in P&G stock in December. "We decided to hold it a short period," recalls board member David Kent. "In the interim, it lost a third of its value." The Cincinnati Symphony Orchestra, the city's largest arts organization, with an endowment of $91 million, saw the value of its P&G stake fall "substantially," says the board's chairman, Pete Strange. "It's an important part of our investments," he says. "We have a significant position in Procter."

Yet there are still P&G loyalists everywhere. Many have been loading up on the stock in recent weeks. It's almost a civic duty. Mayor Charlie Luken, who picked up his small stake—40 shares for each of his three kids—after the 1987 crash, is still a booster, even though, he says, "I thought I had my daughter's last year of college paid for—now I've only got a semester." But he insists, "People remain confident about the company."

David Rice, 55, went to work for Procter just 18 months out of Harvard University's chemistry doctoral program. When he started seriously thinking about retirement a year ago, he decided to wait until he had completed a project at work. That delay cost him $1 million, solidifying his and his wife's decision not to buy a vacation home in Hilton Head, S.C. "We're not going to the poorhouse, but most of us retiring in the next year or two won't be living the lifestyle like we would have otherwise," he observes dryly.

When Procter announced its earnings shortfall, Rice decided to buy some more shares. "I didn't think the news was so terrible," he says. But this time the stock kept falling, all the way to $54. Yet, even as he approached retirement in late April, he wasn't planning to sell off his entire Procter stake. Instead, he figures he'll maintain as much as a quarter of his nest egg in the stock. "I have confidence the company will do well," he says.

It's precisely that attitude that troubles financial planner Michael Chasnoff. "My bet is that when P&G stock gets to $90, everyone will view it as a $125 stock again," he says. "The lesson will be quickly forgotten by many."

The loneliness of the long-distance flyer is a common ailment of today's global executives. Many quoted in this *Wired* magazine story by Warren Berger are no doubt still circling overhead. You can feel their pain, perhaps relive your own pain, and learn helpful tricks of the trade in this unique and lively story that chronicles airborne tedium, bad food, and coping.

Warren Berger

LIFE SUCKS AND THEN YOU FLY

IF HELL IS "the middle seat in the back row of a 757 with the smell of rancid lasagna wafting in the air"—as one frequent-flying Silicon Valley executive recently defined it—then Evan Orensten has at least managed to avoid hell today, what with his reserved aisle seat in front of the wing. Unfortunately, heaven is booked solid.

Orensten, an executive vice president at Razorfish, the hot Web design and consulting firm, has just learned that his Newark-to-London flight is packed, so there's no chance he can talk his way into a freebie upgrade to first class. Sure, he could simply pay more for a first-class ticket, but that usually isn't done at cash-burning yet conspicuously frugal startups like his. The high-tech nouveau riche still tend to fly coach because, as Excite cofounder Joe Kraus says, it's an acknowledgment that "we recently came from the garage and could just as easily go back." The bankers may pay for first class; so may the Microsoft guys who

13

haven't yet bought their own Gulfstreams. Everyone else strives to buy with the masses, get upgraded, and recline with the classes.

Today, there will be no miracles for Orensten, even though he's been known to cadge great seats by plying check-in attendants with Razorfish T-shirts, notepads, CDs, and compliments. ("I'm very good at kissing butt with these people," he admits.) The only other way up would be to cash in a few frequent-flier miles, but Orensten, 33, hoards those like a miser as he marches toward magical status in the 100K club—100,000 miles in the air for the year—which brings with it automatic upgrades and free tickets.

"It's all about the miles, and this isn't worth losing them," he says, smiling and stretching out in United's Red Carpet lounge, resting up for what lies ahead.

Here's what lies ahead: A 7:30 P.M. red-eye, which deposits Orensten in London at 7 A.M. local time, where he checks in to the Lufthansa lounge. He stays only two hours, long enough to stretch his coach-cramped legs, at which point a call reminds him to lurch onto another plane. At 11 A.M. he lifts off to Hamburg, where Razorfish has an office. The gods smile on him—he's upgraded to business class! But the seats aren't much bigger, and the only noticeable difference, he grumbles, is that "you get your mayonnaise sandwich on a plate instead of in a napkin." With the plane aloft somewhere over France, Orensten fires up his laptop and composes some e-mails detailing a few in-flight gripes.

"Movies on last night's flights: *You've Got Mail* (urgh), *Waking Ned Devine* (seen it at least five times) . . . Did not have my low-fat meal, so boycotted and didn't eat. Halfway into my chemically induced sleep I was forced to get up and let someone sit in the empty seat next to me because their video screen didn't work. I asked if they had to see *You've Got Mail* that badly. Decided that I much prefer the 9:30 P.M. flight on Virgin."

After a stay in Hamburg, Orensten flies to Stockholm for a business meeting. Then it's back to London. Then back to Hamburg. Then to Berlin, Frankfurt, New York, and home, which for Orensten is a relative term—that's where he lives only about 25 percent of the time. He has no wife or kids, and his friends are compartmentalized by city: the Paris group, the Hamburg gang, the New York crowd. In an e-mail, I suggest that this is an interesting way to live one's life. To which Orensten replies: "What life?"

Orensten is a "hyperflier," a relatively new species whose members spend more time aloft than aground. They're commonly found swirling in the realms of high-tech, finance, media, and consulting—all the brave-new-world industries that are raging with bull-market energy right now. The hyperfliers' destinations may differ, but their distinguishing characteristics are consistently the same. You can spot them in various ways:

They self-identify by the extent of their flying. Net design consultant Clement Mok is a 150K man, for instance, logging 150,000 miles a year as he crisscrosses the country. There are "200 day" people who fly that many days per year. Hank Nothhaft, chair of Concentric Network, can top all that. He's a three-million-mile guy—three million being his lifetime total of miles logged on American Airlines alone.

They speak in a coded language that has evolved in airport culture. "I'm going from GSO into BOS," reads an e-mail from Nick Shelness, the chief technology officer at Lotus, "then flying out of BOS terminal E on a 20:20 BA to LHR."

They know more than any healthy person should about the legroom and seat pitch on a 757 as compared with, say, a DC-10. "I won't fly a 757 except under extreme duress," says Jeff Drazan, a VC with Sierra Ventures. (He means it, too: To avoid the relatively cramped 757s, he'll switch airlines if necessary.)

They're obsessed with packing efficiently and will go to ingenious measures to travel light—like FedExing clean shirts to their next destination. "Cuts down on baggage," says Nicholas Negroponte of the MIT Media Lab, who pioneered this technique.

They describe outrageous itineraries with nonchalance. "I departed from California to London," says Diane Fraiman, marketing VP at Informix, "then on to Johannesburg, then to Nelspruit—where they have the white rhinos!—then connected in Cape Town, back to Johannesburg, on to London, ending up in San Francisco. A typical week." And they're proud. They share such details expecting to earn admiration, awe, even sympathy. "Telling people how much you fly is a badge of honor," says Vickie Abrahamson, a trend analyst with Iconoculture. "It shows how much you can take."

Though their ranks are constantly swelling, they are, for the most part, solitary. "There is no 'community' in the air," says Larry Downes, an e-commerce expert and author. "Those of us who fly regularly have the kindness to leave each other alone—one less chance for a bad interaction."

Often, they don't look so good. "We know each other by sight," Downes says. "The pallid complexion, red watery eyes, deeply furrowed brow, the look of hunger for home, for edible food and a sleepable bed."

They are everywhere . . . and nowhere. "I don't know what time zone I live in," says Informix CEO Bob Finocchio, a 200K man. "I think I live in some average time zone between New York and Chicago . . . maybe Pittsburgh. I don't know."

It wasn't supposed to be this way. Technology was going to shrink and link the world, and in so doing, render one's physical location practically irrelevant. That's why, just a few years ago, the airlines were fretting about the growth of the Internet, e-mail, and videoconferencing. The ultimate fear: Would business travel become obsolete?

Those worries have vanished in the stratosphere. Even with the tech revolution in full swing, the airlines have been enjoying record-level profits over the last two years. Occupancy rates are higher than ever, and demand for first- and business-class seats is so feverish that some airlines are downsizing coach sections to open more room up front. Rates on nonweekend flights have soared. (Want to fly business class from Los Angeles to London? Try $7,400 round-trip.) For most airlines, the lion's share of profits is coming from hyperfliers—many of whom, like Orensten, are not just users of information technology, but developers of it. In a strange irony, the enemy has become the airlines' best customer. Hyperfliers are the unplanned progeny of the ménage à trois involving technology, global business expansion, and savvy airline marketing.

Why did it happen? Several reasons. As the global economy exploded during the past decade, communications technology fueled the expansion but did not obliterate the need for face-to-face meetings. "Technology allowed businesses like ours to get customers in remote places where we didn't have a physical presence," says Dennis DeAndre of LoopNet, a real estate listings site. "But you still had to get on a plane and go there to really make things happen."

Indeed, technology serves merely as a starting point in long distance business relationships. To do the hard stuff—closing deals, putting out fires, brainstorming, securing financing, kicking butt—you have to materialize on the spot. So the Net actually has put more people in the air, a phenomenon that might be called Saffo's Law.

"If you talk to someone electronically," explains Paul Saffo, a director of the Institute for the Future in Menlo Park, California, "it will inevitably lead to a face-to-face meeting."

Which in turn leads to Saffo's Corollary. "If you hate flying," he says, "kill your computer."

Videoconferencing might have prevented all this, but it hasn't, mainly because most people hate it. "It's a hideous medium," says the Doblin Group's Joe Crump. "People become bizarrely self-conscious, and unnaturally fixated on the person on TV and less on the people in the room." Crump's gripe is echoed throughout the business world, along with complaints about delays in transmission and compatibility problems.

"There's no value in a fuzzy picture of people sitting around a conference table," says T. J. Rodgers, founder of Cypress Semiconductor. "I spent $50,000 installing a system, and now I don't even bother going into the conference room to use it. I'll give you the whole thing for the price of hauling it away."

The final jet-booster of this trend is the airlines' extraordinarily successful frequent-flier programs, which have provided the burgeoning hyperflier culture with its own currency, lexicon, and class structure.

At the heart of it all: the miles. There are ever more ways to collect them and to cash them in. Today, nearly 20,000 businesses in the U.S. are giving away flying miles. Corporations give miles to employees as part of annual bonuses. On the Internet, Netcentives and MyPoints.com offer "click miles" for buying something or for simply completing a marketing survey for retailers like Barnes & Noble. Miles can be cashed in for hotel stays, vacation packages, even non-travel-related perks. Last fall, American Airlines pilot-tested a new program with MCI that trades miles for free long distance phone calls.

When hyperfliers like Orensten talk about miles, it's almost as if they're discussing stock options. Last year, Orensten used his miles for a trip to Australia. "The whole thing cost $30 in tax!" he says in a conspiratorial tone. Nothhaft, of Concentric Network, uses his miles for what he calls "crazy vacations, like taking my family to Hawaii for a football game." Though hyperfliers spend half their lives on planes, it somehow doesn't diminish the appeal of mileage awards, which allow them to spend even more time aloft.

The hyperfliers may think they're getting something for nothing, but they're actually playing the airlines' game. By tightly restricting free flights, airlines have rigged it so that a passenger flying for free almost never displaces a paying customer, and typically costs the airline only about $20 per flight. But to earn that $20 flight, hyperfliers will go out of their way to book all their tickets on one airline, and may waste hundreds or thousands of dollars building their status.

"People will do anything to get to the 100K level," says Mark Kvamme, chair of USWeb/CKS. "We had a guy here who, at the very end of the year, took a golf trip to Arizona for no other reason than to push himself over 100K." According to a University of Georgia study, billions of dollars in corporate money are wasted each year chasing frequent-flier miles.

There is more to it than the perks and free trips, though: It's also a style thing. Rob White, president of United's ad agency, Fallon McElligott, says the airlines have figured out that for some people, the real appeal of frequent-flier rewards "is not that you get more free travel, it's that you're accorded status and recognition. You're recognized as a supremely important traveler."

In other words, you use your miles to move up the food chain. Which means you don't have to stand in line or sit in the back of the plane with those other people, the ones Virgin Atlantic founder Richard Branson cheekily calls "riff-raff." It means you eat pork tenderloin with apple confit, get fussed over by attendants, and, most important, don't get your laptop crushed into your body by the seat in front of you.

It's enough to make even an up-from-the-garage centimillionaire from Silicon Valley desperate for a touch of class.

It's 7 A.M. on a Monday, and, as usual, they're circling testily around the check-in desk for the Nerd Bird, American Airlines' direct flight from San Jose to Austin. The flight didn't even exist until several years ago, when T. J. Rodgers of Cypress Semiconductor wrote to a marketing director at American Airlines. Rodgers pointed out that Silicon Valley travelers were connecting their asses off every day, trying to get to other technology hot spots like Austin, Boston, and New York. *Give us a direct flight*, he told them, *and we will fill it.*

They didn't believe him at first. But a direct flight from San Jose to Austin filled up right away. Soon they added another in the afternoon. A red-eye was added to another Nerd Bird, from San Jose to Boston, and American upped the number of nonstops from San Jose to New York. "We kept adding flights, and they kept filling up," says Tim Smith, a spokesperson for American Airlines.

The Nerd Bird's passengers are often 80 percent tech people, and the flight is legendary for its sartorial level (low), technical quotient (high), and onboard corporate espionage. A sales director for Seagate Technology once boasted in print about how he reached for his briefcase and saw a rival company's business plan under the seat in front of him. No, he didn't steal it, but he did pick it up and read every word before putting it back. Hyperfliers like Dave Sheffler, VP of sales for Advanced Micro Devices, can be seen glancing over their shoulders as they whisper into the air phone. "You have to be careful," says Sheffler. "You never know who's sitting behind you."

Paranoia and deceit notwithstanding, the Nerd Bird is a kind of utopia—almost everyone on board, owing to their miles, has attained some level of privileged status. There are no serfs here, only royalty; when the gate attendant announces, "We'll be boarding our gold and platinum members first," it seems as if everyone rises and heads for the jet. The only stragglers I see during my Nerd Bird trip are people jockeying for last-minute upgrades into first-class, including, I observe, a bearded fellow wearing a ball cap. The gate attendant calls his name and he calmly strolls to the plane. In a few minutes, as I head for my coach seat, I will pass him stretched out in the first row, his morning coffee already served to him (in a real porcelain cup!). Others waiting for upgrades are not so fortunate and mill around the check-in desk, hoping and looking bereft.

Why does it matter so much? Most hyperfliers insist they get more work done up front, but it's really about status. The class structure on airplanes is the most rigid in the Western world.

"It's an incredibly emotional issue," says Christopher Meyer, director of Ernst & Young's Center for Business Innovation and coauthor of the book *Blur*. "Flying first class is a kind of territorial battle among animals. Who's gold, who's platinum, who's got the status and the perks."

"It's unbelievable how strongly class lines are drawn on planes," says Tim Delaney, a renowned ad man. "The curtains separating first class may as well be fucking steel doors."

One might expect that airline snobbery would have no place in the Silicon Valley culture of egalitarian info-revolutionaries, but one would be very wrong. Meyer notes that a big part of the Silicon Valley mind-set involves "being countercultural in a visible way. Wearing jeans and a bomber jacket in first class makes a statement—that first class is where I belong, even though I don't adhere to the conventions."

Delaney, who flies with the Valley crowd often as he travels to his San Francisco office, sums it up this way: "They wear shorts and all that, but they're as venal as anyone from New York."

But while the techies have begun to lust after first class, it's not cool to pay for it.

Most tech companies still have a "coach only" policy on domestic flights, says Silicon Valley travel agent George Oberle. And even if they could, many would be loathe to fork over the premium because it suggests profligacy—and there is always a chance they may run into their banker on the plane. Financiers always fly first class themselves, but they're not impressed by techies who do likewise. "It does not send a good message about how you are spending the money," says Danny Rimer, a senior analyst at Hambrecht & Quist.

Excite's Kraus says: "There's a stigma to buying first class— you're supposed to be able to get it without paying for it." Often, it's the midlevel guys who fly the most and get first crack at upgrades. Which means, sometimes, "you end up with a weird situation in which a company's senior managers are sitting in the back, with the junior guys up front," says Rimer. When that happens, if the juniors are smart, "they give up that front row seat without being asked," says Rimer. Likewise, if someone in the service sector ends up sitting in front of a client, it can be awkward. "I've been in first class and seen a client back in coach, and it makes you feel like a decadent sleazebag," says Doblin's Crump. Sometimes, he says, "you have to fly coach for solidarity."

Walking the aisles of the San-Jose–Austin Nerd Bird, moving from first class to the cattle car, you'd never suspect you were traversing such a social minefield. On a surface level, the only question that seems to matter is: Can we turn on our laptops yet? As we reach cruising altitude, the soft whirring sound of hard drives revving up can be heard all around. When you take the evening

Nerd Bird, the computer screens fill the darkened cabin with an eerie green glow.

Today I'm in the midst of a 16-hour, four-stop circle run around the country: New York to Boston to San Jose to Austin to Dallas to New York. A true hyperflier would not be impressed by this run. (Delaney recently flew 26 hours for a meeting that lasted exactly 30 minutes.) Still, for a groundling, this trip provides a pretty fair taste of the hyperflier life and its routine trials and humiliations. Along the way, I endure stomach-churning turbulence over Boston; a screening of *Stepmom* on the way to San Jose; and sheer, utter chaos in Dallas, where flights, including mine, have been canceled, and packs of elderly people wearing Nikes are cruelly herded from one gate to another for flights that never materialize. I do catch one break along the way; on Austin–Dallas, an airline mistake works in my favor as I get bumped to first class, my lack of status notwithstanding. I sip chardonnay and stretch my legs for an hour. But on Dallas–New York, the gods get even: I'm stuck in the last row, next to two lanky guys with shaved heads who repeatedly punch each other in the shoulder. One is reading *American Psycho* and keeps running across parts that make him laugh.

With all the built-in annoyances—the cancellations, the oddballs, the endless bags of Rold Gold Tiny Twists pretzels—it's little wonder that hyperfliers are world-class gripers. They may be hooked on the miles, but that doesn't mean they're happy junkies. Downes describes flying as "the most unpleasant experience outside of visiting a hospital." Finocchio's had it with the new carry-on rules. "It's not like I'm trying to bring a toaster oven on," he fumes. "I'm talking about garment bags!" GreenTree Nutrition CEO Don Kendall complains that "they keep reducing the seat pitch. You can barely open your laptop. The plane really has turned into the Greyhound bus of the skies."

Grumpiest of all is Faith Popcorn, the famous "trend spotter," who still holds out hope that teleconferencing will slay the mighty airline beast. "You're mistreated at the counter checking in," she begins. "It's impossible to get an upgrade. The food is terrible. The attendants cross their arms while you try to store your bags in first class. The bathrooms are filthy. And don't even think about looking down in that little area where the tray tables are stored. Everybody who flies is going *uchh!* They've had it with the airlines. The airline industry is over."

Air rage may be the next big trend, but the industry outlook is robust. Videoconferencing will have to improve a lot before it has an impact on air travel, and for the near future, that isn't happening.

"The future is already here," says Jonathan Schlesinger, president of Connexus. "The current technology won't change much in 10 years—you'll still see someone on a screen; you still will not be able to touch them or be in the same room." The delivery system may change, perhaps to Internet-based, "but as long as the quality's the same, who cares how it's done?"

Most likely, infotech will continue to be the unwitting ally of airlines. Nothhaft predicts that as satellite feeds improve real-time e-mail and fax and access to the Internet, "we can be more productive on planes—so we'll travel even more." Saffo offers this surreal vision: "We will spend all our time in airplanes, and we will videoconference from the plane with our travel agents on the ground. We'll just go round and round, and the plane will never land."

Assuming that more flight is inevitable, there is, of course, still the hope that the experience will improve through better aero-technology. Someday, we may take off in VTOL (vertical takeoff and landing) planes with swiveling engines and downward jet propulsion. The plane will lift off vertically, which won't require a runway—hence we won't have to wait for the runway to clear. Once airborne, we may be flying at supersonic speed, or we may be in a "hypersoar" plane with an air-breathing engine that accelerates to high altitudes then coasts in space, with the engine re-activating as soon as it reenters the atmosphere. All of this is going to happen, without a doubt, says Stanley Hiller, whose

Hiller Aviation Institute brings together top aviation experts to project future developments.

But it won't happen soon. For now, supersonic travel is impractical and unaffordable (British Airways continues to offer $10,000 seats on the Concorde). Meanwhile, Boeing's explorations of high-speed commercial transport have been shelved; NASA cut funding last January because of noise problems. In other words, "aviation has reached a dead end" in terms of immediate tech advancements. Boeing spokesperson Mary Jean Olsen admits: "For the next 25 years, you can expect planes to stay basically the same in terms of the speed and the way they look." (If anything, you can probably expect planes to become increasingly dysfunctional in the years ahead. As one flight attendant confessed on a recent flight: "We never fly anymore with everything working. Business is so good, they just want to keep the planes in the air. Movies, footrests—if it's not a no-go item, they just leave it broken.")

So this is your life, hyperfliers; deal with it. The airlines, kind souls that they are, will provide one enhancement: They're going to entertain the hell out of you on the plane. Michael J. Wolf, a consultant with Booz-Allen & Hamilton and the author of *The Entertainment Economy*, points out that it's already happening: Last year, Wolf notes, the airlines spent $2 billion on installing entertainment systems.

"Airlines feel they can crowd more people in, as long as they give them something to do in their seats," says Wolf. That means not just 20 channels of movies-on-demand, but other forms of diversion—including gambling (seatback keno and blackjack screens are already being tested). The whole focus "is not to get you there faster," says Wolf, "but to entertain you more, and get more revenue out of you, along the way."

Some hyperfliers are not amused. Downes predicts a war with the airlines. "They've got the guns, but we've got the numbers," he says. Yet this assumes that fliers, who've been splintered by class and set against one another, could somehow unite. Not likely. The more credible scenario is that part of the culture—the most powerful, wealthiest part—will simply secede. You can already see this happening in the Virgin "Clubhouse" at Newark airport, where a pair of unmarked black doors is the gateway to a walled-off community. As I pass through the hushed room inside, there's a gourmet buffet on my right serving marinated sliced beef fillet in a Madeira sauce. To my left, there's an enclosed entertainment booth where a few people are lounging on a sofa watching a James Bond film on DVD with surround sound. (In London Heathrow's version of this lounge, you can practice your turns on a simulated ski slope, or flop face-down for a massage.)

Every attempt is being made to sequester high rollers from the rest of the airport. Directly below us, there's a drive-up window; preferred customers pull up in their limos, and a Virgin attendant walks up to the car, takes the bags from the driver, and hands over the boarding pass. Then you're hustled up a back staircase, like a movie star, into the Clubhouse, and then directly onto the plane. Onboard, the experience of separation continues. In the newest Virgin planes being built now, first-class passengers can descend a staircase into private chambers, with a bed and shower.

Increasingly, too, the more powerful hyperfliers are turning to private jets. And suddenly more can afford it because of jet time-sharing, which "is revolutionizing corporate air travel," says John Hendricks, founder of the Discovery Channel, whose company owns a one-eighth share of a Hawker 1000. With the airlines now pricing business flights through the roof, fractional jets begin to seem reasonable when divided among a group of executives. If you're wondering about the future of jet time-sharing, Hendricks says, consider the fact that Warren Buffett has thrown his money behind Executive Jet, one of the pioneers in the category.

Of course, there's one more option for the elite, which doesn't involve concealed chambers on planes or time-shares in the sky: Stay grounded. "More and more, senior executives are sending the young lions out there," says travel agent Oberle. "They don't want to fly anymore." Iconoculture's Abrahamson concurs: "The upper-level executives are already starting to hire young traveling teams, global employees who don't really have a home."

This is the new, stationary elite—those who use their power to stay put. "The luxury is to have the intellectual capital come to you," says Meyer. "We see it in diplomatic protocol, and in Hollywood. Who-goes-to-whom is important; I believe this all got started with the mountain and Muhammad."

And hyperflying execs are ready to hang up their miles. "Before, I used to fly to meetings for a day," says Lotus's Shelness. "This year I'm saying, 'I'm not going to go. I'll videoconference, I'll get on the phone, I'll e-mail. But I won't go.' I've never really tried this before. At the end of the year, I'll look back and see if it's been a disaster."

But even if the fast-paced business world permits them to cut back, the hyperfliers will face an adjustment on the ground. "We all complain about travel," says Finocchio, "but deep down, we'd be more uncomfortable strapped to our chairs in the office."

Evan Orensten insists he has little choice but to fly on behalf of his growing company, and he isn't ready to land just yet. En route to Stockholm, on his third flight of the day, he writes another e-mail from the clouds: "Where am I?" he writes. "Somewhere over Denmark, I think . . ."

After several years of gee-whiz tales about IPO millionaires, this cautionary story by Michael Hopkins in *Inc.* magazine offered a poignant example of the tide turning. It follows an ambitious 33-year-old who became suddenly rich and then saw everything go terribly wrong before he was eventually shown the door at his company. Step-by-step, the story relates just how the business logic of the "next Bill Gates" proved to be, well, illogical.

Michael Hopkins

PARADISE LOST

THE FACTS, AS THEY SAY, are not in dispute. In January 1998, Doug Mellinger's face graced the cover of this magazine. Over his picture ran the headline "The Next Bill Gates." Mellinger's custom-software-programming business, PRT Group, Inc., had staged a successful initial public offering a month earlier, and in the first two months of 1998 the company's stock was on the rise.

In a nice touch, it rose not in the way the share prices of those unfathomable Internet juggernauts can, but in a way that seemed healthier. It climbed sensibly, sanely, reaffirming the belief of PRT's managers that *Yes, this is no fad here. This is a true reflection of our worth.* From a low of $10 on January 13, PRT went to a high of $21.63 on February 26. Mellinger's stock alone was worth $44 million. The stock held by members of his family amounted to $112 million more. The dream was coming true. Doug Mellinger—who eight years before, with $12,000 in capital, had launched

PRT as a little rent-a-programmer business—was now 33 and rich and a star. It appeared he could do no wrong.

Then things got different.

Over the next year and a half, PRT topped its 1997 sales levels (going from $60 million in 1997 to $85 million in 1998) but made no money—though it had promised Wall Street that it would. Its signature operation, the enchantingly unprecedented "near-shore" software-development center on the island of Barbados, shrank from 360 employees to 80 and bled cash. PRT's stock crashed to $2, less than a tenth of its peak value. And on June 30, 1999, the company announced that Mellinger's handpicked second-in-command, who'd been on the job only a month and a half, was now the new CEO. Mellinger—the wunderkind founder—was out.

Those are the facts; from here the story gets stickier. What went wrong at PRT? How did so promising an enterprise—with a world-class board of directors, blue-blooded partners-cum-customers, and a record of unbroken growth—reverse direction so completely? What lessons can we find in the fall of a once triumphant entrepreneur?

The answers won't come from PRT's current or former leaders. Mellinger co-operated only minimally with the reporting for this article. At press time PRT's new CEO, Dan Woodward, had declined to comment. (Both cited an ongoing shareholder lawsuit as reason enough not to talk.) Mellinger and other PRT representatives lobbied to have *Inc.*'s coverage of the company delayed until after the turnaround tactics now being implemented there had a chance to take effect. "They [Woodward and Mellinger] want to put the past behind them and concentrate on the future—they just want to move on so badly," PRT's media liaison reported. Said a chastened Mellinger, explaining why he couldn't offer a post-mortem just yet: "I can't wait to talk about all the lessons learned, because I think they're phenomenal. I just want to get it [the article] timed out correctly, so we don't have any negative consequences."

But at least two things about Mellinger's tailspin make his

story worth telling right now, even if he and Woodward—the men in the cockpit—aren't yet ready to surrender the black box. One is how fast it all happened, how seemingly without warning. The other is how bracingly it reminds us that the IPO, that lusted-after rite of passage, has an underbelly—a vastly more common flip side. And it's dark.

Imagine it: for Mellinger, the tumble from IPO to exile took barely 19 months—less time than it takes to, say, complete an M.B.A. There he was, with wealth and acclaim and a future promising only more of both, and then, just 19 months later, everything had changed. And as for the sweetness of post-IPO managerial life, consider that of the 248 companies that launched IPOs in the first half of 1998, 145 of them ended the year below their offering price—this in a year when the Nasdaq composite index rose 39.63%. There are no statistics on how many CEOs are dethroned after an IPO, how many whole management teams are erased, but no one considers either scenario unusual—especially today, when companies that miss earnings estimates by even a penny are punished by Wall Street more brutally and swiftly than ever.

True, there are the crazy-IPO examples of Netscape and eBay and Broadcast.com and more. But those are the exceptions. When you dream of your own young company's future—your own rocket ride of an IPO—and think that you, too, will be an exception, remember the numbers, the percentages, the odds. Remember Doug Mellinger.

Nineteen months.

To Mellinger it must seem a lifetime ago, but it wasn't much more than two years back that he sat in the first-class cabin of the daily American Airlines run from New York City to Barbados, and with giddy confidence tried to explain what I was about to see first-hand: a world-class software industry being fabricated almost overnight on a second-world Caribbean island. All thanks to Mellinger's small but suddenly swelling company.

It was this feat on the island that set the company apart as it presented itself for public-market consumption in the fall of

1997. "A home run," Mellinger called the whole idea at the time. "People just can't believe it's been done. I tick off where PRT's facilities are and go past Barbados, and they say, 'What? What'd you just say? Back up. . . .'"

The world Mellinger and PRT created—"the island," it's always called—had been conceived in 1994 in response to a simple but crisis-size problem: the desperate shortage of software engineers in the United States. In the early 1990s, when Manhattan-based PRT was only a $3-million or $4-million business sending programmers out to jobs at clients' facilities, the company struggled to get and keep enough programmers. So did almost every other U.S. company. (American companies still do. There are too few U.S.-bred programmers and too many legal restrictions that prevent a compensating number of foreign programmers from immigrating.) PRT's first solution was to take work offshore—all the way to programmer-rich India. But that country's remoteness and bureaucracy kept clients away. So Mellinger went looking for a more suitable place—a country with more logistical appeal. His list of desired attributes ran to 50 items.

The trouble was, he discovered, no such country existed. Australia, Ireland, China, others—every location he explored was handicapped by distance, inadequate labor, technology shortcomings, or something else equally insurmountable. A reasonable person would have quit the plan. What Mellinger did, instead, was take the step that he knew "would make PRT a whole different company," making a more that no company large or small had ever made.

He decided, preposterously, that since the perfect country couldn't be found, what he would do was "invent" it.

He would choose a blank-slate environment and then import the workers, the customers, the capital, the infrastructure. He'd build a place where, thanks to the talent it housed and the tools it provided and the collaboration it promoted, programmers and clients alike could do the best, most satisfying work of their careers. He would build a miniature United Nations, bringing in people from all over the world and then furnishing them with homes, stocking their refrigerators, handling their bills—providing a whole turnkey life. "I don't want them to have to think about anything but having fun and writing killer code," Mellinger often said. He would build the 21st-century high-tech nation. Which is what, on the island of Barbados, he did.

By the time Mellinger graced *Inc.*'s cover, there were some 350 employees, who had emigrated from some 16 countries, in his next-millennium company town. Highly placed executives at J.P. Morgan and Chase Manhattan, along with a few other customers, were so smitten with the operation and the idea behind it that they not only gave it business but invested $12 million in its construction. Even PRT's relationship with the island itself was news-making: the company had teamed up with government leaders to devise a strategic plan for the country, offered to help rewrite school curriculums, and established public/private joint ventures to install a state-of-the-art high-tech infrastructure. The entire project began to suggest how a tiny developing nation could leapfrog right over the industrial stage of economic evolution into a global technology-based, knowledge-driven future.

It was a great story, and not surprisingly it became the heart of PRT's pre-IPO road show. It dramatized PRT's near-shore solution to the U.S. programming crisis. And it reflected boldness, imagination, and, seemingly, effectiveness that few companies of any age or size could match.

That's how it looked in the heady final days of 1997, anyway. The island was thrumming. Fresh recruits were arriving by the week. Customers and investors alike were lining up to validate the concept with cash. Mellinger, at midcourse, was building a legacy, and anything seemed possible.

Anything, that is, except what happened next.

The 19 months following PRT's IPO were a roller-coaster ride on which almost all the track curved down. I kept in touch with Mellinger off and on throughout that time, noting his thoughts and moods whenever he was willing to describe them. Superficially, at least, some of what went wrong seems clear now. Dozens of interviews with analysts, current and former PRT insiders, and Mellinger's acquaintances have filled in many of the information gaps left by what Mellinger won't yet say or can't yet make sense of. He says he kept a time line annotating the events of those months; one day, though not now, he'll share it, he says. When he does, it won't look happy.

November 20, 1997

PRT Group goes public at $13

The five-month IPO journey was more consuming than even Mellinger's gold-plated advisers had prepared him to expect. There were the lawyers, the underwriters, the dog-and-pony trips to Europe, the 78 separate face-to-face meetings with potential investors, the day-to-day encounters with investment bankers and their "Monopoly money" state of mind. Exhausting. Yet Mellinger was euphoric more often than not. "It was wild," he told me after the road show. On a day in August when I was in his New York City office, he got a phone call from one of his IPO underwriters asking if he wanted a quick piece of some initial offering the firm was floating that day. Sure, Mellinger told him, I'm in your hands. A few hours later the underwriter called back to say that he'd sold Mellinger's position and that the play had netted Mellinger $12,000. A few hours, $12,000. Nothing, really, compared with the millions to come, but still. Mellinger was inside the system now; people were taking care of him. "I always wondered who got to buy these deals," he said when he put down the phone. Now he knew.

At the end of its first day of trading, PRT Group (Nasdaq symbol: PRTG) listed at $13.25.

February 26, 1998

PRT's stock hits historical high, $21.63 . . .
but there's trouble

Just as the total value of the stock held by Mellinger and his family was reaching its high-water mark—$156 million—bad forecasting began to hurt the company. PRT had projected a doubling of revenues, to $120 million, in 1998 and had expanded its programming capacity accordingly. So when five or six anticipated projects fell through in early 1998, PRT was unexpectedly saddled with high fixed operating costs (full-time workers) and a shortfall in offsetting revenues, according to Srinivasan Viswanathan, who has run the Barbados operation since its inception. "The bench—unbilled workers—started growing," Viswanathan recalls. Ironically, PRT had tried to prepare for the opposite problem. "We'd lost business throughout 1997 because we didn't have enough people [programmers on site] to deliver," Viswanathan says. "So we told salespeople, 'Go slow.'" That prudence began to backfire.

March 6, 1998
PRT loses half its market value
In one hour at the opening of trading, PRT's stock dropped $9.56 in the wake of the company's announcement that it would post a first-quarter loss of about $3 million—on quarterly sales of less than $20 million—instead of the small profit it had estimated. In the dreaded calls to analysts the night before ("Worst night of my life," Mellinger later told me) and in subsequent public statements, Mellinger blamed the losses on customer delays in starting scheduled year 2000 projects and other software-development work, delays that left too many PRT programmers sitting idle.

Mellinger and his family saw their net worth fall $70 million. The stock price would never recover.

June 1998
Sales shortfalls worsen
"From mid-1998 onwards," says Viswanathan, "it became clear we would have trouble filling the sales pipeline—not only hitting growth targets but just maintaining current volume." More and more it appeared that the challenge of selling the "near-shore" programming alternative—the very thing Mellinger had focused his energy on creating—was greater than anyone had expected. "The near-shore option turned out not to be as attractive as imag-

ined," says Tarun Chandra, a senior analyst at Punk Ziegel & Co., the observer who has followed PRT closest and longest. It was hard enough getting companies to send their programming work offshore, to places like India, but that alternative was at least well understood.

However, the advantages of PRT's near-shore operation were real enough. Barbados offered a dedicated software-engineering lab that was both low cost and talent rich. Its location made it easy to reach, and customers could work there with a PRT team, undistracted by day-to-day office problems. But the concept was too new for customers to easily embrace. "The uniqueness of the idea made it a tougher sell, with a longer sales cycle, requiring a higher-quality salesperson," observes Chandra. "In an environment where the [information-technology] needs of potential customers change so fast, a long sales cycle is deadly." Would-be clients had too much time to change their minds or run out of budget or get distracted by sudden new priorities.

Complicating the sales challenge further, "the work in Barbados meant selling custom-solutions projects, not [programmer] bodies," says Mark Prieto, a J.P. Morgan vice-president who was lent to PRT throughout the build-out of Barbados. "Instead of asking, 'How many programmers do you need? When do you want them to start?'" says Viswanathan, salespeople needed to understand a client's business well enough to help solve its problems. PRT was offering an entirely different level of customer relationship than most clients had come to expect. In the end, however, says Chandra, "the PRT sales engine never got to a level that could successfully sell Barbados."

August 31, 1998
PRTG down to $5.13

Whenever he tried to explain PRT's challenges to Wall Street, Mellinger was optimistic. But "it wasn't like it was a 'dot-com,' where Doug could say, 'We're not making money—so what?'" notes Prieto. "When they had to report bad results, they got slammed."

By all accounts, the pressure to move the stock changed the way Mellinger and PRT behaved. A panic syndrome set in. "Everyone got reactionary," says one executive who was inside PRT at the time and spoke on the condition of anonymity. "When things started going bad, they just started doing reorganizations." Mellinger, who'd been brilliant at enlisting the talents of others while building Barbados, reverted to "I'm-running-this-company mode," says another insider. The patience he'd always had with missteps—his own as well as others'—had been drained.

September 1998
PRT hit with a shareholder suit
Shareholder litigation brought by the California firm Milberg Weiss—the country's most feared and prolific practitioner of the craft—alleged that PRT falsely portrayed its Y2K capabilities, leaving investors exposed to its stock-price slump. PRT dutifully called the suit meritless and began the dance of negotiation and counterclaim. (At press time the suit remained unresolved.) At September's end, PRTG was trading at $4 a share.

November 1998
Mellinger steps away and does some "soul-searching"
A year after the IPO, Mellinger took a vacation expressly to "reevaluate some things," as he told me afterward. In light of everything he'd been through, he tried to reexamine his own strengths and weaknesses, and to ask himself anew "what it was I wanted." He refused to itemize his conclusions but described the episode—using the word he so often uses to describe things—as "fabulous." It was "painful," he admitted, "but fabulous." As I listened, it was possible to actually believe him.

December 31, 1998
PRT finishes the year with losses of $12 million
Revenues for 1998 were $85 million, a full 43% above 1997's revenues but well short of PRT's $120-million prediction. Employ-

ment in Barbados was down by more than 100 employees, to 250, as underused engineers voluntarily fled, and the momentum that had attracted both programmers and customers to the pathbreaking island setup was gone. Getting the work done "wasn't easy," says Viswanathan. "Morale was tough. There weren't enough new projects, and people saw their colleagues walking out and wondered, 'Should I be doing the same thing?'"

Some 70 percent of the sales staff had turned over in the course of the year and in retrospect it's clear that Mellinger's strengths as a salesman helped mask the company's weaknesses as a sales organization. As CEO, Mellinger had always been able to open doors and close deals with customers "at the CIO level and above," says Viswanathan, something no other PRT representatives—and perhaps not many other small-company CEOs—could do. ("Doug can sell anybody anything," says J.P. Morgan's Prieto.) But as is often the situation at entrepreneurial companies, PRT's growth—and growth projections—called for an ever increasing volume of sales. Eventually, the needed volume exceeded what even a CEO who spent all his time selling could produce. And whenever Mellinger was distracted by other tasks—such as the IPO and the obligations of being a public-company chief executive—the gap between the amount of business he could bring in and what PRT needed grew wider.

PRTG at year's end: $3.

February 9, 1999
Search for new chief operating officer announced

In late winter, Mellinger sounded happier than he had seemed for a while. He seemed relieved. The decision to recruit an outside number two was a by-product, he said, of his November soul-searching. Still, things were far from uncomplicated. The COO title had been held by Mellinger's brother, Greg, and one wondered how difficult it had been—or would become—for the brothers to make their way through changes. Doug Mellinger waved the concern away. "Greg understands," he told me. Included in PRT's news release were these comments by Doug Mellinger: ". . . 1998 was a difficult year for PRT. The revenue shortfalls we experienced appeared initially to be solely a result of project delays by customers. However, as the year progressed we determined that our organizational structure could be improved, our resources utilized more efficiently, and our sales force could improve its productivity." One month later, in a newspaper story, Mellinger would summarize PRT's travail by saying, "It was the classic problem of growing too fast."

May 18, 1999

PRT hires new president and COO

Mellinger devoted much of the spring to considering the more than 80 candidates turned up by a search firm. He interviewed some 20 of them, reduced that list to 8 (each of whom he interviewed for three to five hours), and cut that shortlist to 3, at which point PRT's board got involved. The job ultimately went to Dan Woodward, an EDS executive who, at 38, was only a few years Mellinger's elder. At Mellinger's request, Woodward immediately undertook a "top to bottom" strategic audit of PRT's business. Greg Mellinger, no longer COO, would leave the company before the month was finished.

June 2, 1999

PRT Group initiates turnaround plan

Now things were speeding up. A company press release quoted Woodward announcing a series of cost-cutting measures—including layoffs of 100 people; the relocation of headquarters from Manhattan to Hartford, Conn.; and the shutdown of business activities deemed "tangential to the company's mission." The press release did not mention Doug Mellinger. "When I brought Dan in, I was amazed at his speed, how fast he saw strengths and weaknesses in people and in areas of our business, and how decisive he was," Mellinger told me in July. "I was way too close to it;

it was too personal. I knew we needed to make changes, but an entrepreneur can never know how painful they're going to be."

So the entrepreneur would give way to the manager. Observers both inside and outside the company confirmed Mellinger's instincts. "Clearly, Doug is not someone who should be running a large company," says Rita Terdiman, a Gartner Group research director who followed PRT's progress. "I think Doug is a visionary; I think Barbados was a brilliant model for its time. But if I'm an investor, I might be real happy Dan Woodward is in there now."

On June 2, PRTG ended the day at $2.75.

June 30, 1999

Woodward is named president and CEO of PRT

No one will say what pressures or understandings led to this. Had PRT's board pushed Mellinger to step down? Had Mellinger been planning his escape since November? Was Woodward brought in with the promise that his ascension was a short-order formality? All of the above? Mellinger told me that in June, after a couple of weeks of debriefing with the newly arrived Woodward, he went to Italy on vacation. Once there, he was able to reflect with some perspective on how well Woodward had taken the reins, and he knew the transition should go to the next step without delay.

In PRT's official announcement, Mellinger professed enthusiastic support for the leadership change and stated, "As a major shareholder, I believe that the . . . actions under way should allow the company to achieve its long-term goals." Mellinger, according to the company release, would continue his association with PRT in the newly created position of "nonexecutive" chairman of the board.

"What's *that?*" wondered Punk Ziegel analyst Chandra and others. Documents filed with the Securities and Exchange Commission spelled it out: the nonexecutive chairman "shall have none of the powers of any officer of the Corporation, . . . none of the powers of the chairman, . . . shall not serve as chairman of any meeting, . . . and shall not be authorized to incur any expenses . . .

or to otherwise direct the affairs or management or operations of the Corporation in any manner whatsoever."

It was, by any definition, the end of something.

So what went wrong at PRT? Basic forensics suggest that PRT's troubles were of the sort that could plague just about any fast-growth business: a sales force that was inadequate to an unexpectedly complicated task; a management overfocused on building the production side of the business (the programming machine, in this case) at the expense of the marketing operation; a company overly reliant on the CEO's gift for bringing in business.

But if that's *what* went wrong, understanding *why* it did is a harder call. Here we enter the arena of informed speculation.

Would all of this—or any of it—have happened to Mellinger and PRT if the company hadn't gone public?

"Absolutely not," says Viswanathan. The pressure to meet Wall Street's expectations—expectations nurtured by Mellinger's optimism—turned what might have been just the growing pains of a still-young company into a crisis. "The problem wasn't that sales didn't meet expectations in early 1998, but that we didn't know how to come out of the crisis," says Viswanathan. "And that was a problem of top management"—of which Viswanathan was part. As a public company, PRT's adventuresome, if-we-goof-we'll-just-try-again tactics wouldn't fly. "[Securities] analysts are unforgiving," says Prieto. Miss a projection, and you're cooked.

A couple of months before the IPO, Mellinger had said, "I spend so much time tempering people's expectations when things go wrong or they get frustrated. I tell them, 'Remember how long the trip is and how far we've come.'" But once PRT was public, how far they'd come didn't matter, and the trip could be as short as the weeks remaining until the next quarterly report. "By the time you know something is wrong," Mellinger said after he'd left the company, "it's already too late."

"He discovered what everyone who goes through it does," says Terdiman. "You're a totally different company after going public; nothing remains the same."

Much of the pressure Mellinger felt may have been very personal. PRT's stock slide was "incredibly hard on him—especially because he's got a lot of friends and family who invested in the company," says Brien Biondi, who as the executive director of Young Entrepreneurs' Organization has worked with Mellinger for the past two years. "It's been a painful, emotionally draining time for both him and his wife." In YEO circles, Mellinger's disenchantment with public-company life is well known, not to mention contrarian. "About 10 percent of the companies in YEO are public," says Biondi. "The other 90 percent want to be. 'I want an IPO, I want an IPO'—that's all I hear these young entrepreneurs saying. The enormous personal wealth generated by companies going public in the past four or five years has them thinking of nothing else. But when Doug talks to them, sharing some of the difficulties of being public, he's begging the question, 'Do you really want to go this route?'"

Would PRT have grown at a different, more organic pace if it had remained private? Would it have weathered the ups and downs of learning its business? Quite possibly. Given the chance to do it over again, Mellinger would skip the IPO, I believe. If he or PRT's other owners had wanted to cash out, he'd have followed the advice he's since given to other entrepreneurs: instead of taking the company public, sell it.

In the months since Mellinger's departure, the new leadership at PRT has continued to make changes—adding new senior executives, closing more facilities, and restating the company's strategy, which now focuses on helping clients to extend the life of their computing systems and to make the transition to electronic commerce. Woodward signed a letter of intent to sell off Barbados but in September rescinded it. Whether or not "the island" ultimately remains in the fold, it now functions in a stripped-down mode, with 80 employees and fewer of its all-encompassing company-town practices; it will be run, says Viswanathan, like "a small business," its ambitions humbled.

PRT reported revenues of $37 million for the first half of 1999, down from $41.5 million for the same six months the year before; it lost $11 million (or $18.4 million counting restructuring charges related to severance costs and other onetime expenses). As of September 10, the stock price was hovering just above $2. The company's fate, analysts say, hangs in the balance. "It definitely had a lot of promise, and I would use the word *had*," says an almost wistful-sounding Tarun Chandra. "I think it will eventually get taken out"—sold to a buyer interested in PRT's financial-services-industry connections or its body count.

As for Mellinger, even the observers who testify to how hard the journey has been on him are claiming that he's coming out the other side feeling good. He's begun to play the role of what he calls a "venture catalyst," helping launch e-commerce businesses by providing not just capital but a kind of "SWAT team [of managers] that knows how to do the first six to twelve months of a company," he said in July. He'll do what he loves, he said: stay where he belongs, in the creation end of things. "Doing this is a dream for me," he says.

So it's all OK, then. The fall from one state of grace is, in fact, just the first step in an ascent toward another. That's what Mellinger would have his listeners believe, and maybe it's true. But it's hard for anyone who was there just two brief years ago to ignore the costs that PRT's failures have exacted. A lot of people have lost a lot of money, Mellinger's friends and associates included, and even the preternaturally forward-looking Mellinger must sometimes find that burden a hard one to bear. His brother, Greg, sounds like a man who still hasn't found his footing. "I've been through the exhilaration," he says despondently, recalling the rich promise of earlier times, "and I've been through quite a few moments of despair."

Even Doug Mellinger's own voice, in phone call after phone call, has a weariness and resignation that was rarely present before. But maybe he's just tired. He has reason to be. Maybe the costs have been borne, just as he says, and the future really does look better—even better than it did when PRT's prospects were so bright.

Still, it's hard now not to think of where Mellinger was—where the whole PRT crew was—just a couple of years ago. Maybe it's important to record the distance they traveled from pinnacle to pain as a cautionary tale for the I-want-my-IPO crowd or as a sobering counter-weight to the endless string of stories about company-building success and the dot-com pot of gold.

Once, during the flush of grand feeling in the run-up to the IPO, Mellinger told me about the first dream he could remember having had as a child. "I dreamed of an island," he said, "where I lived." The dream was vague at first, but it kept recurring. As it did, it became more distinct. "My friends were there. My family. I could see it." In Mellinger's mind it became a community, a happy gathering of like-minded souls living fully and well. It became the place people came to. The place where everything meaningful happened.

And that's what Barbados was. That's how the island and everything PRT did there felt to Mellinger at its peak; it felt that good. Mellinger had wanted an island, and he got it. He *made* it.

Now, though, he doesn't go there anymore.

Maybe times don't change. Individual businesses and industries must still "pay to play" if they want government to champion their causes. This scrupulously-researched story by *Time*'s Donald Barlett and James Steele uncovers the protectionist impact of large political contributions from fruit baron Carl H. Lindner Jr. The examination of Lindner's past and present is solid journalism, and the story also shows the personal side of casualties such as small businessman Rick Reinert.

Donald Barlett and James Steele

HOW TO BECOME A TOP BANANA

IN SUMMERVILLE, S.C., Rick Reinert has built a small business called Reha Enterprises that sells bath oil, soap, and other supplies. But now he is selling many of his products, imported from Germany, at no profit or at a loss. This is the result of an order by the U.S. government.

In New York City, Arthur Kaplan, owner of Galaxy of Graphics Ltd., a retailer of decorative prints, has stopped selling the popular English lithographs produced for him by a venerable London art dealer for two decades. This is the result of an order by the U.S. government.

In Somerset, Wis., Timothy Dove, who heads a 17-year-old family business called Action Battery, which sells and installs industrial batteries, has lost a quarter-million-dollar account and faces the prospect of more losses to come. This is the result of an order by the U.S. government.

What's going on here?

Nearly a year ago, the Clinton Administration imposed a 100 percent tariff on the products these three businesses and hundreds of others like them import and sell. That's sort of like charging you $40,000 for a $20,000 Ford Taurus.

What did these folks do to encourage the wrath of the White House? Absolutely nothing. It was what they didn't do that matters. They neglected to make huge campaign contributions or hire high-powered Washington lobbyists to plead their case.

Reinert, Kaplan, and Dove are what the military refers to as collateral damage—unwitting victims of what will go down in economic history as the Great Banana War. Except that for these victims, collateral is up close and very personal.

This is partly the story of Carl H. Lindner Jr. of Cincinnati, a certified member since 1982 of the *Forbes* list of the 400 richest Americans, who has a personal fortune estimated at $800 million and has been a very large contributor to political candidates, both Democratic and Republican.

But mostly this is a story about people who get hurt by contributions, who are paying a steep personal price because of the influence exercised by unlimited money in elections and lobbying. These human casualties are mostly unchronicled, but you can count them in the millions. They are your friends and neighbors.

In simplest terms, Lindner, whose company has dominated the global trade in bananas for a century, was in 1993 frustrated because European countries limited imports of his bananas. He complained to the U.S. government, which complained to the World Trade Organization (WTO), which authorized the U.S. government to retaliate by imposing a stiff tariff—in effect, a tax—on select European goods shipped to this country.

So which goods to attack? President Clinton could have slapped the 100 percent tariff on, say, Mercedes-Benz autos imported from Germany, fine wines from France, or elegant women's shoes from Italy. But that might have provoked retaliation by the Europeans against major American exports. So instead the President chose to punish smaller and less important European companies—companies that furnished bath products to Reinert, prints to Kaplan, and batteries to Dove. In short, the Administration came down with a heavy foot on relatively powerless citizens. People who, like 99 percent of the population, contribute little or no money directly to politicians.

How heavy was that foot? In Reinert's case, the U.S. government raised the tariff on his most popular product, an herbal foam bath, from just under 5 percent to 100 percent. His U.S. Customs bill for the last six months of 1999 spiraled to $37,783 from just $1,851—a 1,941 percent tax increase.

For a small business, that's strong poison. Indeed, when Reinert called the office of U.S. Trade Representative Charlene Barshefsky to describe his plight, an official there expressed amazement. "[They] were very surprised I was still importing," recalls Reinert. "They thought the tariff would cut off the industry—shut it down. That was their intention. They wanted to kill that industry, whatever industry it is." That, naturally, would have meant killing Reinert's business as well.

Reinert did have an option. He could have found a way around paying the tax. Except it would have been illegal. Sort of like people working off the books to avoid paying income tax on their earnings. That's what many small-business people in Reinert's position are doing—fudging their import records. It's polite language for falsifying government documents. Each distinct type of product imported into the U.S. is assigned an individual code number. The tariff is collected on the basis of the code numbers. Thus changing a single numeral in the code will convert a taxable product into one that is not subject to tax.

Are the people doing this comfortable with their deception, which an ambitious federal prosecutor could turn into a conviction accompanied by a large fine and prison sentence? Absolutely not. But it's a matter of survival. Further, they figure, if the U.S. government decides to take care of a multinational business whose owner, his family, and his fellow executives contribute millions of dollars to political candidates and their parties—and to punish small businesses whose owners do not contribute—then why not cheat?

At age 80, Lindner sits atop a corporate agglomeration that includes American Financial Group, Inc., an insurance business (annual revenue: $4 billion); Chiquita Brands International, Inc., the fruit-and-vegetable giant ($2.7 billion); and an array of other businesses, including Provident Financial Group, Inc., a bank holding company (assets: $8 billion); and American Heritage Homes, one of Florida's largest builders.

At American Heritage, Lindner has been a business partner since 1996 with the king of Democratic fund raisers, Terence McAuliffe, described by an admiring Vice President Al Gore as "the greatest fund raiser in the history of the universe." McAuliffe has raised tens of millions of dollars for the Democratic Party, for President Clinton's 1996 re-election campaign, for the President's legal-defense fund, for the President's library, and for Hillary Clinton's New York Senate run.

Since 1990, political contributions of $1,000 or more by Lindner, members of his family, his companies, and their executives have added up to well over $5 million. Most of the money has gone to the Republican Party and its candidates. But at strategic moments, Lindner has made hefty contributions to the Clinton Administration.

The short version of the money story is this: Europe first offended Lindner when it imposed import restrictions on bananas from Latin America, where his plantations are located. Lindner then contributed a quarter of a million dollars to the Democrats. Gore called and asked for more money. Lindner gave it. And then some more. So much more that Lindner had dinner in the White House, attended a coffee klatch there for the truly generous, and slept in the Lincoln Bedroom. Along the way, he periodically met with then U.S. Trade Representative Mickey Kantor and his staff, the officials who ultimately sought the trade sanctions intended to punish the Europeans and force them to give Lindner what he wanted.

Clinton's people weren't the only ones looking after Lindner. Members of Congress—Democrats and Republicans, fund raisers all, beneficiaries themselves of Lindner's largesse—called or wrote or met with Kantor and the President to encourage action on behalf of Chiquita. Trent Lott of Mississippi, the Republican majority leader in the Senate, did it. So did John Glenn, at the time a Democratic Senator from Ohio. And Republican Congressman Jim Bunning of Kentucky, now a Senator. And Charles Stenholm, the Democratic Representative from Texas. And Richard Lugar, the Republican Senator from Indiana. And Mike DeWine, the Republican Senator from Ohio. And, of course, Mitch McConnell, the Republican Senator from Kentucky, who is Congress's most strident advocate of unlimited money in elections.

On April 19, 1999, the U.S. Trade Representative imposed the punitive tariffs on nine types of European goods. To be sure, trade experts outside the European Union generally agree that the restrictive banana policies do violate free-trade rules. Indeed, four global trade panels have reached that conclusion over the years. But restrictive trade policies are hardly peculiar to Europe. The U.S. has its own, notably those that restrict the free access of sugar and peanuts to the American market.

The Clinton Administration has been less than forthcoming about its relationship with the banana baron. In response to repeated *Time* requests for documents relating to the decision to seek the WTO's help with the banana dispute, the U.S. Trade Representative's office stalled, saying it was having trouble coordinating its many files. When it finally began turning over documents last December, many were censored or blank, with the USTR claiming that release of the information would "constitute a clearly unwarranted invasion of personal privacy."

Carl Lindner began investing in bananas in the 1970s, and by 1984 he had acquired a controlling interest in one of America's enduring brand names. Lindner and his family, through their American Financial Group, own 40 percent of the outstanding shares in Chiquita Brands International, based in Cincinnati, Ohio.

Before Lindner bought in, Chiquita Brands was the old United Fruit Co., a ruthless buccaneer that earned a justifiable reputation as a tyrant that bribed officials of foreign governments, used armed force to keep its workers in line, and generally mistreated its thousands of dirt-poor laborers on impoverished Caribbean islands and Central American plantations. All of which helps explain why Chiquita was—and is—the world's dominant banana producer.

But how did it come to pass that the U.S. government launched a trade war over bananas at the expense of small American businesses, especially since the U.S. does not export bananas and Chiquita employs no American production workers?

It started with bananas in Europe. After World War II, the continent's banana market divided into two kinds. Such countries as Britain, France, and Spain limited imports and gave preferential treatment to bananas grown in their former colonies. Thus Britain encouraged banana output in Jamaica, Dominica, St. Lucia; France extended special treatment to bananas grown in the Ivory Coast and the Cameroons. At the other extreme, Germany offered a free market with no import restrictions or tariffs.

Britain and France took the position that banana production was essential for both the economic health and the social well-being of their former colonies. By the late 1980s, about one-third of the work forces on the small island nations were employed in banana production.

Protected banana production, that is. Most of the bananas were grown on small family farms and tilled by hand on hilly terrain and poor soil, with little or no mechanization or irrigation. Yields were far below those in places like Honduras, Guatemala, and Ecuador. In fact, the cost of growing bananas in the Caribbean was twice that for bananas produced on Latin American plantations. Without their favorable entree to Europe, the banana industries of these small islands might have disappeared.

Chiquita nevertheless cracked the British market through its ownership of a British subsidiary, Fyffes Ltd., which grew bananas in the former British colonies. British consumers paid a relatively high price for those bananas, but Chiquita's margin from this trade was still small compared with the profits from its efficient plantations in Latin America. By 1986, as the European Union began to take shape, Chiquita executives hoped the restrictions would be lifted and its low-cost bananas could take over the market. So Chiquita sold off its Fyffes subsidiary.

It would prove to be the first in a series of missteps by the Lindner-controlled company—suggesting at least the possibility that the ensuing banana war was really intended to bail out the Lindners from their costly business mistakes.

Meanwhile, in a tariff-free and quota-free Germany, Chiquita had seized 45 percent of the market. Envisioning the same potential for all of Europe, as well as the former Soviet satellites that were opening up, Chiquita and its chief competitor, Dole Food, decided in the early 1990s to pour more money into production and flood the European market with bananas. With more bananas than buyers, prices—and hence profits—plummeted.

Worse still, the E.U. announced that instead of an open market, which Chiquita had hoped for, it would expand the old system, with quotas and tariffs on bananas brought in from Latin America and preferential treatment for bananas grown in the former colonies. The new rules went into effect on July 1, 1993.

They certainly should not have come as a surprise to Chiquita, the U.S. government, or anyone else. The signs had been clear for years that Europe intended to continue giving preferential status to bananas from its former colonies. An investment report prepared in October 1990 by the Wall Street firm of Shearson Lehman Bros., Inc., predicted that Europe, contrary to Chiquita's hopes, would maintain the status quo for years to come.

Even Chiquita knew at the time what it faced. In its 1992 annual report filed with the U.S. Securities and Exchange Commission, the company acknowledged that "although we will oppose these restrictive policies in the proper legal forums, we are prepared to adapt to this new regulated environment." By this time, Dole, the world's second largest banana producer and Chiquita's only real rival, had hedged its bets and arranged to acquire bananas from those countries with no tariffs and generous import quotas.

Meanwhile, Chiquita's business was tanking. From 1992 to 1994, the company racked up $407 million in losses. Its stock price plunged from $40 to $11 a share. In meetings with government officials, Chiquita laid the blame squarely on the E.U.'s trade restrictions. The U.S. Trade Representative and the rest of the Clinton Administration bought the line, at least officially. And to this day, Chiquita officials insist that's the case. Steven Warshaw, Chiquita's president, told *Time,* "The E.U.'s illegal banana regime is the cause of the company's poor financial results since 1992. It would be absurd to conclude otherwise . . . It is well accepted that the E.U.'s banana regime was specifically designed to expropriate market share from U.S. banana interests to benefit European multinationals and other interests within the European market . . . Our stock price declined precipitously, and our industry has been substantially damaged."

While there is little question that Chiquita's sales would be higher were it not for Europe's quota and licensing system, a close look at company filings with the Securities and Exchange Commission over the past 15 years shows that a good portion of Chiquita's decline is attributable to other causes. In the years it posted record losses, Chiquita said in the SEC reports, its costs "were significantly impacted" by outbreaks of banana disease, bad weather, a strike by workers in Honduras, as well as shipping and operating losses from its "Japanese 'green' banana trading operations."

Banana pricing wars also took a toll, but even more telling, the company ran up its long-term debt so that cash payments for interest charges spiraled from $52.6 million in 1990 to $164.3 million in 1993. Even if Chiquita sales had reached the level the WTO said they would have in the absence of European restrictive policies, the company still would have recorded losses or, at best, a marginal profit. As a Wall Street investment analyst who tracked the banana industry put it in 1992, "We have serious doubts about the abilities of management to deal with the company's problems."

Over the 15 years ending in 1998, with the Lindners in control, Chiquita tallied total sales of $45 billion but profits of only $44 million. That's the equivalent of a $10,000 investment that returns 65 cents a year. Not surprisingly, the company's stock is now trading at less than $5 a share.

In an SEC filing last December, a minority shareholder of Chiquita's reported that the Lindners were pondering an auction to sell off Chiquita. All of which may explain the money trail the Linders left behind in Washington.

Lindner, a nonsmoking, nondrinking, nonswearing Baptist, has been a major supporter of the Republican Party, its candidates and causes. This may account for the less than enthusiastic response that Lindner received when he first took his banana case to the Clinton Administration early in 1993. In fact, at that time the U.S. Trade Representative's internal memos show that bananas were a low priority for the U.S. government. What's more, USTR and State Department officials had given—and would continue to give—repeated assurances to leaders of Caribbean governments that the U.S. supported European preferences for their bananas. And not without good reason. Everyone was fearful that islanders unable to grow and sell bananas would turn to a much bigger cash crop—drugs.

It was against this background that in June of that year, Keith Lindner, then president of Chiquita and one of Carl's three sons in the family businesses, wrote a "Dear Ambassador" letter to Mickey Kantor outlining concerns over Europe's import restrictions. There was little response.

That December, Carl Lindner contributed a quarter of a million dollars to the Democratic National Committee, establishing himself as a generous supporter of both political parties.

Through the early months of 1994, the Lindner lobbying juggernaut concentrated on building congressional support to pressure the Clinton Administration into action. From January to August, lawmakers of both parties bombarded Clinton and Kantor with letters demanding action.

Among the more strident and persistent correspondents were Bob Dole, who would eventually campaign for the presidency aboard Lindner's corporate jet, and John Glenn, who counted Lindner as a campaign contributor.

In January, Dole and Glenn, along with Senator Richard Lugar, wrote to the President calling for "sustained interventions" with European Union officials to make clear that export quotas and licensing "are not an acceptable solution." By August, Dole and Glenn demanded that Kantor initiate a so-called 301 investigation. The name comes from a section of the 1974 trade law that gives the USTR authority to investigate foreign trade practices and impose tariffs in retaliation.

On September 13, Dole arranged a breakfast meeting with Kantor and Lindner. A day later, according to an internal USTR memo, Kantor and his staff had a follow-up meeting with Lindner and his colleagues to discuss "possible strategies" to overturn the European quotas.

Over the years, the USTR has averaged only about five 301 investigations annually. Even rarer are cases in which the USTR has recommended punitive tariffs on the imports of the offending nation. The Chiquita case was rarer still—an instance in which the complaining company was not even a U.S. exporter. Two USTR staff members acknowledged this in a memo to Kantor on October 13, 1994, saying that "if initiated, this investigation would break new ground, as this would be the first time that USTR had ever used Section 301 in connection with a product not exported from the United States but from elsewhere." Nonetheless, the staff members said "we have been persuaded by Chiquita that the practices here do have a significant effect on U.S. commerce." Lawyers for other U.S. corporations disagreed strongly. Natalie Shields, tax and trade counsel for Black & Decker, later captured the logic of the USTR decision this way: "This would inflict substantial harm on one U.S. company in an effort to benefit other U.S. companies which export bananas from third countries."

But the Clinton Administration liked the notion. On Monday, October 17, 1994, Kantor authorized the 301 investigation. That Thursday night Lindner was in the White House, attending a dinner as a guest of the President. And the following week, Al Gore called Lindner, asking for another major donation. Lindner delivered. On November 3, Lindner's American Financial Corp. donated $50,000 to the D.N.C. His Great American Holding Corp. donated $25,000, and his American Money Management kicked in $25,000, bringing the one-day total to $100,000.

At the same time, Senators Dole and Glenn kept the pressure on, urging Kantor in another letter on November 17 to retaliate against the Europeans.

The following month, on December 10, the Lindners again met with Kantor, after which they fired off a "Dear Mickey" letter, thanking him for his efforts.

At year's end, on December 30, James E. Evans, a Lindner executive, contributed $150,000 to the D.N.C., bringing to $250,000 the sum that in one year Lindner, his companies and their executives poured into Democratic coffers.

On January 3, 1995, four days after the latest Lindner-related contribution, Kantor announced "a list of retaliatory actions that he [was] considering against the European Union to counter E.U. policies which discriminate against U.S. banana marketing companies." Specifically, Kantor said he was contemplating sanctions "that would directly hit E.U. firms providing air, maritime, and space transportation services."

On Thursday of the same week, Terry McAuliffe, Bill Clinton's moneyman and Lindner's home-building partner, sent a memo to Nancy Hernreich, one of the President's administrative assistants, summarizing a conversation he had had with the President on fund-raising activities. McAuliffe asked that overnight stays at the

White House be arranged for major contributors; that dates be scheduled for contributors to have breakfast, lunch, or coffee with the President; and that other contributors be included in such presidential activities as golf and jogging.

The next day another aide passed along a memo to Harold Ickes, the President's deputy chief of staff, saying that "Nancy has asked us to follow up on this at the President's direction and his note indicates 'promptly.'" The memo called for "overnights for top top supporters." Accompanying McAuliffe's memo was a 10-person list of those "top top" supporters prepared by McAuliffe. Prominently holding down the No. 2 slot: longtime Republican Carl H. Lindner.

Five weeks later, on February 9, Lindner was in the White House at a state dinner honoring German Chancellor Helmut Kohl. After entertainment by Tony Bennett and a German chorus, Lindner went upstairs to bed. Less than two weeks later, he was back in the White House for coffee.

Throughout this period, Lindner's allies in Congress kept the pressure on the Clinton Administration. On June 21, Senator Dole wrote to Kantor: "I am concerned that time is running out in the banana case. U.S. banana companies are on the verge of suffering even greater irreparable damage as a result of the E.U. and Latin practices."

Kantor scribbled a note in the margin of the letter, addressed to Jeff N.—Jeffrey Nuechterlein, senior counsel to Kantor—and Jeffrey L.—Jeffrey Lang, one of his top aides: "Please give me a way to proceed. Pressure is going to grow. MK."

Kantor says he has no recollection of the note. "I don't remember writing it," he says. Lang doesn't remember it either. He recused himself from the banana dispute, he says, because before his appointment as Deputy U.S. Trade Representative, he represented the European side in the WTO proceedings. Nuechterlein, likewise, doesn't remember anything about it. "I was not involved with bananas substantively," he says.

Dim memories aside, the pressure did indeed grow. On July 19, Carl and Keith Lindner wrote to Kantor again, expressing their dissatisfaction with proposals put forth by the Europeans to resolve the banana dispute. At least in the view of the Lindners, the war should be waged as a joint effort, with Chiquita and its ally, the U.S. government, on one side and the European Union Commission on the other.

On August 3, the four-member Hawaiian congressional delegation sent a letter to Kantor saying they were prepared to talk about possible "international courses of action" against the E.U. As America's only state producing bananas—most were grown for consumption on the islands—Hawaii had an indirect stake in the outcome of the banana war; because Chiquita, Dole, and other producers had flooded the European market, tariffs notwithstanding, the overflow had found its way back into the U.S., driving down retail prices.

The following day, Lindner's American Financial Corp. delivered an additional $100,000 to the D.N.C. A few days later, the Lindners met once again with Kantor. Two months went by. On November 3, the Lindners advised Kantor's staff that it was "very important" they get together for 20 minutes. This particular meeting did not take place, but nine days later, on a Sunday night, Lindner was sitting behind Clinton at a presidential gala in Ford's Theatre.

As 1995 gave way to 1996, the money kept gushing from the Lindner empire, much of it in smaller, harder-to-trace donations. In February a Lindner executive gave $10,000 to the D.N.C., and American Financial Corp. contributed $15,000. In March, Lindner directed $10,000 each to the Minnesota, North Carolina, Tennessee, and Iowa Democratic parties, $15,000 to the Michigan Democratic Party, and $5,000 to the Connecticut Democratic Party. In April he steered $10,000 to the Pennsylvania Democratic Party.

With at least an additional $95,000 of Lindner money in the Democratic Party's bank accounts, the U.S. Trade Representative on May 8 took its banana case to the WTO. At long last, the Clinton Administration was ready to mount a global trade war on Lindner's behalf.

A spokesman for Chiquita dismissed the suggestion that campaign contributions by Lindner had anything to do with the USTR's taking the case. "It is well known that Carl Lindner has been actively involved and a major contributor to candidates and other causes on a multipartisan basis for many decades," he said.

Former Trade Representative Kantor also insisted that contributions played no part in his decision. "The staff made a unanimous recommendation to me that we bring the case," he said.

Of Lindner's contributions, Kantor said, "I couldn't have cared less. It made no difference to us whatsoever. We didn't hear a word from the White House."

Be that as it may, the USTR decision to pursue a trade war over bananas was sharply at odds with its handling of similar agricultural issues. Consider this: today, even with the tough trade restrictions still in place, Chiquita controls 20 percent of the European market. By way of contrast, the USTR has negotiated with Japan to allow American companies a 3 percent share of the Japanese market for rice.

In other words, the U.S. went to war on behalf of one American company that already had 20 percent of a foreign market, and it negotiated to secure 3 percent of another foreign market for the benefit of seven to ten American companies.

Over the next two years, Lindner continued to dispense case to the Democrats. In June 1997, two installments of $10,000 each went to the Democratic National Committee Services Corp. In November he gave $75,000 to the D.N.C. and in February 1998 another $75,000. That was followed by contributions of $10,000, $10,000, $25,000, $50,000, $25,000, and $5,000.

Throughout this period, Lindner and Chiquita enjoyed a close working relationship with the USTR office. Copies of U.S. government correspondence with heads of state in other countries were voluntarily turned over to Lindner. Finally, on November 10,

1998, the USTR proposed 100 percent tariffs on several dozen European imports. The agency said the increased tariffs would be imposed on March 3, 1999, if Europe did not relent and relax its restrictions on Latin American bananas.

The products included pecorino cheese, certain wines, apple juice, bath preparations, candles, furs, coniferous wood, paper boxes, lithographs, cashmere sweaters, women's suits, dresses, skirts, bed linens, scissors, sewing machines, vacuum cleaners, food grinders, windshield wipers, dolls, photographic equipment, chandeliers, glass Christmas ornaments, sweet biscuits, wafers, felt paper, plastic handbags, coffee or tea makers, electric toy trains, greeting cards, stoves, and ballpoint pens.

In short, it was a list of products bearing absolutely no relation to bananas.

While government officials were assuring reporters that the tariffs would never be levied, the U.S.-based companies that would be affected were taking no chances. In all, 42 types of products were targeted for tariff increases and, as it had to do by law, the USTR asked interested parties to respond.

Respond they did, setting off a furious lobbying campaign to try to get off the banana hit list. Companies and politicians showered the agency with letters warning of potential job losses in their districts if the increased tariffs were imposed.

At a USTR hearing on December 9 attended by trade associations and Washington lobbyists, various interest groups spoke out against the tariffs, saying they would cripple or possibly destroy their businesses.

"The imposition of a prohibitive duty on ballpoint pens would have a devastating effect on Gillette's writing-instruments business in the U.S.," a representative for the Gillette Co. warned.

"Subjecting these dolls to a 100 percent duty could well result in the collapse of the entire line of American Girl products," a representative for Mattel cautioned.

"The imposition of a 100 percent duty rate on articles of fur clothing and garments will seriously impact our members, making their garments outrageously expensive, even for a luxury product," declared a representative of the Fur Information Council of America.

Two weeks later, on December 21, products imported by Gillette, Mattel, and fur retailers, as well as those of some two dozen other trade groups and industries that testified at the hearing or lobbied the USTR, were dropped from the list.

More lobbying ensued. On April 19, when the final list was published, most of the goods once proposed for high tariffs had been stricken from the list. Only nine types of products were covered.

In announcing the final list, Barshefsky, who had replaced Kantor as U.S. Trade Representative, reiterated that the higher annual tariffs on European goods were in retaliation for Europe's refusal to change its import rules on bananas.

"It is proof that the system works," she said. "When members [of the WTO] refuse to live by the rules, they will pay a price." There was one major oversight in Barshefsky's reasoning: the wrong people were going to pay the price.

The Clinton Administration salvo aimed at giant European corporations hit Rick Reinert, Arthur Kaplan, Timothy Dove, and other small entrepreneurs, whose only connection to bananas is to eat one every now and then.

Reinert is—or more accurately was—the typical American small-town, small-business success story. He grew up in LaPorte, Indiana, and attended Western Kentucky University before enlisting in the U.S. Army in 1975. He and his wife, whom he met during his Army stint in Germany, started their wholesale bath-supplies business in 1994 out of the family garage in Summerville, S.C., a pine tree–studded bedroom community of Charleston. "We began very meagerly," says Reinert. "We didn't have one account." By knocking on doors, attending an endless parade of trade shows, and selecting the right representatives, they built a solid customer base of some 2,000 stores—gift shops, beauty salons, boutiques, grocery stores, independent pharmacies, and a major drugstore chain. Their most popular items, which they buy from a German supplier and account for 60 percent of sales, are aromatic foam baths scented with herbs from lavender to rosemary. And these items were among the ones singled out by the USTR office for its trade war with Europe over bananas.

Reinert remained blissfully unaware until January 1999 that he was on his way to war. That's when he first heard about the proposed tariffs. "I was at a Portland [Oregon] gift show . . . and I happened to read this little blurb in *Time* about bath products. I thought it was a joke." He investigated. "It was no joke. We were on the potential hit list."

That's when Reinert started writing letters and calling everyone—his Congressman, his Senator, the USTR. It was during one of many conversations with a USTR staff member that he was told, in effect, it was his own fault that he had got caught up in the trade war. After all, the USTR had published a list of the targeted imports in the Federal Register. He should have attended the hearings in Washington, just like Gillette (annual sales: $10 billion) and Mattel ($5 billion). If he had, then Reha Enterprises (less than $1 million) might have been removed from the list as well.

Reinert is still fuming. "That's ridiculous. I mean, do you read the Federal Register? Does anybody in Summerville read the Federal Register?" The trade official suggested Reinert should have hired a lobbyist in Washington to keep him briefed. That one didn't go over well either. "I mean, we've got two kids. It's a small business," says Reinert. "Who in his right mind would come up with stuff like that?"

"We're only [six] years old," Reinert says. "Cash flow is always a problem. Finance is always a problem. But they are just destroying the base of our company."

What other advice has Reinert received from officials in the U.S. Trade Representative office and from the staffs of members of Congress?

He says one official urged him, off the record, to break the law—to change the number on the Customs invoice so it would appear that he was importing goods not subject to the tariff. Reinert demurred. "I could end up in jail for it," he says. "I don't want to be the only one without a chair when the music stops."

Another official chided Reinert for not buying American, a rebuke that angered him. Reinert responded, "'Why don't you go out in your parking lot and count all the Mercedes and Porsches, BMWs, Lexuses, and Toyotas?' I mean, these are just ridiculous arguments."

In response to repeated calls and letters, Reinert heard personally from Barshefsky last August. The news was not good. Reinert, she suggested, was standing in the wrong place at the wrong time when the war started. She explained in her best bureaucratic language that it was legally impossible to remove Reinert's bath products from the tariff list. Said she: "We have examined the question of whether [the USTR office] has the authority to grant exemptions to small businesses, such as yours, that are severely harmed by the increased tariffs . . . We have concluded that the relevant statute . . . does not provide such authority to USTR."

Three months later, in November 1999, Barshefsky told quite a different story when she testified before the Senate Banking Committee concerning the upcoming WTO gathering in Seattle. In response to a committee member who suggested legislation that would rotate products on and off the tariff hit lists, Barshefsky asserted that "I have discretionary authority as it is to alter a retaliation list if that becomes necessary or advisable. So the authority is already there."

None of this is any help to Reinert, Kaplan, Dove, and the hundreds of other small entrepreneurs like them, some of whom have already been forced out of business. Nor is it any consolation for all those who have been caught up in the ripple effect—the peripheral businesses, from trucking companies to local suppliers, who deal with those on the tariff list.

For his part, Reinert continues to wage his battle, writing letters to whoever he thinks just might take an interest in his case. "It's been mentioned to me, you know, from all levels of government, [that] you cannot fight the government. Well, I think you can. It's wrong what they're doing."

The USTR, for its part, insists that the products chosen for high tariffs were intended to "minimize the impact" on Americans and "maximize the impact on Europeans," in the words of Peter Scher, a special trade negotiator. As to how much pressure they have had on Europe, Scher said, "I think it has had an impact. Has it moved the E.U. as far as we want them? No. But it has certainly moved the E.U. to the negotiating table."

Might the tariffs that have squeezed Rick Reinert and other small businesses remain in place another year or two? "Anything is possible," said Scher. "The ball is in the E.U.'s court." Even Chiquita acknowledges that there is little movement toward a settlement. "There is no end in sight," said a company spokesman.

So what does the battlefield look like as the Great Banana War's tariffs approach their first anniversary?

Well, the operators of some small businesses, like Reinert, are limping along from month to month. Other small-business people are filing fraudulent Customs documents to escape payment. Other businesses are doing just fine because their suppliers in Europe agreed to pick up the tariff or it applies to just a small percentage of the goods they sell. In Europe as in America, small businesses have been harmed by the U.S. tariffs. Larger companies have been mostly unaffected. And the European Union has kept in place its system of quotas and licenses to limit Chiquita bananas. Who, then, is the winner in this war?

That's easy. It's the President, many members of Congress, and the Democratic and Republican parties—all of whom have milked the war for millions of dollars in campaign contributions—along with the lobbyists who abetted the process.

A final note. While Lindner had many areas of political interest beyond his battle with the European Union, a partial accounting of the flow of his dollars during the Great Banana War—as measured by contributions of $1,000 or more—as well as lobbying expenditures on the war, shows:

Republicans—$4.2 million
Democrats—$1.4 million
Washington lobbyists—$1.5 million

That's more money than a business like Rick Reinert's will earn in a lifetime.

*—with reporting by Laura Karmatz and Andrew Goldstein
and research by Joan Levinstein*

Perhaps the most influential business article of the past year was this blockbuster by Jack Willoughby of Barron's. The follow-up article is also included. Though there'd been plenty of talk of Internet companies running out of cash, this piece quantified the plight of specific companies (an accompanying table that ran with the initial story is not included because numbers are now outdated). The stock market took these findings to heart, knocking down the stock prices of these companies and changing how the investment community would evaluate their relative strength. Cash and business models now rule.

Jack Willoughby

BURNING UP/
UP IN SMOKE

WHEN WILL THE Internet Bubble burst? For scores of Net upstarts, that unpleasant popping sound is likely to be heard before the end of this year. Starved for cash, many of these companies will try to raise fresh funds by issuing more stock or bonds. But a lot of them won't succeed. As a result, they will be forced to sell out to stronger rivals or go out of business altogether. Already, many cash-strapped Internet firms are scrambling to find financing.

An exclusive study conducted for Barron's by the Internet stock evaluation firm Pegasus Research International indicates that at least 51 Net firms will burn through their cash within the next 12 months. This amounts to a quarter of the 207 companies included in our study. Among the outfits likely to run out of funds soon are CDNow, Secure Computing, drkoop.com, Medscape, Infonautics, Intraware, and Peapod.

To assess the Internet sector's financial position, Pegasus assumed that the firms in the study would continue booking revenues and expenses at the same rate they did in last year's fourth quarter. While this method cannot predict the future precisely, it helps answer a question that has been nagging many stock-market analysts: When will the crowded Internet industry begin to be winnowed?

The ramifications are far-reaching. To begin with, America's 371 publicly traded Internet companies have grown to the point that they are collectively valued at $1.3 trillion, which amounts to about 8 percent of the entire U.S. stock market. Any financial problems at these Internet firms would affect the myriad companies that supply them with equipment, including such giants as Cisco Systems and Intel. Another consideration is that a collapse in highflying Internet stocks could have a depressing effect on the overall market and on consumer confidence, too. This, in turn, could make Americans feel less wealthy and cause them to spend less money on everything from cars to clothing to houses.

It's no secret that most Internet companies continue to be money-burners. Of the companies in the Pegasus survey, 74 percent had negative cash flows. For many, there seems to be little realistic hope of profits in the near term. And it's not just the small fry who are running out of cash. Perhaps one of the best-known companies on our list, Amazon.com, showed up with only 10 months' worth of cash left in the till.

Pegasus was working with the latest public financial data, from December 31, so the table doesn't reflect the fact that Amazon early this year managed to raise $690 million by issuing convertible bonds. But that money will last the firm only 21 months. Moreover, raising fresh funds will be more difficult if Amazon's operating losses continue to mount and its stock price continues to flag.

"What's critical is the stock price," says Scott Sipprelle, cofounder of Midtown Research in New York. "It's only when the stock price comes unglued that the burn rate means anything."

Several signs suggest that the era of "unglued" stock prices is fast approaching. Amazon.com, for example, is trading at about

65, down from its all-time high of $113. Then there's Internet Capital Group, trading at a recent 117, down from a high of 212. Many other net fledglings are in far worse shape. ELoan's shares have plummeted to about 10, from a high of 74.

The broad picture isn't much better. The Dow Jones Internet Commerce Index has fallen 25 percent from the all-time high achieved last April.

Little wonder that so many Net firms are following Amazon's lead and looking for new funding. "The hunt for cash will become more desperate as the reserves deplete," says Greg Kyle, founder of New York–based Pegasus Research International.

Take, for instance, the firm at the top of our list, Pilot Network Services. It was just about at the bottom of its cash hoard when it managed to get a $15 million investment from Primus Telecommunications. To obtain the funds, Pilot had to give Primus a 6 percent ownership stake. At the current burn rate, the cash infusion should last Pilot about 10 months.

VerticalNet, which helps businesses transact on the Internet, had to turn to Microsoft to replenish its dwindling cash supply. In exchange for a $100 million investment, Microsoft is getting a 2 percent stake in VerticalNet and requiring the Internet upstart to use Microsoft's technology.

Medscape, No. 9 on our list, apparently solved its cash problems by agreeing a few weeks ago to be bought by MedicalLogic, Inc., for $733 million in stock

Not all Net firms have been so lucky. Peapod, the fourth company on our list, unveiled crushing news last week. Peapod Chairman Bill Malloy intends to step down for health reasons from the online vendor of groceries. As a result, investors who had agreed to pony up $120 million in financing are backing out of the deal. Peapod has hired Wasserstein Perrella to seek out new investors, but with only $3 million of cash on hand, Peapod's coffers could be empty within a month. That's even sooner than indicated by the financial data that Pegasus used to create its burnout rankings.

Another Net company in disarray is the online music retailer

CDNow, No. 2 on our list. CDNow executives thought their problems were solved when they agreed to a takeover offer of more than $300 million from Columbia House, the mail-order record seller that's jointly owned by Time Warner and Sony. One problem: It turned out Columbia House did not itself generate enough cash to make the merger work. Nancy Peretsman, a managing director at the investment bank Allen & Co., has been hired by CDNow to assess strategic options. Her job may not be easy. CDNow has enough cash to last less than one month, and its shares are trading at 6¾, down 80 percent from their all-time high.

As noted above, a depressed share price limits a company's ability to raise fresh funds. Let's face it, with lots of investors looking at losses on a stock investment, selling more shares into the market can be difficult, at best. A good example is eToys, a toy retailer that came public at $20 and surged to well over $80 amid great public enthusiasm. The concept was easy to understand and promised great riches. But the competition, in the form of Toys R Us, did not roll over and play dead. Toys R Us launched its own Web site, and ardor cooled for eToys. Today shares of eToys repose at 11¾. All those people who bought in at prices ranging from $20 to $80 are none too eager to buy more shares, even at $12. EToys has enough cash on hand to last only 11 more months, so stay tuned.

Even a celebrity like Dr. Everett Koop is not immune. His Web site, drkoop.com, came public at $9 a share, surged to over $40, and has since fallen back to $9. Drkoop.com ranks seventh on our list, with three months' cash left.

Another easy-to-understand e-play that has disappointed investors is FTD.com, the flower retailer. Its shares have wilted to a recent 3⅜, from an all-time high of 12½. FTD.com has about six months of cash remaining.

"That's the problem with these IPO run-ups. They introduce so much hype and emotion, when what's really needed is stability," says William Hambrecht, founder of Hambrecht & Quist, owner of W.R. Hambrecht, a pioneer in offering IPOs to investors

via the Internet. "A volatile price on a new stock kills your ability
to finance in the future. It's very destructive."

Net companies are also finding it more difficult to raise funds
by issuing convertible bonds. One reason: investors in these
instruments are attracted to the possibility that the issuer's stock
price will rise, enabling bondholders to reap a nice profit when
they convert their bonds into stock at some future date. "Slowly
the door's beginning to shut on the pure Internet plays in the convertible market," says Ravi Suria, chief of convertibles research at
Lehman Brothers in New York. Indeed, E*Trade, Amazon.com,
and Ameritrade have had to offer unusually generous interest rates
and conversion terms to sell their latest offerings of convertibles.
With so many Internet stocks well off their highs, the promise of
converting bonds into stocks at a huge profit seems more remote,
making such deals a lot less alluring.

Egghead.com, with an estimated 4.4 months' worth of cash on
hand, recently solved its hunt for capital, but its success may prove
pyrrhic. Although a Bahamian outfit called Acqua Wellington
agreed to invest $100 million in Egghead.com, Acqua plans to
make its investment over a nine-month period, buying up stock at
an unstated discount to the current market. "It's a curious situation, to be sure," says Pegasus's Kyle. And it's yet another sign
that cash is getting more difficult for Net firms to come by.

Investors' distaste for Net stocks is especially prevalent when
the business plans of the companies in question depend solely on
selling goods to consumers. "The business models are coming
under intense scrutiny for companies in the business-to-consumer
sector, because both investors and venture capitalists are skeptical
about the potential for profitability," says Jon A. Flint, founder of
Boston-based Polaris Venture Partners, an initial backer of the
successful Internet company Akamai Technologies.

Could the depression felt in consumer-oriented Net companies
spread to the business-to-business sector? Right now the sector is so
beloved that it hardly seems possible. For instance, a purchasing site
for businesses, PurchasePro, has a mere 10.2 months of cash remain-

ing, yet the stock market totally sloughs it off. Recently, PurchasePro shares touched a spectacular 175, up 2,000 percent from the firm's $8 offering price (adjusted for a split) last September.

Still, don't be surprised if at some point such popular business-to-business stocks go the way of the consumer offerings such as eToys, FTD.com, or drkoop.com. "Many of these B2B companies have strategies that depend upon continuous access to capital," says Kyle. "If any of these firms were not able to raise their cash, the implosion would certainly affect stockholder confidence. We know that B2B stocks have to eventually come down, the question is when: five months or five years from now?"

Don't bet on the latter.

Part of the problem is that the Net companies' founders and early backers are eager to sell their shares while they still can. So far this year, 38 publicly traded Internet companies have tapped the markets for $16 billion in capital through secondary offerings. This represents a fivefold increase in the number of secondary offerings compared with the same period last year. Another key difference is that this year a far larger number of second-round deals involved insiders unloading their shares on the public. This hurts the companies in question because the cash raised by selling shareholders goes right into the pockets of those shareholders, and not into the companies' coffers.

Sure, venture capitalists and other early-stage investors are in the business of selling out at a profit eventually, but large sales of insider stock while a company is still reporting losses can choke off that company's access to fresh capital, thereby diminishing the chances for survival. In the investment world, this is akin to men on a sinking ocean liner pushing women and children aside to commandeer the lifeboats.

"The IPO market used to be available only to seasoned companies where the insiders' exit strategy didn't matter," says Hambrecht. "When you take a company public that still needs capital to continue as a going concern, you are taking a huge risk. Insider selling only makes it harder to raise money."

Venture capitalists, quite rightly, become incensed when their integrity gets impugned. After all, they were behind more than half of last year's 501 initial public offerings. For them, selling down positions to cover startup costs happens to be a business strategy.

The conflict of interest between venture capitalists and the public is well illustrated by the case of MyPoints.com, an Internet direct-marketing firm. With four months' cash left, MyPoints filed to raise $185 million by selling as many as four million shares to the public. At first blush, the offering would appear to refill MyPoints.com's coffers quite nicely. But a closer look reveals that 40 percent of the shares on offer are being sold by insiders. Thus, money seemingly destined for the company gets diverted to insiders.

Another notable insider selloff occurred at the Internet real estate seller HomeStore.com, which at yearend 1999 had enough cash remaining to last a little over a year. The stock came public at 20 in August, rose to a high of 138, and has since slipped to 50. In January, HomeStore announced a $900 million secondary offering, in which the insiders reaped more than half the gross proceeds.

More often than not, venture capitalists sell when retail investors are eager to buy. As noted above, shares of PurchasePro.com recently touched $175. With 10.2 months' cash left, it should be no surprise that PurchasePro recently sold three million shares, one-third of which are owned by insiders.

The evidence shows the race for the exits is especially pronounced among Internet companies. So far this year, in two-thirds of the secondary stock offerings by Internet companies, 25 percent or more of the shares were sold by insiders, according to Comm-Scan. In non-Internet deals, only about one-quarter of the deals involved insider selling of 25 percent or more.

The Internet investing game has been kept alive in large part by a massive flow of money out of Old Economy stocks and into New Economy stocks. Last week's steep slide in the Nasdaq and the sharp recovery of the Dow Jones Industrial Average may mark a reversal of this trend. As illustrated last week, once psychology changes, cash-poor Internet issues tend to fall farthest, fastest.

WHAT A DIFFERENCE three months make. When our cover story "Burning Up" appeared March 20, the technology-laden Nasdaq had just topped 5000 and the initial-public-offerings market still was raining buckets of money on Internet companies. But all that was about to change.

By focusing on Net companies' burn rates—how fast they were depleting their cash reserves—and how long it would take before some would be tapped out, Barron's pinpointed the key risk that many dot.coms faced: They were critically dependent upon a continually receptive stock market to keep funding their furious spending. Since then, the Nasdaq has fallen sharply, the euphoria surrounding initial public offerings has evaporated, and venture capitalists have donned green eyeshades when looking at deals.

"Since the Barron's article, a mantra has developed in board-rooms. The two biggest investor concerns have now become cash and the business model," says Jon Flint, general partner of Waltham, Massachusetts–based Polaris Venture Partners and a lead investor in Akamai. "If companies don't have enough cash for at least 15 months or can't show significant progress by then, private investors are not going to buy in."

In our original 207-company study, we calculated the burn rate for the fourth quarter of 1999, and then projected how long it would take for each fledgling Internet company to burn through its cash. In this issue, we update those estimates, using burn rates for this year's first quarter. We also note what actions these companies have taken since to bolster their financial positions since their last reported quarter.

The good news: Internet companies burned their cash more slowly in the latest quarter. They did consume a hefty $1.15 billion, but that was off 24 percent from the $1.52 billion that went up in smoke in the fourth quarter of 1999, according to an expanded study conducted exclusively for Barron's by Pegasus

Research International. But the heat is still on for more than 60 companies that face the prospect of running out of cash in the next 12 months, according to Pegasus.

Protecting the cash supply has become a No. 1 priority. And with Net companies' revenues rising to $12.5 billion in the first quarter from $10.3 billion in the previous quarter, Pegasus figures the industry's combined cash stash should support it for 13 years, up from eight years at the time our first study was done.

Fewer dot.coms now report negative operating cash flow (earnings before interest, taxes, depreciation, and amortization)—227 in the first quarter, down from 238 in the preceding period, according to Pegasus. Among the nine outfits that turned cash-flow positive in the first quarter were Exodus Communications, Lycos, Ameritrade, and E*Trade.

But of the companies reporting negative cash flow, 29 percent, or 66, stand to run out of cash within the next 12 months, based on their first-quarter numbers, up from 59 three months earlier. To be sure, many of these companies have taken action—radical in many cases—to husband cash. Still, ISI Group tallied some 69 "problem.com" companies in just the past four weeks that were forced to announce layoffs, postpone financings, or close up shop. No doubt many had assumed that capital would continue to be available in infinite amounts and on generous terms forever.

This survey contains 20 more companies than the last one because more corporate disclosures were available and more companies were willing to discuss the cash-burn issue. Seven of the top 10 companies didn't appear in the previous study.

"The numbers clearly show the Darwinian process at work in the Internet," says Greg Kyle, president of Pegasus Research International, which covers the sector for institutions. "The weak falter, while the strong surge ahead. The focus has now shifted from growth-at-any-price to how soon profitability can be achieved."

Many of the new potential burn victims—such as GenesisIntermedia, a Van Nuys, California-based multimedia marketing company, and Convergent Communications, an Englewood, Colorado networking company for small business—already have obtained financing from private sources through small doses of preferred stock or debt. They're Nos. 1 and 2, respectively, on our list.

But, indicative of the profound change in the financial zeitgeist, Net companies are assiduously avoiding the public equity markets. Claimsnet.com, a Dallas-based health-benefit processor ranked No. 11 on our list, said last week that it had finalized a $3 million sale of restricted stock, enough for the near term, according to Paul Miller, chief financial officer. "We're confident of our business model, and we really don't see any sense in raising huge amounts of capital at a time when the public markets are temporarily shut." Cavion Technologies of Englewood, Colorado, No. 35, which helps credit unions patch into the Net, actually withdrew an offering of about two million shares. "We just felt it made no sense" selling equity at depressed prices, says Marshall Aster, chief financial officer. The firm now looks to raise money in the private market.

Indeed, some managements have resolutely put their own money up to buy shares at depressed prices. James Condon, president and chief executive of Reston, Virginia–based CyberCash, an Internet payment services company ranked No. 24, says his directors have added to their holdings. "We certainly have no intention of running out of cash," said Condon as he outlined cost-cutting measures.

Many different types of e-businesses now appear in need of funding. Denver telecommunications concern RMI.net, No. 8, has raised $12 million from a finance company to meet a self-imposed deadline to stop burning cash by yearend. But Westwood, Massachusetts–based RoweCom, No. 7, which manages the purchase and distribution of magazines, journals, and periodicals for businesses, told Barron's it's still looking for fresh money. Earlier this month, it used up some reserves and brought in new private investors to redeem $16.1 million in notes. Venture capitalists backing Sunrise, Florida–based Mortgage.com, No. 18, recruited Stephen Foltz, a former Transamerica executive, as interim chief financial officer to evaluate the various divisions of the company, after the previous CFO departed. Foltz says that Mortgage.com has enough cash for at least the next two quarters.

E-tailers, perhaps more than any other group, have had to raise needed cash. New York–based clothing discounter Bluefly, No. 5, has hired Credit Suisse First Boston to find strategic partners and is talking with bankers about working-capital loans. Westwood, Massachusetts–based e-grocer Streamline.com, No. 15, has also hired an investment banker.

CDNow, the Fort Washington, Pennsylvania, music seller, No. 9, reported that Mexican tycoon Carlos Slim had increased his stake to 9 percent–plus, and said last week that merger talks with several interested parties continue. No. 4 Peapod's $73 million-plus deal with Dutch grocer Ahold appears likely to be completed following an earlier abortive deal. Value America, the electronic e-tailer, No. 6, says an equity infusion has bolstered its prospects, but the share price continues to be hampered by an overhang of stock for sale by deposed former directors.

Naturally, a few managers opted not to discuss plans about burn-rate problems. Pilot Network, an Alameda, California, information security company, No. 13, and US Search.com, No. 14, a Los Angeles–based records search firm, offered no comment. Efforts to reach Audiohighway.com, No. 17, were unavailing.

As with the previous study, some companies took issue with our methodology. New York–based Juno Online, No. 29, says it doesn't even release a burn rate quarter-to-quarter because of the cyclical changes in its business. Steve Valenzuela, CFO of South San Francisco–based PlanetRx, an e-medicine company, No. 19, said: "Our actual cash burn was lower than represented in the first quarter because of a one-time capital investment. Since then, the company has promised to reduce its burn rate by up to 20 percent this year." No. 3 on the list, Atlanta-based bank service firm Net-zee, noted the firm has a $15 million line of credit issued from InterCept Corp., a 34.8 percent shareholder in NetZee, $7.8 mil-lion of which has been drawn down. The credit line—not measured in the Pegasus methodology—plus the money on the balance sheet provides sufficient cash, the company contends. "Your original article caused us untold nightmares because we couldn't find analysts who could understand us," says CFO Rick Eiswirth. "We feel we have sufficient funds to become cash flow-positive by the middle of next year."

Lest we forget, the reason for this new dot.com austerity: a collapse in the price of dot.com equities, which has constricted the size and number of public deals. Since March 10 when the Nasdaq peaked, the public markets have absorbed only 39 Internet IPOs worth $4.2 billion, 23 secondary or follow-on offerings for $6.4 billion, and six convertible deals for $1.7 billion, according to CommScan, a New York statistical information firm.

The market value of Internet stocks has been slashed by 50 percent since their peak—to $693 billion from $1.4 trillion, according to Pegasus. In the meantime, Internet offerings comprise 55 percent of the backlog 202 deals worth $21 billion, out of a total of 368 deals worth $39 billion, according to CommScan. Psychology has changed profoundly. "The long upward ride in technology stocks that has lasted for 10 years appears to be interrupted for a while," says Jay Hoag, general partner of Technology Crossover Ventures, based in Palo Alto, which manages some $2.5 billion and is one of the Internet's more influential investors. "Right now, people are scared.

"March certainly was a wake-up call for venture capitalists who asked: 'Do I stay with my investments, or take my money and go elsewhere?'" adds Hoag.

Others saw opportunity in the chaos. "Clearly, some investment firms used your last story for a shopping list," says Tim DeMello, founder of Streamline.com. "Days after it appeared, we were faxed at least nine term sheets from firms we'd never met. The terms were really onerous, ridiculous. We're now dealing with strategic investors because the private venture firms that four months ago flew out to see us now won't even take our phone calls."

Sales by insiders and other investors while companies seek to raise more equity capital just intensifies the pressure. Says Peter Jackson, chief executive of Orinda, California–based Intraware, No. 45 on the list: "It's tough to have your venture capitalist hold stock for only one or two years, and then flip out to go into another deal, especially when they initially tell you they hold for five years. The early sale gives the impression of a lack of faith in the company management and its direction. It confuses employees, customers, and partners."

While some mourn the end of the euphoria seen at the end of 1999 and in the early months of 2000, many observers welcome a return to a more sober atmosphere. "We're probably in for one more downward motion, but later this summer, we could well have a rally," says William Smith, chairman of Renaissance Capital in Greenwich, Connecticut, which runs the IPO plus Aftermarket fund. "The deals are continuing to come. The best news for our fund has been the declaration by some pundits that the IPO sector has crashed."

Bill Gates isn't just an antitrust target. His foundation, the largest in the world, is targeted for financial requests by just about every cause on the planet. Jean Strouse in this *New York Times Magazine* piece reveals the strategy, deliberations, and enormous amounts of money involved in this Gates family affair. Besides pointing out how big a business-related charity can become, it examines the Microsoft billionaire from an entirely new angle.

Jean Strouse

HOW TO GIVE AWAY $21.8 BILLION

ONE OF THE WAYS in which the very rich are different from you and me is that they become public property. Just about everyone has an opinion about Bill Gates's business tactics, products, motives, character, house—and about what he should be doing with his immense fortune.

Before he began giving money away, people complained that he was a miser. Now that he *is* giving money away, they complain that he's doing it too late, that he isn't giving enough, that he hasn't a clue about what he's getting into, that the projects he is financing are too conservative, too liberal, too big, too small, too safe, too risky, too conventional, too splashy. Or they say he's only doing it to avoid taxes, or to expand Microsoft's markets, or, especially, to improve his image in light of the government's high-profile antitrust suit.

"Bill Gates can't win," says Vartan Gregorian, president of the Carnegie Corporation and a longtime adviser to Gates on the subject of philanthropy. "It's like nineteenth-century anti-Semitism. If the Jews didn't mix into German society, people said they had a parochial, *shtetl* mentality. If they did mix, people said they were trying to pass. More important than why he's doing this is what he's doing. The proof will be in the pudding."

In January, the Bill and Melinda Gates Foundation edged past Britain's Wellcome Trust to become the largest in the world, with assets of $21.8 billion. Even the greatest philanthropists of the past did not give away as much in real dollars over their entire lifetimes as Gates has at the age of 44. According to the Chronicle of Philanthropy, Andrew Carnegie made gifts amounting to $350 million before he died in 1919—a sum that would be worth about $3 billion in today's dollars; and the $540 million that John D. Rockefeller dispensed before his death in 1937 would amount to more than $6 billion today—less than a third of the Gates total so far. As a percentage of the gross national product, Gates's gifts do not yet match those of his predecessors, but he is just getting started.

That Gates began adding to the foundation in huge ($5 billion) increments over the past 14 months, as the government prosecution took its damaging course, led to a widespread conviction that his philanthropy was just part of a public relations campaign. Then, on April 3, Federal District Judge Thomas Penfield Jackson ruled that Microsoft violated the law with "predacious" anticompetitive behavior, and the stock market knocked $80 billion off the company's value. Gates himself reportedly lost $12 billion to $14 billion that day, but the foundation's endowment remains intact: its donations come in the form of Microsoft stock and are immediately converted to cash. What effect, if any, the lawsuit will have on future contributions to the foundation is unclear. Microsoft intends to appeal, and the battle could go on for years.

Gates has always said that, like Carnegie, he will give away most of his fortune before he dies. He plans to make sure his children are well taken care of but doesn't want to leave them the burden of tremendous wealth. Carnegie, however, turned his full attention to philanthropy only after he retired from the steel business at age 65. Gates probably has several decades of earning and giving ahead. He has not set a schedule for dispersing his fortune. In February, Patty Stonesifer, the president of the foundation, said that Gates thought it had reached about the right size for the time being.

Primarily occupied at the moment with his company and his family, Gates has delegated the running of the foundation to his friend Stonesifer, a former Microsoft executive, and to his father, William H. Gates Jr., although he and his wife, Melinda, are actively involved. Well aware that effective philanthropy requires as much time and creativity as building a business does, Gates considers himself "*very* early on the learning curve of this stuff," he says. "There are just an infinite number of things to be figured out." Still, backed by his enormous resources and extraordinary renown (it would be hard to overestimate the power of being Bill Gates), the foundation is already having a major impact—not only on specific projects in the fields of education and global health but also on other wealthy individuals, on the American conversation about philanthropy, and on public policy.

One morning in February, Patty Stonesifer and I drove from Seattle to the Microsoft campus in Redmond to talk with Gates about his philanthropy. He was, of course, looking at a computer screen in his office when we arrived. Emerging from behind his desk, he had on a pale green button-down shirt with the initials W.H.G. in light blue over the left breast, tan slacks, tan socks, and brown basket-weave loafers. On the shelves and walls surrounding his workstation were pictures of Melinda and their two young children, a photograph of Einstein, several framed covers of *The Economist,* and an aboriginal mask from Australia. We sat around a small table in the anteroom—Gates's work and reception areas combined are about the size of a midlevel publishing executive's office in New York. Not exactly what you'd expect for a man whose company had a market value roughly equal to the gross domestic product of Spain.

There was no sign, for the next hour, that the release of Windows 2000 had set off firestorms the previous week, or that lawyers for both sides in the antitrust case were scheduled to make their final arguments the following day. Gates compartmentalizes well. At one point in the conversation he brought up his friend Warren Buffett, who does not intend to give his billions away until he has finished earning them. "Warren thinks it's very tricky to be in a meeting one minute where you're talking about giving away lots of money, and then in the next minute you're thinking about making money," Gates said. "He thinks that's a little schizophrenic, and I hear him. But I've always had partitions where I'm reading about biotech, or working on my job, or learning to play bridge. So, at least so far"—he shrugged and laughed—"it hasn't created any schizophrenia for me."

Gates and Stonesifer have worked together ever since she started at Microsoft in 1988, and they seem entirely at ease in each other's company. She is tall and slim at 43, with brown eyes, pale skin, freckles, and a close-cropped brush of red hair. For years she was the only female executive at Microsoft, and when she retired in early 1997 with Microsoft quantities of money, she didn't need another job. "Patty could sit on a beach for the rest of her life if she wanted to," says one of her friends. She takes no salary for running the Gates Foundation and serves on the boards of CBS, Amazon.com, and Kinko's.

Although they are widely recognized around Seattle, Stonesifer and the Gateses do not stay behind closed doors—they go to movies and restaurants and basketball games—and people come up to Stonesifer in coffee bars and airports with grant proposals and free advice. In the course of working on this article, I've come in for small doses of what she deals with all the time. The heads of five New York institutions suggested that I put in a good word for their financing requests in Seattle. A producer at *60 Minutes* who doubles as an amateur coach asked me, "How would Gates like to supply uniforms for a bunch of 13-year-old basketball players?" Gordon J. Davis, the chairman of Jazz at Lincoln Center: "Find out if he's interested in jazz." A young female editorial assistant: "Ask him if he knows any nice 26-year-old guys."

I repeated these requests to Gates, who laughed, then said, "Well, you know, capitalism has these strange things, where some people have all these resources." Having so much in the way of resources can make it hard to tell what people actually want. When he first met Vartan Gregorian, Gates recalls thinking, "'Ah, why is this guy spending time getting to know me?' First, he was at Brown. So I wondered, does he want a bunch of money for Brown? And then he'd come and see me and we'd talk about what were good causes, or what was going on with foundations." It turned out that Gregorian just wanted to encourage Gates to think about giving money away, not to ask for any.

In those early conversations with Gregorian, Gates was thinking about finding an underfinanced area of scientific research to support. Now the aspects of his philanthropical work that he seems most excited about have to do with redressing tremendous inequities in global health. According to the W.H.O., less than 10 percent of the world's medical research financing is directed at the health problems that afflict 90 percent of the human population. Pharmaceutical companies don't make drugs for people who can't afford them. And millions of children in poor countries die every year from diseases that could be prevented by existing vaccines. The Gates Foundation recently pledged $750 million to a fund that will help buy and distribute those medications in developing countries through a new group called Global Alliance for Vaccines and Immunization (GAVI). "We're in this unbelievable era where you could argue, What's the most amazing thing taking place?" Gates says, leaning forward in his chair. "Is it software technology stuff and the Internet and new forms of communication? Or is it the revolution in biology?"

At the World Economic Forum at Davos, Switzerland, in January, Gates was disappointed to find not everyone as galvanized as he is by the combination of biotechnological innovation, widespread social disparities, and hugely difficult problems that might be solved by the intervention of enormous resources and armies of intelligent people. He sat on a panel that officially inaugurated the global vaccine alliance with Gro Harlem Brundtland of the W.H.O., Carol Bellamy of Unicef, James Wolfensohn of the World Bank, Joaquim Chissano, the president of Mozambique, and Raymond Gilmartin of Merck. It was, Gates said in his office a month later, a colossal bore: "I was sitting there on that panel thinking, We're talking about saving three million lives a year here. It's about *people*. I hate to be critical, but that was one of the least inspirational, least informative panels I've seen."

Though he was by turns voluble, thoughtful, funny, self-deprecating, and serious on a range of subjects, Gates sidestepped my questions about personal motives for his philanthropical choices. The banker J. P. Morgan supposedly once said that a man always has two reasons for the things he does: a good reason, and the real reason (although in his own case he never acknowledged the slightest difference between the two). The "reasons" historically ascribed to philanthropy have ranged from guilt to concern for one's legacy to religious principle to noblesse oblige to plain generosity. It has been widely assumed that the "robber barons" of the Gilded Age tried to buy their way through the eye of the needle with large gifts to libraries, medical research, educational and cultural institutions, and the arts. However, as the historian Richard Hofstadter wrote in the 1940s: "To imagine that such men did not sleep the sleep of the just would be romantic sentimentalism. In the Gilded Age even the angels sang for them."

Maybe, but in fact these men did not believe—regardless of what others thought—that they had earned their fortunes in sinister ways. Rockefeller, Carnegie, and Morgan saw themselves as building great industrial or financial empires and making America rich, and they did not feel that they had to atone for commercial sins or "clean up" their images for posterity by giving money away. This is a very different era, but I would imagine that Gates sees himself as having created extraordinary new technological capacities and widespread public access to information, and as having helped stimulate the phenomenal recent growth of the American economy. That he wouldn't tell a reporter about his "real" reasons isn't surprising. Maybe, like Morgan, he doesn't think they are any different from the "good" ones. And as Gregorian says, it doesn't matter. What he's doing is more important than why.

In early January, I went to Africa with Stonesifer and the foundation's director of global health, Gordon Perkin, to see some of the projects they are underwriting in Ghana, Gambia, and South Africa. Stonesifer had specifically decided not to call on the heads of governments. She wanted to be able to spend her time talking with people "on the ground" about their work—on childhood immunization, family planning, cervical cancer, malaria, the reduction of maternal and infant mortality, and AIDS. Even before we reached Africa, however, it was apparent that you can't travel around the world representing Bill Gates with any degree of anonymity. At 6:30 A.M., as a jet-lagged Stonesifer waited in line at London's Gatwick Airport en route to Ghana, a New York investment banker standing behind her figured out who she was and told her how she ought to be spending Gates's money. When we arrived at the airport in Accra that night, someone was holding up a misspelled sign that said, "Welcome Bill and Malinda Gates Foundation," and a local hustler tried to charge $5,000 for getting some photography equipment through customs.

The foundation does not generally finance direct delivery of health services. Instead, it channels grants through existing organizations, seeking to identify good projects that are already under way and to find new models and strategies that work. This sounds more conservative than it is. All over the world, health care issues are inseparable from politics and economics, and anyone who has worked in developing countries will tell you that the most difficult problem for potentially lifesaving interventions is *delivery*—getting medications and services to the people who need them. The majority of the Gates Foundation's health financing will be directed at improving people's access to existing and newly developing medical technologies. To facilitate that access, the foundation promotes the use of simple tools like vaccines, contraceptives, nutritional supplements, single-use syringes, and diagnostic procedures. At an immunization clinic on our first day in Ghana, Dr. Perkin recognized a small circle on the label of a polio vaccine vial—a warning sign devised by a nonprofit organization he helped found in Seattle called Program for Appropriate Technology in Health. He was delighted when the nurse in charge was able to tell him that the darkening circle meant the vaccine was approaching its expiration date and had to be used right away. Even health workers who cannot read can dispense this medicine.

The Gates Foundation also seeks to support people who are finding innovative ways to approach public health problems and promote major social change. Lynette Denny, for example, whom we saw toward the end of the trip, is a gynecological oncologist working with women in impoverished squatter villages and townships near Cape Town. Most of these women have never seen a gynecologist before, much less had a Pap test. Cervical cancer is the leading cause of cancer death among women in developing countries, but it can effectively be prevented by early detection. Because Pap smears are complicated to administer and expensive to analyze, Dr. Denny's work led her and several colleagues to devise a simple new screening test for cervical cancer. In early January, the Journal of the American Medical Association published a study based on her group's work, showing that the new test detects the precursors of cervical cancer at least as well as the Pap test does. Many questions remain and the research is still under way, but this work could lead to extensive changes in social policy and the saving of millions of lives. Dr. Denny works with the Alliance for the Prevention of Cervical Cancer, which received a $50 million grant over five years from the Gates Foundation in 1999.

Gates has referred to people who don't operate at full mental capacity as having "unused bandwidth." Stonesifer doesn't appear to have any. Throughout the week we spent in Africa she worked from 7 A.M. until midnight every day, talking with people in hospital beds, nursing stations and makeshift doctors' offices, at briefing breakfasts, village councils, private houses, and dinner meetings. When we got back to a van or a plane, the rest of us would be ready to sleep or goof off. Stonesifer and Perkin spent the downtime talking about what they had learned, where they would like to go with it and how they would report back to Bill and Melinda. The book she read on the trip was "The Politics of International Health: the Children's Vaccine Initiative and the Struggle to Develop Vaccines for the Third World," by William A. Muraskin.

For a couple of days in Ghana, most of the people we met had never heard of Bill Gates. As we were about to leave for Gambia, however, Stonesifer got word that Ghana's controversial president, Jerry Rawlings, was coming to the airport to see us off. Rawlings has been a suprisingly outspoken advocate of AIDS education, family planning, economic development, and women's rights. A big man with a broad face framed by a salt-and-pepper beard, he arrived by helicopter. Striding across the tarmac in black jeans, cowboy boots, a black-and-white Nike warmup jacket, and shades, he looked more like a music-industry mogul than a head of state. In the airport lounge he mock-scolded Stonesifer: "Someone like you shouldn't arrive in Ghana without announcing your presence. I'm glad to hear about your noble intentions here. I had to come see you and thank Bill Gates." They talked for a few minutes, then he got around to what Stonesifer calls "the ask." (It is inevitable, and she's not cynical about it; she wants to know what people need.) "What we need in Ghana," said Rawlings, "is to make AIDS testing affordable." Then he stepped back onto the tarmac, signaled the chopper pilot by twirling his finger over his head, and took off.

By the time we reached Gambia, its president knew that Rawlings had met with Stonesifer and wanted an audience as well. It took some delicate negotiating to avoid a diplomatic insult. The lesson Stonesifer drew: political leaders play an important role in what the foundation is trying to do, and its officers can't go in under the radar.

*   *   *

The new headquarters of the Bill and Melinda Gates Foundation offer as sharp a contrast to the stone-and-glass-clad, high-rise, wood-paneled premises of the big East Coast foundations as the new techno-billionaires' dress code does to CEO pinstripes. A two-story tan and gray concrete building, it backs up against a marina on Seattle's Lake Union and is identified only by its street address. (It used to be a check-processing plant, which usually prompts someone to quip that it still is.) Inside, there are ficus trees, an orchid on the receptionist's desk, earth-tone walls, wood and slate-tile floors, several modest executive offices, an open geometry of staff cubicles, and 1,700,000 feet of computer cable.

When I first visited Seattle in early December, Nelson Mandela and his wife, Graca Machel, were in town to raise money for their work in Africa—Mandela and Gates have known each other since 1997—and Stonesifer spent part of a morning showing the couple around the building. At one point on the tour Stonesifer stopped, tapped her fingernail on a polished countertop that looked like stone, and said: "Sunflower seeds. We're testing new materials. It's very Seattle." Also very Seattle is the foundation's lean, informal structure. Last year, when Gates decided to combine two smaller charitable funds into one and increase the endowment, he specifically chose not to enlarge the foursome in charge of ultimate decisions—himself, his wife, his father (CEO) and Stonesifer (president)—and not to appoint a board. He had set up his first foundation in 1994, the year he married Melinda. At a bridal lunch the day before the wedding, his mother, Mary, a prominent civic leader in Seattle, read a letter to the couple saying, in effect, "From those who are given great resources, great things are expected." By all accounts Melinda has played a significant role in directing more of her husband's attention to the world outside Microsoft.

A few months after the wedding, Mary Gates died. Bill's father, who had also been a leader of Seattle's "old" philanthropy—chiefly the United Way—was moving toward retirement from the law firm Preston, Gates & Ellis and volunteered to help his son deal with the floods of requests for money that were coming in. (Although the father is William H. Gates Jr. and the son W.H.G. III, people in Seattle refer to the elder Gates as Bill Sr. and to the Microsoft founder as simply Bill.) Now 73 years old, with genial blue eyes, sparse white hair and big glasses, Bill Sr. is 6 feet 6 inches tall and looks like a combination of his son and Paul Volcker. Bill established the William H. Gates foundation in 1994 with $106 million and added about $2 billion over the next four years. It focused on global health issues and projects in the Pacific Northwest. Until last fall, Bill Sr. ran it out of cardboard boxes in the basement of his house.

Gates enlisted Stonesifer to launch the second foundation, aimed at reducing the "digital divide," early in 1997. She had just left Microsoft, where she had been head of the Interactive Media division; *Time* magazine in 1996 named her one of the 25 most influential people in America. Ready for a change and wanting more time for her two teenage children, she rented an office over a pizza parlor in Redmond and started a management consulting firm. Her first client was DreamWorks SKG. She lasted three months. "Someday I'll write a book called, *My 12 Weeks in Hollywood,*" she says with a laugh. By March she was running the new $200 million Gates library program, which provides computers, Internet access, and training and technical support in low-income communities all over the United States and Canada.

She had no hesitation about returning to the workaholic Gates fold. Raised in a Catholic family in Indiana (she was the sixth of nine children), she has always had a strong sense of social responsibility—she keeps a plastic figure of Jiminy Cricket in her office as a comic reference to her hyperactive conscience. "I loved working with Bill and Melinda at Microsoft, so to be able to use everything we'd learned in technology and turn it to social good, to help shape their philanthropical efforts and give the money back—this job was tailor-made for me." The foundation has proved no less demanding than Microsoft, but she does have somewhat more flexibility about time.

As the two Gates foundations combined and moved into new headquarters last year, they expanded their accounting and public affairs staffs and appointed executive directors for the library program, education, and global health. The Canadian-born Gordon Perkin, director of global health, has more than 35 years of experience in international health and family planning. The foundation's senior advisor for global health is William Foege, a widely revered epidemiologist and former head of the Centers for Disease Control and Prevention, who was part of the international team that eradicated smallpox. In all, the staff now consists of about 130 people, 110 of whom belong to what Gates calls the Internet Peace Corps—a team of young computer trainers who spend about half their time on the road wiring public libraries. Which leaves 20 people for everything else, although the officers consult with 60 to 75 experts in various fields. The Ford Foundation has a staff of 567 worldwide.

Stonesifer and Bill Sr. serve as cochairpersons of the foundation, but she essentially runs it—he doesn't want to be bothered with decisions about hiring, process, and organizational structure. On questions of grant-making, however, she says they are "two in a box—we try not to be at the same meetings since it's unnecessary; that way we get more done." Still, she confesses with a grin, it can be a little weird that "the other person in the box is Dad." Though she is the only nonfamily member of the group, Stonesifer is so close—and so fiercely loyal—to Bill and Melinda that she seems a virtual Gates. How do the foursome handle disagreements? They argue things out, she says: "All of the Gateses, and myself, are strong-minded, strong-willed individuals. That's one reason we get along so well."

Some philanthropy watchers are highly dubious about this all-in-the-family approach. The historian Mark Dowie, who is writing a book on American foundations, recently urged Gates to trade his wife and his father to the Ford Foundation for people with more experience and to set up an executive board with race and gender balance. Gordon Conway, president of the Rockefeller

Foundation, however, has been impressed with the leadership of the new Gates enterprise, finding it "extraordinarily well focused in the health field." And Charles Hamilton, executive director of the Clark Foundation, applauds the agility with which a closely held foundation can make decisions: "I hope Gates will continue to maintain personal control—that he really gets and stays involved."

Gates apparently intends to. He and Melinda set the overall direction and priorities for their giving, and Stonesifer and Bill Sr. report to them constantly—one on one, in four-way meetings, on the phone, and by e-mail, which they call simply "mail." They are rarely all in one place at the same time. Stonesifer travels to New York once a month for CBS board meetings and has been to Davos and India since the Africa trip. The foundation receives more than 3,000 proposals a month, and its public affairs manager, Trevor Neilson, gets about 500 additional personal requests about everything from eviction notices to medical bills to prosthetic limbs. The senior officers, with some staff help, weed out thousands of proposals that do not accord with the Gates aims, then submit lists of projects they would like to finance to Melinda and Bill, who read and talk about the proposals and personally approve every grant over $1 million.

Bill writes questions and comments all over the lists—sometimes saying simply yes (to a request for $40 million) or no, or "tell me more about respiratory diseases," or "why this country?" or "if this does well what's the next step?" His negative response isn't always final: "When I say no," he says with a grin, "somebody usually comes back with, 'Did you really mean to say no on this one?'" Melinda, who does not give interviews to the press, is more closely involved than her husband in the day-to-day operations of the organization. Do the couple have different kinds of input? "Melinda has a strong interest in children and early childhood," says Stonesifer. "Bill is very interested in medical interventions and new tools, in figuring out what is possible with new scientific technology. And they are both passionate about how those areas can work together."

Once Gates made up his mind to create a single large foundation, he began adding to it at the rate of $5 billion a quarter. And
since foundations are required by law annually to give away 5 per
cent of their assets, the directors of this $21.8 billion fund now
have to dispense more than $1 billion a year—not an easy thing to
do well. They insist on careful monitoring to assure that the
money is not wasted or mismanaged. They take a long-term,
strategic view of what their grants can do, and they place strong
emphasis on evaluation prcedures—even though measures of success in the nonprofit world are notoriously hard to come by. Stonesifer says, "I sometimes miss the marketplace, which really kicks
you around when you make a mistake."

At first, the selection process was largely reactive. But as the
foundation's resources have grown, notes Bill Sr., the process has
become more proactive, and the scope of the giving is narrowing
to areas in which the money stands to have the greatest impact—
projects that aim at the causes rather than the symptoms of social
problems. The officers talk a great deal about leverage, impact,
strategy, scale, and the "catalytic dollar" and are determined not to
let their financing drive other sources of money away. On the contrary, they try to use their grants and Gates's celebrity to bring
more partners and dollars to the table.

So far, the Gates domestic programs have drawn more critical
fire than the work in international health. Last September the
foundation announced that it was pledging $1 billion over 20
years to scholarships for minority students—for full-time college
programs and graduate study in engineering, math, science, education, or library science, to be administered by the United Negro
College Fund. In October, the conservative Weekly Standard ran
an article called "Bill Gates, Minority Leader: A Billion Dollars Is
a Terrible Thing to Waste." The argument: that the program
should not be race-based and is an attempt to circumvent recent
anti-affirmative-action rulings in states like Washington and California.

The library-wiring initiative has had critics from the start. It delivers Gateway machines and free Microsoft programs, which led to a wide-spread perception that Gates was using his philanthropy to expand the market for Microsoft, much the way tobacco companies hook adolescents on cigarettes. Stonesifer says, "The only software we donate is Microsoft, but these machines are wide open, and many of the libraries load them up with all kinds of other software." The negative reactions did not cause Gates to reconsider the program, reports Stonesifer, but he and Melinda didn't anticipate the cynicism. "Like the rest of us, they want people to think what they're doing is good." Stonesifer says. "It shouldn't have come as a surprise that one of Bill's first major philanthropical projects would be in the field of technology. All first gifts tend to be something you know about, and he had 20 years of technological expertise."

Gates looks back with some amusement at his belated realization that access to technological information might not be the answer to the world's most serious problems. Microsoft was donating computers to poor communities in Africa in the mid-90's, and during a visit to Johannesburg, Gates went to Soweto where he was proudly shown the town's single computer. As he took in his surroundings, he recalls, he said to himself: "'Hey, wait a minute—there's only one electrical outlet in this whole place.' And yup, they had plugged in that computer, and when I was there, man, that thing was running and everybody was very thankful. But I looked around and thought, Hmm, computers may not be the highest priority in this particular place. I wondered, Who the heck is going to be really using this thing?"

He says it was toward the end of 1998 that he realized—partly through working with Foege and Perkin, and partly through his own reading—how little international attention was being paid to some of the world's most urgent medical problems and how much of a difference his large-scale resources could make. The W.H.O. estimates that malaria kills about two million people a year, nearly half of them children in sub-Saharan Africa, and infects about 200 million more. There has been a 180 percent increase in the number of cases in South Africa over the past year and a dangerous rise in drug resistance to the disease. Roughly 2.3 billion people—more than a third of the world's population—are at risk of infection, but since most of them live in the world's poorest countries and cannot buy expensive drugs, there has been no financial incentive for pharmaceutical companies to develop a malaria vaccine. Piers Whitehead of Mercer Consulting has compared large pharmaceuticals to supermodels: they don't get out of bed and go to work for less than $350 million in annual sales for a single product. According to *The Economist,* the amount of money spent on malaria vaccine research worldwide in 1996 was about $60 million. In June 1999 the Gates Foundation set up a $50 million Malaria Vaccine Initiative. "With one grant," says Gates, "we became the biggest private funder of malaria research. It just sort of blows the mind."

The malaria vaccine research fund creates what economists call a "push" mechanism, providing the means for scientists to conduct studies that would not otherwise be economically feasible. And the foundation is tackling malaria in other ways as well. By putting up $750 million for GAVI, it also gives pharmaceutical companies a "pull" incentive—essentially saying, "If you develop a vaccine, we'll buy and distribute it." It is the medical equivalent of the fairy tale king who challenges his knights to solve some impossible problem, promising that the man who succeeds will marry his daughter. Still, scientists think it will take at least 10 years to find a vaccine against this powerful parasite.

The foundation is also applying the "pull" mechanism to the less glamorous but no less urgent problem of getting childhood vaccines that the industrialized world takes for granted—against measles, whooping cough, tetanus, polio, and diphtheria—to developing countries. It often takes 10 to 15 years for basic vaccines to get to people in poor countries, even though immunization could save millions of lives a year, and administering a $1 shot is much more cost-effective than paying for years of medical care. The $750 million fund will buy and distribute those basic drugs, along with new ones against yellow fever, hepatitis B, and Haemophilus influenza type B. That was the subject of the panel Gates found so disappointing at Davos. Michael Rothschild, dean of the Woodrow Wilson School at Princeton, thinks it "extremely smart of the Gates Foundation to move on all these fronts at the same time. It's hard to think of a more exciting image for science than finding a vaccine for malaria. But figuring out how to distribute a measles vaccine is about as sexy as clearing up the New Jersey Meadowlands."

Twenty-one billion, eight hundred million dollars. It is hard to conceive of that much money. To put the figure in some perspective: as of March 30, 2000, the market capitalization of Apple Computer was $22.5 billion; Gannett's was a little more than $20 billion, J.P. Morgan & Co.'s $21.9 billion and Safeway's $20.5 billion. The Ford Foundation, America's second largest, has an endowment of $14 billion, but its growth, like that of most philanthropical institutions, has come from asset appreciation over time. The Gates Foundation grew by nearly $20 billion in one year. Next to these Olympian sums, the recent charitable gifts of mere mortal billionaires—like the $150 million given to Stanford University by Jim Clark, the co-founder of Netscape, in 1999, or the $134 million that Warren Buffett and his wife, Susan, divided among four organizations—begin to look like pocket change.

The United States has not seen philanthropy on this scale since the era of Rockefeller, Carnegie, Morgan, and Ford. The sources of America's great fortunes have moved west over the course of the century, but as recently as 15 years ago there were no major foundations in the Pacific Northwest. Now venture capitalists and foreign dignitaries go to Seattle for the same reason Willie Sutton robbed banks. And over the past decade, the wealth created by the information technology and telecommunications businesses has been doing for Seattle what the big railroad and industrial fortunes did for New York in the Gilded Age. The city gleams with new or renovated cultural institutions and sports arenas—the Seattle Symphony's Benaroya Hall, the Seattle Art Museum, the SuperSonics' Key Arena, the Mariners' Safeco Field, and an as yet unbuilt waterfront sculpture park. Some of the new multimillionaires are putting personal time and money into social services and public schools. The Gates Foundation has recently given grants ranging from $5,000 for a local AIDS group to $30 million for King County's United Way.

One of the most ambitious of the Gates-financed projects is the New York–based International AIDS Vaccine Initiative. Founded by an intense, 43-year-old physician named Seth Berkley, IAVI identifies promising AIDS vaccine candidates, then brokers deals with drug manufacturers and developing countries to fast-track the candidates into clinical trials. More than 33 million people are infected with HIV worldwide, about 70 percent of them in sub-Saharan Africa, where AIDS is expected to kill more people in the coming decade than died in all the wars of the 20th century. Only a vaccine could stop this devastation. And as with malaria, pharmaceutical companies are not about to spend enormous amounts of money developing a vaccine that is needed primarily by people who can't afford it. But if IAVI supplies the research money, the pharmaceutical company has no major costs to recoup. In exchange for its financing, IAVI expects the company to provide the vaccine at low cost in developing countries or forfeit the rights to the technology. In the United States the company can charge whatever the market will bear. AIDS researchers believe it could take at least a decade to develop a vaccine against this constantly mutating virus, and some think it won't be possible at all.

Nonetheless, Berkley is determined to get human trials under way. The Gates Foundation gave the AIDS vaccine initiative $1.5 million in 1998 in support of a "scientific blueprint." Inaugurated at the international AIDS conference in Geneva in June 1998, the blueprint attracted worldwide attention and brought in additional financing—$325,000 from the British government and another $160,000 from the Elton John Foundation. That fall,

IAVI announced two novel vaccine approaches for Kenya and South Africa and started preparations for clinical trials. Early in 1999 the Gates Foundation granted the AIDS vaccine initiative $25 million to be paid over five years.

Like other Gates projects, this one has critics. Some want more emphasis on forcing pharmaceutical companies to donate huge quantities of therapeutic drugs like AZT to Africa—an issue that is fraught with economic and political complications. Others spoke off the record because their institutions hope to get Gates grants. One prominent AIDS researcher predicts that the vaccine route will prove fruitless—that no one knows what will spark broad immunity and, given the infrastructure problems in Africa, it would be impossible to deliver a vaccine even if science found one. He argues that Gates's support of IAVI is about politics and his image. The foundation, the physician suggests, would do a lot more good handing out condoms on truck routes from Kenya than paying hundreds of thousands of dollars to IAVI bureaucrats.

David Ho, the director of the Aaron Diamond AIDS Research Center, an affiliate of Rockefeller University, disagrees with this point of view. "Vaccines are the biggest thing in AIDS research today," he says, and the vaccine initiative is "a very worthy project" for Gates Foundation support. Dr. Ho, who came up with the concept of the triple-combination drug therapy that has significantly checked the progress of AIDS in the United States and Europe, thinks the freedom Gates has to provide substantial financing more quickly than the N.I.H. is essential. Wouldn't it be interesting, he reflects, "if Bill Gates were remembered in the future more for his philanthropy than for his work with computers?"

David Baltimore, president of the California Institute of Technology and chairman of the AIDS Research Vaccine Committee, says that AIDS research right now is in greater need of new ideas than of more money, but "we can't possibly do too much" about a disease that has "skyrocketed over everything else in importance." He thinks the vaccine initiative is positioning itself at a crucial juncture between drug companies and developing countries, that the candidates it is moving toward trials are good ones, and that science will learn from the research regardless of the outcome.

One IAVI-sponsored vaccine trial is scheduled to begin in Hlabisa, a village in the South African province of KwaZulu/Natal, before the end of 2000. The landscape of undulating hills and neatly planted farms around Hlabisa, 180 miles north of Durban, could be mistaken for Tuscany or Vermont. This beautiful place is the epicenter of South Africa's AIDS epidemic: 38 percent of the population is HIV positive, with the highest incidence among women and men in their twenties. Many of the men leave for months at a time to work in mines near Johannesburg, where they patronize prostitutes or take "town wives" and contract HIV. When they return home they infect their rural wives, who often pass the virus along to babies while nursing. A high rate of sexually transmitted diseases (about 25 percent) enhances the ease of HIV transmission. The community's religious leaders spend most of their time officiating at funerals. "This is not an epidemic," says Dr. Salim Abdool Karim, the principal investigator for the IAVI trial project in South Africa. "It's a catastrophe."

The day we were there the community held a meeting in an open field to discuss preparations for a vaccine trial. Because of its high levels of HIV and STD's, Hlabisa has a relatively well-developed medical system and a strong community advisory board that includes tribal and religious leaders, teachers, and health care and social service workers. The vaccine candidate, started last year with an initial $4.5 million grant from IAVI, is being developed jointly by the South African Medical Research Council, the University of Cape Town, the National Institute of Virology in South Africa, and a biotechnology company in Durham, N.C., called AlphaVax. It is based on the strain of HIV that dominates in this region. The first phase of the trial will simply test the vaccine for safety, using healthy volunteers in the United States and South Africa.

After the community meeting I took a walk with Janet Fröhlich, a tall woman with short dark hair and a strong South African accent who works in Hlabisa as a field coordinator for the Medical Research Council. The vaccine trial has to run in tandem with education and prevention, she said; measures that are perceived as "punitive," like insistence on men using condoms, have failed, and health workers are now trying to teach women how to protect themselves. They are also trying to teach both men and women how to talk about sex and STDs. A soccer game that had been going on during the meeting was still under way. As we stood watching the players, I realized that nearly a third of them will probably be dead in 15 years. Fröhlich said, "If you ask the boys what they know about AIDS, they say: 'We've learned not to sleep with the thin girls. Only sleep with the fat ones.'"

At the white house in March, President Clinton inaugurated his Millennium Vaccine Initiative, which includes a $1 billion tax credit for drug companies to speed up the development of new vaccines and $50 million for the Global Alliance for Vaccines and Immunization purchase fund—and he acknowledged the Gateses' leadership in these areas. The Gates Foundation is a relative newcomer to the field of global health, but in collaboration with others it has helped to create a sense of urgency about a wide range of international health problems, to mobilize vast financial resources, and to bring these issues to the forefront of economic and political debate.

On the subject of his own politics, Gates has refused to characterize himself as conservative or liberal and declines to declare a party affiliation. He contributes to both parties. Last fall he told Sam Howe Verhovek of *The New York Times* that he thinks the Republicans often do a good job of figuring out how to encourage wealth creation while Democrats tend to think more about how to spread wealth around—"and those are both things I think are very important." He went on with a smile: "When people attack the wealth-creation mechanisms, it seems to push me in one direction, and when they don't take spreading the wealth seriously, well, that pushes me in the other direction."

The Gates Foundation has a decidedly liberal agenda—intervening to offset social inequities in health and education—and the online magazine Salon "outed" Gates as a "closet liberal" in 1998 for supporting family planning, gun safety, and organizations that opposed tax cuts in Washington State. The downsizing of federal spending on health and social programs over the last two decades, along with a widespread decline of public confidence in Washington, has steadily shifted responsibility for social welfare issues to state and local initiatives and to private philanthropy. And though some conservatives dislike the Gates Foundation's choices and others think the money would do more good left in the marketplace, many favor this kind of privatization. Edward Crane, president of the Cato Institute in Washington—a libertarian policy center—says: "I applaud Gates for all the wealth he's created. It's his money, and he can do with it whatever he likes."

Times of extraordinary prosperity in America periodically draw national attention to the nature and reach of private philanthropy, raising moral and legal questions about accountability, taxation, spending requirements, and limitations on charitable giving. Susan Berresford, the president of the Ford Foundation, points out that Americans are at once fascinated by and profoundly uneasy about wealth and the power it confers, and she urges her colleagues to welcome increased public scrutiny. Michael E. Porter and Mark R. Kramer have argued in a recent Harvard Business Review that foundations need to improve their performance and justify their tax-exempt status by creating value much the way businesses do. Peter Bienstock, a Princeton, N.J., investor, predicts that the tremendous current flow of money into private foundations is going to create pressure for greater government regulation—that we are moving toward a period of "charitable trust-busting." And Joel L. Fleishman, a law professor at Duke University and president of the Atlantic Philanthropic Service Company in New York, has called for a new federal agency to regulate the nonprofit sector.

Probably the warning I heard most often in conversations about the Gates Foundation had to do with the law of unintended consequences. "Grant-making on that scale is a very difficult art," says Edward A. Ames at the Mary Flagler Cary Charitable Trust, who fears that the people in charge of the "huge new pools of money being turned to philanthropy" may not know enough about "the impact they can have on the fields that are the objects of their generosity."

Richard Gilder, an investment manager, cautions, "Giving is as tough a business as getting." Gilder has done a substantial amount of both. "You can do so much damage," he says. "The rule in philanthropy, as in medicine, should be, 'First, do no harm.'"

The best story about unintended consequences comes from Gordon Conway at the Rockefeller Foundation, who worked as an entomologist in Borneo in the 1960s. In an attempt to control malaria, the W.H.O. sprayed houses with DDT. The campaign did kill mosquitoes and reduced the incidence of malaria, but it had side effects. House lizards ate the dead bugs, then cats ate the lizards and died from the accumulated insecticide. Without cats, the local rat population exploded—rats that could carry plague and typhus. Neighboring states donated cats to the affected upland regions. For the remote interior, the W.H.O. and Singapore's Royal Air Force devised a maneuver worthy of Disney called Operation Cat Drop: they packed cats into perforated containers and sent them plummeting into upland villages by parachute.

The day we drove to Hlabisa in mid-January, the Gates Foundation group took off two hours between 6 A.M. and 8 A.M. for a mini-safari at the Phinda game reserve in Zululand on the eastern coast of South Africa. The high point was a mother cheetah with four cubs, who let us watch her from about 20 yards away for nearly 10 minutes. As we drove back toward the lodge, our guide, Gavin, said that since there is no hunting in the park, the predators tend to take over and kill too many other animals. As a result, the wardens periodically capture some of the big cats and send them off to other parks.

"Is that a good idea?" Patty Stonesifer wanted to know. "To intervene in nature that way?" Gavin said, "Oh, they do it at all the big parks, even Kruger," which didn't really answer the question.

"It's such an enormous responsibility," Stonesifer reflected. "How do you know how far to go?"

A nationwide bacterial outbreak responsible for death and sick-
ness was traced to a Michigan meat plant. These disquieting
excerpts from a five-part series in the *Detroit Free Press* point out
not only the deficiencies of that facility, but also the potential for
similar disasters elsewhere. They outline how health concerns are
commonly overlooked. Warning: It might be best not to read this
well-researched narrative from Jeff Taylor, Janet L. Fix, and Alison
Young immediately before dining.

Jeff Taylor, Janet L. Fix, and Alison Young

A KILLER IN OUR FOOD

WHAT COULD BE MORE WHOLESOME than a
turkey sandwich, more American than a hot dog? We eat them all
the time without much thought. But our assumptions about the
safety of these foods proved to be dead wrong last fall when an outbreak of illness swept the country.

Hot dogs and lunch meats, made in Michigan under such
trusted brand names as Ball Park and Sara Lee, carried a virulent
strain of bacteria that killed at least 21 people, sickened 80 more
and prompted the largest meat recall in U.S. history.

This is the story of that outbreak: how it splintered lives,
shook a reputable company, and sent scientists on a frustrating
quest for clues to a mystery that was never quite solved.

The aftermath left unsettling conclusions. Precooked foods
aren't always ready to eat. Dangerous gaps exist in the food safety
system. And even now, we have no firm answers as to what went
wrong at Bil Mar Foods, the plant blamed for the outbreak.

In this series, you'll learn about sanitation problems inside the massive plant. You'll go behind the scenes with medical sleuths who traced the outbreak through high-tech genetic fingerprinting and old-fashioned instinct. You'll go inside the company boardroom where executives jostled with the tough choice to order the $76-million recall.

And you'll meet the people who paid the highest price, with their health and lives.

Federal regulators say Bil Mar Foods was a typical plant. That may be the most disturbing thing of all.

March 12, 1998

Inside the Bil Mar Foods plant, Borculo, Michigan
The damp room offered a splendid opportunity for bacteria to spread.

Beads of water hovered from pipes and overhead fixtures, splashing down onto two racks of freshly made turkey franks. It was an unappetizing sight, for sure.

But more than that, it was dangerous. Disease-causing bacteria can lurk and grow in condensation droplets. They thrive in a moist environment.

Inspector Brian Ford had seen the problem before.

He and other federal meat inspectors had cited the plant numerous times for condensation buildups. On this morning, the plant was about to be hit twice more for such violations.

Just an hour after Ford found the dripping water at 8:05 A.M., another inspector found condensation buildup elsewhere along the hot dog production lines.

"Fluid was dripping onto exposed franks," the inspector wrote, "and these franks were being conveyed down the line to packing machines."

In his report, Ford noted a particularly disturbing detail—that only 15 minutes before he arrived, a Bil Mar employee had verified that the area was clean, sanitized, and ready for work to continue.

Clean and ready?

At Bil Mar, where workers churned out as much as a million pounds of hot dogs and other meats each day, keeping the plant clean was a monumental job. Bil Mar was the largest meat plant owned by Sara Lee Corp. It often ran seven days a week, producing some of America's favorite foods, including Ball Park hot dogs and Sara Lee Premium deli meats.

To sanitation employees, it seemed that there was hardly enough time to get the work done.

Shawn Maguire couldn't believe the pressure.

Most nights were a race against dawn, as her cleaning crew and others tried to scrape, spray, and cleanse away the greasy residue left each day throughout the huge plant near Zeeland.

The job was exhausting, with so many dirty floors, counters, mixers, vats, conveyors, ovens, and other equipment spread across a main plant bigger than 10 football fields.

Workers were supposed to clean every inch of it, especially surfaces and equipment that touched the hot dogs and other meats. That meant scrubbing meat residue from a lot of hard-to-reach places, and then sanitizing the work surfaces with chemicals against an unseen danger: bacteria.

Maguire, 30, had never worked in a meat plant before she was hired through a temporary agency to work at Bil Mar in April 1998. Before that, she had held a variety of jobs; she had worked at a yogurt plant and driven a school bus.

She hoped to find better pay at Bil Mar, where workers were paid around $10 an hour, and could make a lot more with overtime. For a woman with a young son, that was inviting.

Maguire says she was quickly put in charge of a sanitation team. They worked the graveyard shift, cleaning in the hot dog production area.

They were expected to get the work done in time for the morning start-up, but it was a struggle.

"The sanitation crew that I was working with was horrible," Maguire said. "We were all brand new. And we learned together, and we did the best job we could do."

The crew often got started late because workers who made hot dogs during earlier shifts got behind. That put sanitation crews in a squeeze to finish by morning.

"I would come in and go, 'My God, the chain on this linker is a mess. What have you guys been doing?'" Maguire said, referring to machinery used to form hot dogs into links.

But she knew her crew was trying. "We didn't have time to do what we were supposed to."

As employees tried to keep pace with the demands, they often had inspectors such as Ford looking over their shoulders.

"Brian walked around like he owned the place and he busted us in the frank plant all the time," Maguire said. "We were trying to get contact surfaces clean, and he'd say, 'Hey, there's a speck of meat on the ceiling.' How could he see it? It was 40 feet up. But most of the time he was right."

Maguire's inexperience, and ongoing sanitation problems in the hot dog production area, prompted the company to move her to a job monitoring ovens, she said.

It was more manageable. Even so, she said, she quit in August and returned to the less stressful job of driving a school bus.

The year had gotten off to a shakier start than Bil Mar managers had wanted.

They already were trying to rebound from a costly setback at the end of 1997. That November, the U.S. Department of Agriculture temporarily shut down the plant for ongoing condensation and sanitation problems. The plant had been flagged by the USDA for having too many critical sanitation violations at the time.

A shutdown is a serious action to which the USDA seldom resorts. Thus, there was serious concern at the Chicago headquarters of Sara Lee.

The plant was allowed to reopen the same month, subject to close monitoring by the regulators.

The plant showed some improvement, USDA records indicate, but continued to struggle with sanitation violations as the new year began. In February 1998, Bil Mar Vice President Mary Delrue sent a memo to managers and implored them to cut down on the number of problems being cited by the USDA.

She reminded them that the plant's performance was measured by how often it was written up for food safety violations.

"We control our own destiny," Delrue wrote, adding: "We are very proud of the fact that we are the leading producer of meat products labeled under the Sara Lee brand name. We must do our utmost to protect this brand, along with all of the products we produce, by insuring they are manufactured under the highest quality and food safety standards possible. *Quality Products made by Quality People!*"

During the first six months of 1998, government inspectors cited the plant for 112 violations. Both Sara Lee and the USDA say that was an improvement over the previous year. Most of the new violations were fairly routine slipups. But other lapses were serious.

Inspectors caught workers dropping knives on the dirty slaughtering room floor and returning to work without washing the tools. They found scraps of old meat lodged in equipment that supposedly had been cleaned and sanitized. They discovered slaughtered turkey carcasses stained with excrement, waiting to be processed into lunch meats or hot dogs. They found rust, plastic chips, metal shavings, and other debris in food moving along the processing lines.

At times—just as inspector Ford did when he found water dripping on the hot dogs—inspectors hounded the plant about not correcting problems that kept cropping up.

Inspector Rodney Mueller reached the boiling point on April 1.

After earlier in the day discovering rodent droppings in a spice room, which had been a problem cited before, Mueller ran into another repeat offense in an area where employees were carelessly handling food.

Mueller, in a handwritten note to his supervisor, blasted plant employees for failing to immediately correct problems when they came up.

Mueller said he did "not believe the plant employees should be able to contaminate product by ripping it open and getting dirt on the product, and then just leave it and maybe someone else will catch it. If they contaminate product, it should be either corrected or taken care of."

It was a frustrating time for federal meat inspectors. They were unhappy about a new inspection system that had been put in place at 300 of the nation's largest meat plants.

Bil Mar was in that first wave. The new system, for the first time, put the primary responsibility for food safety on the plant workers and managers and placed USDA inspectors in a backup, spot-checking role. Before, USDA had the primary responsibility for food safety checks.

The USDA was hoping that the plant would take on greater responsibility for preventing and catching problems that could jeopardize food safety.

To do that, the plant had to begin doing more to police itself—while maintaining voluminous records about every critical operation in the plant, from monitoring oven temperatures to keeping cleanup logs.

It was all supposed to make America's meat plants safer. But was Bil Mar up to the challenge?

Fourth of July Weekend
The hot dog lines, Bil Mar

The Fourth of July holiday shutdown was drawing near at Bil Mar, and the plant managers would finally have time to get rid of one of their worst headaches.

Or so they thought.

They had been planning for months to replace a faulty refrigeration unit in the area known as the retail hopper room, where hot dogs bound for grocery stores were sorted before being packaged.

The large, ceiling-mounted unit kept the temperature in the frank room cool. But the piece of equipment had been a lingering problem.

It was one of the chief offenders in the plant's condensation problems.

Bil Mar managers had originally planned to remove the unit in

May 1998. But the removal was pushed back to the July 4 holiday weekend.

The job turned out to be a bear. The chilling unit was so large and bulky that workers had to dismantle it with saws before lugging it out of the plant.

The work may have kicked up a lot of dust around the hopper room and in nearby areas. Workers also tramped through other parts of the plant as they hauled the dismantled cooler away.

Cleaning up the construction mess was critical, to ensure that the room was sanitary when production resumed. The plant did a cleanup, but it may not have been enough.

For most of 1998, Bil Mar's sanitation workers had routinely used testing kits to swab samples from equipment, floors, and other surfaces. The tests detected the presence of a variety of cold-loving bacteria that could thrive in the plant's moist, refrigerated environment. Some of these bacteria were harmless, but one in particular—*Listeria monocytogenes*—could be deadly.

When tests came back positive, as they did from time to time, there was no way to tell whether they had detected harmless or dangerous bacteria. Either way, the bacteria weren't supposed to be there, and a bad sample meant equipment and work surfaces had to be re-cleaned and re-sanitized, then checked again for bacteria.

After the Fourth of July construction was finished and the hot dog lines resumed production, there was a sudden increase in the presence of bacteria.

Over the next six weeks, 11 of the 12 swab samples taken came up positive for cold-loving bacteria. Only three of the previous 12 swabs had detected bacteria in the weeks before July 4.

Maybe the increase involved only harmless bacteria.

Or maybe not.

The only way to know whether the rare and dangerous listeria bug was present was to do more complex testing. Those tests weren't required.

And they were never done.

Monday, July 27
USDA inspectors' office, the Bil Mar plant

As the bad swabs continued, inspectors remained concerned about sloppy cleaning efforts.

On back-to-back days—July 26 and July 27—inspectors forced cleaning crews to return for two to three hours to re-clean dirty areas along the hot dog lines, USDA records show.

Not only were areas unsanitary, plant workers had passed them off in their housekeeping records as being ready for production.

John Stephenson, a senior USDA official assigned to the plant, expressed "major concern" in a memo to Bil Mar Vice President Mary Delrue.

Stephenson noted that the problems weren't confined to the hot dog lines. Other areas of the plant, he said, "appeared to have been neglected for a significant period of time."

Delrue promised that the plant would do better.

Thursday, August 13
The Bodnar home, Memphis, Tennessee

As he had done every day for the past 25 years, 76-year-old John Bodnar pulled out the black loose-leaf binder that served as his diary and prepared to recount the day's events.

Without fail, Bodnar took time daily to jot down the momentous as well as mundane details of life with his wife Helen, the woman he called "Mom." He recorded where they shopped, what they ate, and when they slept. After a quarter of a century, his log runs more than 3,000 pages and fills more than a dozen thick three-ring binders.

On page 2,650, Bodnar recorded what they did the evening of August 13: For dinner, *"we had soup and hot dogs for our meal, watched* Promised Land *and* Diagnosis Murder—*darn mystery is continued next week. Bed by 9:30 for both."*

The Bodnars had met in 1945 at a B29 bomber base in Salina, Kansas: She was in the Women's Army Corps, he was a mechanic. They married within a year. Later he earned a living as a service manager at a Cadillac dealership in St. Louis. After he retired, they moved around the country, eventually settling in Memphis to be near a daughter.

As he aged and his memory faltered, Bodnar found that the log came in handy when he and his wife disagreed over what they had done and when.

"I could always check my log," he said, "to see if I was right."

One thing they didn't share was a love of hot dogs. "I'm not crazy about hot dogs, but Mom sure liked them," Bodnar said. His wife always bought the Ball Park brand "because they were plumper than other brands," he said.

On August 22, when Helen again ate hot dogs, her husband ate other things. *"We ate shrimp, hot dogs and Polish sausage sandwiches and ice cream before bed,"* he recorded in his log.

Over the next two months, Bodnar continued to recount in his journal the ordinary, slow-paced life of a retired couple content to enjoy their garden, their four children and grandchildren, and each other.

For fun, they'd make the four-hour drive in their Saturn to a gambling spot in Tunica, Mississippi. There they'd play nickel slots and enjoy the company of other retirees.

Everything seemed to be going so well. That all changed October 3.

That's when Helen, who had seemed perfectly healthy, crumpled into a pile on the kitchen floor.

"Mom opened the screen door to talk to me—next I heard a big thump. I ran inside and found her lying flat on her back from the stove to the door," Bodnar wrote. *"Helen was as white as a sheet and didn't say anything for about 30 seconds . . . About to call 911 when she started to come to, so I lifted her up and walked her into our bedroom where she put on her gown and laid down on the bed."*

In the middle of the night, Helen woke up, wracked by pain. Her husband took her to the emergency room at St. Francis Hospital, where she was admitted. For two days, doctors ran a battery of tests. But they could find nothing wrong and sent her home October 5.

Within 24 hours, Helen was back in the emergency room and placed in intensive care. Her fever had spiked to 104 degrees and her belly was grotesquely bloated.

"She looked like she was nine months pregnant again," her husband said.

Helen's condition progressively worsened. Doctors suspected meningitis and ordered a CAT scan and spinal tap. They warned her family her chances of surviving were slim.

"The chaplain came in to say a prayer with us," Bodnar wrote. *"Dr. took the spinal tap. Fluid should be clear, but it's cloudy. May be a sign of meningitis, an analysis should show the results."*

By the time the meningitis diagnosis was confirmed, Helen had fallen into a coma. Doctors couldn't lower her fever and she needed a respirator to breathe. In the simplest of language, they explained that Helen had picked up a germ. They didn't use the germ's full name: *Listeria monocytogenes.*

This deadly bacterium can cause several serious conditions, including meningitis.

Over the next few days, the family kept a vigil and prayed. Sister Regina splashed holy water on Helen's forehead as she recited a Hail Mary.

"Helen, please open your eyes," Bodnar wrote in his diary October 14. She never did.

On October 19, Helen's blood pressure plummeted and her heart finally failed.

"Mom lying there peaceful at last," her husband wrote. *"She looks much better with all that equipment removed. I kissed her good-bye, told her that I would see her soon."*

First Week in October
State Health Department, Columbia, Tennessee
Donna Gibbs felt a trace of alarm as she read the report. Two people from Shelbyville had been diagnosed with illnesses caused by *Listeria monocytogenes.*

In her 25 years with the Tennessee Health Department, Gibbs

had seen listeria reports only occasionally, maybe once every four or five months. But she had never seen two cases in one week—let alone in a town of just 14,000 people.

Was this the tip of an outbreak?

Gibbs, a communicable-disease coordinator for 12 counties in south-central Tennessee, was familiar with this germ.

It causes listeriosis and is one of the deadliest food-borne pathogens. It kills a far greater percentage of victims than better-known bacteria such as salmonella and E. coli 0157:H7.

Past listeriosis outbreaks had been linked to certain types of soft cheeses, milk, pâté, and vegetables. Cooking kills *Listeria monocytogenes,* but unlike most other food-borne bacteria, this one thrives and multiplies in the cold.

Since 1985, when the listeria bug killed 48 people during an outbreak in Los Angeles that was linked to contaminated cheese, the number of listeriosis cases had steadily declined. About 1,850 cases are reported nationally each year.

But it's believed that many more people suffer from listeriosis without knowing it. In healthy people, listeria causes symptoms that often are dismissed as the flu—nausea, vomiting, diarrhea. But it can kill the most vulnerable: the elderly, young children, and people with weakened immune systems, such as people with HIV and cancer. It can cause miscarriages and stillbirths.

Concerned, Gibbs called one of the state epidemiologists in Nashville.

"He agreed that two cases were weird, but we had no way to link them," he said.

But Gibbs remained troubled. Food-borne diseases generally show up in clusters. And within two weeks, two more cases of listeriosis landed on her desk.

Gibbs alerted the state epidemiologist again. "What's going on? Something is going on," Gibbs told Dr. Allen Craig, the deputy state epidemiologist. "We've got to find out what's going on."

Craig agreed and fired off an e-mail Oct. 20 to the U.S. Centers for Disease Control and Prevention in Atlanta, urging the federal infectious disease experts to figure out whether Tennessee's listeriosis cases were linked in some way.

While they waited for a reply, Gibbs puzzled over what she knew already. She hoped to find a link between the victims. But what could it be? Three were men—ranging in age from 30 to 60—who had become ill in September and early October. But one case involved an infant.

Gibbs was a go-getter. She started as a typist in 1974 at the Tennessee Health Department and quickly advanced. In the 1980s, when AIDS began its deadly spread, Gibbs went door-to-door warning people about the danger of sexually transmitted diseases.

Gibbs's job was tough on shoe leather, and on the soul. Nobody was happy when she came knocking, and they always knew who it was at the door. A Loretta Lynn look-alike, Gibbs still drives the 1978 ice-blue Corvette she did then. "Even if people didn't know me," she said, "they knew my car."

She knew on Oct. 20 that figuring out which food harbored *Listeria monocytogenes* could be impossible. The bug can take up to 70 days after food is eaten to develop symptoms. And in these cases, there was no obvious link.

The three men lived far apart. They didn't work together, hadn't eaten at the same restaurants.

The two-week-old infant had been rushed in August to a hospital by her parents because she had a 104-degree fever and no appetite. Doctors did a spinal tap and found she had listeriosis.

The infant's case deepened the mystery for Gibbs. "What kind of food could a two-week-old baby and a sixty-year-old man have both eaten?" she wondered. "These four people have absolutely nothing in common."

With the baby's case dating back two months, Gibbs wondered how many other listeriosis cases had not yet been reported to the Health Department. She feared the worst.

Early November
Centers for Disease Control, Atlanta

The e-mail from Tennessee didn't set off any alarms for the nation's top medical epidemiologists at the CDC.

"We get e-mails like the one from Tennessee every week. Most will not turn out to be much of anything, and very few turn out to be an outbreak," said Dr. Paul Mead, who oversees investigations of food-borne illnesses.

Nonetheless, the CDC asked Tennessee officials to send in lab samples for further testing.

"Because of the diffuse nature of food-borne illnesses, a handful of cases in one state doesn't necessarily stand out as a catastrophe," Mead said. "But if twenty states call, you know you have a big problem."

By mid-November, the calls from other states were pouring in.

Besides the four known cases in Tennessee, Ohio had 35 reported cases, Connecticut had 8, New York had 15. (Two people had fallen ill in Michigan, but the cases had not yet caught the attention of state health officials.)

New York officials were especially concerned.

The state had been working with Cornell University scientists to monitor and analyze the genetic makeup of various food-borne bacteria found in New York.

Cornell professor Martin Wiedmann had discovered that half of the state's 15 listeriosis cases shared the same genetic fingerprint. And that mutual fingerprint, later dubbed the E pattern, was extremely rare.

That meant all the victims shared something in common and likely had been sickened by food from the same manufacturer.

Wiedmann, Mead, and the state health officials were convinced: They had a major, multistate outbreak on their hands.

They had to trace its source. Fast.

Listeria monocytogenes could be a virulent killer.

"Twenty to thirty percent of those who get it die," Wiedmann said. "So if you move fast, you may save lives."

Sunday, November 15, 1998

Hills & Dales Hospital, Cass City, Michigan

In their 57 years together, Dottie Eberlein had never seen her husband this sick.

Art Eberlein had always been so vibrant, with a sparkle of mischief in his blue eyes. Even at age 80, the retired high school band teacher had stayed active.

He was a popular figure in his hometown of Sabewaing, a one-stoplight village on the shore of Saginaw Bay, where he directed a 38-piece community band that was a highlight of local holiday festivals.

But now he lay still in a hospital bed, an intravenous line sunk in one arm, his wiry, 125-pound body aching and spent. . . . The tests revealed a rare food-borne bug that his doctor knew about but had never treated before: *Listeria monocytogenes.*

Tuesday, November 24

Michigan Health Department, Lansing

The outbreak was spreading.

But up to now, word still hadn't reached health officials in most states, including Michigan.

Although experts at the U.S. Centers for Disease Control and Prevention had concluded 12 days earlier that an outbreak appeared to be emerging, they had waited for further evidence before sending out a nationwide alert.

In a laboratory at the Michigan Department of Community Health, a fax machine churned out the notice. It warned health departments across the country to be on the lookout for illnesses caused by *Listeria monocytogenes.*

The fax explained that there had been a sharp increase in listeriosis cases in New York, Ohio, Connecticut, and Tennessee.

Michigan health officials checked their records: Only two listeriosis cases had been reported to them in recent weeks, one from October and the other from November. That didn't seem out of the ordinary for a state that annually sees about two dozen cases.

Art Eberlein was one case. The other, dating to early October, involved a young woman enrolled at Western Michigan University in Kalamazoo.

The woman at first just had flu-like symptoms. The next day her roommate found her delirious in their dorm room, according to Dr. Rick Tooker, Kalamazoo County's chief medical officer. She was rushed to the emergency room at Bronson Hospital.

There, doctors discovered she had meningitis, a dangerous swelling of the lining of the brain and spinal cord that can cause coma and death. A culture of fluid taken during a spinal tap revealed that the listeria bacterium was causing the meningitis.

Kalamazoo County health officials began the routine follow-up, quizzing the student about what foods or beverages she consumed.

"Every day, or nearly every day, she'd have a deli turkey sandwich," Tooker recalled in a recent interview.

When Tooker's office first investigated, the significance of the woman's lunch routine wasn't obvious. Later it would become crystal clear. Sara Lee Corp. sponsored the deli stands in dorms across campus, and the meat she had eaten came from Sara Lee's Bil Mar Foods plant, in nearby Borculo.

The woman eventually recovered, Tooker said. She was never publicly identified.

As the state health department reviewed the two cases, there were no obvious links. But following the CDC's instruction, they rounded up lab samples from the two patients and shipped them to Cornell University in New York for genetic fingerprinting, a way of identifying each bacterium's unique structure.

Michigan health officials could have run the tests; they consider themselves pioneers in the technology. But because of cost concerns, the department had a policy of only doing such tests after an outbreak had already been identified in the state.

While the state waited for results from Cornell, the toll of victims was growing in Michigan.

One woman was already dead.

Wednesday, November 25

Clinton Grove Cemetery, Mt. Clemens

On the day before Thanksgiving, Gloria Andrzejewski's family buried her and said their final good-byes.

She was just 56.

An active member of Zion United Church of Christ in Mt. Clemens, where she had served as secretary for 13 years, Andrzejewski was a woman of strong faith. Before her death, the Clinton Township woman had endured a 15-year struggle against multiple myeloma, which causes bone marrow tumors. The condition had weakened her immune system.

And that had made her vulnerable to infections.

So she was no match for a bacterium like *Listeria monocytogenes*.

Andrzejewski died on November 22 at Harper Hospital in Detroit.

Her family and her best friend declined to talk about what happened. Their grief is still too strong.

They didn't learn she had been infected by the listeria bacteria until test results came back after her death.

And they had no idea her death had been linked through genetic fingerprinting to a nationwide outbreak until contacted by the *Free Press* this summer.

Thursday, November 26

A retirement complex in East Lansing

The day after Andrzejewski's funeral, George O'Brian began his own fight against death. It was Thanksgiving Day.

Up to then, O'Brian had enjoyed good health, especially for a man of 94. He was still independent, able to care for himself and get around on his own with the help of a walker. And he could still see and hear well enough to enjoy sports on radio and television, especially broadcasts of his beloved Michigan State Spartans and Detroit Tigers.

After watching football throughout the day, O'Brian began to feel ill. By bedtime, he couldn't get up out of his living room chair. He had a fever of 103 degrees but refused to go to the hospital.

The next morning he was still suffering. That was it. His wife, Mareda, insisted he go to the hospital. At Ingham Regional Medical Center, doctors began treating him with antibiotics. The diagnosis didn't come until three days later: listeriosis.

O'Brian was in agony: Stomach cramps wracked his body. His belly was bloated. His body burned with fever.

O'Brian loved turkey club sandwiches. His wife recalled that she usually bought the Sara Lee brand. Genetic fingerprints would later confirm that he had been infected by the strain of listeria traced to the Bil Mar outbreak.

After weeks in hospitals and a nursing home, O'Brian finally returned home in mid-February. But he never really recovered.

The ravages of the disease stripped him of his independence, leaving him unable to walk or care for himself without assistance. And the illness nearly stole his will to live.

He began to tell his wife of 48 years, "I wish I had died, because the pain is so terrific."

Friday, November 27
Lorain County Health Department, Ohio
Dr. Eileen Dunne had been on a long chase with no reward.

She was new at this kind of work, but she was also tireless and smart. She had joined the U.S. Centers for Disease Control and Prevention just five months earlier as an epidemic intelligence officer.

She worked with Dr. Paul Mead, the CDC epidemiologist in charge of the nationwide listeria outbreak investigation. He had dispatched her to Ohio to look into several listeriosis cases reported there.

Even though Dunne, 33, was a CDC newcomer, she had arrived on the job with substantial credentials. She had nine years of medical training, including an MD in public health from Tulane Medical School, a residency in internal medicine at Oregon Health Sciences University, and specialty training in infectious diseases at the University of Colorado.

Until she began working with Mead on the listeria cases, Dunne had never before investigated a multistate bacterial outbreak. Indeed, this was only her second epidemiological field study.

Dunne initially focused on three cases reported at Anchor Lodge, an upscale nursing home complex in the Cleveland suburb of Lorain, on Lake Erie. Those turned out to be false leads.

The genetic fingerprint of the listeria that sickened the nursing facility's residents didn't match the fingerprint of the outbreak strain. So she shifted direction. Working with the Lorain County Health Department, Dunne decided to go door-to-door and use the phone to question other listeriosis victims who had been interviewed previously, in hope of finding something that was overlooked the first time.

Her persistence paid off with a find that would turn out to be one of the crucial breaks in the investigation.

Dunne and a local health official contacted a woman in Lorain who had given premature birth to a girl in early November. Both mother and child had been diagnosed afterward with listeriosis.

"She remembered making and eating chili dogs on October 3," Dunne recalled in an interview. "But she never got sick."

To Dunne's amazement, the woman had held on to that package of Ball Park hot dogs.

Dunne marveled at how eager the woman was to help, even while dealing with the stress of diapers, bottles, and new motherhood.

"I thought it was neat," Dunne said. "Things were a little crazy for this woman. Her baby was screaming and there was baby stuff everywhere, but she really wanted to help so others didn't get sick."

Dunne packed the hot dogs in ice and shipped them off to the CDC's lab for testing.

Monday, December 14
U.S. Centers for Disease Control, Atlanta
Lots of victims. Not enough answers.

That's how it had been for weeks in the slow-moving investigation to find the source of the outbreak.

But a few important clues were finally emerging.

Health officials, after weeks of knocking on doors and quizzing people about what they had eaten, had hit on a common theme. Many of the 41 known victims had reported eating hot dogs. (Because of a flaw in the CDC's questionnaire, victims were not asked whether they ate deli meat.)

Three hot dog brands stood out—Ball Park, Bryan, and Khan. All were made by Sara Lee.

But Sara Lee was a huge company, with several meat plants producing hot dogs under these and other brand names.

The package of Ball Park franks recovered from the refrigerator of the Lorain County woman offered a strong lead. The manufacturing codes on the package listed their maker as federal plant No. P-261.

Bill Mar Foods in Michigan.

The CDC was still running tests on the hot dogs to determine whether they were contaminated with listeria. Results were still three days away.

But another clue was pointing to Bil Mar.

In New York, experts at Cornell University had discovered some additional samples that tested positive for the outbreak strain of listeria. One came from a sample of Sara Lee chicken deli meat that also was made at the Bil Mar plant.

In his cramped office, Mead reviewed all the data. Too many signs pointed to Bil Mar.

Mead determined it was time to get someone to the plant.

He decided to send Dunne from Ohio. He reached her on December 14 at the Lorain County Health Department, where she was going through patient files.

Usually calm, Mead could hardly contain his excitement, Dunne recalled.

"He said we'd really had a big break," Dunne said.

"He asked if I'd be interested in going to the plant."

Of course, she said enthusiastically. "It was an exciting moment," she recalled. "Something EIS officers live for. You get to play a pivotal role in public health by sleuthing out a very unusual pathogen. It's great to be part of that."

She boarded a plane for western Michigan.

Tuesday, December 15

Days Inn, Grand Rapids

Carrying just the one travel bag she had taken to Ohio, Dunne had arrived in Grand Rapids late the night before. By midday Tuesday, she was back at the airport holding a sign bearing the names of the investigators from the U.S. Department of Agriculture who were to join her in the search.

They headed to a nearby Days Inn and spent the evening until 11 going over evidence the CDC had compiled pointing to the Bil Mar plant, about 18 miles away in Borculo.

Dunne shared details from an update Mead had dispatched by e-mail that day to health departments across the country.

"Dear Colleagues," the Mead memo began. "The pieces of the multistate listeria puzzle appear to be falling into place . . ."

As of that day, the CDC had identified 37 people who got sick in 8 states, including 2 known cases in Michigan. All had fallen ill between August 2 and November 30. All were all infected by the rare E-strain of *Listeria monocytogenes.* The CDC's research had found a common link: Many of the victims had eaten hot dogs, and in particular Sara Lee brands.

There was a sense of urgency. As Mead noted, dangerous food was probably still out there.

"Hot dogs have a long shelf life (decades in my freezer)," he wrote, "and we have good reason to believe that cases are ongoing . . . it is not clear that the company will feel that the data is strong enough to support a recall at this time. WE DESPERATELY NEED ADDITIONAL PRODUCT INFORMATION: brand names, establishment numbers, dates of production for both hot dogs AND deli meats. We ask you to please redouble your efforts to get this information."

A sense of urgency had also finally hit Michigan public health officials.

Test results had arrived from Cornell University proving that the two known Michigan cases—Art Eberlein and the unidentified college student—were part of the outbreak.

"At that point we started calling hospitals asking: 'Do you

have any listeria samples you haven't reported? If you haven't sent them in, please do,'" said Frances Downes, then the state's acting laboratory director.

State law requires doctors, hospitals, and laboratories to report all cases of certain diseases, including listeriosis, to the state, because they can be warning signs of a possible outbreak. But cases often go unreported, as was evident in this outbreak.

After calling Michigan's 15 largest hospitals, the state had uncovered 6 unreported listeriosis cases.

A total of nine Michigan cases ultimately would match the outbreak strain: Three adult residents of an Oakland County group home; a five-year-old Detroit child; an elderly woman in Barry County; the Western-Michigan University student in Kalamazoo; and Eberlein, O'Brian, and Andrzejewski.

It's possible that other Michigan listeriosis cases slipped through the cracks.

There was no way to know.

Wednesday, December 16
Bil Mar Foods plant, north of Zeeland

Dunne and the USDA investigators arrived at the plant shortly after 7:30 A.M. They were met by security and given down-filled coats, white overcoats, boots, and hair nets before being ushered into the plant.

All the layers made the inspectors look 40 pounds heavier. "We looked like obese doctors on rounds," Dunne said.

Dunne was struck immediately by the enormity of the task ahead of her.

"We walked all the way through the plant, and it seemed to take forever," she recalled. "The place was huge."

She saw overhead conveyors carrying boxes of meat throughout the plant. People were walking back and forth. Vehicles hauled boxes from one side of the plant to another.

"Everything seemed to be moving all at once, and I wondered how in the world does everything get orchestrated properly," she said. "It was all unbelievably complex, and I wondered if we'd ever find the cause of the outbreak."

The inspection team was escorted into a windowless conference room, where plant managers had questions for Dunne. They wanted to know why their plant was the target of an investigation.

She explained the reasons and outlined what the investigators wanted to do. Then they got to work.

They scrutinized sanitation procedures, reviewed the steps taken to keep raw and finished products separated, and the hygiene practices of workers. They also took swab samples on equipment and surfaces, looking for listeria contamination, and shipped the samples off for testing. It would be at least a week before the results were back.

So they continued looking inside the plant for ways and places where listeria bacteria could have gained a foothold.

Bil Mar had a slaughtering operation and cooking operation in one plant.

In a large area dubbed "kill and evis," for eviscerate, workers slaughtered thousands of turkeys a day. The slaughtering operation had been around for decades, but Sara Lee had planned to phase it out in 1999.

Slaughtered turkeys are a bacteria haven, as are all raw meats; they can carry a scary assortment of disease-causing bacteria, from salmonella and campylobacter, to deadly E. coli and *Listeria monocytogenes.*

For that reason, workers were instructed to take care when moving about the plant, to prevent the spread of bacteria from raw to cooked foods. They were supposed to change their lablike work coats when they moved from one place to another, rinse their shoes in iodine foot baths, and stop at hand-washing stations.

At the hot dog production lines, Dunne watched the process in amazement as workers emulsified raw meat, squeezed it into skinlike casings, cooked them, and packaged them.

"When I saw hot dogs being made, it turned my stomach, and I think it would turn most people's stomach," Dunne said. "But it wasn't a dirty process, and we found nothing to suggest the process was contaminated."

In making hot dogs and deli meats, two steps were crucial to make them safe.

First, workers needed to cook the products thoroughly. Proper cooking kills bacteria. Second, they needed to make sure the cooked meats were not exposed to contamination before they were packaged. Which meant the work surfaces that came in contact with food needed to be carefully cleaned and sanitized.

After two long days with the federal team on site, plant managers were growing uncomfortable with the intense scrutiny. The tension showed during a second meeting, December 17, between plant officials and the inspection team.

"During this second meeting, several members of the management expressed their concern over having a large number of people in white coats repeatedly walking through the plant and how it might impact on the plant's interests," Dr. Stephen Guryca, one of the USDA officials involved in the inquiry, later wrote in a memo.

But that same day, more evidence was pointing to the plant: The initial tests on the Ohio woman's hot dogs showed they were contaminated with *Listeria monocytogenes*. The CDC's lab needed another two days to complete genetic fingerprinting tests to determine whether it was exactly the same strain as that in the outbreak.

From Atlanta, Mead suggested to Dunne that she ask plant officials about any unusual events in the last six months—plumbing problems, construction work, or other interruptions in the regular routine.

As Dunne talked to plant officials, one thing stood out—a construction job done over the Fourth of July weekend.

A contractor removed a faulty refrigeration unit in the hot dog production area. It had been blamed for some of the condensation problems that federal meat inspectors had cited repeatedly.

The unit was so big that workers had to cut it into pieces to lug it out the door. They hauled out pieces through several corridors, including a main hallway that linked the hot dog production area with other production areas.

"When I was told this, I said, 'Wow, that's kind of important.' Then I talked to Paul, and he said, 'Wow, this *is* kind of important,'" Dunne recalled.

But Bil Mar managers saw things differently. "They said, 'This isn't really so different. We do construction work like this all the time,'" Dunne said. "And they believed they had taken all appropriate steps. They covered everything, shut down production and did a massive cleaning before restarting production.

But this work may have caused listeria bacteria to spread through the plant, Dunne and Mead believed. Their suspicions appeared supported by the plant's own records.

Dunne asked whether the plant was doing microbiological testing. At first she was told no.

But she then learned that workers had taken regular swab samples up until November. When she reviewed the test results, Dunne noticed that, after the July 4 construction, workers recorded a sharp increase in cold-loving bacteria, which could include *Listeria monocytogenes.*

The number of positive samples remained high until the testing ended in November. Company officials later explained that they weren't overly concerned, because the tests showed only the presence of cold-loving bacteria in general and the plant was re-cleaned after each positive test.

Because it can take up to a week to get results from tests that specifically detect *Listeria monocytogenes,* most plants use the more general tests that give results within minutes.

But Mead and his colleagues at the CDC immediately suspected that the work might have spread dust laden with listeria throughout the plant. The refrigeration unit became a suspect. There was one more thing. On December 19 the final results of genetic fingerprinting tests on the listeria from the Ohio woman's hot dogs showed they matched the E-strain fingerprint that was sickening people across the country.

While this was a critical link, it wasn't absolute. Because the package had been open and in the woman's refrigerator for months, it was possible the hot dogs became contaminated there and not at the Bil Mar plant.

Mead knew he needed more than a hunch about the construction dust and an open package of hot dogs if he were going to lobby for a recall of the millions of pounds of Bil Mar products that were still in grocery stores and people's homes.

"We were pretty sure we were right," Mead said. "But we knew it would be devastating if we were proved wrong."

Saturday, December 19, 1999
St. Thomas, U.S. Virgin Islands

Steven McMillan had never been very good at vacations. This one would be no different.

As president and chief operating officer of Sara Lee Corp., McMillan had a reputation as a hard-driving executive whose performance tended to be as exact as his appearance.

In his monogrammed shirts, designer cuff links, and perfectly draped suits, he had the look of a man who was permanently buffed and ready for corporate battle. He had recently announced record sales to shareholders at their annual meeting. In 23 years, McMillan had never failed to make his budget. It was a point of personal pride.

This particular vacation, to the Caribbean island of St. Thomas, had been planned for a long time, squeezed in between a board meeting in Europe and the normal crush of duties that come with leading a Fortune 500 company with $20 billion in annual sales.

McMillan and his wife, Kelly, arrived in the island town of Charlotte Amalie on Saturday, December 19. It was a breathtaking sight: steep rocky shores and emerald green hillsides, floating in a sea of turquoise. And a perfect day: sunny, 83 degrees, the kind of day especially appreciated by a couple escaping the blustery winter winds back home in Chicago.

The McMillans were scheduled to board a cruise ship the next day. At least that was the plan, until McMillan called his office.

Up to then, McMillan had been given only a hint of the trouble that was brewing at Bil Mar. He had heard about it the day before, while attending Sara Lee's employee holiday luncheon at the Four Seasons hotel in Chicago. About 15 minutes before McMillan was to address the gathering, he got a call.

"We may have an issue out at the Bil Mar plant," he remembers being told.

"Well, what have we done?" McMillan asked, in the deep voice that still carries a faint note of his Alabama upbringing.

He was told that the plant had quit shipping meat December 17 after learning that federal officials suspected Bil Mar was linked to a growing outbreak of food-borne illnesses nationwide.

"I was told, 'You know, look, this may be nothing, but stand by,'" McMillan, 53, said in a recent interview with the *Free Press.*

At the time, the concerns didn't seem concrete enough to cancel the trip. But after calling the office from St. Thomas, McMillan was growing uneasy. He found out the Bil Mar situation was still unresolved.

He rattled off questions over the phone, wanting to know what federal officials were saying. "Nobody is really taking any positions," he recalled being told. "Just there is some suggestion that we could have a listeria problem at the plant."

The next day, December 20, McMillan put his wife on the ship alone. He flew the 2,145 miles to Chicago, back to a problem that was rapidly growing into a full-blown crisis.

Sunday, December 20
Sara Lee headquarters, Chicago

While McMillan was in St. Thomas, other Sara Lee executives were holed up in intense meetings at the company headquarters, in the upper reaches of a black skyscraper near the Sears Tower.

The crisis team worked through the weekend, trying to determine how bad things were. The group included executives from the meat division, food safety consultants, public relations specialists, and an epidemiologist.

They had also consulted Dr. Michael Osterholm of the Minnesota state health department, an expert in food-borne illnesses.

His department had traced tainted hamburgers back to school lunchrooms and contaminated herbs to sewage-flooded fields in Mexico. The late King Hussein of Jordan, shortly before his death, even chose Osterholm to be his personal adviser on the issue of bioterrorism.

So when outbreaks emerged across the country, Osterholm tended to be in the loop. And having followed the listeriosis outbreak, he was convinced of one thing: the Bil Mar plant needed to get its products off the market immediately. Too many signs were pointing to the plant as the source of the outbreak, and Osterholm was concerned that more people could be harmed by further delay.

"At that point, clearly it was likely to be the hot dogs," recalled Osterholm, who has since left his state job to form a public health consulting company, which has not done any work for Bil Mar or Sara Lee.

When Bil Mar managers and Sara Lee officials called him around December 17, he was candid: Get a recall started.

Osterholm's message was unsettling—and the lone call for action at that point.

Bil Mar and Sara Lee officials were getting mixed messages.

Neither the USDA, which regulated the plant, nor the Centers for Disease Control and Prevention, which was leading the outbreak investigation, was willing to make that leap just yet.

Federal regulators and health officials had been scouring the Bil Mar plant for five days, taking samples and searching for evidence of what could have caused the outbreak. It would take another six or seven days for the results to come back and answer conclusively whether Bil Mar was the source.

That was frustrating for Sara Lee executives, as they pressed for advice on what to do. They were searching for firm answers, and had even dispatched a contingent to Washington that Friday for a meeting with Thomas Billy, the U.S. Department of Agriculture official in charge of meat plant inspections.

What was said in that meeting would later be a point of dispute.

Sara Lee officials would later say they came away from the meeting with the sense that the government wasn't sure whether a recall was necessary until the test results came back. Billy's staff would say he urged them to consider withdrawing product from the marketplace.

Whatever the case, Sara Lee officials say they were getting unclear signals. That made matters more complicated.

The last thing the company wanted was to leave products on the market that were killing people and making others sick. Yet the company also didn't want to damage a cherished identity by launching an unwarranted—and costly—recall, if Bil Mar wasn't the source.

At Sara Lee, the brand name is everything—a guiding principle recited by top executives as if it were a sacred mantra.

The company reveled in a positive image. Leading business publications heralded Sara Lee as one of the best companies to work for in the United States. Ball Park was the nation's top-selling hot dog brand. Even the company's familiar slogan played on the warm feelings that Sara Lee had tried to cultivate: "Nobody doesn't like Sara Lee."

The Same Day, December 20

Centers for Disease Control, Atlanta

For Dr. Paul Mead and his colleagues at the CDC, the stakes were just as high. The health agency's reputation was on the line.

Mead, one of the top CDC officials investigating the outbreak, had grown increasingly convinced by December 20 that the Bil Mar plant was the source of the outbreak. But without the test results from Bil Mar, he wasn't sure the evidence was strong enough to push for a recall.

"Crying wolf would have massive consequences," Mead said.

"We'd have no credibility the next time there was an outbreak and we wanted a company to recall something."

The dilemma, he said, was the biggest of his career.

Mead was one of the CDC's top epidemiologists, an intense, wiry workaholic with a wry sense of humor. He had devoted his career to the pursuit of elusive pathogens, often flying off at a moment's notice to the suspected source of an outbreak.

One mission might take him to a cruise ship, another to an Indian reservation, another to a church picnic. Always, his job was to figure out what had made people sick.

His office at the CDC was cluttered with mementos collected on those trips. African masks. Mexican weavings.

Mead is not the type of space-suit-clad CDC sleuth often portrayed in movies. Like most epidemiologists, he wears street clothes and often works from a desk, instead of donning a plastic biohazard suit and breathing through tubes while handling killer viruses that threaten to wipe out whole cities.

While others do that work, Mead analyzes their findings and oversees staff in the field who track down victims and ask questions about what they ate and where they were before they got sick. Part of Mead's job is to reconstruct the chain of events.

With Christmas approaching, Mead was once again trapped at his desk, another crisis consuming him. He couldn't be around home to help his wife make holiday plans or do Santa's shopping for their two boys and one girl, ages 2, 4, and 7. Indeed, Mead would end up spending Christmas Eve in his office, working on the Bil Mar investigation.

As Mead reviewed the Bil Mar case on December 20, he saw that the CDC only had circumstantial evidence. But it all pointed to Bil Mar.

The CDC had an open package of Bil Mar hot dogs contaminated with *Listeria monocytogenes*. Mead had surveys of nearly 100 victims, many of whom said they'd eaten hot dogs in the weeks before they got sick. Many recalled the brands of hot dogs they ate—citing mostly Sara Lee brands. Finally, Mead had an open pack of chicken deli meat, made by Bil Mar and contaminated with the outbreak strain of listeria.

But was the evidence strong enough to recommend a recall?

Monday, December 21

Sara Lee headquarters, Chicago

With McMillan back from the Caribbean, Sara Lee executives convened that Monday morning in the boardroom on the 47th floor. The image of Sara Lee founder Nathan Cummings looked on from an oil painting on the wall as McMillan and Chairman John Bryan tried to sort speculation from fact.

Tens of millions of dollars were at stake—and, more importantly, lives.

The company's senior management committee assembled around a massive, polished wood table, big enough for 22 brown leather chairs. The committee normally gathered on Monday mornings to discuss sales results. Crisis management took over the agenda on this day.

They began a daylong search for information, hooking up on conference calls with Bil Mar plant managers as well as industry experts and epidemiologists. One crucial piece of the puzzle was still missing: the test results on meat samples taken from Bil Mar.

"We have no positive tests—clearly no positive tests on product," McMillan recalled. "So the USDA, clearly appropriate in its protocol, was not in a position where they would have required a recall. We'd asked the CDC and their response was kind of, 'We don't do that. We don't suggest recalls.'"

Perhaps that was true, up to then. But whether McMillan was aware or not, the CDC that Monday morning was finally preparing to recommend a recall, even as Sara Lee executives were meeting.

Mead had directed a staff member to draft a memo to Sara Lee, urging the company to recall all hot dogs made after July 4, 1998—the day the refrigeration unit was removed—and to consider recalling all deli meat made after that date, too.

In the three-page memo, dated December 21, Mead outlined

the findings in laborious, scientific terms, then came right out and said the evidence was strong that Bil Mar hot dogs had caused at least one case of listeriosis. Other evidence also suggested that hot dogs from many production dates were contaminated.

The memo struck a note of urgency about the danger of waiting for final test results. "By the time definitive proof is available," the memo said, "more illnesses and deaths will likely occur."

Mead says he informed a Sara Lee consultant on that Monday of his plans to send the recall recommendation to the company the next day, December 22.

Mead's part of the tough call was made. The ball was now in the company's court. "We held our breath and waited," Mead said.

It's unclear what details of the impending memo from Mead were relayed to the Sara Lee boardroom that Monday. But by 3 P.M., the consensus among the Sara Lee crisis team was to wait a day and talk to more experts. The meeting adjourned.

Shortly afterward, McMillan and Bryan began to feel uncomfortable with the decision to wait.

"The chairman and I met privately and kind of concluded we couldn't take the risk," McMillan said. "To the degree that this proved to be accurate—and we were being told it could be another six to seven days before we had tests back—that's six or seven days in which people could be consuming product."

A recall would be costly. The numbers folks provided, in McMillan's words, a rough "back of the envelope" estimate of $50 million to $80 million.

As they weighed the final decision, McMillan says, Bryan and he decided to abide by a set of rules the rest of the way, no matter how rough the going got. "And the guiding rule would be that we would do nothing that would create any risks to health," McMillan said. "To a certain degree, that makes the decision-making process easier."

In the real-life world of corporate bottom lines, where executives live and die by profits and stock values, McMillan and Bryan were taking a big risk. If they were wrong, and Bil Mar turned out to be innocent, the ramifications with stockholders could be devastating.

"And there was a fair amount of conviction we could well be wrong," McMillan said. "But I'd rather justify having been aggressive on the health side than try to justify seven days from now that, well, we were going to save the money and we left the product out."

So, McMillan and Bryan gave the go-ahead: Recall.

All that remained was to decide which products to pull back, and how many pounds. Which was not as easy as it sounds.

At 4 P.M., a select group of crisis team members was called back to the 47th floor, this time to the Braque Room, so named because of the French painter's canvas that once hung there. It was part of a prized art collection owned by Sara Lee, part of which is now on world tour. The room was a smaller meeting chamber with floor-to-ceiling windows that looked out upon the steeple of what Chicago touts as the tallest church in the world.

One decision was obvious. They had to recall hot dogs, given the amount of evidence already pointing to them. And Sara Lee had other plants that could make them.

The harder decision was whether to recall the entire line of Sara Lee's signature premium deli meats made exclusively at the Bil Mar plant.

"The difference between recalling hot dogs and us recalling everything out of that plant is very significant," McMillan said.

Recalling deli meats would put Sara Lee out of that business indefinitely. The company had no other plants that could take over production.

But they couldn't take the risk, either for the public or the company's potential liability.

"So the safest scenario is to recall all of it," McMillan said.

Tuesday, December 22
Bil Mar Foods, Borculo, Michigan
By morning, USDA officials inside the plant had learned of Sara Lee's plans to launch the massive recall, one that could top out at 35 million pounds of hot dogs and lunch meats, more than any other meat recall in U.S. history.

Even with all the evidence gathered by the CDC, some USDA officials still were surprised by the decision. A daily USDA update, filed from the Bil Mar plant at 9:30 A.M., questioned the wisdom of any recall until all the test results were in. Without those results, the update said, a recall "may be premature."

By noon, Sara Lee had set up a toll-free hot line in anticipation of calls from worried consumers once the news got out.

Bil Mar issued a press release announcing the voluntary recall, noting that "specific production lots of hot dogs and other packaged meat products" might contain the listeria germ.

The recalled products included hot dogs and turkey franks, and a variety of deli meats such as ham, smoked turkey, roast beef, and corned beef. They were packaged under numerous brand names—Sara Lee, Ball Park, Mr. Turkey, Gordon Food Service, and others—but all carried Bil Mar's federal ID numbers: P-261 and 6911.

The press release explained that the company had made the decision after consulting with the USDA and CDC. The Sara Lee release stated: "The CDC has indicated that it is studying whether some of these products might contain the listeria bacteria."

That very morning, the CDC's memo to Sara Lee didn't mince words. "Strong evidence suggests that Ball Park brand hot dogs produced on September 17, 1998, at the Bil Mar plant in Michigan were the vehicle for at least one case of human illness from *Listeria monocytogenes* (LM). The outbreak strain of LM was recovered from the placenta of a woman who had a preterm delivery, and from an open package of hot dogs from this mother's refrigerator. The mother reports eating these hot dogs on October 5; preterm delivery occurred on November 7, 1998."

The CDC memo went on to describe the sell-by date and packaging codes from the tainted hot dogs, showing that they were "produced on September 17, 1998, on the #2 retail frank line at the Bil Mar plant . . ."

The CDC memo also outlined evidence that implicated hot dogs and deli meats, made on several other dates at the plant, and cited the mounting toll: 35 illnesses and four deaths in 9 states, including Michigan.

The Sara Lee press release made no mention of that.

As for the USDA—the primary watchdog over Bil Mar and all U.S. meat plants—the department was content to let Sara Lee handle the duty of informing the public. The USDA issued no press release, contrary to its normal policy in such cases.

But at least the news was out. The question was, would consumers get the message in time?

Wednesday, January 20, 1999
Riverside Methodist Hospital, Columbus, Ohio
For eight hours, Lisa Lee endured the pain of induced labor, knowing that one of the twins inside her was dead and the other had no hope of surviving.

Lee, 27, had been so excited about becoming a mother.

She had been pregnant five months. She visited the doctor regularly. She ate properly. She got plenty of sleep.

But then Lee started feeling sick. That was on Saturday, four days earlier. She sought treatment right away at the emergency room of Riverside Methodist Hospital in Columbus, Ohio, and from her own doctor. She was told it was probably just the flu, and, after a night in the hospital, was sent home.

Lee was still recovering in the hospital's intensive care unit when doctors discovered the cause of her miscarriage: infection caused by *Listeria monocytogenes*. Neither Lee nor her fiance, Jonathan Southworth, knew what the bacterium was. A friend visiting later that day put it all together. . . .

The Same Day, January 20
Sara Lee Corp. headquarters, Chicago
On the day Lisa Lee lost her babies, Sara Lee ran newspaper ads across the country, reminding people of the recall. The death toll had grown to 14.

The ad took the form of a letter, signed by Sara Lee Chairman,

John Bryan, and President, C. Steven McMillan. They urged people to check their refrigerators and freezers for recalled products, and not to eat the food.

"We deeply regret this situation," the ad said, "and we continue to make the safety and wholesomeness of our products our number-one priority. Please know that we are working around the clock to address the issues that led us to the decision to announce a recall."

The ad would be the first and only time that top company executives addressed the public about the recall, until McMillan granted a recent interview to the *Free Press*.

McMillan recalled that running the ad was a controversial decision within the company.

By the time it appeared, nearly a month after the recall was launched, publicity had died down. Which was good as far as the company's public relations experts were concerned.

The story of the recall had captured only spotty news coverage. It was the holiday season, and it seemed all other news was overshadowed by the impeachment and trial of President Bill Clinton over the Monica Lewinsky scandal.

So, McMillan said, he and Bryan feared that there might still be many people who hadn't heard about the recall.

In a business where image is everything, deciding to run the ad was far more difficult than deciding to do the recall, McMillan said. The Sara Lee brand name, long regarded as one of the most trusted in the nation, had already been hit hard by the recall and now the company was going to do the unthinkable in the world of public relations.

"The PR people were vehemently against us putting the ad out telling people not to eat our product," McMillan said. "Their view is, 'Look, you went through this thing, you got a lot of publicity, you seemed to survive it, people have forgotten it, it's out of their mind now. For God's sake don't go out and put an ad out reminding all these people.'"

But McMillan and Bryan were taking a longer view. They

wanted customers down the road to have a positive view of how Sara Lee responded to the crisis. They wanted to protect the Sara Lee name.

So they were willing to take the hit, to publish the ads.

It was more than what the nation's food safety watchdogs at the U.S. Department of Agriculture did. They didn't issue their first press release about the recall until January 28—more than a week after Sara Lee's ad and 37 days after the recall began.

And why did the USDA wait so long to warn the public? Because, USDA officials said, the company was handling it.

Late January
Kemper Insurance Co., Lincolnshire, Ill.

Another way Sara Lee handled matters was with a toll-free hot line to answer consumer questions. The company prepared scripts and question-and-answer sheets to help operators deal with callers.

More than 25,000 calls flooded the hot line. The callers were first greeted by a recorded message that listed the products being recalled. Then, callers had the option of talking to an operator. At the height of the recall, more than 4,000 operators were available to take calls.

They had two jobs: To answer questions from those who were afraid of becoming sick—and to give special attention to those who said they already were.

When that happened, the operators instructed them to seek medical help and then transferred them to Kemper Insurance, which portrays itself in advertisements as the cavalry coming to the rescue. The company's toll-free number is 1-800-CAVALRY.

Kemper adjusters sought to get callers to agree to quick settlements and turn over any potentially tainted meat they might still have, plaintiffs' lawyers said.

"They go into their homes and pick up the meat products and we haven't yet been able to get them back," said Kenneth Moll, a Chicago lawyer who represents more than 400 people in what he hopes will become a class-action suit against Sara Lee and Bil Mar.

Moll said he's come across several people who signed papers from the insurance company that bar them from suing, in return for $300 to $400.

Other consumers said they were neither offered money by Kemper nor much help from Sara Lee.

Jean Grabowski, 61, of South Lyon in Oakland County, was among the thousands who sought advice from the Sara Lee hot line. Grabowski called it in mid-January. She had eaten Mr. Turkey hot dogs and hadn't been feeling well since the holidays.

Grabowski was worried. She had been reading articles in the *Free Press* about the outbreak. She knew people had died from the bacteria. And she had been suffering from severe abdominal cramps. Was she in danger?

"I wanted to find out if the hot dogs I had were contaminated because it had the right code on it," she said, referring to the packaging codes.

The person answering the Sara Lee recall hot line asked Grabowski a few questions, she said. Grabowski told the operator that she had eaten the hot dogs and was feeling sick. That, Grabowski recalled, prompted the operator to quickly transfer her to Kemper Insurance—without asking any further questions.

Like thousands of other callers, Grabowski had been routed to risk management workers at Kemper Insurance.

Damage control was under way.

"They asked me if I had any hot dogs left," Grabowski said recently, recounting the conversation this way:

"Yeah, I still have them."

"Are they frozen?"

"Yes."

Grabowski had only eaten two out of the pack before putting them in the freezer. The operator, she said, then made this offer: "We'd like someone to come and pick them up. Keep them frozen until then."

That was fine by Grabowski. Maybe she would find out whether the meat she ate was contaminated.

On February 9, Grabowski received a letter from Kemper

Insurance's risk management department instructing her to complete a claim form and sign a medical authorization form that would allow the company complete access to her entire medical history.

That seemed excessive to Grabowski. "Geesh, they wanted my medical history from the time I was born," Grabowski said.

She set the letter aside. A few days later, she received a call from Kemper saying a woman named Nanette would be coming to pick up the hot dogs. Grabowski, surprised it had taken so long, carefully put the package in a plastic bag, tucked in her name, address, and the claim number she'd been assigned by Kemper and a note asking that she be called with the test results.

On a Saturday morning, February 13, Nanette arrived and took the hot dogs away.

"Will someone call me and let me know if they're contaminated?" Grabowski recalled asking Nanette.

Grabowski says she was assured, "Yes, definitely." But she never heard back, she said.

"The part that upset me is they never contacted me to let me know," said Grabowski, who has been through a battery of unpleasant medical tests. While doctors didn't find listeriosis, she was diagnosed with a spastic colon.

She hired a lawyer, Harvey Chayet of Southfield, who said he wasn't surprised by Grabowski's experience.

"The whole business of this 800 number wasn't set up to help anyone out of genuine concern for their health," Chayet said. "It was set up out of genuine concern for the financial health of Sara Lee."

"They're looking to protect themselves and they're looking to get rid of these claims as cheaply as possible," Chayet said. "The insurance companies are not out there to protect the consumer."

Chayet, who has sued Bil Mar and Sara Lee on behalf of Grabowski and others, said his office was contacted by several people who had already signed Kemper forms, collected a small settlement and were now barred from suing.

Kemper officials declined to comment. Theresa Herlevsen, a Sara Lee vice president, acknowledged that Kemper sought to settle claims and collect food for testing, but said there was an earnest attempt to keep people informed of test results when they requested them.

Law offices of Kenneth B. Moll & Associates, Chicago

Ken Moll was in his element. Basking before the TV cameras, he began his attack on Sara Lee with a calm smile.

On this day, Moll had just filed a motion with a state court in Chicago seeking a judge's approval for a nationwide class action on behalf of people who said they had been harmed by Bil Mar products.

He was quickly becoming Sara Lee's newest nightmare.

Moll had invited the press to his offices on the 37th floor of a skyscraper called Three First National Plaza—which also happens to be home to Sara Lee, based nine floors above the conference room where Moll was holding court.

As he laid out the highlights to his case Moll read excerpts from the diary of John Bodnar, whose wife Helen died from the outbreak, and spoke of the suffering endured by many others.

And for that, he said, Sara Lee would pay.

"The reimbursement alone could cost $2 billion for Sara Lee," he said.

Moll had made a career of being a major irritant to big companies like Sara Lee.

He saw himself as a guy who succeeded the hard way. He grew up poor in rural Wisconsin and was dubbed a real-life Rainmaker a few years back on Court TV. The reference was to a young lawyer in the John Grisham novel of the same name who successfully took on a large insurance company that refused to pay for a potentially life-saving bone-marrow transplant.

When Moll was just a year out of law school, he represented a 5-year-old boy who was brain-damaged by a reaction to the DPT vaccine and won a $4.5-million award. It was cited at the time as the largest award of its kind for a vaccine liability case.

Since then, he had been one of the lead lawyers in breast-implant litigation against Michigan-based Dow Corning; taken on the tobacco industry; and sued the makers of the diet drug combination fen-phen.

Among other cases, he also sued Hostess for allegedly selling Twinkies filled with asbestos-contaminated cream. And he went after the organizers of the infamous fight between Mike Tyson and Evander Holyfield, when Tyson bit Holyfield's ear. Moll contended that ticket-holders and pay-per-view customers didn't get their money's worth.

Moll never shunned publicity. Colleagues at a firm where he worked before had nicknamed him Mr. Hollywood. And to the chagrin of his adversaries, Moll loved taking his cases to the media. Over the years he appeared on national television shows ranging from the *McNeilLehrer Newshour* to the *Jenny Jones* show, where he has been a guest several times.

In prepping for his battle against Sara Lee, Moll obtained a court order to allow him to tour the Bil Mar plant on March 2. Dressed in jeans and cowboy boots, before going into the plant he gave a brief press conference at a diner just down the road from the plant in Borculo. As TV cameras rolled, he offered his theories on how the meat became tainted.

One possibility: That workers tracked bacteria as they moved back and forth between the turkey slaughter operation and the processing areas. Another: Fans installed near a storage room for spoiled and other inedible food scraps may have spread the bacteria. And still one more: That dirty equipment provided a breeding ground for bacteria.

"The big issue here is cross-contamination," he said.

With that, he and his hired entourage of experts, former Bil Mar employees, and a video and still photographer sped off to the plant. It was a scene that would still have Sara Lee brass grumbling months later—annoyed by this lawyer who had never even been in a meat plant, yet acted as if he had all the answers.

"We've all learned a lot more about listeria than we ever

expected to at this stage," said McMillan, the Sara Lee president. "And one thing we've learned is there is a huge amount that is not known about listeria, which added to the uncertainty that was kind of prevalent—and continues to be prevalent."

EPILOGUE

In June, the U.S. Centers for Disease Control and Prevention issued its summary report on the Bil Mar outbreak and recall.

The conclusion: It's impossible to say exactly what triggered the outbreak, but it is probable that the deadly listeria bacteria were present in the plant prior to July 1998 and were spread on dust particles during removal of a refrigeration unit over the Fourth of July weekend.

The final human toll in 22 states: 80 people sickened and 21 dead, including 6 babies miscarried or born dead. Most victims were elderly. Many had other medical problems: diabetes, kidney disease, lupus.

THE VICTIMS

John Bodnar of Memphis, Tennessee, whose wife Helen died of listeriosis October 19, is suing Sara Lee Corp.

Art Eberlein of Sebewaing has fully recovered from his November 1998 bout with listeriosis and again directs the Unionville-Sebewaing Area Band.

George O'Brian of East Lansing, who was rendered almost helpless by a case of listeriosis, died on July 1 of heart failure. He was 95.

Lisa Lee and **Jonathan Southworth** of Columbus, Ohio, who lost twins when Lisa suffered a miscarriage, are active members of an infant-loss support group, which they say helps them deal with their grief.

SARA LEE'S COST

Sara Lee Corp. continues to pay a huge financial toll:

- The recall itself cost $76 million.
- Meat sales dropped about $200 million in the 6 months after the recall.
- While the stock market overall was rising, Sara Lee stock has dropped 19 percent to $22.50 since the Dec. 22 recall. That means the company is worth $4.7 billion less than it was in December—$20.3 billion now, $25 billion then.

CHANGES AT BIL MAR

The Bil Mar plant, closed at the time of the recall, resumed production of deli meats on March 3 under close scrutiny by USDA inspectors and new safety measures adopted by Sara Lee. The hot dog lines are being reconfigured; no date has been set for a restart.

Although the USDA listed the size of the recall at 35 million pounds, Sara Lee executives said they only expected to recover about 16 million pounds. A final USDA audit of the amount of meat returned to the company has not been released, but company officials say they recovered close to what they expected.

A federal grand jury in Grand Rapids is investigating whether there was criminal wrongdoing at Bil Mar.

THE PRODUCTS

Sara Lee deli meats are still missing from shelves of some supermarkets that sold them before the recall, including the Meijer and Farmer Jack chains. Sara Lee officials say the deli meats, made only at Bil Mar, have returned to 80 percent of stores that carried them prior to the recall. Ball Park hot dogs, made at other Sara Lee plants, are widely available and sales are running at record levels, the company says.

THORN APPLE VALLEY

Sara Lee was strong enough to survive a huge recall. Southfield-based Thorn Apple Valley was not. On January 22, a month after the Bil Mar recall, a Thorn Apple plant in Arkansas recalled 31 million pounds of meat products for the same reason—*Listeria monocytogenes.* Already unprofitable and only one-fortieth the size of Sara Lee, Thorn Apple Valley filed for Chapter 11 bankruptcy protection in March. By July, it had been sold to IBP.

THE SCIENTISTS

At the CDC in Atlanta, **Dr. Paul Mead** has worked since the outbreak on a major report on food-borne illnesses and their cost. The report is expected to be released soon.

Dr. Eileen Dunne continues her work as an epidemic intelligence officer at CDC. Recent assignments have taken her to Maine to investigate a case of E. coli 0157:H7, and to the Ivory Coast to help an international team evaluate water for bacterial contamination.

Every reporter longs for entrance into places where he or she isn't totally welcome. Writing for *The New Yorker,* Ken Auletta became the first journalist to crash the party at investment firm Allen & Company's annual five-day retreat for the "who's who" of CEOs. While his straightforward journalistic style dutifully relates the casual chatter and organized events he encountered in Sun Valley, Idaho, it also deftly reveals the personal, quirky, and often childlike characteristics of those who wield power.

Ken Auletta

WHAT I DID AT SUMMER CAMP

Summer camp is a chance for a kid to play, to forge friendships, to escape his parents. For a media mogul, the five-day Sun Valley, Idaho, camp conducted for the past seventeen years by the investment firm Allen & Company offers similar advantages. There is a head counsellor and there are activity directors; each day has a morning activity period, canteen, then playtime and evening programs. The session culminates in an awards ceremony. This year, for the first time, an outsider, a reporter, was permitted to attend. This is my diary.

Tuesday, July 6

There was no sweaty, noisy bus ride. Most of the three hundred or so adult guests and the hundred and thirty children accompanying them have come by private jet. By the end of the day, the fleet of Gulfstreams and Falcons parked on the tarmac is bigger than the air force of most of the Benelux countries. Waiting on the tarmac for each guest is a guide wearing shorts and an Allen & Co. shirt. The guides greet us by name (they memorized our faces from pictures we sent), fetch luggage, and direct us to our rented cars. My guide is Bob Dean, the vice-president of the risk-arbitrage department at Allen & Co.

To read the guest list is to savor the class list in *Lolita* but then to recognize the cast in the pages of *Forbes.* Among the CEO-ish men and women arriving are Paul G. Allen, a co-founder of Microsoft, and now of Vulcan Ventures; C. Michael Armstrong, of AT&T; Jeffrey Berg, of International Creative Management; Jeffrey P. Bezos, of Amazon.com; Michael R. Bloomberg, of Bloomberg L.P.; Warren E. Buffett, of Berkshire Hathaway; Stephen M. Case, of America Online; Michael Dell, of Dell Computer Corporation; Barry Diller, of USA Networks; William T. Esrey, of Sprint; William H. Gates III, of Microsoft; Donald and Katharine Graham, of the Washington Post Company; Andrew S. Grove, of Intel; Christie Hefner, of Playboy Enterprises; John S. Hendricks, of Discovery Communications; Nobuyuki Idei, of Sony; Steven P. Jobs, of Pixar Animation Studios and Apple Computer; Robert L. Johnson, of BET Holdings; Mel Karmazin, of CBS; Jeffrey Katzenberg, one of three DreamWorks SKG partners; Geraldine B. Laybourne, of Oxygen Media; John C. Malone, of the Liberty Media Group; Thomas Middlehoff, of Bertelsmann AG; Jorma J. Ollila, of Nokia; Sumner M. Redstone, of Viacom; Oprah Winfrey, of the Harpo Entertainment Group; Robert Wright, of NBC; and Jerry Yang, of Yahoo!

The camp is referred to, without irony, as "a family gathering," but the family has got quite big. Robert Strauss, the former Democratic National Chairman, has been a friend of Herbert Allen, the patriarch of the investment bank that bears his name, for 35 years. "I've been to every one of these," he tells me. "The first one was the best: thirty-five people and one speaker—me!" Strauss, who is eighty, loves coming here, and not just because his Washington law firm can garner clients here. "There's a bunch of people here I know are not the nicest people in the world," he says. "But *here* they're nice." Here is the Sun Valley Lodge, which is just outside the town of Ketchum, six thousand feet above sea level. The lodge was built in the thirties by Averell Harriman and his Union Pacific Railroad's millions. One begins to imagine this sort of gathering at the turn of the last century. Did Rockefeller go rafting with Carnegie?

When guests arrive, a small Allen & Co. army is waiting to pamper them. For the children, 90 of whom are 12 or younger, there are 75 babysitters and 20 activity directors, plus 20 nannies brought by the guests themselves.

Also awaiting each guest are two thick folders. In one are the daily schedules, for adults and for children. From Tuesday through Saturday, guests will be offered tennis, golf, fly-fishing, whitewater rafting, skeet shooting, massages, mountain biking. The kids may have an even better schedule: an ice-skating party, a wagon ride, a horse show, tennis clinics, a Wild West show, kickball, fishing, relay races, a raft trip, pizza and ice cream. Media moguls say that their sons and daughters have made lifelong friends here, engaging in junior networking.

Dress is casual. Except for Steve Jobs and Lachlan Murdoch, who often wear Bermuda shorts, jeans are the uniform of choice. Peter Barton, who once ran Liberty Media and stopped by this year to say hello to friends, points out that you can spot the regulars because they "move with calculated indifference" as they enter the lobby of the lodge; first-time guests enter and glance about like startled rabbits, clearly "titillated," he says. Regulars also bring sweaters, for the mountain air is chilly at night; first-timers like me catch colds. Photographers for Allen & Co. circulate at tonight's outdoor barbecue, taking pictures of the guests.

Wednesday, July 7

Each morning's activity period consists of two or three presentations in the large conference center. These are preceded by a 6:45 A.M. buffet breakfast, which is eaten at round tables seating ten. The photographs taken the previous night fill two walls of the auditorium; everyone seems to be smiling.

Today, the first corporate presentation is by Charles B. Wang, the chairman and CEO of Computer Associates International, a five-billion-dollar enterprise. Sony makes the second presentation.

Howard Stringer, the CEO of Sony America, says that Sony will ship seventeen million PlayStation game consoles this year; the new PlayStation II has enough microprocessing power to rival Microsoft's operating system and Intel's chip. When Stringer's boss, Nobuyuki Idei, speaks, he hastens to say that "Sony is basically a hardware company." Not that Idei was fooling Intel or Microsoft; it's just that a kind of Kabuki civility reigns at camp.

As does loot. Stringer has gifts for everyone: a digital Sony AM/FM stereocassette Walkman; a Discman; or a digital tape recorder. Last year, Microsoft gave away copies of their expensive WebTV. Millionaires stampede to snatch one—sometimes two—of Sony's elegant white shopping bags. They are motivated by what appears to be lust, and perhaps because it's almost playtime.

Twenty-five rafts wait at an embankment of the Salmon River, each manned by a professional guide and equipped with life jackets and oars. Herb Allen demands an additional accessory—three empty water buckets; he is determined to start a water fight. Water fights are a tradition. The former Sony America president Mickey Schulhof stopped in Ketchum to buy aluminum water cannons that squirt water great distances, and he hid them in his clothes. Who'd a thunk!

Everyone is laughing as we drift or bounce down the river, and notice Allen & Co. photographers perched on rocks. Ambulances quietly follow our progress. They were almost needed several years ago, when Rupert Murdoch fell in and quickly floated downstream and out of sight. He managed on his own to get to shore, but he'd had to scramble over the rocks and his legs were bloodied. This incident did not retard his enthusiasm for water sports and competition; indeed, when hikes were organized Murdoch is said to have hustled to the fore and stayed there, leaving his wife and others chugging after him. (This year, only a new wife and a honeymoon kept Murdoch away from camp.)

Thursday, July 8
There are other leadership retreats: the Bilderberg conference; the World Economic Forum, in Davos; Bohemian Grove; investor

conferences. Allen & Co.'s retreat, though, is longer than most. It is also confined mainly to a single industry—communications. And, most distinct of all, it includes families. There's one other difference, as Sumner Redstone points out: "This conference has a host in Herbert Allen"—a single figure who dominates, even as he shies away from the stage.

Many CEOs have been attending the camp for most of its 17 years, and, in addition, Allen has a large extended family. He has sons and nieces and nephews of his own and sons and daughters of close friends who work for Allen & Co. There are people he always invites because they're old friends: Bob Strauss and his law partner, Vernon Jordan, of Akin, Gump; former Vice-President Walter Mondale; former Senator Bill Bradley, who is running for President; Meredith and Tom Brokaw; Diane Sawyer; the producer Ray Stark, who first introduced Allen to Sun Valley; the actress Candice Bergen; the director Sydney Pollack. Then, he has people who always came when they headed powerful organizations, and he makes sure they keep coming, even though they're no longer in charge, such as James Robinson, the former CEO of American Express, and Frank Biondi, the former CEO of both Viacom and Universal. Allen gets upset at those who misbehave. A couple of years ago, Ronald Perelman both brought his own security detail and hired locals to protect him. No other CEO comes with an aide, not to mention a security army, and Allen was mightily offended.

Allen, 59, is an unusual head counsellor. Unlike most investment bankers, he is a billionaire, yet in a business of salesmen he acts like a buyer. Day and night, he wears a cap pulled down to his ears. During the morning presentations, he sits off to one side near the front of the stage; he invites junior bankers to introduce all the speakers. One of the morning's presenters is an unshaven, black-turtlenecked Steve Jobs. Jobs talks about the importance of stories, of marrying technology and storytelling skills. Most computer geeks, he says, don't get it. "Silicon Valley thinks 'creative' is a bunch of guys sitting in a condo thinking up dirty jokes." But Hollywood, he says, doesn't get it, either. "Hollywood thinks technology is something you buy."

After the break, and more gifts, the first of two socially relevant panels is scheduled. Entitled "Unparalleled Prosperity and a Troubled Society," the panel is moderated by the charming Donald Keough, who joined Allen & Co. after serving as president of Coca-Cola. Little new ground is broken here, to say the least. Keough contrasts America's vibrant economy, where the "creation of wealth is incredible," with what he calls the "dark side to our society." Does the media, he asks, bear some responsibility for the violence?

The first speaker, Geraldine Laybourne, says, "There aren't enough fingers in this room to point at all the causes." Then she does what every panellist but Steve Case, of AOL, would do: change the subject. She says she wants to mention another problem: the "digital divide," or the gap between rich and poor in access to the Internet.

CBS's Mel Karmazin talks about going to high school in Hell's Kitchen. "There are more things we can do," he says, but the major culprit is guns, not the media. (The gun people have their own camp—and blame the media.) Barry Diller says, somewhat enigmatically, that although his job "is to entertain people," he also has "editorial responsibility." Steve Case adopts the bleakest view: "Obviously, things are getting worse, not better." Eighty per cent of teenagers who are on AOL say that what happened at Columbine could happen in their school. The media, he says, has to stop hiding behind the First Amendment. The central issue, he says, is this: Do we sacrifice profits to downplay violence? No one picks up this challenge.

Keough asks Barry Diller about the "Jerry Springer Show," which Diller's network owns. "We had said, 'Let's shut the show down,'" Diller says. But his network couldn't, because, internally, various executives had made mistakes. So he tightened the rules— no violence, period. The issue for him, Diller says, is that executives have to "be vigilant."

"You don't get credit for it," Karmazin says, congratulating Diller—and himself. CBS's radio stations, Karmazin continues, don't play gangsta rap. "We're expressing our First Amendment right not to play it." The Allen sessions are polite, so no one mentions that Karmazin's CBS distributes and airs the famously profane Howard Stern radio and television programs.

Laybourne laments media violence, then changes the subject again, boasting that Oprah Winfrey is planning to do a show for Oxygen, "so that we can help lead women in a positive direction." Redstone introduces a note of unhappy reality: "One of our responsibilities is to make fiscally sound decisions." Translation: The shareholders come first. And Keough, at the end, inexplicably assures everyone, "No one here ducks his responsibility."

In years past, Allen & Co. banned the press. Lately, it has allowed reporters on the grounds of the campus but keeps them away from all meetings, breaks, recreation, and evening activities. For many years, I'd asked Allen to allow me to cover the camp, and this year he relented, asking only that I display discretion by not poking a tape recorder into the faces of campers, for example. I was on the guest list both as an author and as a writer for this magazine.

Shyness with the press does not include the fourth annual photograph of media movers, to be taken on Friday by the photographer Annie Leibovitz for *Vanity Fair.* Allen takes care to tell guests who inquire that he has nothing to do with who is selected. Allen & Co. simply gives the magazine the guest list, and editors choose their own media élite. Thirty-two will make the Media All-Star team and appear for tomorrow's session; as hard as Allen tries to shake the perception that he influences the list, various campers intensely lobby him to be included in the picture. (After this year's photograph is taken, Allen will turn to Leibovitz and say, "*Vanity Fair* has been great to us . . . this is my last picture." "Never say never," Leibovitz will tell him, gently. "I'll say it," Allen will reply.)

When I get back to the lodge after tennis this afternoon, the elevator door opens and Sumner Redstone, whom colleagues often describe as self-absorbed, appears. He does not say hello or pause but announces, "You can see me on CNN. I'm on now!"

Why do they come to camp? Clearly, campers have fun. But there are other reasons: "Insecurity is one motivation," Peter Barton answers. "It says you're a player. The inviter here is the kingmaker. If you're here, it says to everyone else that you're in the game." That's only one motivation, he continues. "The presentations are brain food. You're socializing with people you dream to have a social opportunity with. And at the same time you know that your wife and kids, who are with you, are separately having a wonderful time."

They come, said Howard Stringer, of Sony, because of the peculiar nature of the communications industry. "Everything changes so fast. No one can keep up with innovation or transactional options. This is the only place where all the information-technology leaders converge." Major business deals have been orchestrated, or provoked, at this retreat. It was here, over golf, in 1995, that Michael Eisner made his first pitch to buy Cap Cities/ABC, culminating three weeks later in a nineteen-billion-dollar acquisition. It was here, after negotiations had collapsed earlier, that Rupert Murdoch reached an agreement in 1996 to purchase Ron Perelman's television stations. It was here, in 1997, that Murdoch and Gerald Levin of Time Warner ended the feud between their companies.

A number of CEOs get in touch with the people they want to see before arriving and pack their schedule tight with appointments. Sony's Idei, who was here for only two days, had a plan that kept him mostly indoors. Thomas Middelhoff, of Bertelsmann, flew to Sun Valley from Germany, a trip that took 18 hours. He was able to schedule meetings in Sun Valley that spared him from taking many separate trips.

On Friday morning, Michael Armstrong, of AT&T, makes the first presentation. He looks like a picture-perfect CEO. Dressed in a beige crew-neck sweater over a blue oxford shirt and tan slacks, Armstrong is a commanding presence, his left hand in his pocket, his right resting on the podium, his voice deep. He offers startling facts, including this one: Since he was hired by AT&T, less than two years ago, he has spent 140 billion dollars to acquire companies and to relieve AT&T of its dependence on long-distance tele phone service, which is a slow-growth business.

After a break, there is a panel entitled "The Internet and Our Lives," which is moderated by Tom Brokaw and consists of Jeff Bezos, of Amazon.com, Jerry Yang, of Yahoo!, Jay Walker, of Priceline.com and Michael Dell, of Dell Computer. Is the Internet another tulip craze? (No.) Will retail shopping survive? (Yes.) Do brand names matter in this strange new world? (Maybe.)

Friday evening is usually when the camp's awards ceremony takes place. This is the occasion for Jack Schneider, one of Allen's partners, to get up and roast the various campers, giving out mock awards, such as a Team Viagra T-shirt. This year, Allen cancelled the roast. Schneider thinks that it's because there were reporters who might learn what he said, and it might be embarrassing; Allen says that it's because the group is so big that the remarks would lose their intimacy, and, besides, he's tired of the same jokes.

Something else has changed the mood: the center of gravity at Sun Valley has shifted from old media to new. Jokes about Michael Ovitz are passé. So this year's buffet dinner on the lawn beside the pool is less raucous. There are no speeches. At one table, Melinda and Bill Gates dine with Gates's rival Steve Case and his wife, Jean, and are joined by the president of Walt Disney International, Robert A. Iger, and his wife, Willow Bay, and by Susan and Michael Dell. Michael Ovitz, who has not been very visible and who has been here for only two days, sits beside Katharine Graham.

Saturday, July 10
At 7:30 A.M., Herb Allen speaks for the first time, introducing his friend of three decades, Bill Bradley. "Why Bill Bradley? The only answer I have is to invoke personal privilege." Bradley is relaxed, comfortable, and focused as he speaks about children and family

structure to a crowd of potential campaign donors that could finance a government, not to mention a candidate. At 8:30 A.M., Warren Buffett speaks. A shambly man, in a beige V-necked sweater over a red flannel shirt and wrinkled tan slacks, the legendarily shrewd investor gives a talk, with slides, centered on overvalued stocks. The stock market is no god, he suggests. In the short run, the market "is a voting machine," he says. "In the long run, it's a weighing machine," and what carries the most weight is a stock's value, not its hype. He believes that the stock market today is inflated, and unlikely to continue its meteoric rise. He flashes on the screen a chart of the *Fortune* 500 companies that constitute 75 per cent of America's corporate wealth. In 1998, corporate profits totalled $334.3 billion, yet the market value of these companies was ten trillion dollars. No way, he cautions, will this market value continue to rise as it has. Then he clicks to a slide marked "U.S. Horse Population." In 1990, there were seventeen million horses; in 1998, only five million. The lesson: Don't forget the losers.

Buffett tells the story of the oil prospector who died and went to Heaven. He asked St. Peter for a place, but St. Peter said there was no more room in the pen set aside for oil prospectors because there were too many of them in Heaven.

"Do you mind if I say four words?" the oil prospector asked.

O.K., St. Peter said.

"Oil discovered in Hell!" the oil prospector cried.

With that, the prospectors all fled, and St. Peter said, "The pen's all yours."

"No, I think I'll go along with the rest of the boys. There may be some truth to that rumor."

Buffett says, "That's how I feel about the stock market."

The camp farewell takes place at dinner at the River Run Lodge, which is tucked into the side of a ski mountain. It's a sit-down dinner, and Herbert Allen chooses to sit with his old friends: Ray Stark, Candice Bergen, Sydney Pollack, and Allen's son Herbert, among others. Wearing jeans and a purple shirt, Allen, who is rail-thin, steps to the microphone and begins thanking people, starting with Stark, who is now 83, all the speakers, and members of the Allen & Co. "family." It is a heartfelt note on which to end. No summer camp, however, concludes without a talent show, and after dinner Susie Buffett, with her husband, Warren, bouncing along to the rhythms of the Big Band sound, belts out four songs. Then it's back to the lodge for an ice-skating show, followed by a fireworks display. Something Buffett has said sticks in my mind: "If it weren't for Herbert, my family wouldn't get a summer vacation."

Going undercover can take many forms, and in this case Barbara Ehrenreich of *Harper's* wasn't afraid to get her hands dirty. She worked three weeks as a maid. Her inside look at the operation of a large maid service raises serious questions not only about the methods used in the cleaning industry, but also the growing class distinction between today's client and worker. The author showed great imagination in pursuing this unusual but important story.

Barbara Ehrenreich

MAID TO ORDER—
The Politics of Other Women's Work

I N L I N E with growing class polarization, the classic posture of submission is making a stealthy comeback. "We scrub your floors the old-fashioned way," boasts the brochure from Merry Maids, the largest of the residential-cleaning services that have sprung up in the last two decades, "on our hands and knees." This is not a posture that independent "cleaning ladies" willingly assume—preferring, like most people who clean their own homes, the sponge mop wielded from a standing position. In her comprehensive 1999 guide to homemaking, *Home Comforts,* Cheryl Mendelson warns: "Never ask hired housecleaners to clean your floors on their hands and knees; the request is likely to be regarded as degrading." But in a society in which 40 percent of the wealth is owned by 1 percent of households while the bottom 20 percent reports negative assets, the degradation of others is readily purchased. Kneepads entered American political discourse as a tool of the sexually subservient, but employees of Merry Maids, The Maids International, and other corporate cleaning services spend hours every day on these kinky devices, wiping up the drippings of the affluent.

I spent three weeks in September 1999 as an employee of The Maids International in Portland, Maine, cleaning, along with my fellow team members, approximately 60 houses containing a total of about 250 scrubbable floors—bathrooms, kitchens, and entryways requiring the hands-and-knees treatment. It's a different world down there below knee level, one that few adults voluntarily enter. Here you find elaborate dust structures held together by a scaffolding of dog hair; dried bits of pasta glued to the floor by their sauce; the congealed remains of gravies, jellies, contraceptive creams, vomit, and urine. Sometimes, too, you encounter some fragment of a human being: a child's legs, stamping by in disgust because the maids are still present when he gets home from school; more commonly, the Joan & David–clad feet and electrolyzed calves of the female homeowner. Look up and you may find this person staring at you, arms folded, in anticipation of an overlooked stain. In rare instances she may try to help in some vague, symbolic way, by moving the cockatoo's cage, for example, or apologizing for the leaves shed by a miniature indoor tree. Mostly, though, she will not see you at all and may even sit down with her mail at a table in the very room you are cleaning, where she would remain completely unaware of your existence unless you were to crawl under that table and start gnawing away at her ankles.

Housework, as you may recall from the feminist theories of the Sixties and Seventies, was supposed to be the great equalizer of women. Whatever else women did—jobs, school, child care—we also did housework, and if there were some women who hired others to do it for them, they seemed too privileged and rare to include in the theoretical calculus. All women were workers, and the home was their workplace—unpaid and unsupervised, to be sure, but a workplace no less than the offices and factories men repaired to every morning. If men thought of the home as a site of leisure and recreation—a "haven in a heartless world"—this was to ignore the invisible female proletariat that kept it cozy and humming. We were on the march now, or so we imagined, united against a society that devalued our labor even as it waxed mawkish over "the family" and "the home." Shoulder to shoulder and arm in arm, women were finally getting up off the floor.

In the most eye-catching elaboration of the home-as-workplace theme, Marxist feminists Maria Rosa Dallacosta and Selma James proposed in 1972 that the home was in fact an economically productive and significant workplace, an extension of the actual factory, since housework served to "reproduce the labor power" of others, particularly men. The male worker would hardly be in shape to punch in for his shift, after all, if some woman had not fed him, laundered his clothes, and cared for the children who were his contribution to the next generation of workers. If the home was a quasi-industrial workplace staffed by women for the ultimate benefit of the capitalists, then it followed that "wages for housework" was the obvious demand.

But when most American feminists, Marxist or otherwise, asked the Marxist question *cui bono?* they tended to come up with a far simpler answer—men. If women were the domestic proletariat, then men made up the class of domestic exploiters, free to lounge while their mates scrubbed. In consciousness-raising groups, we railed against husbands and boyfriends who refused to pick up after themselves, who were unaware of housework at all, unless of course it hadn't been done. The "dropped socks," left by a man for a woman to gather up and launder, joined lipstick and spike heels as emblems of gender oppression. And if, somewhere, a man had actually dropped a sock in the calm expectation that his wife would retrieve it, it was a sock heard round the world. Wherever second-wave feminism took root, battles broke out between lovers and spouses over sticky countertops, piled-up laundry, and whose turn it was to do the dishes.

The radical new idea was that housework was not only a relationship between a woman and a dust bunny or an unmade bed; it also defined a relationship between human beings, typically husbands and wives. This represented a marked departure from the more conservative Betty Friedan, who, in *The Feminine Mystique,* had never thought to enter the male sex into the equation, as either part of the housework problem or part of an eventual solution. She raged against a society that consigned its educated women to what she saw as essentially janitorial chores, beneath "the abilities of a woman of average or normal human intelligence," and, according to unidentified studies she cited, "peculiarly suited to the capacities of feeble-minded girls." But men are virtually exempt from housework in *The Feminine Mystique*—why drag them down, too? At one point she even disparages a "Mrs. G.," who "somehow couldn't get her housework done before her husband came home at night and was so tired then that he had to do it." Educated women would just have to become more efficient so that housework could no longer "expand to fill the time available."

Or they could hire other women to do it—an option approved by Friedan in *The Feminine Mystique* as well as by the National Organization for Women, which she had helped launch. At the 1973 congressional hearings on whether to extend the Fair Labor Standards Act to household workers, NOW testified on the affirmative side, arguing that improved wages and working conditions would attract more women to the field, and offering the seemingly self-contradictory prediction that "the demand for household help inside the home will continue to increase as more women seek occupations outside the home." One NOW member added, on a personal note: "Like many young women today, I am in school in order to develop a rewarding career for myself. I also have a home to run and can fully conceive of the need for household help as my free time at home becomes more and more restricted. Women know [that] housework is dirty, tedious work, and they are willing to pay to have it done. . . ." On the aspirations of the women paid to do it, assuming that at least some of them were bright enough to entertain a few, neither Friedan nor these members of NOW had, at the time, a word to say.

So the insight that distinguished the more radical, post-Friedan cohort of feminists was that when we talk about housework, we are really talking, yet again, about power. Housework was not degrading because it was manual labor, as Friedan thought, but because it was embedded in degrading relationships and inevitably served to reinforce them. To make a mess that another person will have to deal with—the dropped socks, the toothpaste sprayed on the bathroom mirror, the dirty dishes left from a late-night snack—is to exert domination in one of its more silent and intimate forms. One person's arrogance—or indifference, or hurry—becomes another person's occasion for toil. And when the person who is cleaned up after is consistently male, while the person who cleans up is consistently female, you have a formula for reproducing male domination from one generation to the next.

Hence the feminist perception of housework as one more way by which men exploit women or, more neutrally stated, as "a symbolic enactment of gender relations." An early German women's liberation cartoon depicted a woman scrubbing on her hands and knees while her husband, apparently excited by this pose, approaches from behind, unzipping his fly. Hence, too, the second-wave feminists' revulsion at the hiring of maids, especially when they were women of color: At a feminist conference I attended in 1980, poet Audre Lorde chose to insult the all-too-white audience by accusing them of being present only because they had black housekeepers to look after their children at home. She had the wrong crowd; most of the assembled radical feminists would no sooner have employed a black maid than they would have attached Confederate flag stickers to the rear windows of their cars. But accusations like hers, repeated in countless conferences and meetings, reinforced our rejection of the servant option. There already were at least two able-bodied adults in the average home—a man and a woman—and the hope was that, after a few initial skirmishes, they would learn to share the housework graciously.

A couple of decades later, however, the average household still falls far short of that goal. True, women do less housework than they did before the feminist revolution and the rise of the two-income family: down from an average of 30 hours per week in 1965 to 17.5 hours in 1995, according to a July 1999 study by the

University of Maryland. Some of that decline reflects a relaxation of standards rather than a redistribution of chores; women still do two thirds of whatever housework—including bill paying, pet care, tidying, and lawn care—gets done. The inequity is sharpest for the most despised of household chores, cleaning: in the thirty years between 1965 and 1995, men increased the time they spent scrubbing, vacuuming, and sweeping by 240 percent—all the way up to 1.7 hours per week—while women decreased their cleaning time by only 7 percent, to 6.7 hours per week. The averages conceal a variety of arrangements, of course, from minutely negotiated sharing to the most clichéd division of labor, as described by one woman to the *Washington Post:* "I take care of the inside, he takes care of the outside." But perhaps the most disturbing finding is that almost the entire increase in male participation took place between the 1970s and the mid-1980s. Fifteen years after the apparent cessation of hostilities, it is probably not too soon to announce the score: in the "chore wars" of the Seventies and Eighties, women gained a little ground, but overall, and after a few strategic concessions, men won.

Enter then, the cleaning lady as *dea ex machina,* restoring tranquillity as well as order to the home. Marriage counselors recommend her as an alternative to squabbling, as do many within the cleaning industry itself. A Chicago cleaning woman quotes one of her clients as saying that if she gives up the service, "my husband and I will be divorced in six months." When the trend toward hiring out was just beginning to take off, in 1988, the owner of a Merry Maids franchise in Arlington, Massachusetts, told *The Christian Science Monitor,* "I kid some women. I say, 'We even save marriages. In this new eighties period you expect more from the male partner, but very often you don't get the cooperation you would like to have. The alternative is to pay somebody to come in. . . .'" Another Merry Maids franchise owner has learned to capitalize more directly on housework-related spats; he closes between 30 and 35 percent of his sales by making follow-up calls Saturday mornings, which is "prime time for arguing over the fact that the house is a mess." The micro-defeat of feminism in the household opened a new door for women, only this time it was the servants' entrance.

In 1999, somewhere between 14 and 18 percent of households employed an outsider to do the cleaning, and the numbers have been rising dramatically. Mediamark Research reports a 53 percent increase, between 1995 and 1999, in the number of households using a hired cleaner or service once a month or more, and Maritz Marketing finds that 30 percent of the people who hired help in 1999 did so for the first time that year. Among my middle-class, professional women friends and acquaintances, including some who made important contributions to the early feminist analysis of housework, the employment of a maid is now nearly universal. This sudden emergence of a servant class is consistent with what some economists have called the "Brazilianization" of the American economy: We are dividing along the lines of traditional Latin American societies—into a tiny overclass and a huge underclass, with the latter available to perform intimate household services for the former. Or, to put it another way, the home, or at least the affluent home, is finally becoming what radical feminists in the Seventies only imagined it was—a true "workplace" for women and a tiny, though increasingly visible, part of the capitalist economy. And the question is: As the home becomes a workplace for someone else, is it still a place where you would want to live?

Strangely, or perhaps not so strangely at all, no one talks about the "politics of housework" anymore. The demand for "wages for housework" has sunk to the status of a curio, along with the consciousness-raising groups in which women once rallied support in their struggles with messy men. In the academy, according to the feminist sociologists I interviewed, housework has lost much of its former cachet—in part, I suspect, because fewer sociologists actually do it. Most Americans, over 80 percent, still clean their homes, but the minority who do not include a sizable faction of the nation's opinion-makers and culture-producers—professors, writers, editors, politicians, talking heads, and celebrities of all sorts. In their homes, the politics of housework is becoming a politics not only of gender but of race and class—and these are subjects that the opinion-making elite, if not most Americans, generally prefer to avoid.

Even the number of paid houseworkers is hard to pin down. The Census Bureau reports that there were 549,000 domestic workers in 1998, up 9 percent since 1996, but this may be a considerable underestimate, since so much of the servant economy is still underground. In 1995, two years after Zoe Baird lost her chance to be attorney general for paying her undocumented nanny off the books, the *Los Angeles Times* reported that fewer than 10 percent of those Americans who paid a housecleaner reported those payments to the IRS. Sociologist Mary Romero, one of the few academics who retain an active interest in housework and the women who do it for pay, offers an example of how severe the undercounting can be: the 1980 Census found only 1,063 "private household workers" in El Paso, Texas, though the city estimated their numbers at 13,400 and local bus drivers estimated that half of the 28,300 daily bus trips were taken by maids going to and from work. The honesty of employers has increased since the Baird scandal, but most experts believe that household workers remain, in large part, uncounted and invisible to the larger economy.

One thing you can say with certainty about the population of household workers is that they are disproportionately women of color: "lower" kinds of people for a "lower" kind of work. Of the "private household cleaners and servants" it managed to locate in 1998, the Bureau of Labor Statistics reports that 36.8 were Hispanic, 15.8 percent black, and 2.7 percent "other." Certainly the association between housecleaning and minority status is well established in the psyches of the white employing class. When my daughter, Rosa, was introduced to the wealthy father of a Harvard classmate, he ventured that she must have been named for a favorite maid. And Audre Lorde can perhaps be forgiven for her intemperate accusation at the feminist conference mentioned above when we consider an experience she had in 1967: "I wheel my two-year-old daughter in a shopping cart through a supermarket . . . and a little white girl riding past in her mother's cart calls out excitedly, 'Oh look, Mommy, a baby maid.'" But the composition of the household workforce is hardly fixed and has changed with the life chances of the different ethnic groups. In the late nineteenth century, Irish and German immigrants served the northern upper and middle classes, then left for the factories as soon as they could. Black women replaced them, accounting for 60 percent of all domestics in the 1940s, and dominated the field until other occupations began to open up to them. Similarly, West Coast maids were disproportionately Japanese American until that group, too, found more congenial options. Today, the color of the hand that pushes the sponge varies from region to region: Chicanas in the Southwest, Caribbeans in New York, native Hawaiians in Hawaii, whites, many of recent rural extraction, in Maine.

The great majority—though again, no one knows exact numbers—of paid housekeepers are freelancers, or "independents," who find their clients through agencies or networks of already employed friends and relatives. To my acquaintances in the employing class, the freelance housekeeper seems to be a fairly privileged and prosperous type of worker, a veritable aristocrat of labor—sometimes paid $15 an hour or more and usually said to be viewed as a friend or even treated as "one of the family." But the shifting ethnic composition of the workforce tells another story: this is a kind of work that many have been trapped in—by racism, imperfect English skills, immigration status, or lack of education—but few have happily chosen. Interviews with independent maids collected by Romero and by sociologist Judith Rollins, who herself worked as a maid in the Boston area in the early Eighties, confirm that the work is undesirable to those who perform it. Even when the pay is deemed acceptable, the hours may be long and unpredictable; there are usually no health benefits, no job security, and, if the employer has failed to pay Social Security taxes (in some cases because the maid herself prefers to be paid off the books), no retirement benefits. And the pay is often far from acceptable. The BLS found full-time "private household cleaners and servants" earning a median annual income of $12,220 in 1998, which is

$1,092 below the poverty level for a family of three. Recall that in 1993 Zoe Baird paid her undocumented household workers about $5 an hour out of her earnings of $507,000 a year.

At the most lurid extreme there is slavery. A few cases of forced labor pop up in the press every year, most recently—in some nightmare version of globalization—of undocumented women held in servitude by high-ranking staff members of the United Nations, the World Bank, and the International Monetary Fund. Consider the suit brought by Elizabeth Senghor, a Senegalese woman who alleged that she was forced to work fourteen-hour days for her employers in Manhattan, without any regular pay, and was given no accommodations beyond a pull-out bed in her employers' living room. Hers is not a particularly startling instance of domestic slavery; no beatings or sexual assaults were charged, and Ms. Senghor was apparently fed. What gives this case a certain rueful poignancy is that her employer, former U.N. employee Marie Angelique Savane, is one of Senegal's leading women's rights advocates and had told *The Christian Science Monitor* in 1986 about her efforts to get the Senegalese to "realize that being a woman can mean other things than simply having children, taking care of the house."

Mostly, though, independent maids—and sometimes the women who employ them—complain about the peculiar intimacy of the employer-employee relationship. Domestic service is an occupation that predates the refreshing impersonality of capitalism by several thousand years, conditions of work being still largely defined by the idiosyncrasies of the employers. Some of them seek friendship and even what their maids describe as "therapy," though they are usually quick to redraw the lines once the maid is perceived as overstepping. Others demand deference bordering on servility, while a growing fraction of the nouveau riche is simply out of control. In August 1999, *The New York Times* reported on the growing problem of dinner parties being disrupted by hostesses screaming at their help. To the verbal abuse add published reports of sexual and physical assaults—a young teenage boy, for example, kicking a live-in nanny for refusing to make sandwiches for him and his friends after school.

But for better or worse, capitalist rationality is finally making some headway into this weird preindustrial backwater. Corporate cleaning services now control 25 to 30 percent of the $1.4 billion housecleaning business, and perhaps their greatest innovation has been to abolish the mistress-maid relationship, with all its quirks and dependencies. The customer hires the service, not the maid, who has been replaced anyway by a team of two to four uniformed people, only one of whom—the team leader—is usually authorized to speak to the customer about the work at hand. The maids' wages, their Social Security taxes, their green cards, backaches, and child-care problems—all these are the sole concern of the company, meaning the local franchise owner. If there are complaints on either side, they are addressed to the franchise owner; the customer and the actual workers need never interact. Since the franchise owner is usually a middle-class white person, cleaning services are the ideal solution for anyone still sensitive enough to find the traditional employer-maid relationship morally vexing.

In a 1997 article about Merry Maids, *Franchise Times* reported tersely that the "category is booming, [the] niche is hot, too, as Americans look to out-source work even at home." Not all cleaning services do well, and there is a high rate of failure among informal, mom-and-pop services. The "boom" is concentrated among the national and international chains—outfits like Merry Maids, Molly Maids, Mini Maids, Maid Brigade, and The Maids International—all named, curiously enough, to highlight the more antique aspects of the industry, though the "maid" may occasionally be male. Merry Maids claimed to be growing at 15 to 20 percent a year in 1996, and spokesmen for both Molly Maids and The Maids International told me that their firms' sales are growing by 25 percent a year; local franchisers are equally bullish. Dan Libby, my boss at The Maids, confided to me that he could double his business overnight if only he could find enough reliable employees. To this end, The Maids offers a week's paid vacation, health insurance after 90 days, and a free breakfast every morning consisting—at least where I worked—of coffee, doughnuts, bagels, and bananas. Some franchises have dealt with the tight labor market by participating in welfare-to-work projects that not only funnel employees to them but often subsidize their paychecks with public money, at least for the first few months of work (which doesn't mean the newly minted maid earns more, only that the company has to pay her less). The Merry Maids franchise in the city where I worked is conveniently located a block away from the city's welfare office.

Among the women I worked with at The Maids, only one said she had previously worked as an independent, and she professed to be pleased with her new status as a cleaning-service employee. She no longer needed a car to get her from house to house and could take a day off—unpaid of course—to stay home with a sick child without risking the loss of a customer. I myself could see the advantage of not having to deal directly with the customers, who were sometimes at home while we worked and eager to make use of their supervisory skills: criticisms of our methods, and demands that we perform unscheduled tasks, could simply be referred to the franchise owner.

But there are inevitable losses for the workers as any industry moves from the entrepreneurial to the industrial phase, probably most strikingly, in this case, in the matter of pay. At Merry Maids, I was promised $200 for a 40-hour week, the manager hastening to add that "you can't calculate it in dollars per hour" since the 40 hours include all the time spent traveling from house to house—up to five houses a day—which is unpaid. The Maids International, with its straightforward starting rate of $6.63 an hour, seemed preferable, though this rate was conditional on perfect attendance. Miss one day and your wage dropped to $6 an hour for two weeks, a rule that weighed particularly heavily on those who had young children. In addition, I soon learned that management had ways of shaving off nearly an hour's worth of wages a day. We were told to arrive at 7:30 in the morning, but our billable hours began only after we had been teamed up, given our list of houses for the day, and packed off in the company car at about 8:00 A.M. At the end of the day, we were no longer paid from the moment we left the car, though as much as fifteen minutes of work—refilling cleaning-fluid bottles, etc.—remained to be done. So for a standard nine-hour day, the actual pay amounted to about $6.10 an hour, unless you were still being punished for an absence, in which case it came out to $5.50 an hour.

Nor are cleaning-service employees likely to receive any of the perks or tips familiar to independents—free lunches and coffee, cast-off clothing, or a Christmas gift of cash. When I asked, only one of my coworkers could recall ever receiving a tip, and that was a voucher for a free meal at a downtown restaurant owned by a customer. The customers of cleaning services are probably no stingier than the employers of independents; they just don't know their cleaning people and probably wouldn't even recognize them on the street. Plus, customers probably assume that the fee they pay the service—$25 per person-hour in the case of The Maids franchise I worked for—goes largely to the workers who do the actual cleaning.

But the most interesting feature of the cleaning-service chains, at least from an abstract, historical perspective, is that they are finally transforming the home into a fully capitalist-style workplace, and in ways that the old wages-for-housework advocates could never have imagined. A house is an innately difficult workplace to control, especially a house with ten or more rooms like so many of those we cleaned; workers may remain out of one another's sight for as much as an hour at a time. For independents, the ungovernable nature of the home-as-workplace means a certain amount of autonomy. They can take breaks (though this is probably ill-advised if the homeowner is on the premises); they can ease the monotony by listening to the radio or TV while they work. But cleaning services lay down rules meant to enforce a factory-like—or even conventlike—discipline on their far-flung employees. At The Maids, there were no breaks except for a daily ten-minute stop at a convenience store for coffee or "lunch"—meaning something like a slice of pizza. Otherwise, the time spent driving between houses was considered our "break" and the only chance to eat, drink, or (although this was also officially forbidden) smoke a cigarette. When the houses were spaced well apart, I could eat my sandwich in one sitting; otherwise it would have to be divided into as many as three separate, hasty snacks.

Within a customer's house, nothing was to touch our lips at all, not even water—a rule that, on hot days, I sometimes broke by drinking from a bathroom faucet. TVs and radios were off-limits, and we were never, ever, to curse out loud, even in an ostensibly deserted house. There might be a homeowner secreted in some locked room, we were told, ear pressed to the door, or, more likely, a tape recorder or video camera running. At the time, I dismissed this as a scare story, but I have since come across ads for devices like the Tech-7 "incredible coin-sized camera" designed to "get a visual record of your babysitter's actions" and "watch employees to prevent theft." It was the threat or rumor of hidden recording devices that provided the final capitalist-industrial touch—supervision.

What makes the work most factorylike, though, is the intense Taylorization imposed by the companies. An independent, or a person cleaning his or her own home, chooses where she will start and, within each room, probably tackles the most egregious dirt first. Or she may plan her work more or less ergonomically, first doing whatever can be done from a standing position and then squatting or crouching to reach the lower levels. But with the special "systems" devised by the cleaning services and imparted to employees via training videos, there are no such decisions to make. In The Maids' "healthy touch" system, which is similar to what I saw of the Merry Maids' system on the training tape I was shown during my interview, all cleaning is divided into four task areas—dusting, vacuuming, kitchens, and bathrooms—which are in turn divided among the team members. For each task area other than vacuuming, there is a bucket containing rags and the appropriate cleaning fluids, so the biggest decision an employee has to make is which fluid and scrubbing instrument to deploy on which kind of surface; almost everything else has been choreographed in advance. When vacuuming, you begin with the master bedroom; when dusting, with the first room off of the kitchen; then you move through the rooms going left to right. When entering each room, you proceed from left to right and top to bottom, and the same with each surface—top to bottom, left to right. Deviations are subject to rebuke, as I discovered when a team leader caught me moving my arm from right to left, then left to right, while wiping Windex over a French door.

It's not easy for anyone with extensive cleaning experience—and I include myself in this category—to accept this loss of autonomy. But I came to love the system: First, because if you hadn't always been traveling rigorously from left to right it would have been easy to lose your way in some of the larger houses and omit or redo a room. Second, some of the houses were already clean when we started, at least by any normal standards, thanks probably to a housekeeper who kept things up between our visits; but the absence of visible dirt did not mean there was less work to do, for no surface could ever be neglected, so it was important to have "the system" to remind you of where you had been and what you had already "cleaned." No doubt the biggest advantage of the system, though, is that it helps you achieve the speed demanded by the company, which allots only so many minutes per house. After a week or two on the job, I found myself moving robotlike from surface to surface, grateful to have been relieved of the thinking process.

The irony, which I was often exhausted enough to derive a certain malicious satisfaction from, is that "the system" is not very sanitary. When I saw the training videos on "Kitchens" and "Bathrooms," I was at first baffled, and it took me several minutes to realize why: There is no water, or almost no water, involved. I had been taught to clean by my mother, a compulsive housekeeper who employed water so hot you needed rubber gloves to get into it and in such Niagaralike quantities that most microbes were probably crushed by the force of it before the soap suds had a chance to rupture their cell walls. But germs are never mentioned in the videos provided by The Maids. Our antagonists existed entirely in the visible world—soap scum, dust, counter crud, dog hair, stains, and smears—and were attacked by damp rag or, in hardcore cases, by a scouring pad. We scrubbed only to remove impurities that might be detectable to a customer by hand or by eye; otherwise our only job was to wipe. Nothing was ever said, in the videos or in person, about the possibility of transporting bacteria, by rag or by hand, from bathroom to kitchen or even from one house to the next. Instead, it is the "cosmetic touches" that the videos emphasize and to which my trainer continually directed by eye. Fluff out all throw pillows and arrange them symmetrically. Brighten up stainless steel sinks with baby oil. Leave all spice jars, shampoos, etc., with their labels facing outward. Comb out the fringes of Persian carpets with a pick. Use the vacuum to create a special, fernlike pattern in the carpets. The loose ends of toilet paper and paper towel rolls have to be given a special fold. Finally, the house is sprayed with the service's signature air freshener—a cloying floral scent in our case, "baby fresh" in the case of the Mini Maids.

When I described the "methods" employed to housecleaning expert Cheryl Mendelson, she was incredulous. A rag moistened with disinfectant will not get a countertop clean, she told me, because most disinfectants are inactivated by contact with organic matter—i.e., dirt—so their effectiveness declines with each swipe of the rag. What you need is a detergent and hot water, followed by a rinse. As for floors, she judged the amount of water we used—one half of a small bucket—to be grossly inadequate, and, in fact, the water I wiped around on floors was often an unsavory gray. I also ran The Maids' cleaning methods by Don Aslett, author of numerous books on cleaning techniques and self-styled "number-one cleaner in America." He was hesitant to criticize The Maids directly, perhaps because he is, or told me he is, a frequent speaker at conventions of cleaning-service franchise holders, but he did tell me how he would clean a countertop: first, spray it thoroughly with an all-purpose cleaner, then let it sit for three to four minutes of "kill time," and finally wipe it dry with a clean cloth. Merely wiping the surface with a damp cloth, he said, just spreads the dirt around. But the point at The Maids, apparently, is not to clean so much as it is to create the appearance of having been cleaned, not to sanitize but to create a kind of stage setting for family life. And the stage setting Americans seem to prefer is sterile only in the metaphorical sense, like a motel room or the fake interiors in which soap operas and sitcoms take place.

But even ritual work takes its toll on those assigned to perform it. Turnover is dizzyingly high in the cleaning-service industry, and not only because of the usual challenges that confront the working poor—child-care problems, unreliable transportation, evictions, and prior health problems. As my longwinded interviewer at Merry Maids warned me, and my coworkers at The Maids confirmed, this is a physically punishing occupation, something to tide you over for a few months, not year after year. The hands-and-knees posture damages knees, with or without pads; vacuuming strains the back; constant wiping and scrubbing invite repetitive stress injuries even in the very young. In my three weeks as a maid, I suffered nothing more than a persistent muscle spasm in the right forearm, but the damage would have been far worse if I'd had to go home every day to my own housework and children, as most of my coworkers did, instead of returning to my motel and indulging in a daily after-work regimen of ice packs and stretches. Chores that seem effortless at home, even almost recreational when undertaken at will for twenty minutes or so at a time, quickly turn nasty when performed hour after hour, with few or no breaks and under relentless time pressure.

So far, the independent, entrepreneurial housecleaner is holding her own, but there are reasons to think that corporate cleaning services will eventually dominate the industry. New users often prefer the impersonal, standardized service offered by the chains, and, in a fast-growing industry, new users make up a sizable chunk of the total clientele. Government regulation also favors the corporate chains, whose spokesmen speak gratefully of the "Zoe Baird effect," referring to customers' worries about being caught paying an independent off the books. But the future of house-cleaning may depend on the entry of even bigger players into the industry. Merry Maids, the largest of the chains, has the advantage of being a unit within the $6.4 billion ServiceMaster conglomerate, which includes such related businesses as TruGreen-ChemLawn, Terminix, Rescue Rooter, and Furniture Medic. Swisher International, best known as an industrial toilet-cleaning service, operates Swisher Maids in Georgia and North Carolina, and Sears may be feeling its way into the business. If large multinational firms establish a foothold in the industry, mobile professionals will be able to find the same branded and standardized product wherever they relocate. For the actual workers, the change will, in all likelihood, mean a more standardized and speeded-up approach to the work—less freedom of motion and fewer changes to pause.

The trend toward outsourcing the work of the home seems, at the moment, unstoppable. Two hundred years ago women often manufactured soap, candles, cloth, and clothing in their own homes, and the complaints of some women at the turn of the twentieth century that they had been "robbed by the removal of creative work" from the home sound pointlessly reactionary today. Not only have the skilled crafts, like sewing and cooking from scratch, left the home but many of the "white collar" tasks are on their way out, too. For a fee, new firms such as the San Francisco–based Les Concierges and Cross It Off Your List in Manhattan will pick up dry cleaning, baby-sit pets, buy groceries, deliver dinner, even do the Christmas shopping. With other firms and individuals offering to buy your clothes, organize your financial files, straighten out your closets, and wait around in your home for the plumber to show up, why would anyone want to hold on to the toilet cleaning?

Absent a major souring of the economy, there is every reason to think that Americans will become increasingly reliant on paid housekeepers and that this reliance will extend ever further down into the middle class. For one thing, the "time bind" on working parents shows no sign of loosening; people are willing to work longer hours at the office to pay for the people—housecleaners and baby-sitters—who are filling in for them at home. Children, once a handy source of household help, are now off at soccer practice or SAT prep classes; grandmother has relocated to a warmer climate or taken up a second career. Furthermore, despite the fact that people spend less time at home than ever, the square footage of new homes swelled by 33 percent between 1975 and 1998, to include "family rooms," home entertainment rooms, home offices, bedrooms, and often bathrooms for each family member. By the third quarter of 1999, 17 percent of new homes were larger than 3,000 square feet, which is usually considered the size threshold for household help, or the point at which a house becomes unmanageable to the people who live in it.

One more trend impels people to hire outside help, according to cleaning experts such as Aslett and Mendelson: fewer Americans know how to clean or even to "straighten up." I hear this from professional women defending their decision to hire a maid: "I'm just not very good at it myself" or "I wouldn't really know where to begin." Since most of us learn to clean from our parents (usually our mothers), any diminution of cleaning skills is transmitted from one generation to another, like a gene that can, in the appropriate environment, turn out to be disabling or lethal. Upper-middle-class children raised in the servant economy of the Nineties are bound to grow up as domestically incompetent as their parents and no less dependent on people to clean up after them. Mendelson sees this as a metaphysical loss, a "matter of no longer being physically centered in your environment." Having cleaned the rooms of many overly privileged teenagers in my stint with The Maids, I think the problem is a little more urgent than that. The American overclass is raising a generation of young people who will, without constant assistance, suffocate in their own detritus.

If there are moral losses, too, as Americans increasingly rely on paid household help, no one has been tactless enough to raise them. Almost everything we buy, after all, is the product of some other person's suffering and miserably underpaid labor. I clean my own house (though—full disclosure—I recently hired someone else to ready it for a short-term tenant), but I can hardly claim purity in any other area of consumption. I buy my jeans at The Gap, which is reputed to subcontract to sweatshops. I tend to favor decorative objects no doubt ripped off, by their purveyors, from scantily paid Third World craftspersons. Like everyone else, I eat salad greens just picked by migrant farm workers, some of them possibly children. And so on. We can try to minimize the pain that goes into feeding, clothing, and otherwise provisioning ourselves—by observing boycotts, checking for a union label, etc.—but there is no way to avoid it altogether without living in the wilderness on berries. Why should housework, among all the goods and services we consume, arouse any special angst?

And it does, as I have found in conversations with liberal-minded employers of maids, perhaps because we all sense that there are ways in which housework is different from other products and services. First, in its inevitable proximity to the activities that compose "private" life. The home that becomes a workplace for other people remains a home, even when that workplace has been minutely regulated by the corporate cleaning chains. Someone who has no qualms about purchasing rugs woven by child slaves in India or coffee picked by impoverished peasants in Guatemala might still hesitate to tell dinner guests that, surprisingly enough, his or her lovely home doubles as a sweatshop during the day. You can eschew the chain cleaning service of course, hire an independent cleaner at a generous hourly wage, and even encourage, at least in spirit, the unionization of the housecleaning industry. But this does not change the fact that someone is working in your home at a job she would almost certainly never have chosen for herself—if she'd had a college education, for example, or a little better luck along the way—and the place where she works, however enthusiastically or resentfully, is the same as the place where you sleep.

It is also the place where your children are raised, and what they learn pretty quickly is that some people are less worthy than others. Even better wages and working conditions won't erase the hierarchy between an employer and his or her domestic help, because the help is usually there only because the employer has "something better" to do with her time, as one report on the growth of cleaning services puts it, not noticing the obvious implication that the cleaning person herself has nothing better to do with her time. In a merely middle-class home, the message may be reinforced by a warning to the children that that's what they'll end up doing if they don't try harder in school. Housework, as radical feminists once proposed, defines a human relationship and, when unequally divided among social groups, reinforces preexisting inequalities. Dirt, in other words, tends to attach to the people who remove it—"garbagemen" and "cleaning ladies." Or, as cleaning entrepreneur Don Aslett told me with some bitterness—and this is a successful man, chairman of the board of an industrial cleaning service and frequent television guest—"The whole mentality out there is that if you clean, you're a scumball."

One of the "better" things employers of maids often want to do with their time is, of course, spend it with the children. But an underlying problem with post-nineteenth-century child-raising, as Deirdre English and I argued in our book *For Her Own Good* years ago, is precisely that it is unmoored in any kind of purposeful pursuit. Once "parenting" meant instructing the children in necessary chores; today it's more likely to center on one-sided conversations beginning with "So how was school today?" No one wants to put the kids to work again weeding and stitching; but in the void that is the modern home, relationships with children are often strained. A little "low-quality time" spent washing dishes or folding clothes together can provide a comfortable space for confidences—and give a child the dignity of knowing that he or she is a participant in, and not just the product of, the work of the house.

There is another lesson the servant economy teaches its beneficiaries and, most troublingly, the children among them. To be cleaned up after is to achieve a certain magical weightlessness and immateriality. Almost everyone complains about violent video games, but paid housecleaning has the same consequence-abolishing effect: you blast the villain into a mist of blood droplets and move right along; you drop the socks knowing they will eventually levitate, laundered and folded, back to their normal dwelling place. The result is a kind of virtual existence, in which the trail of litter that follows you seems to evaporate all by itself. Spill syrup on the floor and the cleaning person will scrub it off when she comes on Wednesday. Leave *The Wall Street Journal* scattered around your airplane seat and the flight attendants will deal with it after you've deplaned. Spray toxins into the atmosphere from your factory's smokestacks and they will be filtered out eventually by the lungs of the breathing public. A servant economy breeds callousness and solipsism in the served, and it does so all the more effectively when the service is performed close up and routinely in the place where they live and reproduce.

Individual situations vary, of course, in ways that elude blanket judgment. Some people—the elderly and disabled, parents of new babies, asthmatics who require an allergen-free environment—may well need help performing what nursing-home staff call the "ADLs," or activities of daily living, and no shame should be attached to their dependency. In a more generous social order, housekeeping services would be subsidized for those who have health-related reasons to need them—a measure that would generate a surfeit of new jobs for the low-skilled people who now clean the homes of the affluent. And in a less gender-divided social order, husbands and boyfriends would more readily do their share of the chores.

However we resolve the issue in our individual homes, the moral challenge is, put simply, to make work visible again: not only the scrubbing and vacuuming but all the hoeing, stacking, hammering, drilling, bending, and lifting that goes into creating and maintaining a livable habitat. In an ever more economically unequal culture, where so many of the affluent devote their lives to such ghostly pursuits as stock-trading, image-making, and opinion-polling, real work—in the old-fashioned sense of labor that engages hand as well as eye, that tires the body and directly alters the physical world—tends to vanish from sight. The feminists of my generation tried to bring some of it into the light of day, but, like busy professional women fleeing the house in the morning, they left the project unfinished, the debate broken off in midsentence, the noble intentions unfulfilled. Sooner or later, someone else will have to finish the job.

Day trading in the desert while tuned into CNBC is business as usual for the wealthiest investor outside of the United States. As *Fortune's* Andy Serwer found, Saudi Arabia's Prince Alwaleed seamlessly mixes tradition with new technology, interrupted only by the occasional all-night card game. Besides portraying the global appeal of tech investing, this detailed story gives the reader entrance into the grand lifestyle and thinking process of the prince.

Andy Serwer

TECH IS KING; NOW MEET THE PRINCE

PRINCE ALWALEED bin Talal bin Abdul Aziz al Saud has just had an epiphany. "Murdoch should sell the Los Angeles Dodgers," he shouts, which is the way he talks when he thinks he's onto something. "It is not a core asset like TV and the movies—it drags those businesses down," he says, gesturing excitedly. At least I think he's gesturing excitedly. I can't really tell. It's the middle of the night, and the prince and I are moving on foot across a vast stretch of desert in central Saudi Arabia. Actually, we're almost jogging. The prince walks very, very fast, and I've already fallen twice.

For the prince this is a pretty routine Wednesday night. He's bound to have strong opinions about Murdoch; he holds nearly $900 million of News Corp. stock and therefore owns a piece of the Dodgers. As for walking fast, well, keeping up with him in any endeavor is a challenge. And yes, he stays up all night and goes on treks across the desert. It helps him unwind. Usually he goes solo, but tonight he has taken me along, mostly, I think, to see whether I can make it back in one piece.

There are poisonous snakes here in the Ramah region, some 60 "clicks" northeast of Riyadh, though apparently they're hibernating now. What about getting lost? Not a chance. First of all, you can easily see the monstrous banks of lights at the prince's weekend desert camp three miles back (the weekend is Thursday and Friday in Saudi Arabia). But even if we managed to wander over the horizon, the prince carries a Motorola Star TAC that his boys can track off a radio signal beamed from a 240-foot tower back at camp.

The camp, in fact, bristles with technology. Sure, there are tents, a couple of dozen camels, and Bedouin retainers who might have stepped right out of the pages of T. E. Lawrence. But there are also mobile phones, faxes, printers, PCs, laptops, and a $700,000 custom Chevy Suburban communications truck. There's a satellite uplink too—in part so the prince's kids can play around on AOL when they visit. (He also happens to own about $600 million of AOL stock.)

When we finally return from our nighttime walkabout, the prince leads me to one of the campsite's open-air living rooms: an expanse of rugs half the size of a football field, bordered by big cushions against which card-playing Bedouins lean. Pots of tea and coffee simmer on grills above two fire pits. A half-dozen hooded hunting falcons roost silently on perches hammered into the bone-dry earth. And there are TVs. With the prince, there are always TVs. To the left of his carpeted command post, one big-screen behemoth carries Bloomberg. On his right, another has CNBC. A little 13-inch job at his feet is turned to the ART network (Arab Radio Television, which is part-owned by the prince). The prince monitors all three. Suddenly something on CNBC catches his eye. It's a story about Goldman Sachs analyst Rick Sherlund's making negative comments about Microsoft. The prince grabs the phone and starts up in rapid-fire Arabic. The only words I can make out are "Rick Sherlund" and "Microsoft" and "Bloomberg." It takes just 15 minutes for an aide to stride over with a fax of the Bloomberg story with Sherlund's comments. At 3:30 in the morning. In the Saudi desert.

By now you're probably somewhat familiar with Prince Alwaleed, the Saudi royal who made his first billion buying a bundle of Citicorp stock when the bank was on the brink in the early 1990s. But the prince isn't just some wealthy oil sheikh who happened to hit one home run in the stock market. Though that richly appreciated Citi stock remains the cornerstone of his portfolio, over the past decade the prince has systematically created a global empire of investments in brand-name companies, worth, he says, some $17 billion. Today Prince Alwaleed, 44, has become a member of the upper-echelon billionaire elite. He's not quite in the same league as Gates (who is?), but he's right up there with Michael Dell and Steve Ballmer. In fact, partly because years of recession and turmoil in Asia have eroded so many great fortunes there, it now appears that the prince is the richest businessman in the world outside the U.S.

The prince has also become one of the world's leaders of the information technology industry. As an investor, he holds about $2 billion of Apple, Motorola, AOL, and Teledesic. Which is a paradox, because the prince is a committed value investor, and value investors don't usually own tech stocks. But Alwaleed bought these shares when they *were* values, finding entry points when they were "hammered," to use his term. And at this very moment the prince is hungrily eyeing another handful of tech stocks for a possible pounce.

But Alwaleed is more than simply an investor in tech. He has also become the first mover, as they say, in bringing digital technology to the Arab world, backing an Arab Web portal, an ISP, and a huge satellite wireless network.

Prince Alwaleed doesn't just invest in and fund technology, he swims in it! When Motorola first came out with the Star TAC, the prince ordered 200 of them for himself, his family, and friends. But he quickly ran out. So he bought another 200. And then another 100, and so on, until he'd bought and given away 700 phones. "There is a revolution going on here in the Middle East, just like America and Europe; only we are behind, of course, in telecommunications, in technology, and the Internet," the prince says. "So we'd like to prepare ourselves."

It makes sense that the prince should be one of the most wired men on the planet—more so than any of his billionaire peers or, for that matter, any Nethead slouching around Silicon Valley. Remember, this is a guy who lives in Riyadh, Saudi Arabia, exactly 8,091 miles from Palo Alto. He can't just go over to Buck's in Woodside and network, right?

At one point I remark to the prince that in contrast with most American billionaires, who take pride in understanding their wealth these days—Steve Ballmer could pass for a $600,000-a-year senior executive at Merck—His Highness seems to truly live like a billionaire. The prince nods his head and smiles: "I live too happily, for sure," he says. "I love it." And why not? If your lot in life happens to be "billionaire prince," why not live like a billionaire prince?

Let's start with the palace. Completed earlier this year at a cost of $130 million, and located within Riyadh, the style is, well . . . How about "modern Arabian palace"? As we come to the gate (the guy driving says, "Open, sesame"—really!), it swings open to reveal a 20-foot-high wall-of-water fountain and a broad avenue lined with palm trees. The palace itself looks a bit like the world's swankiest Four Seasons, which is not a coincidence, since the prince owns 24 percent of the luxury hotel chain.

Inside, a 75-foot-high foyer is framed by dual winding staircases. There is ballroom after dining room after living room after bedroom wing after gymnasium. In all, 317 rooms, 400,000 square feet. At one point several of us actually got lost in the prince's closets. The palace has 520 TVs (somewhere Elvis is smiling), 400 phones, and eight elevators. And of course swimming pools (indoor and out), a screening room that beats David Geffen's hands-down, a bowling alley, tennis courts (indoor and out), and an Astroturf soccer field (that's outdoors). The staff, all 180 of them, carry walkie-talkies. All this for the prince, his new (third) wife, Princess Kholood, 22, and his two children from a previous marriage: Prince Khalid, 21, and Princess Reem, 17.

Even with two kids around, the palace doesn't feel very lived in. After our tour, which takes more than two hours, we meet up with the prince and describe a certain room and ask him about it. He turns to an aide and asks, "Which one is that?"

A man with a house like this must own some airplanes, right? Five or six Gulfstreams, maybe? Actually, no. He has no use for them. They're too small. When the prince travels, he takes along a couple of dozen people. This is a man who needs Boeing planes. He has a 737 and a 767. And a chopper and a 288-foot yacht, once owned by Adnan Khashoggi, which the prince bought from Donald Trump (during one of Trump's financial hammerings, of course). The boat is usually parked off the Côte d'Azur in the summer and serves as the prince's warm-weather retreat. As for other homes, he has none. Zip. When he travels, he stays at one of his hotels. The Four Seasons. The Plaza in New York (he owns 41 percent). The Fairmont in San Francisco (17 percent). Or the soon-to-be-reopened George V in Paris (100 percent).

Prince Alwaleed is the grandson of King Abdul Aziz al Saud, who created modern Saudi Arabia by uniting the kingdom in 1932. The prince's father, Prince Talal, brother of the current King Fahd, was sort of a black sheep of the Saudi royal family; he married the daughter of the Lebanese Prime Minister and ran off to Egypt for a time.

To this day the Saudi royal family is one of the most wealthy and secretive families on earth. It rules Saudi Arabia (or the "kingdom," as the country is often called) absolutely. The nation's economy is almost completely reliant on the price of a single commodity, which has been depressed for years. Its society is one of the world's most conservative—there is little political freedom, the press is censored, and women do not appear in public unless veiled and escorted. Many members of the royal family—including the prince—favor loosening these strictures. Some people, including elements of the Western political establishment, fear change would stir up Islamic fundamentalists and disrupt the status quo, i.e., the mutually beneficial exchange of oil for dollars. It is a very delicate balancing act.

Like every member of the Saudi royal family, Prince Alwaleed started life with silver prayer beads in his hand. But far more than any other member of this clan, the prince took his monthly allowance and ran with it. He graduated from Menlo College, south of San Francisco (at that time a favorite school for rich Saudis) and then got a master's degree in political science from Syracuse University. Though there are some who suggest that he is a conduit for the investments of other members of the royal family, the prince says he made his early millions speculating in real estate in Riyadh and trading stocks. If so, he must have had a real knack, because by early 1991 he was wealthy enough to snap up some $790 million of Citicorp stock. It was a master stroke, and that single position is up more than tenfold.

The prince wears traditional Arabic garb in the Arab world and Western clothes everywhere else. He stands about 5-foot-8 and weighs 140 pounds and has a slight tick whereby he jerks his head. He is prone to a bit of exaggeration and has a sizable ego. Perhaps that is understandable: Every week scores of Bedouins line up to kiss his shoulder (a greeting and a sign of respect for royal family members), read poems of adulation, and ask for money.

Though he's a bit brisk at first, the prince soon warms up, telling jokes in accented English. He seems most at ease with his Bedouin crew. They razz him, and he razzes them back—throwing cookies, for instance, at one old guy (either 95, 100, or 105, depending on whom you ask) who warbles some ancient desert love song.

They say the prince is loved in Saudi Arabia (there are no taxes in the kingdom, but the prince says he hands out $60 million a year in charity—that's off around $500 million of annual income). He is respected by those who work for him, though he's incredibly demanding; he's been known to delay an employee's paycheck after a failed white-glove inspection of his palace. "If you work for the prince, you are on call 24 hours a day, 365 days a year," says one of his top aides. The staff of Kingdom Holdings, as the prince's company is called, numbers only 20 or so professionals, mostly American-educated Middle Easterners (Saudis, but also Lebanese, Egyptians, and Palestinians) who manage his investments, hotel operations, and construction projects. Some are also stock traders and investors who have become wealthy in their own right.

It might be tempting to view the prince as an investor who was born on third base and thinks he hit a triple. Certainly he's not in Warren Buffett's league when it comes to analyzing financial markets and securities. Nor does he possess the technological expertise of a Gates or a Dell. But give the man credit: The prince knew enough to buy 6.2 million shares of Apple in March of 1997, when it was trading for about $18 a share. Today Apple sells for $96.That's nearly $500 million of profit in some 30 months in a high-profile stock that was sitting right there in front of everyone. As Citigroup co-CEO Sandy Weill observes, "You sure can't argue with results."

In the desert, at the prince's camp, the phone rings. The prince snatches it out of the cradle. "Yes. That's good. Yes," he says, then hangs up. "That was Paul Collins, vice chairman of Citigroup. Rubin is coming to Citigroup; it will be on the news right now." And 20 minutes later, so it is. Right there on CNBC.

Take a look at the prince's portfolio, and a couple of points jump out at you right away. First, the overwhelming majority of his holdings are plunked down in three stock groups: media, technology, and banking (he owns about 150 million shares of Citigroup, or 4.4 percent of its stock, worth $8 million, which is why he got the courtesy call from Collins). If you were to travel back to 1990 and pick three sectors of the world economy to invest in, you couldn't do much better than that. What makes this even more impressive is that Alwaleed is a value investor who bought what are really growth stocks when they were cheap. He didn't get suckered into metal producers, for instance—which have always looked cheap but have gone nowhere—or oil, about which the prince says he knows nothing. Did he zero in on tech, media, and banking by design? "Yes and no," says the prince. "I really came to these groups because of the companies. I am always looking for the same thing: global companies with a brand name that are basically healthy but that have had a hiccup. That is what led me to these companies."

What the prince really is, of course, is a very successful portfolio manager. If you look at the world's richest men, they sort of fall into two camps. In one camp are the founders, like Gates and Dell, who have created their wealth from one great business. The prince falls into the second, which includes men like Buffett and Philip Anschutz, whose great skill is not managing business but deploying capital. Depending on how you look at it, the prince, as the great globalist of the group, either has it harder or easier than the others, since he has the whole world as his investing canvas. And he does have poles planted all over the world these days. North America. Asia. Europe. Africa. The Middle East. He has significant holdings everywhere. Well, almost everywhere. The prince didn't get snookered into Russia. "We went to Moscow, and there was nothing," he says, shaking his head. "Nothing."

One of the fictions of investing is that diversification is a key to attaining great wealth. Not true. Diversification can prevent you from losing money, but no one ever joined the billionaire's club through a great diversification strategy. Most often great wealth is created by making bold, concentrated bets. For instance, nearly half of the prince's $17 billion fortune sits in Citi stock. On Nov. 3, a $1 billion chunk of Citi stock was traded, and some immediately speculated that the prince was selling. Not so. In fact it would have been tricky for the prince to sell then, because the day before,

Sandy Weill and his wife, Joan, had visited with him in Saudi Arabia. Though the prince is not an insider and can therefore buy or sell anytime—which is partly why he chooses not to sit on any corporate boards—it would look very bad for Weill if the prince sold 18 million shares after a prolonged and private audience with Citi's cochairman.

The prince says he is delighted with Citi (interestingly, the bank has had strong ties to the Saudi royal family for decades). Bob Rubin's arrival, he says, "adds major credibility to our bank. But I do not believe he will succeed Sandy." As for the future of Citi, the prince says what you'd expect from someone who owns a yachtload of shares: "I believe Citigroup is a $100 stock. The full potential of the merger has yet to take place. Also cost reduction. And when the markets begin accepting that Citigroup is a global bank not susceptible to small increases in interest rates, that it grows 15 percent to 20 percent every year, then the P/E multiple goes up from 15 to 20. I am patient. I have been hammered twice with Citibank, very badly. I'm a long-termer. I'm not a seller." Remember, if the prince does hang on to all of his Citi stock, then for all practical purposes, where Citi's stock goes, so goes the prince's fortune. During my visit Citi stock moves from $46 to $53, adding about $1 billion to his net worth. No wonder he's in a good mood.

But many of the prince's big non-Citi holdings, particularly his tech stocks, have also been on a hot streak lately. A quick review: We've already mentioned how he jumped into Apple in early 1997. Why? Was that because he saw Jobs had come back? "No," says the prince, "that was before Jobs returned [Jobs' redux was July 1997]. I looked at Apple and said, This company has an incredible name. It can't just evaporate. Worst-case scenario, it would be a candidate for a takeover. Some companies did talk to me about taking over Apple. One of them is Oracle—Mr. Ellison. The other I can't name." Was it IBM? The prince won't say. "When Jobs came back, he proved how lousy, bad, and disastrous the management was. All the people between Jobs No. 1 and Jobs No. 2 were lousy." The prince tells of meeting Jobs in Cupertino,

Calif., two years ago. "He ran up with a new iMac. That Jobs, he is different." So is the prince in this one for the long haul too? "For the long haul."

In October of 1997, with the markets doing their usual fall swoon, the prince made two other big bets on tech, buying pieces of Netscape and Motorola. At first neither move looked particularly astute. He bought some six million shares of Motorola at around $76, and over the next 12 months the stock promptly fell all the way down to $38. Abracadabra, the prince is out some $228 million. You know the story about Motorola: bad chips, bad phones, bad management moves. But since that low last year, the stock has headed due north, soaring to about $90 in early November. So now the prince has a $538 million stake in Motorola, and abracadabra, he's up $82 million. "Sure, that stock could have stayed down for three or four years, but when we analyze a company we really do it, so we knew that we had a plan, and thank God we were proven right."

Not that the prince hasn't had issues with Motorola. They come up when I ask him about his 15 percent stake in Teledesic (Craig McCaw's ambitious wireless network based on a series of satellites), which he bought for $200 million and which is now worth $300 million. "Teledesic is feeling the hurt right now because of problems with Iridium and Globalstar, which I was offered to invest in and didn't, thank God. Teledesic is fundamentally different because it is broadband, the Internet in the sky. And because it is voice and data and possibly video. It is well financed, no leverage, and is backed by incredible people. Now, frankly speaking, this may not make those people happy over at Motorola, but Motorola was one of the causes of the collapse of Iridium. They made a lot of money by selling technology to this company. They were milking it completely. And I told [Motorola CEO Chris] Galvin that, when he came to see me last week."

As for Netscape, it too went south after the prince bought four-plus million shares for $130 million. But then last fall, after

AOL announced it was buying the browser company in a stock swap, Netscape shares began climbing. This spring, when the deal was completed, the prince's Netscape holdings were exchanged for four million shares of AOL, now worth $600 million. "Netscape to me was just like Apple. It was down, but it wasn't going away. Again, I thought maybe a takeover. Actually, in my meeting with Barksdale, I told him, 'Why don't you think of a takeover by some company?' He said, 'Well, we don't rule it out, Prince.' I am in AOL by default, but I don't mind. It's one of the only Internet companies that makes money. My average cost is $30, and the stock is $150. I'm happy."

Okay, but what about some of the prince's greatest misses? Yes, he has some very high-profile duds. Like Planet Hollywood. The prince sank some $110 million in that debacle, which has been whittled down to $40 million—though he now owns 20 percent of the company and is convinced it will rebound. (Disney apparently was sniffing around recently, looking to buy the All-Star Cafe chain, which is part of the same company.) And speaking of Disney, the prince's investment in Euro Disney has pretty much gone nowhere, so that's a $320 million investment just spinning its wheels—though he does stay chez Mickey when he's visiting Paris, while the George V is being renovated. Daewoo has also been a bust, though it will likely be restructured. And then there's Donna Karan. He put in $20 million, which is now down to $13 million. What in the world did he see there? "It was for my daughter," the prince confesses. "She's my partner in that one." (And, in fact, Princess Reem's quarters are festooned with DKNY.) All told, the prince's losses in these investments—both realized and unrealized—are somewhere around $150 million, which is not so bad, considering it about equals his gain in any one of his big recent winners. "This is a portfolio," says the prince. "Of course that happens."

The only non-Saudi part of his empire that the prince's company actually manages is the hotel properties. In fact his hotel people, based in Riyadh and New York, are busy expanding in the

Middle East, as well as looking to consolidate their holdings into what might turn out to be a publicly traded entity not far down the road. But how're they doing managing the hotels? Pretty dang well, if you believe Warren Buffett. In May, Buffett wrote the prince about his stay at the Plaza: "You have restored the Plaza to its former luster—indeed your managers have enabled it to surpass its previous heights—and I congratulate you." (After the prince responded, Buffett wrote back, "In Omaha, I'm known as the 'Alwaleed of America'—which is quite a compliment.")

As it turns out, some of the prince's biggest moves lately have been in European media stocks. (It's worth noting here that his News Corp. stock has been treating him royally of late, up to $300 million over the past two years.) He recently bought 3 percent of Kirch Media of Germany. Together with his 3 percent stake in Mediaset, the big Italian TV and publishing company, that brings his European media holdings to more than $500 million. The prince also owns small bits and pieces of all kinds of stuff. Like 5 percent of TWA. And 3 percent of Saks. And 5.5 percent of Saatchi & Saatchi.

The prince repeatedly says that he thinks the U.S. stock market is overvalued, which is vexing for him, because obviously it is the venue that has the greatest appeal for him. It's where the big companies are. The marquee names. The big brands. The liquidity. And yet, even with stock prices so high, there's a group of about six to eight large, globally branded, down-but-not-out companies that the prince is monitoring. He's watching three or four of them like a falcon. Think about it for a while, and you can pretty much figure out which ones they are.

Spend some time outdoors in Saudi Arabia in the middle of the day, and you begin to see why the prince is such a night owl. A visit to some of the prince's construction projects gives me a taste of a typical Saudi afternoon: not a cloud in the sky, temperature hovering around 97 degrees Fahrenheit. In the shade. And this is fall. On the outskirts of Riyadh the light is so bright that the world is reduced to white and tan. Your eyes beg you to put on sunglasses. But we leave the swelter as we enter a nearly completed school the prince is building, a $90 million construction project—built, like everything else in Saudi Arabia, by hundreds of workers from Pakistan, Bangladesh, and India. Though the unemployment rate in the kingdom is said to be as high as 30 percent, Saudis are not keen on construction work.

In some respects the school will be no different from schools built here for decades, conforming to rigid Islamic precepts separating male and female students. But look closer, and you'll find that the school will be as cutting-edge as anything built in Seattle or San Francisco. At the school's core is a gigabit Ethernet backbone network, run on the latest hardware from Cisco. (That company will train technicians and teachers.) Every student will have an iBook and Internet access. The construction manager proudly shows off the ports in the classrooms' floors.

The prince is helping to bring the Internet economy to the Middle East and North Africa. A drop-in-the-bucket market, you say. Syria, for instance, doesn't even have mobile or paging yet. Well, yes, but the Middle East does have at least one attribute that the boys on Sand Hill Road will find compelling: one language. There are some 270 million Arabs in the world, spread mostly across the Middle East and North Africa, all speaking Arabic. Sure, disposable income is only a fraction of Europe's, but at least you don't have the problem of trying to wire up the Greeks to the Danes.

Turns out that much of the digital-communication action in this part of the world is run through a company 25 percent owned by the prince (surprise, surprise), called Silki La Silki. Translation: cable and no cable (like Cable & Wireless). "Also, the name is like music in Arabic," says company president Abdul Aziz Al Hagbani. (Like music in English too, I tell him!) Silki La Silki controls an ISP called PrimeNet, headquartered in a dusty office building in downtown Riyadh. Walk in the door, and . . . voilà!, a real ISP, complete with six Sun Enterprise 450 servers, Cisco routers and cache engines, and Oracle database software. Customers? Well, only 7,500, and I happen to pop in during prayer time, so traffic is down to a trickle, but volume is growing faster than Saudi Telecom can handle.

Besides building pay-phone networks in Syria and Saudi Arabia, Silki La Silki is also working on a satellite network that will blanket 99 countries in the Middle East and Africa. But the really exciting piece of this company could be Arabia Online (go to arabia.com), an Arab portal. Through Silki La Silki, the prince recently bought 50 percent of this business, which is run by Ramzi Zeine, a Jordanian out of Amman, for $1.2 million. (That's *million*.)

Now, think about that. Arabia Online has about 400,000 unique users each month and is growing the way a popular new Web site should. Zeine is talking to American VCs right now, and then he'll look for strategic partners (i.e., including a big U.S.-based portal); he hopes to take this company public on Nasdaq as soon as next year. A similar proposition like StarMedia (a Latin portal) has a market cap of $1.9 billion. Say Arabia Online—which unlike StarMedia has virtually no competition—has a market cap only half as big (and, remember, 270 million Arabs). Then that 50 percent stake the prince bought for $1.2 million would be worth $475 million. Could be one of the prince's biggest hits ever.

As the Middle East inexorably—albeit slowly—gets wired, the prince stands to make out coming and going. The populace will buy Macs and Moto phones. They will dial in to the Internet through his telecom networks, using his ISP. And they will log in to AOL and Arabia Online. Talk about setting yourself up for the next millennium!

The prince, though, is wired already. His world is powered by a pair of Compaq servers linked to four T-1 lines hooked up to a network node in Boston. The prince requires that he have T-1 or equivalent access pretty much all the time. Not just in Riyadh or the desert camp, but on his boat, on the planes, and in hotel rooms—everywhere. Here is a partial laundry list of IT equipment required on all of his trips: HP 1100 printer, Canon Multipass C5500 fax/copier, IBM 380D laptop, IBM 600E laptop, Sony laptop, Kodak Digital camera, two Motorola walkie-talkie sets, Motorola phone sets, Iridium phone set, and so on. And then there's one more piece of hardware, the one his staff finds most terrifying. Everywhere the prince travels, he brings an ordinary touch-tone phone, just like the ones he has at home. The No. 1 speed-dial button is programmed to ring at the palace, and when the prince hits that button, anytime, anywhere in the world, he expects to get the palace. Period. Needless to say, this tiny little request keeps his travel and telecom guys in a state of absolute telecom panic. (As in, it's 3 A.M. in Kuala Lumpur. "Quick, where's the satellite uplink?")

The prince's infatuation with technology is really the product of two deeply conflicting desires. He wants to live in Saudi Arabia. And he wants to be in touch with everything in the world instantaneously. Sometimes this results in operations right out of James Bond. Not long ago he sent Hisham Fleihan, head of his travel staff, to the Bentley factory in Crew, England, to check out some new cars. Fleihan brought along his new Sony Vaio with its Integrated Swivel Motion Eye Camera. Fleihan snapped pictures of the Bentleys with the Vaio and then immediately e-mailed them back to the prince for his perusal. "I travel in advance of the prince and take pictures of the hotels for him to see with the Sony," says Fleihan. We could all use a guy like Fleihan and his Vaio.

But in the end, the prince is always happiest back at his desert camp. For him, staying up all night watching business news and poring through periodicals is relaxing. And as the hours wear on toward dawn, we are still very much in never-a-dull-moment territory. I'm taken over to a caravan of camels and given a milking lesson (drink right out of the pail!). And finally the all-night Bedouins' card game is winding down. The Bedouins get paid hundreds of dollars a day by the prince, just for being a member of the posse. (Nice work, if you can get it. But you can't.) The guys often play cards for a big pot of prize money, but tonight the prince has announced that the winner gets a new car. Over the hours, the number of Bedouins playing shrinks until we're down to a final four. Sometime around 4:30 A.M., a portly fellow bounds straight up in the air from a seated position on the carpet. He rushes the prince and gives him a big hug. Yes, I think we have a winner here! Then comes dawn, and the prince's cleric calls the faithful to prayer. A huge breakfast, including fish and hot dogs, awaits us on the floor of a tent. The prince will sleep a few hours after that and then begin another endless day.

There is so much about the prince that's difficult to fathom. But then again, he comes from a different place, almost a different time. Here is a man who began his life not far removed from the era of *Seven Pillars of Wisdom* and is now thriving in the Digital Age. It's the prince's world, and from his perspective it all makes perfect sense. And as Sandy Weill says, you sure can't argue with results.

President Trump wasn't in the cards this time around, but Chris Byron in *George* magazine places "the Donald's" aborted political campaign within the context of his other attempts to over-inflate his image. The richer Trump makes himself appear, Byron reasons, the more money he can borrow. His wealth, projects, vocabulary, and women are carefully placed under the microscope here.

Chris Byron

BEHIND TRUMP'S POLITICAL FLING

IN THIS WORLD, everything is stage-set perfect. The attendant who parks your car is young and handsome. The receptionist who announces your arrival looks like the parking attendant's twin sister. Mr. Trump's "manservant"—Tony, by name—stands ready to welcome you; he is a dead ringer for Bruce Wayne's aging butler in Batman. The only giveaway that all is not as it seems on the day of my arrival is the animated discussion taking place between Tony and the receptionist, Tracey, as I enter. It went like this:

> Tracey: "I don't want to call him. I'm afraid. He's in a yelling mood."
> Tony: "Go ahead. You've been working here for two years, and he hasn't killed you yet, has he?"

Whereupon Tony turns to me and says, "Mr. Trump will be with you momentarily. Meanwhile, make yourself at home." He gestures toward the "living room," actually the astonishing Grand Salon, and I enter. By and by Donald Trump presents himself before me and proceeds to hold court on topics ranging from his wealth ("huge") to his presidential ambitions ("we're considering the situation carefully").

As it happens, there is one other element to the proceedings that is not easy to overlook: the arrival, midway through the meeting, of a half-naked fashion model wrapped in a towel about the size of a dinner napkin, who approaches the two of us and joins the discussion. I'll get into what happened next in due course—and in detail—but, for the moment, it is enough to say that this is what I had waited a decade, and now had come a thousand miles, to see and hear and discover for myself: whether the official billionaire rascal of American real estate is indeed serious about running for president, or whether his campaigning is a publicity ploy to improve his bottom line.

When a friend recently asked Trump why he was running, Donald laughed—apparently only partly in jest—and answered, "It's a good way to raise the rents." My goal was to find out whether he was (a) as rich as he claims to be, (b) as serious about running for president as he suggests, and (c) as cynical as that "raise the rents" answer makes him sound.

What I found, in the end, was what I suppose I had suspected all along—that the answer to all three questions is ultimately "no." But so what? Whether Trump is even a fraction as rich as he says (which is almost certainly not the case) or stands any chance at all of becoming president is ultimately a nitpick. When it comes to understanding Donald Trump, what's most important is to grasp what matters the most to him, and that is how well he's been performing in his lifetime starring role of living rich as the best revenge—and on that score he's basically retired the cup.

For nearly a quarter century now, Trump has held himself forth before the public as an enduring testament to the Cerebrus-like proposition that (a) ostentation is its own reward and (b) what you've got is less important than what people think you've got—whether you've got anything or not. And who cannot admire the

finesse with which he's pulled it all off—even to the point of twice
in his life transforming a fling at presidential campaigning into a
profit-making opportunity?

At the dawn of the third millennium, Donald Trump is America—a creation of limitless possibilities, ever reinventing itself,
bold, noisy, juvenile, shallow, obsessed with material gain, but
with a smile to the world as wide as all outdoors. Who can't like a
country like that, or admire a businessman who has invented himself in its image? If America is a Great Country, then Donald
Trump is a Great Guy. It's as simple as that.

In a culture that exists on the come, in which debt and desire
are the interchangeable images in the pop art called the American
Experience, it was Trump, after all, who in the mid-1980s bought
the Mar-a-Lago estate in Palm Beach—one of the most ornate,
lavish, overwrought residences in the world—for next to nothing
down. (Donald says it was $1 million down.) Then, to save it from
seizure by creditors as his business empire crumbled, he turned it
into a kind of real-life Love Boat for status-hungry businessmen
you've never heard of. Trump sells memberships to the place for
$100,000 a pop, which is not a bad way to pay the bills.

In those cable-TV infomercials in which real estate promoter
Carlton Sheets shows America's late-night insomniacs how to buy
real estate for almost no money down, then turn it into income-
producing property, Donald Trump is the ultimate model—the
man who actually did it. He lives like a billionaire by simply bor-
rowing the money, and betting that the endless bounty of the
American economy—and his own endlessly flowing blather and
blarney—will bail him out.

It takes nerves of titanium to attempt that kind of a stunt even
once in your life, let alone to pull it off successfully time after time
until it becomes your whole career. But that is precisely what
Trump has done: He's made living like the richest man in America
seem at least as good as actually being that person. To quote a line
from the comic Billy Crystal's send-up of Latin film idol Fernando,
"It's better to look mahvelous than to feel mahvelous."

The only really intriguing question left about Donald Trump

today is this: Will he seriously pursue the Reform party's nomination for president, or is all his talk just part of his self-promoting act, as he swells himself up, larger and larger, until the dimensions of his majesty block out even the sun?

As I write this, I don't know the answer for sure. Maybe Trump doesn't either. But whether he ratchets up his campaign or bows out is beside the point. One need only revisit his history to see what this—his second flirtation with the White House since the late 1980s—is all about: In a presidential election year built of bathtub rings and name-the-leader-of-Azerbaijan foreign affairs tests, Trump stands apart as the candidate who manifestly and obviously is in it for the money. Or, as Trump boasted to *George,* "I'm the only one who makes money when he runs." To dispel all doubts, he added, "I got a fortune for the book I came out with. Also, I'm the highest-paid speaker out there. I'm making 12 speeches this year at $100,000 each." Not to mention his other profit-making angles.

It is perhaps a measure of the current American temperament that few people seem to regard his obsession with money as diminishing his qualifications for the job in any way. It is as if wealth and leadership in America have become flip sides of the same coin, so that the ostentatious display of the former is now seen as a way to demonstrate competence in the latter.

If so, Trump is certainly a man for his time, for rarely does one encounter a person more devoted than he—through good times and bad, from triumph to failure and back again—to the narcissistic lifelong adoration of his reflection in the mirror of high finance. That is where we found him nearly 35 years ago, as a young man fresh out of the Wharton School at the University of Pennsylvania, working in his father's real estate office in Brooklyn while yearning to join the fast-track crowd of East Side socialites across the river in Manhattan.

Now, at the age of 54—after two failed marriages and a humiliating $900 million prepackaged bankruptcy—that is where we find him, still seeking, Gatsby-like, to impress the impressionable with his closets of monogrammed shirts, while holding himself forth to the world as a possible candidate for president of the United States. As he told ABC TV's Cokie Roberts recently, "If you look at the other candidates—give me a break. Now, I made billions of dollars. Do you think that they would have made billions of dollars? I don't think so."

Trump is, in fact, hardly as wealthy as he claims to be—a condition that has dogged him for his entire adult life. He is the only even semiofficial candidate for president who has a private plane—a vintage Boeing 727 jet—registered in the offshore tax-haven domicile of Bermuda. "I play by the rules," Trump said to me at Mar-a-Lago, "and the rules say I can keep a plane in Bermuda, so I do."

Trump likes to create the impression that he owns the General Motors building in New York City, but when questioned on the matter, he agrees that he actually owns only half of it. And it is mortgaged, so, for all practical purposes, he owns very little of it. In addition, he owns only 40 percent of the Trump Tower project he is now constructing near the United Nations—and the stakes of both he and his 60 percent majority partner in the project are dwarfed by the debt on it held by a German bank. Many of his other high-profile projects of years past have disappeared in bankruptcy proceedings, or his interest in them has been sharply reduced.

Even the beautiful 26-year-old model, Melania Knauss, whom he paraded around as his potential first lady until their recent breakup, is something of an illusion. The press has taken to describing her as a fashion "supermodel," in much the way they uncritically fawned over his first wife, Ivana, as a top model and an "Olympic skier," two images that Trump did much to help cultivate. But just as Ivana seems to have been, at most, a barely known model prior to hooking up with him, Melania Knauss was largely unknown prior to her yearlong romance with Trump. She earned a good living, to be sure. But her status as a supermodel, whatever that means, was bestowed by the media only after Trump began incessantly introducing her that way as she hung on his arm at public functions.

As with everything else about Donald, you can hear the jingle of coins in the background. In reality, Melania Knauss is represented by a modeling agency owned by Trump, T Management. Since beginning her high-profile life as Trump's love interest, Knauss has seen her day rate double, from $5,000 a day two years ago to $10,000 a day now. And because she is represented by Trump's agency, 20 percent of her modeling fees go to Trump, who also collects another 20 percent from agencies and publishing companies that hire her. That is an even richer take-off than Trump took from the labors of his second wife, Marla Maples, whose short-lived career as a Broadway actress blossomed from her association with Trump. He pocketed 30 percent of her earnings.

Nonetheless, once every decade or so Trump begins reminding folks that millions upon millions of them would like nothing better than to have him as their president, and up rockets his public image—and his income. Up go the sales of whatever ghosted autobiography he happens to have in the stores at the moment, up go the rental values of his apartments, in come more day-tripping gamblers lured to his Atlantic City casinos—in short, up goes the market price of the most valuable, and promotable, possession Trump has: his name.

Then, like the Kenny Rogers character who "knows when to hold 'em, and knows when to fold 'em," he simply places his cards facedown on the table, sweeps his winnings into his lap, and exits the quadrennial poker game without ever showing his hand— namely, the obligatory audited personal financial statement, required of serious candidates, that would reveal how modestly wealthy, relatively speaking, he really is. *Forbes* magazine currently pegs his net worth at $1.6 billion, but the magazine's editors say the total could be far lower. They do know, however, that much of his wealth is not from his own wheeling and dealing, but simply represents the Queens, New York, apartment buildings he inherited from his father, Fred.

Be that as it may, Trump's many critics have already dismissed his political ambitions as being half-hearted, self-indulgent, and (roll the drums for this one, please) Not Serious—the ravings of a confused rich man in the grips of a midlife crisis.

But that misses the point because, when it comes to Donald Trump, the name of the game isn't delivering the goods; it's the Art of the Process.

Trump has already come out so far ahead financially that actually becoming president would be a setback. Sure, he'd get to live in the White House and fly around on Air Force One. But he's already got the run of Mar-a-Lago (which may be more garish but is certainly bigger than Casa Blanca), and he's got his own plushed-out Boeing 727. Worse, if he did, by some miracle, become president of the United States, he wouldn't be able to run his businesses anymore, and would have to scrape by on a rotten $400,000 a year, courtesy of the American taxpayer. No one who knows Donald Trump can imagine him allowing others to take over the management of his business and financial affairs for a single minute.

We could therefore say, with only slight poetic license, that in his second flirtation with the presidency, Donald Trump is in a race he's already won. Says Michael Bruneau, senior vice president of the Lund Group, a boutique New York public relations firm, "In almost no time at all, Trump has graduated from the gossip pages to *Meet the Press*. I tuned in Don Imus on the radio the other day and heard Dan Rather describe Trump as a 'really smart guy.' This kind of endorsement is so huge that its value is incalculable. If I were Donald's flack, I'd send him a bill that even he would choke on."

New York advertising personality Jerry Della Femina agrees. "What's it worth for a casino operator to get himself transformed into presidential material?" asks Della Femina. "I dunno, $500 million maybe?"

But Jack O'Dwyer, the dean of New York public relations men, says he thinks Trump is playing a dangerous game by toying with the presidency. "Publicity is like a football," says O'Dwyer. "You never know which way it's going to bounce next. One false move and he could have the whole country laughing at him."

In the short-attention-span theater of American politics, what

O'Dwyer and others forget, of course, is that Trump has been down this road before, and the more he travels it, the better he gets at avoiding the potholes. In his recitation of events, the genesis of his current presidential sort-of campaign was when a real estate trade publication carried an article last fall that described him as presidential timber. Almost instantly, says Trump, his office was besieged with calls—from Barbara Walters, Dan Rather, everyone—all wanting to know if he was planning to run. So Trump just tossed the ball to his good friend and "great guy," Republican party campaign adviser Roger Stone, who decided to test the waters by setting up an exploratory committee.

A plausible scenario? Sure, except that it bears an eerie resemblance to certain events that unfolded 13 years ago. That's when Trump invented his "Trump for President" stunt. Back then, in the autumn of 1987, his goal was to gain national recognition to stimulate sales of his first book, *Trump: The Art of the Deal.* And he recruited many of the same characters who are involved this time, too, most notably Stone, the Republican campaign apparatchik who's been his Washington, D.C., lobbyist for the past 18 years. The campaign even featured a softball segment on 20/20, hosted by Barbara Walters, and a Stone-concocted "open letter" on U.S. defense policy, which ran in *The New York Times.* Then, when Trump's book leaped onto the best-seller list for the next 48 weeks, Donald's campaign for the presidency faded away until nothing remained but the smile of a Cheshire cat.

Thirteen years later, memories as well have faded, and a whole new set of media acolytes have emerged to play his foil. There's Stone Phillips and Tim Russert, both of NBC, nodding dutifully to Trump's pronunciamentos on tax policy in set-piece interviews. There's Chris Matthews and Geraldo Rivera sounding awestruck when each in turn asks him how rich he is—and he answers that, frankly, he really doesn't know how many billions he's got.

I asked *Washington Post* media critic Howard Kurtz to explain the press's groveling approach to the Trump candidacy, and he said, "Donald Trump is a master at finding the media's G spot. He knows journalists go gaga over the idea of a gold-plated developer running for president with a superbabe on his arm. And reporters are all too happy to suspend disbelief—about his finances and his campaign—so they can ride on the Trump jet and chronicle the Trump lifestyle, which is a lot more interesting than writing about Steve Forbes."

Meanwhile, lurking just offstage, we once again find the indefatigable Stone, cobbling together talking-point papers on everything from taxing the rich to negotiating trade deals with Japan. In January, Stone told the Associated Press that "if" Trump decides to run, he'll conduct a "fireside chat" with the American people on all the major networks in the spring. The idea is for Trump to spend part of the $10 million of his money that he's earmarked for his race for the Reform party nomination on a five-minute block of the same time slot on all five major networks: CBS, NBC, ABC, CNN, and Fox.

Whatever happens on the TV front, Renaissance Books is shipping book four of the FrankenTrump saga, his campaign manifesto, *The America We Deserve,* to stores, and Trump is hawking it hard.

When Donald Trump and I first came face-to-face a decade ago, it was a rather oddly orchestrated get-together. Word reached him, via a mutual acquaintance in the media, that I was preparing to write a column vouchsafing the opinion that, his blustering, blowhard self-absorption notwithstanding, he was probably a net positive for New York—at least, insofar as the local economy was concerned. Scarcely had this pearl of medium-priced wisdom dropped from my lips than he was on the phone with me, telling me what a "great guy" I was and how much he had admired my writing over the years. Then he invited me to his office on Fifth Avenue to hear those very sentiments expressed directly from his lips.

I recall two things in particular about that meeting. His entire office wall, large enough for at least a half-court game of jai alai, was covered end-to-end and top to bottom with framed magazine photographs of himself. Also, he spent most of the meeting explaining to me how wealthy he was, as evidenced by the nightly gambling take at the Taj Mahal in New Jersey ("the greatest casino resort in the world!") and his ownership of a 282-foot yacht that had previously belonged to Saudi Arabian arms dealer Adnan Khashoggi.

I also remember that no sooner had I returned to my office, a 15-minute walk from his headquarters on Fifth Avenue, when a messenger arrived with a note. Inscribed on paper so heavy it could have been parchment, the note told me how much he, Donald, enjoyed a book I'd recently written and how he'd already recommended it to two of his "top friends." Not long afterward, I wrote a column that nonetheless suggested that Mr. Trump had a lower net worth than many believed. A decade went by without another peep or glance in my direction from the man.

During that time, Trump's businesses and two marriages collapsed, various properties slid into bankruptcy, and he was forced to sell his yacht as well as his airline (he had once owned the old Eastern Airlines shuttle service from New York to Washington, D.C.). His ownership of the Plaza Hotel was stripped from him, he lost his mansion in Greenwich, Connecticut, and he even wound up having to turn his treasured Mar-a-Lago into a spa open to the paying public.

From having had the run of Mar-a-Lago's 118 rooms as his own palatial romper room, Trump was reduced to living quarters in a single wing, managing the rest in the manner of a threadbare British duke who is forced to raise funds by turning the ancestral barony into a drive-through zoo where weekenders from London come to pay a few quid and gaze at the rhinos and giraffes. From a man with a claimed net worth of more than $1.5 billion, he had emerged as America's most preposterously enormous deadbeat. In the midst of all this, he and Marla Maples were walking down Fifth Avenue one day and passed a panhandler on the street. Trump looked at her and said, "That guy's better off than I am. At least he's got nothing. I'm $900 million in the hole."

One way or another, Trump's problems can all be traced to his involvement in the gambling business of Atlantic City—the source of most of the cash and calamity in his life over the past 20 years. Atlantic City had been the arena in which he found the glamour and the cash flow to concoct his image as a kind of early Howard Hughes. But the siren song of the slot machines and craps tables was also the reason for his collapse into a prepackaged bankruptcy reorganization—from which he emerged as only a minority owner in a business he once owned outright. The fiasco in Atlantic City also led to the bank-directed reorganization of his real estate holdings, reducing him to little more than a manager of buildings he once owned.

Yet, by 1997, Trump was back, more boastful than ever, recalled to life in one of the shrewdest maneuvers in the history of high finance. Convinced by his top adviser and chief financial officer, Stephen Bollenbach—who had been hired away from Holiday Corp. at the behest of Trump's creditors—that the banks to which he owed billions needed him even more than he needed them, Trump negotiated what turned out to be a highly beneficial bankruptcy deal. In it, he agreed to shed various real estate holdings and lifestyle accoutrements in return for being permitted to keep the wildly indebted Atlantic City casino and hotel properties that had gotten him in trouble in the first place.

Trump's reasoning? Although the gambling industry was then in recession, as was most of the economy, both he and Bollenbach figured the Atlantic City market was destined to recover in a big way, if for no other reason than its close proximity to the New York, Philadelphia, Baltimore, and Washington, D.C., markets.

Then, having maneuvered the banks out of any role in his casino operations, Trump began issuing yet more debt while siphoning off the resulting cash and rebuilding his real estate empire all over again.

In June 1995, he tapped into the Wall Street equity market, bundling one of his Atlantic City properties—the Trump Plaza Hotel—together with some blue-sky plans for a riverboat gambling operation outside Chicago, and taking the thing public in a complex IPO transaction. In the deal, Trump sold 60 percent of the resulting company to the public for $140 million, at an offering price of $14 per share—a transaction that boosted the market value of his stake in the company to $93 million.

This offering, plus a 15.5 percent junk bond issue, raised nearly $300 million for Trump Hotels & Casino Resorts, and as the company's largest single—and controlling—shareholder, Trump was suddenly back in the game.

Soon deals were flying in all directions. First came Trump's move to climb out from under his money-losing 50 percent stake in Atlantic City's Taj Mahal. The Taj, a minaret-domed complex spread over 17 acres that is visible from far out at sea, had cost Trump $675 million in junk bond financing, but wound up cannibalizing business from his other gaming properties from the moment it opened. So he sold the business to Trump Hotels & Casino Resorts for $40.5 million in company stock. Then, several months later, he did the same thing with the third—and weakest—of his Atlantic City properties, the Trump Castle. He dumped that one on the public company for $133 million more in stock and cash.

Along the way, there were more junk bond financings and more debt reshufflings—and with each one, more millions seemed to tumble into Trump's personal pocket. As Trump himself confessed in book three of the FrankenTrump saga: "If truth be known, without Atlantic City it is highly unlikely that Random House would have asked me to write this book, because it was the tremendous cash flow from Atlantic City that enabled me to escape the tough times of the early 1990s."

But what was good for him was not so good for his shareholders. By siphoning off cash, Trump weakened the very casino operations that had saved him from ruin. In the process, the public's stock in Trump Hotels & Casino Resorts crashed from a high of $35 per share three years ago to around $3 per share now, as nearly $2 billion of debt was piled back onto the balance sheet.

"Look, I'm telling you, I've let that situation slide, okay?"

Trump said to me at Mar-a-Lago. "But I'm going to be getting involved in it big-time right after the first of the year." Then, as if to reassure me that things were okay with him personally, even if his investors had gotten soaked, he added, "Anyway, it's only a small portion of my wealth. You want to be looking at the real estate, really."

That, unfortunately, is easier said than done, since Trump, who seems obsessed with sticking his name on anything he comes within 20 feet of, has hidden his real estate interests—especially the debt on them—behind blanket after blanket of anonymous corporate filings and then goes to almost comical lengths to reassure the curious that he's got nothing to hide.

Author Harry Hurt III, whose definitive biography—*Lost Tycoon, The Many Lives of Donald J. Trump* (W.W. Norton, 1993)—infuriated Trump for its page after page of unflattering revelations, quotes one Trump executive as saying regarding the company's real estate finances: "It was all a shell game. We never had any unencumbered cash. We were always creating new partnerships and corporate entities to shift the money around. We were always robbing Peter to pay Paul."

In *Lost Tycoon,* Hurt tells of a 1988 Trump scheme to inflate himself from the status of a borrowed-to-the-hilt, low-millions real estate developer into the ranks of an actual, out-and-out billionaire. Why? All the easier to borrow more money from gullible bankers to keep his deal machine spinning. To that end, Trump had his organization prepare a bogus net worth statement that pegged his worth at $3.7 billion by wildly inflating the value of his assets, and then circulated it to the press. The ploy helped convince *Fortune* to proclaim him an authentic billionaire that autumn, and that publicity in turn helped him secure the financing to buy the Eastern Airlines Shuttle and, thereafter, the Taj Mahal.

A decade later and Trump was up to the same tricks. Having been dropped from *Forbes* magazine's list of America's 400 richest people in 1990, not to reappear again until the turnaround in

Atlantic City and his IPO for Trump Hotels & Casino Resorts in 1996, Trump wasted no time in trying to boost his net worth as calculated by *Forbes*'s editors. "He spent close to an hour with me trying to get our estimates up," says Laurence Minard, the former editor of the "*Forbes* 400" issue. "It was astonishing. He haggled over everything."

Minard's colleague Peter Newcomb, who directs the research for the list, now adds, "We're currently putting his worth at $1.6 billion, but it is very difficult to know. Much of his money seems to be coming from nothing more than real estate he inherited from his father."

The Trump Tower project, now under way on Manhattan's East Side, near the United Nations, is an example of how little he stands to profit from even the largest of his undertakings. Trump has repeatedly described the project—the world's largest residential high-rise—as "my 90-story" building. Actually, he owns only 40 percent of the 70-story project, with a Korean real estate company holding the majority stake. Furthermore, deed records on file at the New York City registrar's office show that the majority partner, Daewoo 845 UN LLC, put up part of $65 million in what amounted to earnest money, after which a German bank, Hypo Vereinsbank, agreed to put up $295 million. Bottom line: If all the units are sold at the asking price specified in the loan document, Daewoo stands to make at least $89 million and Trump will get upwards of $60 million.

Now, $60 million may not sound like much for the "world's largest residential building," but it is hardly chump change, to be sure. Moreover, there is a way for Trump to do far better. He might convince would-be apartment buyers to pay more—a lot more—for the units than the loan committee at Hypo Vereinsbank figured they're worth. In other words, he could talk up their prices with endless references to how valuable they must be because Trump himself is the builder.

And what better way to boost the cachet of the Trump name than to infuse it with the marbled permanence of the Republic itself? Will anyone pay $39 million for an apartment overlooking the factories of Long Island City in Queens, which is what Trump maintains a buyer has agreed to pay for a duplex apartment, as yet unbuilt, atop the Tower? It certainly doesn't hurt for would-be buyers to know that the "owner" of the project may be the next president of the United States. That alone can help justify what amounts to raising the rents, as Trump joked to his pal.

There's another secret to Trump's supersalesmanship: his limited vocabulary. Although Trump has yet to deliver a single stump speech on any topic, his appearances in one-on-one television interviews have already positioned him as a new-millennium "man of the people"—which is to say, an affable fellow whose enthusiasms come out, New York–fashion, as effective grade school grunts. His three favorite adjectives, which he attaches impulsively to almost anyone he has ever met, or any issue, institution, building, or other thing about which he holds an opinion are: "great," "tremendous," and "incredible." Whether it's idiotic to think of such a man representing American interests in the capitals of the world or not, it's undeniably entertaining to listen to him.

To Trump, the Seminole Indians are "great guys, you should meet them." Rudolph Giuliani is "a great mayor." New York governor George Pataki and his wife, Libby, are "two great people." Frank and Kathie Lee Gifford are "two great people" also. Any banker who has ever lent Trump money is "tremendously talented." Marriage is "an incredible institution." So is the New York City Police Department. Mike Tyson is a "great fighter." The Empire State Building is both "great" and "tremendous." So are the Taj Mahal, the Plaza Hotel, and several other buildings. New York Stock Exchange chairman and CEO Richard Grasso is "a great guy"; so is singer Tony Bennett. Trump's ex-wife Ivana is "a great woman." Estée Lauder is "a great lady." Liberace was a "great man." And Ted Turner and Ron Perelman are, like the Seminoles, both "great guys."

On the other hand, when Trump wants to criticize someone, the put-downs that seem to leap most effortlessly from his lips have to do with that person's physical appearance. Reporters who criticize him aren't simply "aggressive" or "obnoxious" or "pushy," but downright "unattractive" physically: *New Yorker* writer Mark Singer, author Harry Hurt III, *Vanity Fair* writer Marie Brenner.

The language says it all. In Trump's world, there are no shades of gray—just huge or not huge, vast or not vast, supermodel-beautiful or ugly and unattractive.

Yet no one seems to care, and why should they, for how is this any different from the movies, or fame, or America itself? To Donald Trump, America is the perfection of material possibilities of utter neatness, utter lavishness, utter cleanliness, utter wealth. He is Madonna stuck in a 1980s time warp, the Material Boy who never grew up.

Such was the baggage I brought with me when I stepped into the Grand Salon (a.k.a. the living room) of the Mar-a-Lago mansion in Palm Beach and waited for Trump to present himself.

The room itself is so vast that inviting someone to sit down and be comfy, as Trump's butler did to me, seems rather like being encouraged to pull up a chair and chill out in the main entrance of the Metropolitan Museum of Art. The soaring, 20-plus-foot ceilings are covered in handworked copper reliefs of angels and cherubs, the walls are paneled in oak and mahogany wainscoting, with intricately worked enamel tiles. There are gold leaf and brass inlays on everything. This isn't a living room; it's like walking inside some kind of colossal Fabergé egg—the Romanoffs brought to life by P. T. Barnum.

Off to one side, behind a grand piano so dwarfed by the scale of everything that it seems almost a toy, is the entrance to the "library." It is a library with no books, just a wet bar against one wall, and, nearby, a framed oil portrait of Merriweather Post. She looks old, pinch-lipped, and mean—not the kind of person to whom a tyke would come running, shouting, "Granny, Granny, can you tell me about the olden days?" And, gazing back opposite her on a far wall is—what else?—a portrait of Trump ("the Trumpster," as Tony the manservant refers to him when Trump is not around). In the painting, the Trumpster is tricked out in a white tennis sweater, with his mop of sandy hair tousled as if he'd just come in from a love game, set, match with Rudy Valle.

Tony approaches and says, "Mr. Trump will be with you in five minutes." He gestures toward a sofa the size of a yacht and says, "He will sit there, at the right end. You can sit on the chair next to him."

Why that particular arrangement? Because the seat on the sofa presents Trump to all who enter the club, as if he were on some kind of overstuffed throne—a throne by which it is impossible to pass without acknowledging the man ensconced upon it. Adding the ornamental touch of a person in a chair to the side (that would be me) simply adds to the effect: The duke of Mammon is holding court.

And then, suddenly, there he is: the Trumpster, or the Donald, or whatever you want to call him, resplendent in a blue Brioni suit and an open-collar white shirt.

"Chris," he says, extending a hand that belies his Howard Hughes–like phobia of shaking hands. "It's been a long time, no? And you haven't changed a bit." (Two sentences into the interview and he's winning already. I haven't changed in 13 years? Okay, Donald, where do I sign?)

We are there to talk about politics, business, and his presidential ambitions, but somehow the topic keeps coming back to money and how well his real estate ventures are doing. There's his 72-story art deco office high-rise (a kind of knocked-down version of the Empire State Building) at 40 Wall Street. Trump bought it for $1 million down a few years back and now says it's fully rented and worth $400 million. (On the other hand, a spokesman for the City of New York's Buildings Department says 40 Wall Street has a market value of $55 million. Trump says the department's numbers are absurd. But why dwell on any of that?)

There's his project over by the U.N. Trump says it's more than 50 percent rented already and will wind up generating a profit of $500 million, implying that it will all be his. (In fact, it seems that 60 percent of whatever remains after all the bills are paid will go to Trump's partners in the project, not to him.) Trump says that if the project performs well enough, he'll get the 60 percent, not his partners. So why dwell on that either?

There's his project on the West Side, a project on Park Avenue . . . there's this project, then that project. Just when it seems as if he's determined to run through them all, as if on cue, who should emerge in the grand living room before us, wrapped in a Turkish towel in drop-dead defiance of the club's dress code, than supermodel Melania—all dewy fresh and wet from the spa. I'm an ordinary sort of guy, to be sure . . . just a working-stiff reporter, and Donald had figured me to a tee. For here was this vision, emerging from nowhere, wrapped in a towel you could have fit into a Taj Mahal tote bag, trying to clasp it to her naked-ness with one hand while shaking my hand with the other, and saying, "I'm so flattered to meet you. Donald has told me so much." And I'm thinking, Oh sure, I'll bet he has—and while we're on the topic, can I just see what's under that towel?

Unfortunately, a moment more and she is gone, gliding out the double-hung doors onto the veranda and the rear lawns, disap-pearing into the enveloping embrace of Palm Beach's morning mist. And there I am, watching her leave, thinking, I want to be that mist. No, actually, I want to be the Turkish towel. No, the hell with all that: I want to be Donald Trump!

Soon, more characters make their appearance. Through the door waltzes Patricia Duff—not in a Turkish towel—on her way to the spa. (I'm thinking, Why don't we just move this interview into the spa?) Donald smiles wanly, and as soon as she's out of earshot he turns to me and says, "That bitch had some nerve, the way she treated Ron Perelman."

By and by, more members enter and acknowledge the great one, but mostly they turn out to be people even Donald doesn't know. There's a little, fat fellow named Jerry who's in the carpet business. He approaches with a funny story about how come Sears couldn't make a go of it in the catalog business and what that foretells for Internet outfits like Amazon.com. Says Jerry, "I'm telling you, people would buy stuff and then send it back. Sears had a billion dollars' worth of shit that got sent back." After he leaves, Donald turns to me and says, "Jerry's a great guy, I'm telling ya, one of the best." But when I ask his last name, the Trumpster goes blank. He says, "I dunno . . ."

That's how it turns out for a lot of Mar-a-Lago's allegedly swanky, gilded, jeweled, and gowned clientele: They're people you've never heard of, faces you've never seen before, names you forget as soon as you hear them. There's somebody named Seymour (or was it Sid?) Cohen, who, Donald wants me to understand, is big in New York real estate (not as big as Donald, mind you, but big enough), "a real mother . . . ," as Donald puts it. The trouble is, being a medium-big mother . . . —real or otherwise—in New York real estate won't get you a sofa spot on Jay Leno's show or anywhere else: Let's hear it for Sid Cohen, the toughest son of a bitch in the Kew Gardens rent-stabilization game? I don't think so.

This, then, is Mar-a-Lago, filled with members like Jerry and Sid (or was it Sy?) who think that a $100,000 membership fee is a quick and painless passport to the Palm Beach glamour they read about in the Shiny Sheet but never get access to in their lives. Amortized over 20 years, it's not even all that expensive to catch a glimpse of Melania flashing her towel act for a reporter, or listen to wax museum "stars" like Michael Bolton and Paul Anka sing on the weekends? Hey, life is short, so what the hell, live a little!

And that, in the end, is Donald Trump himself: Life is short, live a little. No one needs to remind the Trumpster what fate awaits him if interest rates rise and the economy turns south: It could be curtains all over again for the Trump magic act. Even in America, there's more to life than fast talk and extravagant dreams—you need people who are willing to hand over cold cash (or, at least, be able to borrow it from somewhere) in order to buy into your dream of minaret-domed gambling palaces that reach to the sky, of Fabergé eggs with soaring ceilings, of women with legs as smooth and flawless as polished marble . . . none of which is possible when interest on the long bond rises, money grows tight in all the wrong places, and, suddenly, life becomes payback time.

But Donald Trump didn't want to think about that a decade ago, and he doesn't want to think about it now. Why should he? When Mario Cuomo proclaimed Bill Clinton America's Comeback Kid at the 1992 Democratic convention, he didn't know the meaning of the words. In the world of Comeback Kids, you've got Arkansas pols and their bimbos, and then there's Donald Trump, the Comeback Guy of all time, who by the art form of his personal life has managed to turn every failure he has ever endured into spectacular, gilt-edged success. Why should tomorrow be any different? It's morning in America, the dawn of a new millennium, and life is good—especially when it's lived on the cutting edge of airbrushed perfection, where all the women are flawless and beautiful, and all the grandest buildings bear your name . . . and by simply pretending to run for president, you can raise the rents and never have to awaken from your dream at all.

When an injustice is supposedly corrected, it is often put out of sight and mind. This story by Scot Paltrow of *The Wall Street Journal* reports that thousands of blacks who bought insurance policies in the 1940s through 1960s in the South continue to pay higher premiums than whites. It also provides a somber history lesson in race-related pricing. The *Journal* has been in the forefront of reporting stories of economic inequity.

Scot Paltrow

PAST DUE: In Relic of '50s and '60s, Blacks Still Pay More for a Type of Insurance

IN 1964, James D. Crane went to work selling life insurance door-to-door for Independent Life & Accident Insurance Co. On his first day, his district manager in Gadsden, Ala., handed him two books, with two different sets of premiums. Mr. Crane says he recalls his new boss's exact words as the man held up each book in turn: "You write the white people out of this, and the niggers out of this."

The premiums in the second book were about 25 percent higher.

Independent Life's rate book for 1960 backs Mr. Crane's memory. It describes "non-Caucasians" as "substandard risks" and gives tables showing that African-Americans were to be charged a little more than 25 percent above what whites were for the same amount of insurance.

It wasn't an isolated case. Records coming to light show that racial discrimination in the industry was endemic at least into the 1960s, as in the wider society. Then, under pressure from the civil-rights movement and laws it spawned, insurers in the mid-1960s stopped overtly charging separate rates for whites and blacks when writing life-insurance policies.

Now, however, Florida investigators looking into the current practices of five companies have made a startling discovery: In the decades since they dropped their explicit race-based system, some insurers never reduced the higher premiums of African-Americans who had bought policies under the old system.

Instead, hundreds of thousands of blacks who bought policies from the 1940s through the 1960s in the South are still paying higher rates, in some instances more than a third higher, according to documents obtained by the Florida insurance department and lawyers representing blacks in suits filed last year against at least seven insurers.

Moreover, while companies officially stopped using race-based premiums when they sold new policies, former actuaries and agents say in interviews that in some cases the practice continued for a decade or more under another guise.

The life-insurance policies at issue are small ones sold door to door by agents who also come by each week to collect the premium of just 25 cents to a dollar, usually in cash. Burial insurance, this is commonly called, because low-income people often buy it so their families can afford a funeral. Its more formal name is industrial life, a term dating from its origins in England, when the small policies were sold to the "industrial," or working, class. Most companies have stopped selling new weekly-premium policies in favor of similar ones with monthly premiums—still often collected in person.

Although the old policies' premiums are small, the additional amount charged to blacks has added up over the decades to at least tens, and more likely hundreds of millions of dollars, say Florida insurance officials and lawyers for policyholders. And the higher rates have been charged to many people living well below the poverty line.

Most companies that sold the policies have long since been

taken over by larger insurers. Independent Life, for which Mr. Crane worked, was bought about 30 years later by American General Corp. of Houston. American General says it "has never, and will never, condone such reprehensible behavior." The company estimates that 350,000 customers are still paying such rates. It says it is taking immediate steps to cease collecting the excess premiums currently paid by African-Americans, which it estimates at $500,000 a year.

The Florida insurance department believes the figure is much higher. In any event, at stake for companies are not just current premiums but whether the companies might someday have to pay back, with interest, higher premiums that African-American customers have paid since the 1960s. The same question applies to the hundreds of thousands of policies that have become "paid up" in recent years or where the insured has died.

Four other companies, besides American General, that Florida is investigating decline to discuss the issues in any detail, citing the inquiry, but all deny any wrongdoing. They include units of Torchmark Corp., Unitrin Inc., and the Netherlands' Aegon NV and ING Group.

All now face civil suits from policyholders, as do two others: Mutual Savings Life Insurance Co. of Decatur, Ala., and Atlanta Life Insurance Co. The suit against Atlanta Life, a company founded by African-Americans, doesn't accuse it of racial bias in premiums but of targeting "impoverished, unsophisticated, and minority" customers with products giving them little or no economic benefit. Atlanta Life calls the suit "baseless."

The companies don't dispute that race-based rates were once commonly used to sell industrial-life policies. In court filings, the insurers generally argue that they were providing coverage to people who otherwise couldn't get any, and some say dual life-insurance rates were legitimately based on blacks' significantly shorter life expectancies. They also cite statutes of limitations, which, in fact, have already led to the dismissal of one suit, that against Torchmark's Liberty National Insurance unit.

Little red books gathering dust at the College of Insurance library in New York give an idea of how open insurers were about all this. Little Gem Life Chart books, once published annually by National Underwriter Co. in Cincinnati, listed various insurers' rates for industrial life. For some, the tables said standard rates applied to "white risks only." For example, the 1960 Little Gem shows that Gulf Life Insurance Co. of Jacksonville, Fla. (now also part of American General), had separate rates for "White risks" and "Negro risks." For 30-year-old males, the premiums were 36 percent higher for blacks than for whites.

Often, the customer had to keep paying premiums for life, although some policies became paid-up at age 65 or 80. The terms were such that most buyers of industrial-life policies, black and white, would pay more in premiums than the policies ever paid in death benefits, and the difference was of course greater for those paying the higher premiums charged to blacks.

John Bratcher of Bradenton, Fla., bought such a policy from National Standard Insurance Co. in 1957, for a 50-cent weekly premium. It sounds small, but Mr. Bratcher, who is black, was earning only about $40 a week mowing lawns, and "it was hard just making enough to buy something to eat," Mr. Bratcher says. He was about 46 then.

Today Mr. Bratcher is 90. He and his 65-year-old wife, Mattie, live in a tiny, dilapidated house, its bare yard furnished with child-size chairs discarded by the school where Mrs. Bratcher is a cafeteria worker. For a policy that will yield $152 when he dies, Mr. Bratcher has so far paid more than $1,000 in premiums. A third of that was a racial surcharge, estimates Christa L. Collins, his lawyer, who is suing two insurers on his behalf.

Mrs. Bratcher fishes out a six-inch stack of policies. Receipts show she has been paying $311 a month in premiums on more than 50 policies on herself and the Bratchers' descendants. She says the household income is $1,030 a month, on which she and Mr. Bratcher support a developmentally disabled daughter and five grandchildren who live with them.

Why buy so many policies? Mrs. Bratcher says the agents said they would cover the cost of funerals for the Bratchers and their family members. "I see so many people having to borrow money to be put away, and I didn't want my children to have to be saddled with that," Mrs. Bratcher says.

The discovery that blacks were still paying higher rates on old policies grew out of a broader inquiry—focused on current practices—in which Florida insurance officials are investigating complaints that the companies offer inferior coverage to low-income minorities or try to avoid paying claims. No charges have been filed so far. But "what we have discovered is that African-Americans who have these old policies are continuing to pay premiums on a race-differentiated basis," says Florida Insurance Commissioner Bill Nelson.

His department served subpoenas on five companies in October. The policyholder suits, in federal courts in Florida and Alabama and in Florida state court, were filed a couple of months later by law firms led by James, Hoyer, Newcomer & Smiljanich in Tampa, Fla. Among laws they cite is a federal civil-rights law passed after the Civil War, which the Supreme Court has said bars using race as a factor in setting the terms of any contract.

There is no doubt that when the policies were being written, blacks' life expectancies were significantly shorter. For life insurers, a shorter life expectancy means higher risk of loss. In a 1944 book, Metropolitan Life actuary Malvin E. Davis wrote: "The race of the applicant . . . has an important bearing on prospective longevity. Nonwhite races have been found to have much higher mortality than white persons, which should be considered in underwriting."

U.S. government data show that in 1955, the difference in life expectancy between whites and blacks was almost seven years. Today, it is about six years.

But as early as the 1950s, it was becoming clear that the life-expectancy gap had less to do with race than with such factors as lower incomes and poorer medical care. That put the rigid system of race-based rates at odds with a cardinal principle of underwriting, that equal risks should be treated equally. For instance, a rural black who might live in no worse circumstances than a rural white neighbor still had to pay 20 percent or 30 percent higher premiums.

Mr. Crane recalls that, while selling for Independent Life in the mid-1960s, he had to give white customers the better rate regardless of their living conditions. "I had a lot of white people that should have gotten a substandard rate," he says. "They lived much worse than some of your black people." Mr. Crane says he quit in disgust in 1966 over the practices. He now is a part-time Baptist minister who works with prisoners.

Actually, by 1960, all states had adopted an Unfair Trade Practices Act, prohibiting "any unfair discrimination between individuals of the same class and equal expectation of life in the rates charged for" life insurance. References to race were gone from the Little Gem books by 1961. Regulators and actuaries drew up a single industrial-life mortality table that soon became mandatory in nearly all states. In court documents and in response to questions, most companies now being sued or investigated say race-based rates were eliminated in the mid-1960s on new policies.

But some former company officials and agents say in interviews that certain companies secretly continued to do race-based underwriting, in updated form. "I can tell you that race-based underwriting did not disappear in the 1960s," says Andrew C. Stratton, a former manager of actuarial services at Life Insurance Co. of Georgia.

He says in an interview that when he arrived at the Atlanta company in 1972, its rate books had no overt references to race, but in practice, all blacks who bought weekly-premium policies were charged more. He says there were two rate tables for those policies, "W" and "A," and blacks were charged from table A, which had higher premiums.

"The practical effect was different rates for the two races," Mr. Stratton says, adding: "When I left the company in 1981, I'm pretty sure it was still going on."

Life of Georgia (now a unit of ING) says that it has never used race-based rates, so it could hardly have continued the practice in the 1970s, to say nothing of failing to rescind such rates for decades. It also says its rates were approved by each state in which it sold insurance.

While all the insurers deny liability, they are taking divergent tacks.

American General confirms that many of its small life-insurance subsidiaries charged different rates to whites and blacks through sometime in the 1960s, in most cases stopping many years before it acquired them. It says it wasn't aware that people were still paying such rates on old policies until the Florida probe began. Why not? An American General executive who declines to be identified says the policies contribute only about 2 percent of revenue and earnings, and "it's a block of business that we simply have not focused on."

American General, besides ceasing to collect blacks' excess premiums, has held settlement talks with plaintiffs' lawyers and the Florida insurance department. It intends to discuss with the department what if anything to do about reimbursing policyholders for excess premiums paid in the past, or the family members of deceased black policyholders. People close to the Florida insurance department say the talks have been in a fragile state recently.

The other companies being sued and investigated have given no sign they are willing to negotiate or to rescind race-based premiums on decades-old policies. One, United Insurance Co. of America, rejects the charge of discrimination, noting that its own president, Don M. Royster Sr., is an African-American. Mr. Royster says that "we proudly serve the low- and moderate-income members of society who are largely ignored by the rest of the insurance industry."

United, now owned by Chicago-based Unitrin, also says it has consulted with a leading industrial-life actuary, Tommy Bowles, and that he has assured it its practices were sound. The 83-year-old Mr. Bowles, a former insurance-company CEO, sees no problem with the rates. "Who would say rates based on color is wrong?" Mr. Bowles asks. "I don't agree with that." If whites and blacks have different mortality rates, then their premiums ought to be different, he says, adding that the only reason companies stopped charging separate rates on new policies was that mortality differences narrowed.

Mr. Bowles says that he has done extensive consulting for companies that sold industrial life, and that after they ceased charging race-based rates on new policies, as far as he knows none of them ever lowered rates to blacks who had purchased under the old system of dual rates.

Companies also make the point that whatever they did, they did while regulated by state insurance authorities. The general counsel of Florida's insurance department, Dan Sumner, doesn't disagree. He says it is almost certain that Florida insurance commissioners in the 1940s, '50s, and '60s, and their counterparts elsewhere, knew of and at least tacitly approved the race-based rates. Most states don't specifically approve premiums but do review each type of policy.

No other state has joined Florida's investigation. "No one on my staff has made me aware of any concerns about any kind of racial discrimination" in life-insurance premiums, says Georgia Insurance Commissioner John Oxendine, adding that if complaints arose, he would definitely look seriously at them.

One other point companies raise might be called the tenor-of-the-times defense. "Racial discrimination is and was an abhorrent aspect of our collective American heritage," says Liberty National in papers filed in federal court in Alabama. The Torchmark unit— which declared industrial-life policies paid-up in the 1980s to avoid the collection costs—acknowledged in court papers that through about 1965, it charged race-based rates on many policies. But the suit against it, Liberty National argued, unfairly sought to punish the company "not for its current practices, but for the alleged 'sins of the fathers.'"

Whether this moved the court is unclear. As he dismissed the suit on statute-of-limitations grounds, Judge H. Dean Buttram Jr. wrote that "to the extent that the plaintiffs' allegations reveal a moral lapse by Liberty National, that company has a moral obligation to remedy the damage done." But he said he could enforce only legal obligations, not moral ones.

Many new companies seem to rely more on salesmanship than anything else. This story by *Business Week's* John Byrne tells of a new
retailing paradigm at dot-com start-up Value America that sounded
too good to be true, and couldn't be executed. It meticulously lists
the outrageous expenditures and CEO aggrandizement that, left
unchecked, proved capable of hurtling a firm into bankruptcy.

John Byrne

THE FALL OF A DOT-COM

ON A BALMY DAY last April, Craig A. Winn, a onetime
housewares salesman, momentarily became a dot-com billionaire.
As the stock in his e-tailing startup, Value America Inc., ascended
from its initial public offering price of $23 a share to a giddy high
of $74.25 on April 8, 1999, it became clear that the charismatic
entrepreneur had tapped into the mind-set of the New Economy.
Investors flocked to his idea of a "Wal-Mart of the Internet" where
shoppers could order jars of caviar along with their gas barbecues
or desktop computers. And why not? Winn had already signed up
some big-time investors, including Microsoft co-founder Paul
Allen, financier Sam Belzberg, and FedEx Chairman Fred Smith,
whose names added cachet to the venture.

When the stock settled down that day at $55 a share, the
three-year-old, profitless company was valued at $2.4 billion. Yet
the 45-year-old Winn maintains that he was overcome with
melancholy as he watched shares trade that first day. "I felt fear

and anguish," he said recently. "I believe the company was genuinely worth the IPO value. When the stock shot up to three times the IPO price, I recognized that this was not reasonable. You are never closer to your greatest failure than when you are at the moment of your greatest success. I was very humbled by it."

Winn's unease was prescient. In the 12 months since the IPO, Value America has gone from euphoria-inducing heights to a struggle for survival. In late March, auditors expressed doubt that the company could survive as a going concern. Nearly half of Value America's 600 employees have been fired. With the stock now trading at $2 a share, investors have lost millions. The obligatory shareholder class action has been filed. And Winn, founding CEO and entrepreneur extraordinaire, has been ousted by an all-star board that includes Fred Smith, former Newell Rubbermaid CEO Wolfgang Schmitt, and celebrated headhunter Gerard R. Roche. "A year ago," bemoans one insider, "we were infallible. Now, it's a complete crash and burn."

The company says it is in "advanced discussions" with potential investors and expects to gain sorely needed cash within a few months. "Rumors of its demise might be a little premature," says William D. Savoy, a Value America director who manages Paul Allen's personal finances. "It's not over yet."

Value America's rise and fall is emblematic of an era of unbridled optimism and outright greed. Possibly only during a period of unprecedented valuations and a seeming suspension of the rules of finance could someone of Winn's background amass the following and the finances to get a company off the ground as quickly as Value America took flight. For most of his stint at the company, Winn, who collected a salary of $295,000 a year, had little of his own money at risk. His business experience consisted mainly of leading another public company into bankruptcy. His technology experience: nil. Winn and his company practiced New Economy values with a vengeance. A massive ad budget was spent well in advance of any profits. Yawning losses were excused as a necessary evil in the pursuit of market share. There was a rush to take an untried company public at the height of the investor frenzy for new dot-com stocks.

But the Value America saga goes beyond the excesses of the Internet era. Serious questions are also being raised about alleged gross mismanagement, abuse of corporate funds, and the sometimes erratic and bizarre behavior of Winn, who asked that the money-losing company finance his personal jet and who dreamed out loud of running for President. "There have been a fair amount of decisions and expenditure of funds that were questionable," says director Schmitt. (Winn counters that the plane was needed because of the company's location in Charlottesville and that the board approved of it.) "Everyone figured he was more a genius than crazy," says a former senior executive at Value America. "As time went on, everybody got more concerned."

One thing Craig Winn, a salesman at heart, could do is spin a good tale. His story of a "frictionless" business model was perfectly attuned to the times. Winn's cyberstore was supposed to harness every efficiency promised by the Web to create a new paradigm in retailing. His breakthrough idea? The store would carry no inventory and ship no products. Instead, it would pick up orders from consumers and immediately transmit them to manufacturers who would ship IBM computers and Knorr soups, Panasonic televisions and Vicks Vapo Rub, direct to customers. It featured more than 1,000 brand names, many in multimedia presentations online.

The story was mesmerizing, the execution somewhat less so. Insiders say Winn tried to do too much, too soon. Computers crashed. Customers waited and waited to get orders filled. Discounting and advertising drained cash and wiped out any chance of profitability. Returned merchandise piled up in the halls of the company's offices. "They got going too fast," says Smith. "They got unfocused." Winn disagrees. "In the Internet world, no one is willing to invest in a company that grows slowly," he argues. "Go find an Internet company that said it was going to be methodical."

In retrospect, the story's most surprising aspect is how long the public—and the board members—continued to believe in Winn.

For the boyish-looking entrepreneur, with his sandy hair and perpetual smile, the world of the Net seemed a natural fit. He was always a man, say friends and colleagues, who looked to the future, and he certainly had a way with words. Associates say that Winn would drive to work with the radio off, practicing the slogans that would give his sales pitches a New Economy resonance, even if the precise meaning was unclear. He grandly called his e-tailing venture "the marketplace of the millennium." He described his concept as "alliances of consumption with alliances of production." Above all, he intoned, Value America permitted "friction-free capitalism." A colleague said Winn called his practiced pitches "the Art of Emphasis."

Winn quickly embraced the worst excesses of the New Economy, particularly the notion of building a business empire where sales—not profits—came first. He spent money lavishly, running through the company's cash as if it were unlimited. In an era when not-yet-profitable dot-coms burned through giant ad budgets, Value America spent even more, second only to E*Trade Group in the size of its marketing budget in the first nine months of 1999. For the year, its ad spending hit $69.6 million. Taking a page from the Lee Iacocca playbook, Winn filmed a series of commercials last June starring himself—at a time when Value America could hardly afford the cost of TV airtime. Winn says the idea to do the spots came from outside public-relations experts.

Other expenditures were even harder to understand. Winn agreed to purchase a 34.4-acre expanse of land for $5 million where he planned to build a multimillion dollar headquarters. The property was later appraised at less than $2 million. It cost the company $400,000 to get out of the contract. Winn disputes that valuation and says the building was needed. After a newly recruited CEO discouraged Winn's purchase of a corporate plane, Winn and co-founder Rex Scatena spent $650,000 for a downpayment on a Hawker 800 anyway. With board approval, they began expensing their trips to the company and put two pilots on the payroll at a cost of $250,000 a year. In 1999 alone, the cost of the plane to Value America was $800,000. Winn now claims the company still owes him and Scatena the $650,000 downpayment, which he says the board agreed to cover. Scatena could not be reached for comment.

Meanwhile, as investors anted up more cash to keep Value America going, Winn began taking money out. During one investment round, in the summer of 1998, when Microsoft founder Paul Allen put in $15 million, Winn sold some of his own holdings, pocketing some $5.7 million. Allen, who declined comment, knew of the sales at the time. "There were extenuating circumstances," says Savoy, declining to go into further detail.

The splashy expenditures hid some fundamental problems with Winn's business model. In signing up as many vendors as possible, there was little regard to whether their products were suited for sale via the Web. Many manufacturers simply weren't capable of shipping a single box of Tide or a bottle of Advil. They had no experience in dealing directly with consumers. Glenda M. Dorchak, a 24-year veteran of IBM who is now CEO of Value America, says she tried ordering a pair of toothbrushes. It took weeks for the package to arrive, and when it did, it was one toothbrush short. Indeed, Winn's basic premise of eliminating the middleman never happened. Most orders were handled by the ultimate middlemen: old-fashioned distributors.

Still, at the height of the company's success last April, Winn seemed neither humbled nor melancholy. He started voicing political ambitions, even a desire to become President of the U.S. Winn told colleagues he planned to withdraw from the company in order to run for lieutenant governor of Virginia. That, he said, would give him a platform for a Presidential bid in 2008. Winn dismisses those stories and says he had given up his Presidential aspirations "a long time ago." He also began cultivating relationships with politically connected conservatives, including former

Education Secretary William S. Bennett, who joined his board last summer, and Reverend Jerry Falwell, who was invited to buy shares in the Value America IPO under the friends-of-the-company provision. While other dot-coms might have a "chief evangelist," Winn had a "chief of staff," Mick Kicklighter, a retired three-star general who traveled everywhere with his boss, taking notes.

Although Value America is just months from running out of cash, Winn is set for life. He lives just three minutes from the company's Charlottesville headquarters on a 150-acre estate, where he has built a Greek Revival mansion modeled on George Washington's Mount Vernon. Both Winn and Scatena, who served as outside counsel to Winn's earlier bankrupt venture, have been feverishly dumping their stock since being forced out of the company in November. Winn has personally realized cash gains of about $53.7 million and still has an additional $15.5 million worth of stock. Winn's backers have not fared so well. Allen has lost roughly $50 million, according to public filings. The personal and company losses of FedEx founder Smith approach $8 million.

So where were the directors during this debacle? Many of them were still being recruited in the months following last April's IPO. Savoy and Smith came on soon after the offering, but Schmitt, Roche, and Bennett joined during the summer. When an executive-suite coup erupted in November, they had barely settled into their roles. Directors contacted by *Business Week* say they acted appropriately and still express confidence in the company.

Winn shows little regret about the fate of Value America or of the well-heeled backers who believed in him. He cheerfully meets with a reporter in his "carriage house" to recount his role in this New Economy cautionary tale. Seated in a brown leather club chair before a massive stone fireplace and a crackling early-morning fire, with his yellow lab, Crystal, at his side, he looks the picture of country aristocracy.

Life wasn't always so comfortable. Winn says that in his first year as a manufacturer's rep, in 1978, after graduating from the University of Southern California, he was painfully shy and worked 90-hour weeks to earn just $12,000 for the year. He had joined his gregarious father in a housewares venture. The younger Winn was raised on the business, which his father ran from a home office next to the kitchen, in Sierra Madre, Calif. From the age of five, Winn says, he knew he wanted to sell. He proved a quick study. Within a few years, he had bought out his father and was pulling down a six-figure salary. His success brought him a house perched on the edge of the Pacific Ocean, a sailboat, and a big bank account.

It also brought him greater ambition. In 1986, Winn founded Dynasty Classics Corp., a maker of lighting products. Four years later, with annual sales of nearly $100 million, he brought the company public. Within eight months, however, after revealing a fourth-quarter loss, the stock fell from a high of $18.50, to under $4. In October 1993, Dynasty filed for Chapter 11 bankruptcy. Russell Schreck, a turnaround consultant who became president of Dynasty after the filing, blamed the problems on "a lack of structure and discipline. You had an entrepreneur who grew the company very quickly, but he hit a brick wall. There was a lack of accounting."

Winn has a different view. He says the company was forced to file for bankruptcy only after Wal-Mart Stores Inc. reneged on a deal to help fund the production of $25 million worth of lamps and other products. Wal-Mart says it doesn't comment on vendor relations. "I was not without blame," recalls Winn, who grows misty-eyed as he tells the story. "I was at the helm of the company and there were any one of a hundred things that I could have done better." Remarkably, though, given Dynasty's fate, Winn feels he was underappreciated. "When things go south, there is an element in society today that is very vile. You get to see the underbelly of people." Winn says he met the payroll out of his own pocket for a time, but never received any thanks.

Over the next couple of years, as interest in the Internet began to heat up, Winn dreamed of the ultimate sales company, one that would advertise, market, and take orders but never handle the merchandise. Eventually, he cranked out a 250-page business plan for Value America, and on July 4, 1996, he and a few friends and partners moved their families to Charlottesville to launch it.

Winn and Scatena anted up about $150,000 each in the startup and began to furiously hire the talent necessary to make a go of it. A big break occurred in December 1997, when Winn persuaded the Union Labor Life Insurance Co. in Washington, to invest $10 million in Value America. Winn quickly paid himself $150,000 from the proceeds, saying that his initial cash outlay had been a loan. Six months later, an even bigger break occurred. Through the insurer's contacts, Winn gained a meeting with Paul Allen and William Savoy in Seattle and persuaded Allen to put $15 million into the company, giving Winn's fledgling business a $300 million valuation—and instant credibility.

The IPO of last April took place well before Value America had begun to prove its mettle. But Winn had tried to take it public even earlier. In September 1998, only three months after Allen's investment, Winn tried to cash in on the connection with a $75 million offering. But the IPO market had temporarily dried up. When his bankers told him he'd have to accept a lower price for the stock, Winn cancelled the offering.

It was a crushing blow, but Winn says he gained encouragement from Intel Corp. founder Andrew S. Grove, whom he had met through a mutual friend. At a dinner shortly after the failure, Winn says that he told Grove of his troubles. "He put his arm around me and said 'I believe in you. You're going to do well, and you're going to live to see far brighter days.'" Grove says he was supportive but doesn't recall the details of the dinner.

Few outside the company knew how badly things were going. Value America was struggling to meet its growing payroll. It began delaying its payments to manufacturers. "We played vendor bingo," says one former executive. "Whenever they complained, we paid."

Dorchak confirms that, strapped for cash, the company was forced to delay payments. Winn and Scatena loaned the company $550,000 in late September 1998. Then Winn led what insiders termed a "pass the hat" round that raised $7 million more. Winn didn't invest more money himself because, he says, SEC rules prevented him from doing so. Winn says that what he did was far more selfless. "We got no stock or anything for our loan," he says. "That was genuine charity there." Both he and Scatena took repayment of their loans before the end of the year.

Despite the scare, Winn and Value America won lots of publicity, partly a payoff from the millions spent on ads in *The New York Times* and other newspapers. In February 1999, *CEO* magazine dubbed him "the prince of e-commerce," just months after his company nearly went belly-up. "Princes rise and fall," says J. P. Donlon, editor in chief. "If this was bullshit, I thought, it was platinum." The buzz attracted more money and big names.

Fred Smith was one. Smith had often expressed skepticism about e-commerce, but he believed that Winn had the ideal business model. "I thought this was one of the best things I've seen," recalls Smith. In January 1999, Smith committed $5 million of his own money and $5 million of FedEx's money to the venture. Allen, meantime, put in $50 million more.

As the new money and the support of other big backers, like Gary Winnick of Global Crossing Ltd. and financier Sam Belzberg, rolled in, Value America began to operate less like a business and more like a cult. "When you're around him, you get caught in the swirl," says one former manager. "It's like drinking Kool-Aid." Winn would gather his employees and speak for a full hour at a time, promising that everyone standing before him would someday be a millionaire. At one session, recalls employees, he stood on top of railroad ties on a chilly May morning in the parking lot and spoke for an hour about his life and career. "As he talked, the sun rose higher in the sky and the air became warm and comfortable," remembers Tom Matthew, who wrote product descriptions for the company's Web site. "I wondered if Craig had planned it that way."

It was an exciting place to work, even if the hours were horrendous and the inconveniences many. "People were stacked on people," recalled Melissa M. Monk, vice-president for sales. "It looked like an anthill." Sales soared from $134,000 in 1997 to $42.3 million in 1998. But the losses rose just as fast. After losing $425,000 in its startup year of 1996, the company lost $2 million in 1997, $64.8 million in 1998. Few investors worried about the red ink: Net companies were supposed to lose money to gain scale and clout in a frenzied marketplace.

Winn decided he needed help in managing the torrid growth. Before going public on April 8 last year, he recruited the head of U.S. Office Products Co., Thomas Morgan, to become chief executive. Morgan, 46, a mild-mannered man, had met Winn on a golf course and was hoping to sell him his line of office products. Instead, Winn persuaded him to leave his job as CEO of a $4 billion company and take a flyer with a Net startup. Winn remained chairman, but Morgan was supposed to be the professional manager who would run Value America's day-to-day operations.

The IPO was a huge success, creating dozens of paper multimillionaires, including Morgan. "It was phenomenal," he remembers. "It was a high for everyone in the organization." That evening, Winn celebrated by arriving in a limo with his wife, Katherine, for a celebratory dinner at the local country club.

The celebration proved short-lived. Winn, say insiders, had trouble giving up control to his new CEO. Although Winn denies it, several present and former executives say he frequently undermined Morgan and continued to micromanage nearly everything. "There was never a major decision he was not involved with," says Morgan. "Craig would just do what he wanted to do and informed me after the fact." Winn disputes this, maintaining that he largely focused on developing outside alliances. Winn promised to give more authority to Morgan over the next three months, but the shift never materialized.

Meantime, in its zeal to meet the unrealistic expectations of

Wall Street, the company was making ever more desperate and wasteful marketing deals. The company paid Yahoo! Inc. $4.5 million for a year's worth of Web site ads that several insiders say brought in less than $100,000 of revenue. The company spent $1 million for a booth at Comdex, the computer show, hoping to sign up 100,000 potential Value America customers. Instead, the event brought in only 16,000. Winn argues that most of the decisions were made by Morgan and Dorchak, who as president was responsible for marketing and sales. He said he was against another deal to pay $750,000 to sponsor Dennis Conner's America's Cup yacht. "We kept spending money like it was going out of style," says one former top executive.

Investments in more fundamental areas were more scarce. "The Web site was perpetually slow, outdated, and uncommonly difficult to navigate," recalls ex-employee Matthew. Instead of fixing the problem, Matthew said, the company focused on meeting its financial numbers. "We needed to do X amount of business this quarter and add X number of products to the site so the stock price would stay high and we would all be millionaires. Who cared that the store ran like molasses or that order tracking was virtually unmanageable." Through the end of last year, Value America still got over half its revenues from customers dialing in by phone. Winn maintains that the computer systems worked well and that appropriate investments were made in them. Adds CEO Dorchak: "It's like icing a cake that hasn't been baked. We had someone here who was just icing an unbaked cake."

To drive revenue and keep the stock inflated, the company introduced ValueDollars, which consumers could use for 50 percent off the cost of purchases. The discounts virtually assured that the company would lose money on every sale it made. By last summer, Value America was handing out 1,000 ValueDollars with the purchase of a $1,000 color TV. "It was uncontrollable," says Nick Hoffer, senior vice-president for marketing. "It was crazy."

Inside the company, chaos was rampant. Winn, insiders say, ran the place on daily whims. He spent $1.8 million on a Christmas catalog that didn't get into the mail until late November. "That was one of the projects of the day," says Hoffer. Winn says the delay resulted because the marketing department failed to follow his May directive to work on the catalog, which he says, was largely paid for by the brands. Toward the Christmas holiday season, the company advertised a Sega Genesis game at $199. At that price, with ValueDollars added, every sale was below cost. Even more troublesome, Value America secured only 1,200 units. Orders the first day reached 1,500 units and eventually topped out at 6,000. To meet demand, the company sent employees to Toys 'R' Us and other stores to buy the product off the shelf. "We fulfilled every order, at a huge cost," recalls Dorchak.

Although Winn spoke grandly of his inventoryless model, in the third quarter of 1999 alone Value America recorded an inventory writedown of $350,000. How was that possible? To secure the supply of some goods, Winn had to agree to purchase such products as Compaq and Toshiba computers that later were sold below cost, resulting in a writedown. Meanwhile, many orders, insiders say, were transmitted to vendors by fax or e-mail, a far cry from the instantaneous computer-to-computer model Value America had promised.

Meanwhile, Morgan was growing ever more frustrated waiting for Winn to resign as promised. Winn still occupied his corner office, triple the size of Morgan's. On November 1, Morgan walked into Winn's office and resigned, but the entrepreneur persuaded him to stay by promising to come up with a plan to leave. Just 10 days later, after a four-hour meeting in which Morgan aired a list of grievances, the founder finally agreed to give up the chairman's job immediately. At least that's how Morgan remembers it. Winn says he only agreed to think about the issues. That Sunday, November 14, Winn asked a colleague at Value America to go to his log cabin on his estate and get a two-page, handwritten document he had drafted. The memo, left on a table in the cabin, stated that Winn was stepping back into the CEO's job.

When Morgan saw the document that night, he was dumb-founded. He confronted Winn the next morning, then contacted a director before taking a holiday to give the board time to act. Finally, Smith, Roche, and other directors began interviewing senior managers in the company. On November 23, the Tuesday before Thanksgiving, the board voted to fire Winn. Schmitt was named chairman, while Dorchak, 45, was named CEO when Morgan quit for good.

Dorchak now finds herself trying to pick up the pieces. The promotions helped to increase revenues last year fourfold, to $182.6 million. But losses of $175.5 million nearly equaled its sales and have led to a liquidity crisis. The market capitalization of the company is now less than $100 million—below its valuation during the first round of venture financing, in 1997. Meanwhile a shareholder lawsuit alleging that the company made misrepresentations to inflate the stock is pending in U.S. District Court. The company says the claims are without merit.

Since taking over in November, Dorchak has restructured to focus on electronics, technology, and home-office supplies and has laid off nearly half of the payroll. But Dorchak has her own critics who point out that the day after announcing the layoffs, she chartered a private plane at a cost to Value America of $25,000 to spent New Year's in Arizona. She says she did so after working 26 hours straight and missing the last flight out of Charlottesville.

Dorchak's hopes for survival hinge on her ability to sell investors a new game plan. She plans to market Value America's technology to other companies eager to sell products over the Net. "The business model the company has today is the model it should have had all along," says director Savoy. "Attempting to deal directly with consumers probably wasn't the smartest idea on their part."

At a time when lots of Net bubbles are bursting, the humbling of Value America is a fitting postscript to an age fast fading. While such failures may be a price the market must pay to break new ground, the lesson here is simpler: In a period of near mania, almost anyone can find buyers for a house of cards if he has a good enough pitch.

Sitting in his very sturdy mansion, which he calls Windom Hall, with majestic views of the Blue Ridge Mountains, Winn wants his millions and the last word. "Not only is the company nearly bankrupt," he says, "its current management is morally bankrupt. They have chosen to recreate history."

Some history.

The magnitude of the demonstrations in Seattle against the World Trade Organization caught an entire world by surprise. But what if it occurred in your own back yard? This story by *The Seattle Times*'s David Postman, Lynda V. Mapes, Alex Fryer, and Sally MacDonald notes that many early warning signs were completely overlooked. It also studies the dynamics of the long, hard organizing work by a coalition of groups that was to catapult trade issues from the boardroom to the streets.

David Postman, Lynda V. Mapes, Alex Fryer, and Sally MacDonald

WHY WTO UNITED SO MANY FOES

THERE WERE PLENTY OF WARNINGS that World Trade Organization demonstrations could bring trouble to Seattle. The "Battle in Seattle" T-shirts on sale a week before the meeting, for example, were certainly a clue.

But maybe city officials could be excused for underestimating the size and power of the crowds.

After all, who could have predicted that a five-year-old organization that deals with trade, tariffs, and countervailing duties and has a 22,500-page list of rules for selling of goods and services could fill Seattle's streets with protesters?

And how, in a time of unprecedented economic growth, could so many people be so angry about an organization designed to foster even more prosperity?

The answers have to do with both politics and cultural change.

The biggest demonstrations were the result of nearly a year's work by a coalition headed by a Ralph Nader group, major industrial unions, and environmental organizations. They succeeded in turning the seemingly bloodless issue of free trade into a major organizing and fund-raising tool for a variety of liberal groups.

"Trade was always the province of the corporate elite—it was shiny-pants trade lawyers and government diplomats—and we changed that," said Gary Hubbard, public-relations director for the United Steelworkers of America union. Labor showed that in Seattle, with massive, peaceful marches and rallies of tens of thousands of union members.

The vast reach of the WTO made it an easy target. Protesters could pick their causes, from protecting clean air, sea turtles, and dolphins to halting job exports and pest imports, from curbing child labor to eliminating beef hormones and genetically modified food.

It might be hard to imagine a protester with a sign reading "The International Monetary Fund kills butterflies" or 200 people dressed as sea turtles marching against the World Bank. But environmentalists turned out by the thousands against the WTO last week.

"The greenies have tried to organize campaigns around the World Bank for 15 or 20 years now and have never ignited 1 percent of the people that are organized around the WTO," said Dan Seligman, director of the Sierra Club's Responsible Trade Program.

The fast pace of commercial and technological change, which has made it possible to move capital around the world with a mouse click and driven a superheated economy hailed by President Clinton and other free-trade advocates, also leaves people feeling insecure even amid plenty, according to many analysts.

"This ought to be, objectively, the best time for Americans in history," said Haynes Johnson, a Pulitzer Prize–winning journalist who has written several books about U.S. culture and politics.

"There's no war, no visible crisis, no Great Depression. People aren't jumping out of windows. There's no Hitler, no Stalin—there's not even communism anymore. Kids aren't under their desks, practicing how to hide from the bomb. And there's this showering of wealth."

But, Johnson said, not everyone is sharing in the bounty, and many are uneasy about a general loss of trust in institutions.

"There's a profound uncertainty about the pace of change and the uncertainty of where the wonders of the global world are taking us. There is, beyond the roaring good times, an uneasiness about the pace of life. . . . It's a cutthroat world," Johnson said.

Despite worries that vandalism and clashes with police may have obscured their message, WTO opponents left Seattle with some successes. They put the controversies of free trade in the public eye, and when the meeting adjourned Friday without an agenda for the next round of trade talks, some delegates credited or blamed the mass opposition they could see from their hotels.

These protests, unlike those in the 1960s, seemed targeted more at multinational corporations than at governments.

Vandals smashed the windows of Starbucks, McDonald's, NikeTown, and Old Navy. During a demonstration in front of The Gap, a protester burned a pair of khakis to protest the company's labor record.

But on Thursday, after some demonstrators hauled down a U.S. flag at the King County Jail, others intervened, and in the end the flag was hoisted back up the pole.

Passionate demonstrations are nothing new for the WTO. When the group met on its home turf in Geneva last year, there were thousands of demonstrators and dozens of arrests, and restaurant and store windows were smashed.

In June, there were also protests, including violent ones in London, to protest globalization.

But last week's demonstrations in Seattle were, by all accounts, the largest anti-free-trade rallies ever in America. And the cause was not spontaneous combustion.

The organizing that eventually brought tens of thousands of protesters to Seattle began with congressional approval of the North American Free Trade Agreement in 1993. Unions fought fiercely against NAFTA, and its passage drove a wedge between labor and its friends in the Democratic Party.

It also brought unions into an alliance with environmental groups.

"NAFTA became a major political fight, not a trade fight," said William Daley, secretary of commerce. "Nobody read it, no one knew what the hell it meant."

After NAFTA, Ralph Nader's Global Trade Watch began putting together the Citizens Trade Campaign, a coalition of labor, environmentalists, consumer groups, and churches. It was an effort led by veteran Naderite Lori Wallach and her sharp-tongued deputy and longtime political organizer, Mike Dolan.

"I used to hate the Nader people. I despised them," said Chuck Harple, political director of the Teamsters union. "Now I revere Lori Wallach."

Relations with the environmental movement also changed.

"It's weird," Harple said. "We fight so much with the environmentalists, but we also realized that we are both fighting against the (Clinton) administration—the bigger evil."

Harple said that since James Hoffa became Teamsters president, "We kept on saying to Jim, 'Keep an eye on this.' Jim Hoffa gets trade. It's a passion for him."

Hubbard, of the United Steelworkers, said Dolan and Wallach encouraged the unions to get involved in the fight that eventually spelled defeat for the Multilateral Agreement on Investments, a controversial WTO proposal that was intended to open global financial markets.

Environmentalists were among the first critics of the push for global free trade. The Sierra Club's Seligman, Seattle attorney Patti Goldman, and others have been working on the issue for most of the decade.

And when the WTO announced earlier this year that it would meet in Seattle, Nader organizer Dolan began booking hotel rooms and scouting locations for protests yet to be organized. He arrived in Seattle months before the meeting.

"I was afraid we wouldn't have time to educate people quick enough to mobilize a massive demonstration," he said. "This has been the best single opportunity to build this effort in the U.S. since I've been involved with trade."

The conservative critique of the WTO, delivered most prominently by Reform Party presidential candidate Pat Buchanan, claims the trade body is a step toward one-world government.

By contrast, WTO critics on the left, while talking about the loss of U.S. sovereignty and jobs, want to see global enforcement of their agenda of tougher labor and environmental standards.

Environmental groups put much of their focus on the WTO's closed deliberations, condemning the "faceless bureaucrats in Geneva" who rule over global trade disputes in secret.

Gary Chamberlain, an ethicist at Seattle University, thinks that message from the street protests resonated with Americans who believe in access to government power.

"Until they open the doors at the WTO, what do people have but the streets?" Chamberlain asked. "People sense there aren't any rules to this global economy and that what rules there are are being made by corporations. The WTO is setting the rules, but in whose favor?"

Before the WTO meeting, its supporters knew that free trade was becoming an increasingly hard sell. Commerce Secretary Daley traveled the country on an educational tour trying to sell the WTO and Clinton's open-market agenda. He was dogged by protesters at every stop.

Al From, president of the centrist Democratic Leadership Council and a strong free-trade advocate, said free trade is a target because its benefits are diffused but the negatives are concentrated.

"When people celebrate a factory opening, they don't tie that to trade, but when a factory closes, everyone focuses on the jobs that might be going elsewhere," From said. "The micropolitics of anecdotes tends to overwhelm the macropolitics of opportunity and progress."

L. Craig Johnstone, a senior vice president of the U.S. Chamber of Commerce, added, "I think there is a latent suspicion born of America's traditional xenophobia and propensity toward isolationism."

But, he said, "it may also be born in the uncertainty associated with the technological changes we are going through in the business world and the fact that people's jobs are a little less sure than they were before, and they tend to tag that onto trade."

Anti-free-trade activists think Seattle has energized the movement and will help keep the coalition alive.

"For the first time, you had a major negotiation held in an American city that was confronted with an angry, mobilized, broad coalition," said Seligman of the Sierra Club.

Environmentalists will continue to push for an official voice in trade talks, within both the administration and WTO. Labor wants to stop Congress from lifting trade restrictions on China and doesn't want to see that country enter the WTO.

But it's difficult to measure the staying power of the discontent displayed in Seattle, said Andrew Kohut of the Pew Research Center for People and the Press.

Surveys by the center in Washington, D.C., found enthusiasm for globalization of the economy highest among those making $75,000 a year or more. But Kohut said even those at the lower rungs of the economy are hopeful their situation will improve. He sees broad opposition to the WTO catching fire only if people begin to lose hope.

"The issue is whether this event and all the coverage it's had will engender some shift in opinion and rile up people who are anxious," Kohut said. "My guess is probably not."

Nader's Dolan, though, is giddy with the prospect of resuming his drive to build the coalition and thinks it will be easier to raise money.

"After our success here, I'm going to the bank on this," Dolan said. "I'm going to several banks."

The New Economy has infected virtually every aspect of today's business. Michael Lewis, writing in *Business 2.0*, ponders the new ideas about new wealth and why "making it big" no longer carries a stigma as it has throughout history. The possibility that something could be a bubble, he contends, doesn't mean that it doesn't have an impact. He offers an explanation as to why our old compass doesn't help us find direction as it once did.

Michael Lewis

BOOM OR BUST?

THE QUESTION HAS BECOME so irritatingly familiar: If the United States stock market boom is a "bubble," when will it burst? But it still stumps those who should have some answers. Alan Greenspan himself can't seem to make up his mind on the subject. Two years ago, the chairman of the United States Federal Reserve was telling investors that the Net Boom was triggering "irrational exuberance"; 3,000 points on the Dow later, he's saying that the stock market is fairly valued, that there is no need to raise interest rates because high technology is "transforming the American economy."

A big problem with the debate is the distinction between "bubble" and "real." A bubble, if it lasts long enough, has real effects. The Internet Boom began with Netscape Communications' public offering in August 1995, and so has already lasted longer than the U.S. involvement in World War II. Spend four and a half years hurling tens of billions of dollars at thousands of entrepreneurs intent on wreaking havoc with the economic and social order and you will leave a permanent mark, even if many of those billions wind up being wasted on fruitless ventures. Experiences shape societies, just as they do people.

Consider the generation of Americans born after 1968, once known as Generation X. In the early 1990s, Generation X, with its vague antimarket sentiment which mistook sloth for moral superiority, was shaping up as one of the most annoying groups of young people in history. Movies (*Reality Bites, Slacker*) celebrated their relentless alienation, and unless you happened to be one of them, it was difficult to sympathize.

Then came the Internet Boom, which offered even alienated young people the chance to get really rich, really fast. In a flash, the noisiest and most ambitious members of Generation X—who just minutes before were whining about the Baby-Boomer obsession with money and status—were scrambling to make millions. In a short few years an entire generation of young, restless Americans became ideologically indistinguishable from their elders. Having given themselves over so completely to the coarser capitalistic lusts, they cannot go back. You can only sell your soul once.

There are many changes that have been ushered into American life by the Internet boom. Some of them are dramatic shifts in the structure of the economy; others are more subtle shifts in people's basic attitudes. Many of these changes will endure—even if the boom is a bubble, and even if the bubble bursts tomorrow. Herewith, a few examples:

BIRTH OF THE NEW ENTREPRENEUR

In an article in the November/December 1999 issue of *Harvard Business Review,* Professor William Sahlman pointed out a curious new pattern of behavior in his students. In years past Harvard Business School graduates tended to seek careers on Wall Street and in management consulting. Now, for the first time anyone can remember, they want more than anything else either to be entrepreneurs, or to work closely with entrepreneurs. Nearly 40 percent of the Harvard Business School Class of 1999 went to work either at startups or venture capital firms.

You might think the Harvard Business School an unlikely place to find entrepreneurs. After all, entrepreneurs tend to stand apart from the crowd, always searching to find a new way to look at the economy. Much of the benefit of attending the Harvard Business School is the membership it grants you to the crowd, and its shared vision of the economy. When the Harvard MBA loses his job, he still has (a) a glittering credential that demonstrates basic aptitude for any old corporate job; (b) a proven willingness to subordinate himself to collective enterprise; and (c) a network of former classmates to help him out. Why bother defraying the risk in economic life by attending the Harvard B-School if upon graduation you intend to take a flying leap into the unknown? Indeed, why bother going to business school at all if you intend to start a business?

One obvious reason for the new ambition of Harvard B-School graduates is that the New Economy has taken the risk out of risk. The Internet Boom has spawned so many wildly successful new companies that "entrepreneur" is no longer a euphemism for "trying something small and insignificant that will probably fail because he couldn't get a job with Goldman or McKinsey." At the Harvard B-School reunion of 2004, when a member of the Class of 1999 tells a fellow classmate that he is an entrepreneur, he won't find the classmate looking over his shoulder for someone more important, as the entrepreneur may well be the most important person in the room.

The downside of entrepreneurship has improved along with the upside—and this change is probably permanent. The boom has educated a lot of people on the meaning of the word. As a result, entrepreneurial failure is not as great a setback as it once was. The belief that an honest entrepreneurial failure only better equips you for future entrepreneurial success has spread from Silicon Valley to the greater economy. Entrepreneurs are now allowed mulligans. And since founding a dud of a small company looks better on your resume than being a cog in some big, profitable concern, why not go for it?

But there is something else going on here: The entrepreneur now enjoys a new, higher status in American life. This is not merely a result of a rising stock market. It follows directly from structural changes in high finance, as well as a big new idea about the economy, both of which were bubbling along for some time before the Internet Boom brought them to a head.

THE DEMOCRATIZATION OF CAPITAL

The signature trait of the Net boom has been its from-the-ground-up quality. Little guys no one had ever heard of have created companies worth billions of dollars more or less overnight. This was possible only because they have had access to capital that, for little guys, is unprecedented. There has been a near total collapse of the old financial order, in which a person, if he wished to borrow money, must have already had money.

The explosion in capital available for new ventures—and for the new people who create them—is a natural extension of trends that were up and running by the early 1980s, when Michael Milken raised capital for all sorts of implausible characters (T. Boone Pickens, Nelson Peltz) who wanted to take over big corporations. The reason this change has taken place is simple: It pays. By the end of the 1980s Milken may have been personally discredited but his ideas about finance had triumphed in the marketplace. In particular, Milken believed that high-risk debt was systematically undervalued, and therefore a good investment, if accumulated in a diversified portfolio. There is now a huge junk-bond industry that did not exist before.

By the end of the 1990s, Silicon Valley venture capitalists had proved a similar point: High-risk equity was also systematically undervalued in the marketplace, and therefore a good investment, if accumulated in a diversified portfolio. As a result, there is now a huge pool of venture capital searching for the new new thing.

Of course, venture capital has existed as long as capitalism. But until very recently it was a tiny backwater of a business. Today it is an enormous, systematized industry, and is likely to remain so. The $6 billion of venture capital funds invested in the United States in 1993 had swelled to $40 billion by last year. But even those numbers underestimate the boom in capital available to entrepreneurs. In 1993, according to Venture One, the average company went public after six and a half years of venture capital funding. In 1998, thanks to the public willingness to invest in companies that had yet to prove their worth with profits, the number had fallen to 2.6 years, 2.2 for Internet companies. Why? Stock market investors—and not just day traders—have educated themselves a bit on the risks and rewards of earlier-stage investing. This in turn enables the venture capitalists to get their capital back three times as fast, and each venture capital dollar goes three times as far.

A curious consequence of the democratization of capital is the demise of the Wall Street Man: Capitalism is eating the capitalists. Who would have thought that from the heart of capitalism would rise anticapitalist propaganda? Turn on the television and it isn't long before you see ads for an online brokerage firm telling you to fire your stockbroker, since his advice is worthless. The same will soon be said about the high-end brokers: investment bankers.

In just a few years, a status revolution has taken over the financial world. At the same time that the entrepreneur leapfrogged the venture capitalist, the venture capitalist leapfrogged the investment banker. A successful venture capitalist makes 10 times the money of a successful investment banker. Investment bankers now suck up to venture capitalists, rather than the other way around. Young people fresh out of business school go into investment banking usually after they have been rejected for jobs at venture capital firms.

When capital is democratized it is also demystified. And once it is demystified it is no longer the job of a Master of the Universe to raise it. Ask a venture capitalist what he does for a living. He'll offer you a long, complicated explanation. He'll stress the advice he gives to entrepreneurs, the employees, and managers he recruits to the companies he backs. He'll even brag about having sold products. What he'll never mention is his central function: collecting capital from investors and handing it out to entrepreneurs. Venture capitalists are insulted if you suggest that they are "merely" providers of capital. The reason for their relentless posturing is that capital is becoming a commodity, as are the people who supply it, and *they know it.*

One day not long from now, entrepreneurs will get capital by posting a business plan on the Internet. And what, then, will be the role for venture capitalists?

When capital is treated as just another commodity, instead of some sacred trust, all sorts of other things happen. For one, the people who enjoy access to capital are no longer viewed as members of an exclusive club, since there is a new feeling in the air that everyone, in theory, has access to it. Which brings us to another more or less enduring change in social attitudes that has gotten a great big push from the Internet Boom: Getting rich quickly is no longer even the slightest bit controversial. Ten years ago I published a book about Wall Street, *Liar's Poker,* and spent six weeks racing around the country to persuade people to buy it. It was a war out there in the heartland. Hostile takeovers, leveraged buyouts, junk bonds, savings and loan restructuring—you couldn't talk about any of it without stirring up a lot of anger and resentment. Book reviewers, television interviewers, letter writers, lecture hall questioners, and radio call-ins spoke with one voice: Wall Street people should be ashamed of their money. Indeed, I was routinely expected to be ashamed of myself for having been one of them. (I did my best to comply.) Even people prone to think the best of their fellow man were unwilling to entertain a more nuanced view of new Wall Street money. On the *Today Show,* after I explained to Jane Pauley what I had done for a living, she smiled sweetly and said, "Now, your mother didn't raise you to be that way."

A few months ago I published a book about Silicon Valley, *The New New Thing,* and once again spent six weeks racing around the country to persuade people to buy it. This time it was a cakewalk. There was not a peep of protest about the new rich, or their methods. They were heroes.

On the surface, this was a bit odd. Silicon Valley in the 1990s made Wall Street in the 1980s look like the low-stakes poker table. Silicon Valley tycoons raked in each week more than all but a few of the greatest Wall Street deal makers made in their entire careers. They thought in terms of not millions but billions of dollars. What's more, the ambition of Silicon Valley Man had thrown the entire society into turmoil, even more violently than the ambition of Wall Street Man had done a decade earlier. By the end of last year most industries were scrambling to respond to the challenges posted by fly-by-night startups. People feared for their jobs. And yet for some reason this did not translate into resentment or anger. I didn't hear a word about moral and social consequences of Internet Man because no one wanted to talk about them. All people wanted was stock tips.

Something important has changed, and it affects even those who have not gotten rich. A person who missed out on the Wall Street bonanza could say to himself: "Well, I may not be rich, but at least I'm not a jerk." A person who has missed out on the Internet Boom is left with no such consoling thought. Either you are rich, or you are a chump. As *New York Times* columnist Maureen Dowd has pointed out, people no longer feel guilty for making a lot of money. They feel guilty for *not* making a lot of money.

The new morality of money has implications for the social structure. For instance, new money is now more widely admired than old money. Obviously, the Internet Boom hasn't single-handedly poisoned the prestige of old money—the poison was slow, it required many doses—but it may have administered the final dose. The snobbery of old money depended on the idea that there was something dirty about *making* money. No one even pretends to believe this anymore. The money that has been made during the Internet Boom is as free of taint as new money has ever been. (A phrase you never hear anymore is "nouveau riche"; as it occurs to no one that there is anything wrong with it.) The new logic of money is: the newer, the better. Jerry Yang's money is more fashionable than Gordon Moore's.

Old money had its value system, which has also largely died. (Who now speaks of noblesse oblige?) Ultimately, I think it was killed off by economics.

NEW IDEAS ABOUT NEW WEALTH

John Maynard Keynes famously said that even the most practical man of affairs is usually in the thrall of the ideas of some long dead economist. That's still true. The idea that has seized the American business mind is that innovation is the source of all wealth.

This is not a wildly original notion and, in retrospect, it is astonishing that it took so long for it to catch on. Still, as recently as 1985, you could get your graduate degree in economics without ever once considering the role of innovation in the economy. (I know because I did.) Economic growth was widely thought to be a matter of the proper level of government spending, or a high personal savings rate. Innovation, like changes in tastes or fashion, was an "externality," or a "supply shock." Left outside the models, it never entered into the discussion.

In the late 1980s, a new idea gathered a head of steam. A small group of economists subsequently dubbed New Growth Theorists argued that innovation was not merely an important factor in economic growth but *the* most important factor. Stanford University Professor Paul Romer, who wrote several papers on the subject in the mid-1980s, summarizes their views for the layman when he says that "wealth is just another word for change."

It took about a decade for the ideas of New Growth Theorists to become conventional wisdom in the academy; the Internet Boom sealed victory out in the real world. Faith in the importance of innovation is at the bottom of the great, inchoate shift in attitudes toward technology, and the entrepreneurs responsible for turning technology into business. When people think of economically important technology at the moment they tend to think of information technology. But the idea can be generalized to other technologies, and it will.

During the Internet Boom, the ideas of the New Growth theorists have percolated into the brains of policy makers. "In a real sense today we do have a new economy in the United States," Treasury Secretary Lawrence Summers said in January at the World Economic Forum in Davos, Switzerland. "With surpluses and with the progress we have made in information technology." As a result, all sorts of people who might not otherwise have given the matter a second thought are now looking for excuses to spur innovation and change. In his State of the Union address U.S. President Bill Clinton proposed to spend an additional $3 billion of tax revenues on basic research and development grants for university professors.

Big-business people have also been infected. As a group, they have always had a love-hate relationship with innovation. In theory, they know they should love it, since it creates new businesses. In practice, nothing is more threatening to their immediate interest, which is staying right where they are, on top. A lot of the attributes of the Serious American Executives who preside over big businesses—modesty, discretion, gray suits, Republican Party membership, the belief that "prudence" and "caution" are primary values rather than questionable traits—are antithetical to the New Economy. Today, the best-selling book at management consulting firms—as good a proxy as any for the conventional wisdom inside *Fortune* 500 companies—is Clayton M. Christensen's *The Innovator's Dilemma*, which seeks to explain to big companies how they can be as innovative as small ones. Why do you think that is?

Indeed, it's hard to list all of the putative core beliefs that Serious American Executives have abandoned in their adoption of

New Economy values. In their own way they have sold out as completely as the Generation Xers who quit slacking to take jobs flacking for dot-coms. For instance, the once tight-lipped big-time CEO is not a publicity whore. Turn on CNBC or CNN any day between 9:45 A.M. and 4:05 P.M. and you will find businessmen, who just a few years ago refused on principle to return journalists' phone calls, painted an eerie shade of orange and yakking away about their successes as inanely as supermodels.

All in all, there is something like a new ideology that has accompanied the Internet Boom. The changes that the Internet Boom have wrought are all of a piece. If you celebrate innovation, you call into question the status quo. If you glorify the entrepreneur, you denigrate the Organization Man. If you make capital freely available, you disempower the capitalist. If you place a higher value on change, you place a lower value on preservation. If you place an absurdly high value on the future, you place an absurdly low value on the past.

These changes all spring from a single belief—or perhaps it is a suspension of disbelief—that the future will not just be better than the present, but so much better that it will be unrecognizable. After all, that is the sentiment that is at the bottom of the bubble—if it is a bubble.

More than anything, the ideology of the Internet Boom is designed to sustain it. In the midst of gold rushes there are always skeptics who point to past gold rushes and say, "Look how similar these times are to those and look, further, how badly they ended."

Our times are more immune than most to this sort of plea, as they don't value the past, or its lessons. The message of these times is embedded in the stock market and in the minds of the people who are engineering the boom. It is: The future will be so different than the past that the past cannot serve as a point of reference. There is no point examining track records when the race is no longer run on a track.

Attention consumers: A discipline known as account planning that centers on "the brand" means just about everything to the advertising business these days. Many of its adherents also bestow considerable historical and cultural significance to it. Thomas Frank in this *Harper's* article attends a conference of "hip" account planners and comes away with intriguing stories, including Nike's attempt to become a friend of rebel skateboarders.

Thomas Frank

BRAND YOU: BETTER SELLING THROUGH ANTHROPOLOGY

Advertising is a means of contributing meaning and values that are necessary and useful to people in structuring their lives, their social relationships, and their rituals.
    —from a British pamphlet introducing Account Planning

IT IS AN EASY THING, I admit, even in this high noon of the bull market, to scoff at the dot coms, the hedge funds, the silicon millionaires, the day traders, and all the other ephemera of prosperity. But beneath all the prodigious bubbling, counsel the wise, stands an institution as solid and reliable as U.S. Steel: the Brand. But the Brand is a complex thing, not easily understood by the earthbound and the pessimistic. Its power is not a matter of simple force, of the workery brawn celebrated in WPA murals; nor does our faith in the Brand resemble the naive patriotism of the early Cold War. The brand, correctly understood, is a relationship, a thing of nuance and complexity, of irony and coy evasiveness. We are at once skeptical of consumer culture and more ravenous consumers than ever, easily seeing through the clumsy sales pitches that convinced our parents and grandparents, and yet continuing to hum the Lite-Brite jingle to ourselves more than fifteen years after it ceased appearing on TV. Brands are special things to us Americans, interactive myths that earn our loyalty through endless repetition and constant adjustment by people of learning and subtlety.

I have spent some time in the company of those people, the individuals charged with overseeing the brand relationship. They call themselves "Account Planners," and although their field is a relatively new addition to the organizational flowcharts of Madison Avenue, Account Planning has already captured the imagination of "New Economy" enthusiasts everywhere. Its Stalinist-sounding name notwithstanding, Planning is insurrectionary stuff. Not only is it identified with the sort of places where future-envisioning "change agents" are always making heroic revolution on the old rules but its every advance hastens the achievement of full consumer democracy, that imagined free-market utopia wherein each empowered customer can make his or her voice heard in the great public agoras of shopping mall or Internet.

One of the first things I learned after arriving last July at Boston's Westin Hotel was that one did not come to gatherings of Account Planners dressed in a gray flannel suit. I had hoped to make myself inconspicuous by wearing the stereotypical adman's costume of the 1950s; I accomplished exactly the opposite. Not only were a majority of the Planners female and a good number of them British, but I appeared to be the lone square in an auditorium full of high-budget hipsters. They had arrived at the Westin in white synthetic T-shirts stretched tightly over black brassieres, in those oblong spectacles favored by European intellectuals, in hair that had been bleached, bobbed, and barretted after the Riot Grrl style. The men, for their part, wore four- and five-button leisure suits and sported corporate goatees and pierced noses. One group of

Planners periodically donned bright red fezzes; another set wandered around in camouflage. The sight of so much visible extremeness did what it no doubt was intended to do: it threw me, in my obsolete garb, into instant and compound self-doubt.

There were fully 750 people at the Account Planning Conference, a number that seemed to startle everyone. The previous year's gathering was said to have been more "radical" but drew only around 500; a year before that it was an intimate affair of only 300. Planning has about it the air of a youth subculture that is on the cusp of going mainstream: It began in Britain in the corporate-revolutionary days of the 1960s and until quite recently had attracted only a handful of American initiates. But now, as talk of revolution once again blazes through the nation's office blocks, even the less tuned-in agencies are setting up Planning Departments, a fact that seemed vaguely to annoy several of the younger Planners I spoke to. One of these actually warned me against "Fake Planners," agency opportunists who know no more about the mystery and the mission of Planning than they do about Altaic verb conjugation. No one actually came right out and complained that Planning's newfound popularity in the American hinterland meant that it had lost its edge or sold out to The Man, but the feeling was difficult to miss.

What has permitted Planning to infiltrate the world of American business with so little notice, I suspect, is its name. The term "Account Planning" seems almost designed to disguise the profession as just another unremarkable component of the "Fordist" order (a term that was actually used in one Planner's presentation). But we live in an age of public skepticism and heightened sensitivity to every subtle shading of the advertising form, and it is not enough simply to dream up a pleasant-sounding jingle and a sleek-looking logo back at corporate headquarters. In a time when markets are routinely understood as the ultimate democratic form, as an almost perfectly transparent medium connecting The People with their corporations, Planners function, or believe they function, as interpreters of and advocates for the popular will. Planning thus turns out to be virtually the opposite of what its name implies. I would hear again and again over the course of the weekend how advertising people must change their ways to acknowledge the fact of market democracy, how they must abandon their various fixed ideas, how they must "talk to consumers" and initiate an "agenda-free discussion" and "let consumers direct your plan." And to assist them in "uncovering the rational and emotional components of a product's Brand Essence," as one Planner's job description read (yes, with caps in the original), Planners enlist any number of audience-research techniques. I would hear about getting at the Essence of the Brand with the help of techniques such as "beeper studies," "fixed-camera analysis," "shadowing," "visual stories," brainstorming sessions with celebrities, and, of course, focus groups, which some Planners seem to invest with an almost holy significance.

Account Planning is postmodern cultural democracy come home to Madison Avenue complete with all its usual militancy against master narratives and hierarchical authority, its cheerleading for the marginalized, its breathless reverence for the wisdom of everyday people, and its claim to hear the revolutionary voice of the subaltern behind virtually any bit of mass-cultural detritus. Only one thing seems to be wrong: these enthusiastic, self-proclaimed vicars of the vox populi are also, almost to a person, paid agents of the *Fortune* 500.

The Planners were addressed on the first day of their conference by Gerry Laybourne, the former head of Nickelodeon and occupant of the no. 20 spot in *Fortune*'s list of the "Fifty Most Powerful Women in American Business," who was introduced as someone "known for creating incredibly profitable media brands by always putting the consumer first." A woman who confessed to having "epiphanies" during focus-group sessions and who referred to target demographics as "constituents" for whom she aimed to "make life better," Laybourne embodied Account Planning's combination of corporate power and effusive, hyper-democratic populism.

Perched on a tall stool and gently prompted by the solicitous questions of a Planner associate, she described for us the bleak world of TV programming before the dawn of Laybourne, a time when her former employer "believed you should shout down a pipe" to reach your audience. At this the audience murmured scornfully: they knew it was all about listening, respect, dialogue, interactivity—and they knew what was coming next. Laybourne described the Nickelodeon focus group in which the revelation had come:

> [W]e asked kids a very innocuous question: "What do you like about being kids?" And in four different rooms, with these kids who were ten years old, we got a barrage of stuff back. "We're afraid of teenage suicide, we've heard about teenage drunk driving, we've heard about teenage pregnancy, we're terrified about growing up, our parents have us programmed, we're being hurried, we don't have a childhood."
>
> So I stopped the research and I said, "Just go in and ask them what Nickelodeon can do for them." And in all four groups: "Just give us back our childhood." . . . And that became our battle cry. That became our platform.

Now, with childhood back in the hands of its rightful owners, with access to *Rugrats* and *Bewitched* assured in perpetuity, the demographic battle lines had been drawn and fortified.

"We were clearly on the side of kids," Laybourne continued, "clearly their advocate, and we were never going to turn our backs on them."

But the work of empowerment-through-listening went on. There were other demographics to liberate, and Laybourne told the Planners how she and her new organization, Oxygen Media, were preparing to launch a new "entertainment brand" for women, a segment of the population that sounded just as lovable in Laybourne's telling—as misunderstood, as monolithic, and as desperate for accurate media representation—as the kids themselves. Although the exact nature of the programming to which Laybourne's new brand was to be affixed remained mysterious throughout her talk, she did let drop that the ideal medium for it would be the Internet, which she described as a living embodiment of her notion of democracy through dialogue. Growing audibly indignant, Laybourne switched into protest mode, railing against the arrogance of those who

> think that they can put a structure on this thing. But the Internet is an organism, and they are trying to put mechanisms on top of an organism. *It won't work.* It's too powerful. Once people taste freedom—this is the United States of America, we've got that in our blood. This is a revolution that will be led by kids . . . and I hope women as well.

No revolution is complete without reactionaries, real or imagined, and so Laybourne let us know where she and her brand drew the line, stopped listening, and started excluding—namely at Southern Baptism, which had recently made the subjection of women an official element of its credo. "I don't think that our brand is going to appeal to those Southern Baptist men," she remarked tartly. The ad execs erupted in laughter and applause.

But in the revolution against institutional hierarchy that continues to embroil the republic of business, Laybourne was a moderate and slow-moving Girondin compared with the Jacobins of the British St. Luke's agency, which had dispatched Planner Phil Teer to inspire his American comrades with tales of upheaval and progress at "the agency of the future." St. Luke's was nothing less than a syndicalist agency, its ownership shared uniformly by each employee. Teer was said to have come to advertising only after working as a critic of the tobacco industry, which bestowed upon him a credibility that not even Laybourne's focus-group epiphanies could match. His irreverent, self-effacing way of talking won the instant enthusiasm of the audience. He showed us slides that contained the word "fuckin'." He spoke in a working-class Scottish accent, which, he acknowledged, made him difficult for Americans to understand but which also demonstrated the progress of the revolution: "It used to be, a year ago, we always sent nice, middle-class, Oxford-educated, public school boys to talk at conferences for St. Luke's." Surely this was the real thing at last.

Teer did not disappoint. He passed the next hour alternately extolling the artistic idealism that burned at his agency and tersely proclaiming the slogans of the business revolution. "If we stop exploring, we'll die," he said. "Work is leisure," read one of his slides. "Transform people," insisted another, flashing on the screen while Teer told of the liberation of the admen: the story of the security guard who now "dances to jazz funk as he does his rounds," the former suit-wearing executive who is now "a shaven-headed DJ." Not only had St. Luke's freed its employees to participate in the subculture of their choice, but it had also invented such boons to productivity as "hot desking," a system in which people worked wherever they wanted in the company's unstructured office. "Abolish private space, and you abolish ego," Teer proclaimed. Even agency performance reviews had been revolutionized (the chairman was reviewed by a receptionist), apparently along the lines of the criticism/self-criticism sessions once fashionable on the Maoist left. But the people of St. Luke's were less interested in smashing the state than in "killing cynicism."

Not surprisingly, the ads produced by syndicalist admen turned out to imagine the brands in question as the contested terrain of social conflict. For Ikea, St. Luke's had imagined a cultural revolution in which the women of England rise up against chintz, a symbol of the old order as loathsome as cold desks or middle-class public school boys. "Chuck out that chintz. Come on, do it today," ran the jingle, sung to acoustic guitar accompaniment. The Planners boisterously endorsed the call for People's War on chintz with waves of enthusiastic cheering.

*   *   *

After the Planners had talked enough chaos and revolution for one day, they descended on gleaming, polished escalators past the Palm steak restaurant, the elite pen shop, and the indoor waterfall, and were ferried by buses disguised as trolleys to the Massachusetts State House, where they were welcomed by a platoon of men dressed in Revolutionary War uniforms and ushered up to one of four or five open bars dispensing microbrews and Maker's Mark.

"*Anyone* can make an identical product," one adman told me as we relaxed in a gallery of patriotic artifacts from Boston's heroic period. "*Why* do we choose one over another?" I listened to assorted rumors about Red Spider, the mysterious Scottish Planning consultancy whose representatives had conducted an extremely exclusive all-day training session at the conference. I was told by one Planner that your company's check must clear the bank before Red Spider will even leave Scotland; by another, that Red Spider never distributes anything that has been written down; by a third, that their instruction is done in a mystical master-to-acolyte approach; by a fourth, that their instruction takes a simple fiction-writing-seminar approach; and by a fifth, that in fact Red Spider *will* distribute things that are written down, it's just that the guy who was supposed to bring the written materials got sick.

Many Planners are former graduate students from the social sciences, a woman from a Chicago-area agency told me. It's "Margaret Mead meets the Marlboro Man." A man in two-tone glasses from one of the more creative New York agencies informed me that Planners are outsiders in a Peyton Place industry, both ethnically and institutionally.

"That's the *mystique* of the Swiss Army Knife," came an earnest voice from a nearby table. "Now, when you put that on a sweatshirt . . ."

For me, the most telling fact about Account Planning is that its practitioners do not speak of it as a job or a workaday division of agency labor. Planners refer to what they do—and almost universally, it seems—as "the discipline." The academic pretensions that the word carries are intentional: even casual talk at the conference, although not academic jargon per se, was often phrased so as to imply familiarity with academia, with other "disciplines," with realms of learning and expertise that lay far beyond the usual narrow purviews of Madison Avenue.

A number of senior Planners, I was told, hold advanced degrees in various very sophisticated fields. One Planner related to me how "my insight on the meaning of [a brand] came from evolutionary psychology." Another compared the goings-on at his agency to the intellectual freedom and self-questioning that takes place at universities. Gerry Laybourne had told us that "this whole planning process" she was undertaking prior to launching Oxygen made her "feel like I've been in graduate school." And again and again I came across the word "ethnography," used sometimes to describe what is normally called "market research" and on other occasions as a handy, compact definition of the discipline itself.

The only bona fide Ph.D. I came across at the conference, however, was Rick Robinson, a social psychologist whose speech had introduced the Planners to E-Lab, the Chicago-based consultancy he headed. Robinson littered his talk promiscuously with juicy bits of academese. He repeatedly reminded the assembled admen of his postgraduate credentials, implied that he spoke both German and ancient Greek, read a quote from anthropologist Clifford Geertz (in which Geertz himself quotes Max Weber), and asked us not to confuse a book he wrote with a similarly titled one by Aldous Huxley. He told us about "theories of narrative behavior" and prefaced one story by remarking, "If this is Perception 101, I apologize."

In some hotel ballroom in some distant city, perhaps, Babbittesque businessmen were still inspiring one another with exhortations to think positively and with crude pep talks evolved only slightly from the half-time originals. Maybe they were still cursing the "tenured radicals" who had distracted our youth from their rightful concerns with leaders and forward passes. Here, though, the arcana of cultural studies and anthropology were exactly what the Planners had come to absorb. It was helpful to think of the brand as a myth, Robinson said, a primal tale of hero and archetype. Unfortunately, though, most brands were related to consumers haphazardly: "disparate" and "distributed" were the terms Robinson actually used, meaning that a company's 30-second commercials didn't always dovetail with consumers' actual experiences of the product in question. And so Planners, whose job it was to transform these bits and pieces into what Robinson called "a mythic whole," were sometimes forced to call in the heavy intellect to put things right.

Enter E-Lab, which, as its promotional literature puts it, "specializes in providing a deep understanding of everyday experience through a variety of innovative, ethnographic methods." Robinson described some of them for us: questioning people about products while they're actually using them, mounting cameras in stores or homes so that the ethnographers can observe exactly how we go about buying coffee or watching TV. As Robinson showed us slides from the latter operation, distorted and grainy like surveillance-camera views of convenience-store holdups, his language of benign academic understanding morphed into a language of imperial control. A brand's myth is everyday experience for consumers, he noted, and "if you can understand experience, you can *own* it."

This rather starling remark was the closest anyone at the conference would come to the sort of sales-through-domination language that was once such a standard part of advertising-industry discourse. It had now been fully forty years since Vance Packard used a bookful of such manipulative talk to send the industry into the public-relations tailspin from which it has never really recovered. In those days, advertising executives were in the habit of comparing themselves to scientists: they were "engineers of consent," as one famous title had it, masters of applied psychology who were as certain of which sales pitches worked and which didn't as the lab-coated Authorities who peopled their works. In the Sixties, and partially in response to the tidal wave of doubt whipped up by Packard's accusations, admen changed their minds: now they were artists, temperamental geniuses whose intolerance for order and hierarchy was shared by the insurgent consumers they imagined clamoring to purchase all those cars, cigarettes, and air conditioners. These days, with the media world grown as fragmented as the American demographic map, the sales fantasy du jour is anthropology.

It is important to distinguish this professional fiction of the Planners from more standard corporate anthropology: all those practical efforts to increase productivity by studying shop-floor behavior, or to avoid "insensitivity" when building a new factory in some distant clime. Those varieties of corporate anthropology require real anthropologists, formally trained scholars who, the literature on the subject warns, tend to bring all sorts of troublesome "values" to the job with them. The admen here were as much anthropologists as their forebears were scientists when they donned white lab coats and sat for the cameras before a bookcase full of Encyclopaedia Britannicas. What they had taken from anthropology was attitude alone.

And for good reason. Anthropology allows advertising to do what it does in the democratic language of sensitivity and empowerment. To understand production and consumption as "rituals" is to remove them entirely from the great sweep of history and enlightenment, to place them beyond criticism. To understand demographic groups as "tribes," and admen as sympathetic observers, is both to celebrate the relationship and to ensure that any resulting exchange takes place in a rigorously circumscribed context. The business writer Tom Peters coined the phrase "the brand called you" to describe techniques for career building; applied to advertising, the phrase acquires a much creepier significance. What the Planners are planning is, quite literally, you.

"Chaos" had been last year's planning buzzword, and this year it seemed to boast two discrete schools of elaboration. Adepts of a happy chaos foresaw opportunity everywhere, whereas those theorizing a pessimistic chaos believed that extinction lurked around every corner. Either way, Account Planning was being touted as a crucial navigating tool, a compass without which clients would either fail to profit from chaos or fail to avoid chaos's pitfalls.

Ted Nelson of the Mullen agency cleaved to the happy chaos camp. With a series of slides depicting fractals, the growth of musical genres, and a tangled landscape of strip-mall signs, he impressed upon a small audience in a hotel conference room the notion that "life is getting complicated." Clearly brands "based on consistency" were, like the master narratives invented by all those dead white males, in for some pretty rough debunkings; meanwhile, brands that dared to acknowledge and accept chaos could prosper. As Nelson got carried away with his subject, "chaos" began to sound less like an unavoidable state of affairs and more like a rosy and ultra-democratic utopia that Planners needed to work desperately to bring about. Until the day that Planning was practiced as he had counseled, Nelson warned, "the existing paradigm will not be subverted."

Others understood "chaos" differently, as something closer to "evasion" or, simply, the "cynicism" denounced by so many of the conference's dominant paradigm subverters. And confronting that evasiveness, that cynicism, that towering doubt was, ultimately, what Planners were charged with doing.

No brand had enjoyed more success over the years than Nike, with its ubiquitous swoosh and its creepy soft-totalitarian Nike-Town shops in the big cities. At the same time, no brand had suffered as much for its accomplishments. In the wake of revelations about its labor practices and its unpleasant encounters with Michael Moore and *Doonesbury,* Nike had gone from signifying athletic excellence to symbolizing everything that was wrong with global capitalism: multi-millionaire athletes and starvation wages in Indonesia. So it was inevitable, perhaps, that as the Account Planning Conference drew to a close, we should all have been brought together into one room to hear two dramatic accounts of Nike's recent travails and of the heroic work of the Planners to whom the company had turned.

One day, Nike had decided to sell special shoes to skateboarders. But there was a problem. Not the obvious problem of whether or not skateboarders actually required special shoes but the problem of skater resistance. As Kelly Evans-Pfeifer of the Goodby, Silverstein agency spun the tale, the problem when Nike "decided to get into the skateboarding market" was that "skateboarders did not want them there." Skateboarding, it turned out, was "an alternative culture" populated with difficult people who "don't really like this attention they're getting from mainstream companies." The cultural task the Planners faced was not to decide whether this hostility was deserved or warranted but to liquidate it:

> [T]he objective for the advertising was not to reach a certain sales goal but rather it had a more basic, grassroots task, which was that it needed to begin to start a relationship between Nike and skateboarders, and make skateboarders think that it wasn't such a bad thing that Nike was going to get involved.

Nike had wanted the agency to run commercials featuring superstar skaters doing tricks at skating arenas, but the Planners at Goodby saw through that in an instant: the thing to do was to talk to "real" skaters, who do their tricks on the outdoor walkways, planters, and banisters of corporate America. And what the Planners found was that skaters believe that they are the victims of a culture war all their own, that they are persecuted unjustly by intolerant cops and suburban city councils. The key to bringing skaters into the brand's fold, then, was to transform Nike from an enemy into a sympathizer, "to acknowledge and harness all those feelings of persecution." The ads that resulted asked, amusingly, what it would look like if other athletes were harassed and fined the way skaters so routinely are. In focus groups done to test the commercials, Evans-Pfeifer told us, skaters "came in completely hostile to Nike: 'Nike's the man, they don't know anything.'" But, post-viewing, "they said, 'God, man, that's totally coming from a skater's view. That's awesome that that's going to be out there.'" This was a campaign with "grass-roots objectives," she reminded us, and it garnered "grass-roots results." The Nike 800 number, ordinarily a conduit for complaints, she said, began to receive a shower of congratulations: skaters asked for a copy of the commercials to show during their court dates. Then she displayed the cover of the May 1998 issue of *Big Brother*, a skateboarding magazine, and proudly related to us the campaign's crowning victory: in an issue denouncing "corporate infiltration" of the subculture, the publication had singled Nike out for praise.

Pamela Scott and Diana Kapp, another team of Planners from the same agency, began their presentation by reminding us how "Nike has been stewing in a bit of negativity for the last couple of years." "We realized that there was a distance and certainly a disconnect that [young people] were experiencing with the brand," the Planners told us. Again that dread cynicism was tearing people and their brands apart! The Planners rolled up their sleeves and prepared to "address this negativity by reinjecting authenticity and credibility back into the brand." To make their advertisements effective, Scott and Kapp needed to find a sport as distant as possible from Nike's traditional advertising approach, discredited now with its excesses of money and celebrity. So they set about studying high school girls' basketball and packaging it into an elaborate pitch for the Nike brand. The two ad women told us how they embarked on an ethnographic fact-finding tour throughout the South, "inner-city Philly," and other regions where authenticity can be mined cheaply and plentifully. They narrated with the enthusiasm of a post-vacation slide show how they had encountered all manner of curious "rituals" among the girl athletes they found and how they had come across "the most unselfconscious laughter you've ever heard"; they played a recording of an exotic-sounding high school cheer and showed us black-and-white photos of serious-looking teenagers staring past the camera like Dust Bowl farmers in a Dorothea Lange picture. And then they told us how they went about putting that authenticity to work for Nike.

NCAA rules forbade the agency to film an actual high school team, so the agency invented a replica team to reenact the unsullied love of sport that the Planners had witnessed on their tour. A group of high school–age girls was duly recruited and dispatched to basketball camp, where they were assigned to "build their own relationship, their own sisterhood, that we could reflect with great authenticity on film." The squad was dubbed the Charlestown Cougars and made the subject of intentionally low-budget-looking commercials that document the team's arduous, unsung road to a fictitious state championship. The commercials stretched to push all of our authenticity buttons: the timeless black-and-white imagery, the heroic slow motion at crucial points, the unpolished voice-overs, the women's voices humming church spirituals in the background. Consumers, the duo assured us, found the authenticity convincing. We heard of Web-site hits and plaintive messages from real-life high school girls. But the campaign wasn't to be judged in terms of Nike sales alone, the adwomen insisted, for the ads were about "raising consciousness" as well. They worked not merely commercially but "to build role models for young girls." The audience of Planners erupted once more.

When I was in graduate school, it was a pedagogical given that the turn from studying the makers of culture to examining the way culture was received and experienced was a liberating development. Liberating not merely in the sense of scholarly opportunity, in that it was now permissible to study subjects that had formerly been considered unworthy; this stuff was *politically* liberating as well. Certainly the new pedagogies had all the right enemies: Southern Baptists, undersecretaries from the Reagan Administration infuriated by textbooks' failure to pay homage to national heroes, newspaper columnists angered to derangement by the parade of sin at the MLA. As the culture wars got loudly under way, what was less frequently remarked upon were the sundry ways in which the rhetoric of cultural studies mirrored the new language of market research.

Today, though, it is impossible to overlook. What we are wandering into at this fin de siècle is not "culture war" but a strange cultural consensus between business and its putative opponents, a consensus in which both sides agree on the obsolescence of social class and heavy industry and in which both sides shamelessly abuse the language of popular consent. It is a consensus in which even the most stridently radical of disciplines feed ever more directly into the culture industry, in which it no longer surprises anyone when Ogilvy & Mather trawl for anthropology Ph.D.s who have "no ideological or moral objections to consumption/materialism." As is the way with all such things, it is a consensus that seems impossible to resist.

Prizes distributed, conference adjourned, and several hours still before my plane back to the Midwest, I walked out of the Westin Hotel and down Newbury Street. It was eighty degrees and sunny, a great day for being seen in a public place with a Penguin Classic. I wandered past the Boston Public Library and on into the magic landscape of sunglass boutiques, Au Bon Pains, record stores and vegetarian restaurants, and the slow churn of Lexuses and BMWs. Before me lay that gorgeous parade of commerce where anthropology grad students mingled comfortably and understandingly with less enlightened shoppers, where the old conflicts were as meaningless as the heavy, oxidizing statues of abolitionists on the next avenue over.

Even the Tufts-educated barman smiled. In fact, he was ecstatic at my presence. Next year he would be moving on to the State Department, maybe, or Morgan Stanley. But this year was good enough for him. He complimented my choice of Famous Grouse over Dewar's. He meant to see to it that my Scotch-drinking experience was a peak one. Three times did the goateed counter guy at the Burger King (Boston University) inquire whether I had been provided sufficient salt. I floated down the street in my new green tie, past the Armani Exchange where the Planners in fezzes were dining at a sidewalk café, giggling and gesturing, rocking backward and upward in crescendoing paroxysms. I could feel my journalistic cynicism fall from me like the unsubtle enthusiasms of my youth, and we were all of us as one under the empowering gaze of Ronaldo, exotic of the moment, who looked hopefully down on us from the windows of NikeTown.

Because there's good money in building and running prisons, for-profit companies are increasingly entering the field. Barry Yeoman's story from *Mother Jones* takes an in-depth look at Corrections Corporation of America's operations in Youngstown, charging that society is often receiving a bargain-basement form of incarceration from such firms. Understaffing and lax security are among the weaknesses he encountered.

Barry Yeoman

STEEL TOWN — Corrections Corporation of America Is Trying to Turn Youngstown, Ohio, into the private-prison capital of the world

BOB HAGAN was reading his e-mail one July afternoon when the telephone rang at his home in Youngstown, Ohio. "If you have a police radio, turn it on," a friend told the 51-year-old former locomotive engineer. Hagan went down to the basement, hauled out his old scanner, and listened to the news: Six prisoners had escaped in broad daylight from the Northeast Ohio Correctional Center and were still at large. The inmates had cut a four-foot hole in the prison's fence during outdoor recreation, then maneuvered through three rolls of razor ribbon without being detected. No alarm went off, and the officers patrolling the perimeter didn't notice anything amiss.

Hagan, a Democratic state senator who serves on a corrections oversight committee, knew the prison couldn't be trusted to handle the emergency safely. Unlike most prisons, which are government run, the Youngstown facility is managed by Corrections Corporation of America, a multinational company based in

Nashville that makes its money running lockups. Since it opened the prison in 1997, CCA had repeatedly demonstrated the dangers of allowing businesses to operate prisons for profit. The company staffed the facility with guards who had little or no experience in corrections—and then imported 1,700 of the most violent inmates from Washington, D.C., to fill what was supposed to be a medium-security prison. CCA left metal equipment everywhere, which the prisoners quickly stripped and fashioned into weapons. During the first year alone, 20 prisoners were stabbed and two were murdered. The inexperienced staff resorted to tear gas and humiliation to keep order. Sick and injured inmates received inadequate medical treatment. "Knowing what I know now," Youngstown mayor George McKelvey later told reporters, "I would never have allowed CCA to build a prison here."

Now, as Hagan listened to the latest crisis on his scanner, he knew someone had to monitor the search for the escapees. He called his son inside from playing baseball, then jumped in his car to drive the seven miles to the prison. "We're in real trouble," he thought, steering past Youngstown's ruined landscape of abandoned steel mills. The city had once led the nation in steel production, but on that summer afternoon, the shuttered industrial buildings seemed like little more than convenient hideouts for escaped convicts. "God, I'm gonna see them," Hagan said to himself, peering into the shadows of buildings.

When Hagan reached the prison, he found local and state police scrambling to make up for lost time. The company, it turned out, had waited at least half an hour before notifying authorities of the escapes, giving the inmates a significant head start. "The warden had his jackbooted Ninja guys, all dressed in black, running through the woods—untrained and unprepared to pursue dangerous criminals—before they notified the police," Hagan recalled later. When CCA finally did call for help, it offered such sketchy information that police didn't know how to respond. Well after the inmates fled, a Youngstown officer radioed the dispatcher, asking if anyone knew when the men had escaped. "Negative," came the response. "Still in a state of mass confusion up there."

The company exhibited no such confusion, however, about how to secure its bottom line. Despite the high-profile escapes and killings in Youngstown, CCA announced last year that it wants to add 500 beds to the private prison—and build two more facilities nearby to incarcerate another 5,000 prisoners. If the expansion is approved, 1 in every 50 residents of Youngstown and the surrounding two-county area would be an out-of-state inmate. The plan suits many elected officials, who are desperate for an economic boost to a region hardened by the loss of its steel industry. But some residents are taking a closer look at what has transpired at the for-profit prison over the past three years—and what will happen if CCA succeeds in making their quiet corner of Ohio the private-prison capital of the world.

Not since slavery has an entire American industry derived its profits exclusively from depriving human beings of their freedom—not, at least, until a handful of corporations and Wall Street investors realized they could make millions from what some critics call "dungeons for dollars." Since the 1980s, when privatization became the rage for many government services, companies like CCA and its rival, Wackenhut Corporation, have been luring elected officials with a worry-free solution to prison overcrowding. Claiming they can lock people up cheaper than government can, the companies build cells on speculation, then peddle the beds to whatever local or state government needs a quick fix for its growing criminal population. "It's a heady cocktail for politicians who are trying to show they're tough on crime and fiscally conservative at the same time," says Judith Greene, a senior justice fellow at the Open Society Institute, a foundation chaired by philanthropist George Soros.

Over the past decade, private prisons have boomed. Corporations now control 122,900 beds for U.S. inmates, up at least eightfold since 1990. The reason is simple: With antidrug laws and stiffer mandatory sentences pushing the prison population above two million, and governments strapped for capital to build new cells, for-profit prisons seem to offer plenty of cells at below-market prices. "If it could not be done cheaper than the government does it, then we wouldn't be in business now," says Brian Gardner, warden of the CCA prison in Youngstown. "We believe in giving the taxpayer the best deal."

In fact, research indicates that governments save little or no money by contracting out their prison business. In 1996, the U.S. General Accounting Office reviewed five studies of private prisons and found no "substantial evidence" that for-profit institutions save taxpayer dollars. A more recent report commissioned by the U.S. attorney general notes that private prisons attempt to save money by cutting back on staffing, security, and medical care.

No company has benefited more from this private-prison boom—or been so plagued by understaffing, high turnover, and lax security—than CCA. The company, which controls half of a billion-dollar industry, now operates the sixth-largest prison system in the country—trailing only California, Texas, the U.S. Bureau of Prisons, New York, and Florida. Founded in 1983, CCA has never wanted for business. It now manages 82 prisons with 73,000 beds in 26 states, Puerto Rico, Great Britain, and Australia—raking in $365 million during the first three quarters of 1999.

Yet from the very beginning—when inmates from Texas escaped through the air-conditioner slots of a motel the company used as a makeshift penitentiary—CCA has engaged in cost cutting that jeopardizes the safety of prisoners, guards, and communities. In two Georgia prisons, the company's neglect of medical care and security amounted to "borderline deliberate indifference," according to a 1999 state audit. In Colorado last year, a number of female guards left alone with hundreds of male inmates admitted having sex with prisoners in exchange for protection. And at a South Carolina juvenile facility, children were hog-tied and beaten by an overworked, undertrained staff, according to a lawsuit filed in federal court. "They were grabbing the kids and slamming their heads into walls, slamming them into the floors," says Gaston Fairey, an attorney representing one of the children.

What's more, escapes from CCA prisons have been rampant. According to one survey, at least 79 inmates fled CCA facilities nationwide between 1995 and 1998—compared to nine escapes from California prisons, which have more than twice as many inmates. Many of the breakouts could have been prevented, a report prepared for Attorney General Janet Reno concluded, if CCA had simply learned from its previous mistakes and "implemented preventive measures."

In Youngstown, a class-action lawsuit by prisoners has forced the company to improve conditions. But CCA, which declined to speak with *Mother Jones,* remains unapologetic. When local residents expressed concern after the prison break, the company simply shrugged it off. "It's nice if your community is happy with you—that's an extra," CCA founder Doctor Crants told reporters. "But the business is built around providing a valuable service to our customers."

On a snowy morning in January, traffic is light enough on Youngstown's Center Street Bridge that it's possible to park a car in the right-hand lane and look out over the industrial waterfront. In either direction, the Mahoning River is crisscrossed with train tracks and dotted with the occasional crane and ore pile. The hulking horizontal carcass of the Youngstown Sheet & Tube Campbell Works, a steel mill that once employed 5,000 people, dominates the far distance. And there are "brownfields" everywhere: weedy, asbestos-poisoned lots where other mills, and other railroad lines, no longer exist. There's a dark silence to the place—a silence Youngstowners recognize as the sound of economic stagnation.

A quarter-century ago, more trains passed under Center Street than under any other bridge in America. Often, in the dead of night, Bob Hagan would sit at the helm of one of those trains, picking up steel destined for Detroit's auto plants. Coming into Youngstown, he'd see slag pits full of molten metal, so hot that they cast a light bright enough to read by. "When it was good, the graphite floated by and the coke dust followed," he says, "and you knew there was employment."

That sooty prosperity ended September 19, 1977, the day Sheet & Tube announced it would shut down the Campbell Works. The closing triggered a domino effect: In the next few years, mill after mill shut down or announced massive layoffs, eliminating an estimated 60,000 jobs in the metropolitan area. Once-stable neighborhoods crumbled as Youngstown's modest clapboard houses fell into disrepair. Thousands of homes were torn down or put up for sale at rock-bottom prices. The taverns where steelworkers once drank and gambled went belly up, transforming Youngstown's main north-south thoroughfare into a sad strip of payday-loan businesses, discount furniture stores, and abandoned buildings.

By the mid-nineties, with unemployment still in the double digits, Youngstown was desperate for any job it could land. So when the world's largest private-prison company offered to employ 350 people, local officials welcomed it with tax breaks and free water and sewer hookups. As the new prison went up on the edge of town, it looked much like an old steel mill, only surrounded by razor wire. And it held the same promise for the men and women who applied for the $24,600-a-year jobs CCA offered.

But it didn't take long for disillusionment to set in. The day Victoria Wheeler reported for work as a guard, she recalls, the company "explained that these were going to be very, very bad inmates." CCA was negotiating a $182 million contract with the District of Columbia, which was scrambling to transfer some of its most unmanageable inmates out of a crumbling prison complex in Lorton, Virginia. Margaret Moore, director of the D.C. Department of Corrections, told the local newspaper that Youngstown's newest male residents would be "young, aggressive, and violent."

The first inmates arrived on May 15, 1997—courtesy of a transport company owned by CCA. Many of them were classified as maximum security, in violation of CCA's agreement with the city. Half came without case histories or medical records. And according to the report prepared for the U.S. attorney general's office, they arrived in such large numbers that they completely overwhelmed the prison. Inmates needed bedding and toiletries; they needed health screenings; their property needed to be inventoried and distributed. The prison's skeletal crew couldn't possibly accommodate so many new arrivals—900 in the first 17 days—especially after they discovered that may of the men's possessions hadn't arrived from D.C. "It was chaos," Wheeler says.

Angry and frustrated, some new arrivals refused to return to their cells one day until they received their personal property. When inmates in one unit threatened to "trash the place," prison officials ordered a full-scale teargassing of four cell blocks through a hatch on the roof. The gas, intended for outdoor use, blackened the blocks where it was dropped. "The entire pod was smoked out. You couldn't see through the gas," recalls Anthony Beshara, a former guard. Even after the men returned to their bunks and the prison's security chief gave an "all-clear" signal, court records show, the assault continued. "Three for good measure!" an assistant warden announced as the canisters fell.

Then came the murders. In February 1998, 25-year-old inmate Derrick Davis died in a brawl over a Tupac Shakur tape. He was stabbed a dozen times and bled to death while awaiting attention; the prison was so short-staffed that there was no officer on the floor. Less than three weeks later, 23-year-old Bryson Chisley was stabbed repeatedly while one of Davis's assailants—who had not been separated from other inmates—held him down.

According to the report commissioned by the attorney general, CCA responded to the Chisley murder with a "reign of humiliation directed indiscriminately at the entire inmate population." Clad in helmets and riot gear, the company's Special Operations Response Teams (SORT) burst into living units, forced the inmates to strip, and made them lie or kneel naked on the floor with their legs shackled and their hands cuffed behind their backs. They were ordered not to move or speak for an hour while the riot squad searched and often ransacked their rooms. Men's rectums were probed by employees who had no medical training. When one inmate momentarily looked away from the wall, says an officer's report, "I sprayed pepper spray on my glove and wiped it on his face." Such extreme procedures, the report concluded, "would be uncalled for in any circumstance."

"It seemed like they were trying to take their frustrations out on us," says Tati King, a bearded, broad-shouldered 28-year-old who sports both a tattoo of a pit bull and a knit blue-and-tan Muslim skull-cap. "A lot of racial comments were made: niggers this, can't stand you D.C. guys." King later refused to return to his cell to protest not having received a religious meal for four days. "Next think I know," he says, "maybe 20 or more SORT team members told me to strip down and get naked." After slamming him to the floor, King says, officers took him to a segregation unit in shackles. "They had me walk the distance of a football field and a half, stark naked," he says.

If CCA intended the show of force to make the prison more secure, it didn't work. That summer, six inmates escaped on a bright afternoon and one remained at large for several weeks. According to a report by the D.C. Corrections Trustee responsible for monitoring the private prison, everything that could have gone wrong did. A metal detector broke, a motion detector malfunctioned, and the outside yard went unsupervised for 40 minutes. (One staff member was inside playing Ping-Pong.) At the time of the break, there were 219 prisoners in the yard. "Fortunately," the trustee reported, "large numbers of inmates did not choose to . . . follow the route of these six."

Youngstown residents were alarmed by the escapes, but even those most experienced in community organizing didn't know how to take on a far-flung corporation like CCA. "Once the private prison opened, there didn't seem to be a heck of a lot that one could do to tear it down," says Staughton Lynd, an educator and labor lawyer with four decades of experience as an activist, dating back to his stint as director of the Mississippi Freedom Schools. Some residents put their energy into developing a visitation program to help prisoners' families make the 600-mile round trip from Washington. Senator Hagan pushed a bill through the legislature putting tighter restrictions on for-profit prisons.

Then came the bombshell that sparked a grassroots movement—not just in Youngstown, but for 50 miles up and down Ohio's eastern border. In May 1999, Rep. James Traficant Jr. signed a "memorandum of understanding" with Doctor Crants, CCA's founder, agreeing to help the company site two more prisons in his district. The new lockups would each house at least 2,500 inmates, more than tripling the number of private-prison beds in the valley. The Democratic congressman also promised to push for a 500-bed expansion in Youngstown, saying the plan would generate 1,400 jobs and $200 million in taxes.

Officials in five communities expressed interest in the new prisons, and two immediately became front-runners. In the small city of Campbell, where CCA is eyeing the site of the old Sheet & Tube blast furnace, several hundred people turned out for a meeting at a Catholic church to angrily protest the private prison. Many residents voiced their opposition by supporting the insurgent mayoral candidacy of Juanita Rich, an administrator at an assisted-living center. A staunch CCA critic, Rich missed the runoff by six votes.

But it's in Wellsville, an old manufacturing village of 4,500, where the resistance has been most determined. Located across the Ohio River from the northern panhandle of West Virginia, Wellsville and its environs were once dotted with industrial potteries, including one that, at its peak, churned out 10 million plates of Fiesta dinnerware in a single year. But like Youngstown an hour north, Wellsville declined as factories cut back or went out of business. "It's been a tough go," says Mayor Joseph LaScola. "A lot of our people are working in McDonald's, Wendy's, some of the stores in the outlying areas." At one point village officials declared a fiscal emergency, laid off workers, and shut down a fire station. "There wasn't hardly enough money to close down the town," LaScola says.

So when the mayor learned that CCA needed two more host communities, he made sure Traficant knew that Wellsville had the perfect site: some cleared farmland up a twisting cattle road, on a hill overlooking many of the riverfront industries that have closed down. "This would bring close to $2 million a year to our town," says LaScola. "Most of our residents—a large number—are retirees and low income. Anything that looks like it would be a benefit financially, I have to take a serious look at."

In an area devastated by layoffs, the mere promise of added employment was enough to sway some residents to support the prison. "It's about time for Wellsville to progress," Evelyn Springer, a retired teacher, declared at one public meeting. "You can't stay back in the fifties and forties."

But others in Wellsville were furious at how quickly their elected officials bought into CCA's lavish promises, despite the company's dismal track record in Youngstown. The lure of jobs and taxes, they felt, was offset by the hidden costs of prison privatization.

Janice Gartland, a 37-year-old office worker at a medical services company, had never been involved in politics before a neighbor told her about Traficant's proposal. But the idea of a for-profit prison didn't sit well with her. "I have a pretty big problem with using inmates as a commodity," Gartland says. "When you say a person's worth x dollars, and you have to make sure they're fed and medically provided for within that x-dollar range, then something's going to suffer. You're looking at that person as, 'How can I make a profit from them?'"

Gartland and other residents attended a city council meeting to hear Traficant speak—and they didn't like what they heard. The plainspoken congressman defended his alliance with CCA in a long, defensive speech that had council members nodding in agreement. "I would love to bring you Saks Fifth Avenue. I would love to bring you United States Steel," Traficant said. "And this is certainly controversial indeed. But who employs our people? . . .

Who pays for our schools? . . . So I'll take your political shots, but I'll bring the opportunity."

Looking for a voice in the decision, Gartland and her neighbors decided to take the fight to the ballot box. Those who opposed the prison campaigned for a referendum prohibiting the village from extending sewer lines to any correctional facility that housed out-of-state inmates. Through last summer and fall, they canvassed door-to-door, warning neighbors about CCA's track record. They met with union leaders, who object to low-paying jobs at for-profit prisons. And they hooked up with Staughton Lynd, who was bringing together CCA opponents from around the region through an organization called the Prison Forum. Meeting in Youngstown, Forum members shared information about privatization, listened to experts from around the country, and offered one another support.

Fired up by the gatherings, Wellsville activists tried to meet with their elected officials, but were repeatedly rebuffed by the mayor and his allies on the council. LaScola acted as if residents weren't in the council chambers, often ignoring their questions. He refused to recognize Bob Hagan during one meeting, ordering the senator bodily ejected for speaking at the microphone during a recess. He told prison opponents that his line of reasoning was "above you, and you would never understand it." At one meeting, when a woman introduced herself as a resident of a neighboring township, the mayor said, "I'm happy for you. I hope you stay there."

The small town never recaptured its civility after that. HEY ESCAPEES, said a hand-lettered sign posted immediately after one meeting. TURN RIGHT, 2ND HOUSE DOWN ON LEFT, MAYOR'S HOUSE. GO STEAL HIS CAR, HOLD HIM HOSTAGE . . . AS HE IS US. Wellsville's police chief responded by telling federal authorities that prison opponents had threatened to kill LaScola—a charge that leaders of the anti-prison referendum call ludicrous. "They were making us into this radical, dangerous group," says Diane Dinch, who manages a local video store.

As the election approached, opponents picked up the pace,

sponsoring two public forums and continuing their door-to-door campaign. Through Traficant, CCA responded by offering more and more money to Wellsville: a nightly "bed tax" for each inmate, scholarships for local college students, an upgraded sewer system. The company even promised to allow correctional officers to unionize, something it had firmly resisted in Youngstown.

On Election Day, the initiative to block the prison lost by 35 votes. Some opponents blamed the confusing wording on the ballot: Voting "yes" meant opposing the prison. But Janice Gartland also believes that CCA capitalized successfully on the village's desperate financial straits. "We lost support the minute they started throwing dollar figures around," she says.

As residents campaigned to stop CCA, prisoners were also fighting back. In May 1999, inmates at the Youngstown prison won $1.65 million in a class-action lawsuit settlement with the company. Under the terms of the agreement, CCA agreed to pay damages to prisoners, improve security and medical care without cutting back other programs, and pay for an independent monitor to check company abuses. The settlement solves "the worst of the abuse," says Alphonse Gerhardstein, the inmates' attorney. The maximum-security prisoners have been shipped out. Sworn enemies are kept apart. The company has built three new guard towers and put up additional fences. And the prison sponsored more than 50,000 hours of staff training last year, in areas such as conflict resolution and escape prevention.

The Youngstown facility currently appears to enjoy the institutional calm of a well-behaved high school, with murals on the cinderblock walls, monitors in every hallway, and well-stocked classrooms where inmates learn wiring, masonry, and commercial cleaning. And the prison's current leadership tries to distance itself from the earlier debacles. "The past is the past," says assistant chief Jason Medlin. "That was a different administration, a different system altogether."

But Gerhardstein warns that the improved conditions shouldn't be taken as proof that the company—much less the industry—has reformed. After all, he says, it took a lawsuit, new legislation, a renegotiated contract with the city, a monitoring program, and a whole lot of bad publicity just to get CCA to improve conditions at one facility.

For now, negotiations over the proposed expansion have been stalled by CCA's current financial upheaval. Last year, the company merged with a real-estate trust it set up called Prison Realty that was exempt from $50 million in federal income taxes. But the scheme to boost profits even higher wound up backfiring: Prison Realty missed its year-end dividend payment to shareholders last winter, and its stock price has plummeted from $20 to $4 a share.

The cut-rate prices have some heavy hitters on Wall Street hoping to cash in on private prisons. In December, Bank of America teamed up with two high-powered investment firms to offer Prison Realty and CCA an infusion of $350 million—in exchange for as much as 25 percent of the action and four seats on a new 10-member board of directors. The investors are led by the Blackstone Group, a leverage buyout firm with plenty of political connections and annual revenues of $15 billion. Its chairman, former Nixon commerce secretary Peter Peterson, is best known for his recent crusade to privatize Social Security.

Some CCA shareholders have balked at approving the Blackstone deal, which they fear would dilute the value of their shares. But there's no question that some of Wall Street's most respected firms see an opportunity to profit from punishment. "CCA is the market leader in a growing industry," says Thomas Saylak, senior managing director of Blackstone. The infusion of capital, he adds, will enable CCA "to maximize growth prospects."

Investors aren't the only ones who consider the company's current woes a temporary setback in an otherwise lucrative industry. Paul Marcone, chief of staff to Rep. Traficant, insists that negotiations for the proposed expansion in Youngstown will reopen soon. "CCA has had some organizational shake-ups," he says, "but now the company is focused more on expanding."

That expansion, many residents fear, would make Youngstown as synonymous with prisons as it was with steel a quarter-century ago. "We may have concentrated the sun's rays somewhat, but it's not clear if we've started a fire," says Lynd, whose Prison Forum is launching a campaign called Schools, Not Jails. Lynd and other opponents want to keep the debate above the level of "not in my backyard"—to convince the public and policymakers that it's both unethical and counterproductive to turn incarceration over to the private sector.

"We can't put somebody in the Black Hole of Calcutta, or the Gulag Archipelago, just because they've done something wrong," says Bob Hagan. "When money's your main motivation, you forget one major lesson: that these people are coming out. If you don't create rehabilitated prisoners, but you only create profit for your shareholders, then you have failed at a system that's supposed to protect society."

Experts questioned whether powerful executives Sanford Weill of
Travelers Group and John Reed of Citicorp could coexist after
their giant financial firms merged. They were right. This inside story
by Charles Gasparino and Paul Becket of *The Wall Street Journal*
gives a move-by-move look at the intricate corporate chess game
that Reed lost because his style clashed with Weill's. The story
paints an especially vivid portrait of Weill's temper.

Charles Gasparino and Paul Becket

ALONE AT THE TOP:
How John Reed Lost the Reins of Citigroup
to His Cochairman

IN LATE FEBRUARY, when John S. Reed announced his
retirement as cochairman of Citigroup Inc., it looked like a benign
end to one of the most storied careers in U.S. finance.

It wasn't.

In fact, Mr. Reed, a master corporate chess player, found himself on the losing end of an 18-month struggle with his cochairman, Sanford Weill, an equally celebrated corporate infighter—and
in this case at least, a better one.

Mr. Weill and Mr. Reed rocked the business world in April
1998 when Travelers Group, Inc., run by Mr. Weill, agreed to
merge with Citicorp, run by Mr. Reed. Valued at $83 billion, it
was the largest corporate merger ever at the time. It created a
unique financial-services powerhouse, combining such household
names as Citibank, Travelers, and Salomon Smith Barney. Mr.
Weill and Mr. Reed, both giants in their fields with egos to match,
would run the new colossus jointly as cochairmen. Despite some

initial turmoil, the deal is now widely viewed by investors as a success. Since the merger closed in October 1998, Citigroup shares have risen about 170 percent, surpassing the roughly 120 percent increase in the Standard & Poor's 500 index.

But behind the scenes, things ran less smoothly. By the end of their partnership, Messrs. Weill and Reed were deeply—and on occasion bitterly—at odds. In recent months, Mr. Weill had made clear to at least one associate his intention to wrest control of the company. After Heidi Miller, Citigroup's chief financial officer, announced her resignation in February to join Priceline.com, an e-commerce outfit, Mr. Weill blamed Mr. Reed.

"Godd—, is this because of John?" Mr. Weill asked over the phone to Ms. Miller, say Wall Street executives with knowledge of the discussion. No, Ms. Miller replied; the Priceline offer was just too good to pass up. But Mr. Weill remained furious—and vowed to get rid of Mr. Reed.

Mr. Weill declined to comment for this article, as did Mr. Reed. Ms. Miller has told colleagues that the growing tensions between her two bosses helped trigger her decision to leave Citigroup.

Power-sharing agreements between executive heavyweights often collapse, and many observers had predicted at the time of the merger that the one between Mr. Weill and Mr. Reed couldn't last. At bottom, their split wasn't about disputes over direction or strategy—though there were some, on things ranging from Citigroup's Internet approach to its new employee benefits plan. The larger problem, say insiders, was a simple personality clash: Mr. Weill, the brash, instinctive dealmaker; Mr. Reed, the reserved and famously analytical management whiz. Ultimately, that clash amplified the impact of a number of relatively small differences of opinion and style, undermining each man's tolerance for cooperating at the top.

Moreover, some people who know Mr. Weill say it just wasn't in his nature to share power forever. "Sandy needs to run Citigroup like you and I need to breathe," says one longtime colleague of Mr. Weill's.

The fissure came to a head at a special board meeting in late February. Mr. Reed, 61 years old, insisted that he and Mr. Weill, 67, should leave the firm together after finding a successor. Mr. Weill wanted to stay. A tumultuous meeting ensued. Eight hours later, Mr. Reed was out of a job.

One key influence: Robert Rubin, chairman of Citigroup's executive committee. After a director asked the former Treasury Secretary if he would like to run the firm, he demurred, but came to Mr. Weill's defense. Mr. Rubin called on the board to have Mr. Weill run the firm solo while the company finds a successor, according to a person familiar with the matter. (Mr. Rubin declined to comment.)

Now, speculation is swirling inside Citigroup that Mr. Weill has no intentions of relinquishing control anytime soon. This, even though the board has appointed a search committee to find a successor within two years. And Mr. Weill already has powerful support to remain at the helm: Prince Alwaleed bin Talal, one of Citigroup's largest shareholders, says he "doesn't see anyone but Sandy running the show for the foreseeable future."

Last year, the two met at Prince Alwaleed's desert camp in Saudi Arabia and became "very close," the prince says. "I think I can convince Sandy" to stay, he says. "I am willing to be a leader in this" effort. "My prediction is that he will stay longer."

Meanwhile, there is no clear successor inside the firm to fill Mr. Weill's shoes if and when he leaves Citigroup. Mr. Weill, with Mr. Reed's blessing, pushed out Jamie Dimon, Mr. Weill's longtime protege and heir apparent. And in some ways, the rift between Mr. Reed and Mr. Weill can be traced to the firing of Mr. Dimon, who fell out of favor with Mr. Weill and left amid a management shake-up in the fall of 1998.

Mr. Reed agreed with the move at the time, people at the company said. But later, as his working relationship with Mr. Weill began to deteriorate, he had some second thoughts. In April 1999, during a Citigroup consumer-group conference in Florida, Mr. Reed acknowledged that losing Mr. Dimon was a mistake. "Any time you lose someone that talented, that's unfortunate," Mr. Reed said, according to a person familiar with the matter.

When Mr. Weill heard about that remark, he was livid. "What will Mike Carpenter think?" he fumed, according to a Wall Street executive with knowledge of the matter. (Mr. Carpenter became cohead of Citigroup's global corporate and investment bank after Mr. Dimon's departure.)

Though the two men usually agreed on the big picture, the almost diametrically opposed ways each went about reaching conclusions on key corporate issues rubbed the other the wrong way, insiders say. They say Mr. Reed, highly analytical and organized, often wanted detailed reports and studies; Mr. Weill frequently made his decisions on gut instinct. And strategic differences did emerge. For instance, the co-chairmen argued over the work of eCiti, an internal laboratory to dream up products and strategy for the company's Internet efforts. Mr. Weill thought each of Citigroup's numerous units should control its own Web strategy; Mr. Reed wanted Internet strategy centralized under eCiti—Mr. Reed's pet project.

By last summer, Mr. Weill and Mr. Reed weren't speaking to each other much, Citigroup executives say. In July, seeking to patch things up, the two formally agreed to divide their duties, with each taking jobs to match his strengths. Under the plan, Mr. Reed headed the firm's Internet and technology efforts. Mr. Weill was in charge of the firm's "operations," such as investment banking, sales, and trading.

Meanwhile, Mr. Weill moved to embrace key executives within the organization, including those regarded as loyal to Mr. Reed. In the fall, Mr. Weill asked Citibank veteran Victor Menezes, cohead of the global corporate and investment bank, to act as his guide in an unusual undertaking. Not far from the Taj Mahal in India, a robed Mr. Weill, accompanied by Mr. Menezes and other friends, rode a horse to a Hindu ceremony, where he and his wife renewed their marriage vows.

Insiders began noting that Messrs. Weill and Reed no longer

openly joked together in front of the troops. During one meeting last summer, as Mr. Reed expounded about an internal program he championed to improve service, one of his lieutenants observed that one Citigroup unit had achieved 2.3 "sigmas," a middling quality grade. Mr. Weill, no fan of management-theory jargon, cracked with a smile: "How many sigmas was that?" The group erupted in laughter; Mr. Reed remained silent, according to a person who was there.

At another meeting, Mr. Weill asked Mr. Reed to explain how the effort generated profits. "Can you quantify the bottom line?" Mr. Weill asked. When Mr. Reed began, Mr. Weill rolled his eyes, said one person who witnessed the exchange. When it was Mr. Weill's turn to speak, Mr. Reed started reading, the person said.

By late last year, Mr. Reed clearly was thinking about his future, people at the firm say. After hearing about General Electric Co. Chairman John Welch's intention to retire in April 2001, Mr. Reed told associates that Citigroup needed to map out an orderly process as well. He thought that he and Mr. Weill should leave together while the company was thriving. He also said it should be a board decision, and even mentioned Mr. Dimon as a candidate who ought to be considered for the top post, company insiders say.

But by then, the cochairmen's fractious relationship had taken its toll on Citigroup's senior managers. In January, Robert Lipp, head of Citigroup's global consumer business, frustrated over what he viewed as Mr. Reed's continued meddling in Citigroup's consumer operations, told Mr. Weill he would retire, people familiar with the matter say. Mr. Weill openly blamed Mr. Lipp's desire to leave on Mr. Reed. Mr. Weill also confided to executives that he was frustrated with the power-sharing arrangement. Through a spokesman, Mr. Lipp declined to comment.

A few weeks later, at a senior management committee meeting in Arizona, the issue came to a head. On the first day, executives debated the shortcomings of eCiti, the firm's Internet research arm, overseen mostly by Mr. Reed. The second day was dubbed the "What's wrong with us?" session, and senior managers poured out complaints about having to report to two feuding bosses.

"Pick any hill and we'll go up any hill, but we just can't go in two different directions," Mr. Menezes told them, according to a witness. (Mr. Menezes, through a spokesman, declined to comment.) Mr. Lipp was even more direct: Reporting to two bosses isn't working, he said.

Mr. Reed and Mr. Weill seemed to be taken aback. When the session was over, Mr. Reed vowed to managers that he and Mr. Weill had heard their gripes and would "sit down next week and talk" about their relationship. Mr. Weill nodded in agreement.

In late February, Messrs. Weill and Reed called a special board meeting in New York. They met under the guise of discussing a pending acquisition—cover, in case word of the meeting leaked to the media.

The meeting would be about much more. In his presentation to the board, Mr. Reed proposed that he and Mr. Weill leave at the same time, once a successor was in place, he later told an associate. By the time he wrapped up his presentation, Mr. Reed thought he had won enough board support to push his plan through.

Mr. Weill balked, and was supported by Mr. Rubin. Since Mr. Rubin joined the firm, the two had grown close. Mr. Rubin argued that it would be bad for the company if they both left, and better if Mr. Weill stayed to focus on running the businesses, a person familiar with the meeting says. Mr. Weill, Mr. Rubin said, was capable of operating the company alone with his help, this person says.

Yet some board members voiced their doubts. One asked Mr. Rubin: "Would you be willing to take the post?" He declined.

The board deliberated privately for several hours after Messrs. Reed, Weill, and Rubin were asked to leave the room. Messrs. Reed and Weill watched golf on television. Mr. Rubin watched basketball.

Inside the boardroom, tensions were mounting. Franklin Thomas, a board member of the old Citicorp, assumed the role of chairman. "Each person on the board had a different thing to say," says one director.

As the hours stretched on and Mr. Reed waited, he became increasingly fed up. He thought, "I'm not going to stick around to save the world," according to the account he later gave an associate. Eventually, Mr. Thomas emerged from the boardroom with a proposal: Mr. Reed could stay on as nonexecutive chairman, while Mr. Weill became the sole chief executive (the two had been co-CEOs as well as cochairmen). Mr. Reed declined. "It wouldn't be good for the company," he told Mr. Thomas, according to an associate of Mr. Reed. Mr. Thomas returned to the board room, and shortly thereafter the board made its unanimous decision: Mr. Reed would retire. Mr. Weill had won.

Days later, Mr. Reed made one parting request: that he be given "most favored nation status," or the same departure perks, such as a secretary and a company car, as Mr. Weill when Mr. Weill leaves. The board has yet to take up the request.

It didn't take long for Mr. Weill to consolidate his power, even in areas formerly under Mr. Reed's purview. Soon after Mr. Reed announced he would retire on April 18, Mr. Weill sent a memo to executives announcing the formation of a new Internet Operating Committee, headed by Vice Chairman Deryck Maughan, to "better integrate, coordinate, and promote all of our Internet activities across all our global businesses."

Last week, Mr. Reed finished his farewell tour in London, meeting for the last time Citigroup officials with whom he worked during his career. Earlier this week, Citigroup held a cocktail reception at Citigroup's headquarters in honor of the soon-to-be former cochairman. Mr. Weill was in Brazil.

Last month, Mr. Weill himself was the guest of honor at a party thrown to celebrate his 67th birthday, with some family and friends at Citigroup's main office. The party had a biblical theme. Mr. Weill played the role of Moses, wearing a false white beard and robe. "We have been lost for two years now wandering in the desert," said Citigroup General Counsel Charles Prince, who acted as master of ceremonies, according to people familiar with the event.

"Now Moses saves us," Mr. Prince added, "and brings us to the Promised Land." Later, he observed: "You know, Sandy, that Moses was never allowed to enter the Promised Land."

Mr. Weill just laughed.

Genome became a popular term once scientists announced they'd taken impressive steps toward unlocking the human DNA code, but it's becoming big business as well. Richard Preston of *The New Yorker* profiles controversial and rambunctious Craig Venter of Celera Genomics Group, whose company is aiming for big revenues as it supplies the genomic information it expects will be in demand in the future. Besides probing biotechnology, the story delves deeply into Venter's personal and professional background.

Richard Preston

THE GENOME WARRIOR

"CRAIG VENTER is an asshole. He's an idiot. He is a thorn in people's sides and an egomaniac," a senior scientist in the Human Genome Project said to me recently. The Human Genome Project is a nonprofit international research consortium that since the late 1980s has been working to decipher the complete sequence of nucleotides in human DNA. The human genome is the total amount of DNA that is spooled into a set of twenty-three chromosomes in the nucleus of every typical human cell. It is often referred to as the book of human life, and most scientists agree that deciphering it will be one of the great achievements of our time. The stakes, in money and glory, to say nothing of the future of medicine, are huge.

In the United States, most of the funds for the Human Genome Project come from the National Institutes of Health, and it is often referred to, in a kind of shorthand, as the "public project," to distinguish it from for-profit enterprises like the Celera

Genomics Group, of which Craig Venter is the president and chief scientific officer. "In my perception," said the scientist who was giving me the dour view of Venter, "Craig has a personal vendetta against the National Institutes of Health. I look at Craig as being an extremely shallow person who is only interested in Craig Venter and in making money. Only God knows what those people at Celera are doing."

What Venter and his colleagues are doing is preparing to announce, in the next few days or weeks, that they have placed in the proper order something like 95 percent of the readable letters in the human genetic code. They refer to this milestone as First Assembly. They have already started selling information about the genome to subscribers. The Human Genome Project is also on the verge of announcing a milestone: what it calls a "working draft" of the genome, which is more than 90 percent complete and is available to anyone, free of charge, on a Web site called GenBank. It contains a large number of fragments that have not yet been placed in order, but scientists in the public project are scrambling to get a more complete assembly. Both images of the human genome—Celera's and the public project's—are becoming clearer and clearer. The human book of life is opening, and we hold it in our hands.

A human DNA molecule is about a meter long and a twenty-millionth of a meter wide—the width of twenty hydrogen atoms. It is shaped like a twisted ladder, and each rung of the ladder is made up of four nucleotides—adenine, thymine, cytosine, and guanine. The DNA code is expressed in combinations of the letters A, T, C, and G, the first letters of the names of the nucleotides. The human genome contains at least 3.2 billion letters of genetic code, about the number of letters in two thousand copies of "Moby Dick."

Perhaps 3 percent of the human code consists of genes, which hold recipes for making proteins. Human genes are stretches of between a thousand and fifteen hundred letters of code, often broken into pieces and separated by long passages of DNA that don't code for protein. It is believed that there are somewhere between thirty thousand and possibly more than a hundred thousand genes in the human genome (there's great puzzlement about the number). Much of the rest of the genome consists of blocks of seemingly meaningless letters, gobbledygook. These sections are referred to as junk DNA, although it may be that we just don't understand the function of the apparent junk.

The conventional route for announcing scientific breakthroughs is publication in a scientific journal, and both Celera and the public project plan to publish annotated versions of the human genome later this year, perhaps in *Science*. It is even possible that they will announce a collaboration and publish together. Although right now the two sides look like armies maneuvering for advantage, the leaders of the Human Genome Project have consistently denied that they are involved in some kind of competition.

"They're trying to say it's not a race, right?" Craig Venter said to me recently, in a shrugging sort of way. "But if two sailboats are sailing near each other, then by definition it's a race. If one boat wins, then the winner says, 'We smoked them,' and the loser says, 'We weren't racing—we were just cruising.'"

I first met Craig Venter on a windy day in summer nearly a year ago, at Celera's headquarters in Rockville, Maryland, a half-hour drive northwest of Washington, D.C. The company's offices and laboratories occupy a pair of five-story white buildings with mirrored windows, surrounded by beautiful groves of red oaks and tulip-poplar trees. One of the buildings contains rooms packed with row after row of DNA-sequencing machines of a type known as the ABI Prism 3700. The other building holds what is said to be the most powerful civilian computer array in the world; it is surpassed only, perhaps, by that of the Los Alamos National Laboratory, which is used for simulating nuclear bomb explosions. This second building also contains the Command Center, a room stuffed with control consoles and computer screens. People in the

Command Center monitor the flow of DNA inside Celera. The DNA flows through the Prism machines 24 hours a day, seven days a week.

That day last summer, Venter moved restlessly around his office. There had been a spate of newspaper stories about the race to decode the complete genome, and about the pressure Celera was putting on its competitors. "We're scaring the shit out of everybody, including ourselves," he said to me. Venter is 53 years old, and he has an active, cherubic face on which a smile often flickers and plays. He is bald, with a fuzz of short hair at the temples, and his head is usually sunburned. He has bright-blue eyes and a soft voice. He was wearing khaki slacks and a blue shirt, New Balance running shoes, a preppy tie with small turtles on it, and a Rolex watch. Venter's office looks into the trees, and that day leaves were spinning on branches outside the windows, flashing their white undersides and promising rain. Beyond the trees, a chronic traffic jam was occurring on the Rockville Pike. Celera is in an area along a stretch of Interstate 270 known as the Biotechnology Corridor, which is dense with companies specializing in the life sciences.

Celera Genomics is a part of the P.E. Corporation, which was called Perkin-Elmer before the company's chief executive, Tony L. White, split the business into two parts: P.E. Biosystems, which makes the Prism machine, and Celera. Venter owns 5 per cent of Celera's stock, which trades, often violently, on the New York Stock Exchange. In recent months, the stock has been tossed by waves of panic selling and panic buying. Currently, the company is valued at three billion dollars, more or less. At times, Craig Venter's net worth has slopped around by a hundred million dollars a day, like water going back and forth in a bathtub.

"Our fundamental business model is like Bloomberg's," Venter said. "We're selling information about the vast universe of molecular medicine." Venter believes, for example, that one day Celera will help analyze the genomes of millions of people as a regular part of its business—this will be done over the Internet, he says—and the company will then help design or select drugs tailored to patients' particular needs. Genomics is moving so fast that it is possible to think that in perhaps 15 years you will be able to walk into a doctor's office and have your own genome interpreted. It could be stored in a smart card. (You would want to keep the card in your wallet, in case you landed in an emergency room.) Doctors would read the smart card, and it would show a patient's total biological-software code. They could see the bugs in the code, the genes that make you vulnerable to certain diseases. Everyone has bugs in his code, and knowing what they are will become a key to diagnosis and treatment. If you became sick, doctors could watch the activity of your genes, using so-called gene chips, which are small pieces of glass containing detectors for every gene. Doctors could track how the body was responding to treatment. All your genes could be observed, operating in an immense symphony.

Venter stopped moving briefly, and sat down in front of a screen and tapped a keyboard. A Yahoo! quote came up. "Hey, we're over 20 today," he said. (Celera's stock has since split. Adjusted for today's prices, it was trading at ten dollars a share; last week, it was trading at around seventy dollars a share.) I was standing in front of a large model of Venter's yacht, the *Sorcerer,* in which he won the 1997 Trans-Atlantic Race in an upset victory— it was the only major ocean race that Venter had ever entered. "I got the boat for a bargain from the guy who founded Land's End," Venter said. "I like to buy castoff things on the cheap from ultra-rich people."

Venter went into the hallway, and I followed him. Celera was renovating its space, and tiles were hanging from the ceiling. Some had fallen to the floor. Black stains dripped out of air-conditioning vents, and sheets of plywood were lying around. Workmen were Sheetrocking walls, ripping up carpet, and installing light fixtures, and a smell of paint and spackle drifted in the air. We took the stairs to the basement and entered a room that held about 50 ABI Prism 3700 machines. Each Prism was the size of a small refrigerator and had cost three hundred thousand dollars. Prisms are the fastest DNA sequencers on earth. At the moment, they were reading the DNA of the fruit fly. This was a pilot project for the human genome. The machines contained lasers. Heat from the lasers seemed to ripple from the machines, even though they were being cooled by a circulation system that drew air through them. The lasers were shining light on tiny tubes through which strands of fruit-fly DNA were moving, and the light was passing through the DNA, and sensors were reading the letters of the code. Each machine had a computer screen on which blocks of numbers and letters were scrolling past. It was fly code.

"You're looking at the third-largest DNA-sequencing facility in the world," Venter said. "We also have the second-largest and the largest."

We got into an elevator. The walls of the elevator were dented and bashed. Venter led me into a vast, low-ceilinged room that looked out into the trees. This was the largest DNA-decoding factory on earth. The room contained a hundred and fifty Prisms— forty-five million dollars' worth of the machines—and more Prisms were due to be installed any day. Air ducts dangled on straps from the ceiling, and one wall consisted of gypsum board.

Venter moved restlessly through the unfinished space. "You know, this is the most futuristic manufacturing plant on the planet right now," he said. Outdoors, the rain came, splattering on the windows, and the poplar leaves shivered. We stopped and looked over a sea of machines. "You're seeing Henry Ford's first assembly plant," he said. "What don't you see? People, right? There are three people working in this room. A year ago, this work would have taken one thousand to two thousand scientists. With this technology, we are literally coming out of the dark ages of biology. As a civilization, we know far less than 1 per cent of what will be known about biology, human physiology, and medicine. My view of biology is 'We don't know shit.'"

Celera's business model provokes some interesting questions, and some observers believe the company could fail. For instance, it appears to be burning through at least a hundred and fifty million dollars a year. But who will want to buy the information the company is generating, and how much will they pay for it? "There will be an incredible demand for genomic information," Venter assured me. "When the first electric-power companies strung up wires on power poles, there were a lot of skeptics. They said, 'Who's going to buy all that electricity?' We already have more than a hundred million dollars in committed subscription revenues over five years from companies that are buying genomic information from us—Amgen, Novartis, Pharmacia & Upjohn, and others. After we finish the human genome, we'll do the mouse, rice, rat, dog, cow, corn, maybe apple trees, maybe clover. We'll do the chimpanzee."

One day at Celera's headquarters, I was talking with a molecular biologist named Hamilton O. Smith, who won a Nobel Prize in 1978 as the co-discoverer of restriction enzymes, which are used to cut DNA in specific places. Scientists use the enzymes like scissors, chopping up pieces of DNA so that they can be studied or recombined with the DNA of other organisms. Without the means to do this, there would be no such thing as genetic engineering.

Ham Smith is in his late sixties. He is six feet five inches tall, with a shock of stiff white hair and a modest manner. "Have you ever seen human DNA?" he asked me, as he poked around his lab.

"No."

"It's beautiful stuff."

A box that held four small plastic tubes, each the size of a pencil stub, sat on a countertop. "These four tubes hold enough human DNA to do the entire human-genome project," Smith said. "There's a couple of drops of liquid in each tube."

He held up one of the tubes and turned it over in the light to show me. A droplet of clear liquid moved back and forth. It was the size of a dewdrop. Then he held up a glass vial, and rocked it back and forth, and a crystal-clear, syrupy liquid oozed around in it. He explained that this was DNA he'd extracted from human blood—from white cells. "That's long, unbroken DNA. This liquid looks glassy and clear, but it's snotty. It's like sugar syrup. It really is a sugar syrup, because there are sugars in the backbone of the DNA molecule."

Smith picked up a pipet—a hand-held device with a hollow plastic needle in it, which is used for moving tiny quantities of liquid from one place to another. His hands are large, but they moved with precision. Holding the pipet, he sucked up a droplet of DNA mixed with a type of purified salt water called buffer. He held the drop in the pipet for a moment, then let it go. The droplet drooled. It reminded me of a spider dropping down a silk thread.

"There the DNA goes, it's stringing," he said. "The pure stuff is gorgeous." The molecules were sliding along one another, like spaghetti falling out of a pot, causing the water to string out. "It's absolutely glassy clear, without color," he said. "Sometimes it pulls back into the tube and won't come out. I guess that's like snot, too, and then you have to almost cut it with scissors. The molecule is actually quite stiff. It's like a plumber's snake. It bends, but only so much, and then it breaks. It's brittle. You can break it just by stirring it."

The samples of DNA that Celera is using are kept in a freezer near Smith's office. When he wants to get some human DNA, he removes a vial of frozen white blood cells or sperm from the freezer. The vials have coded labels. He thaws the sample of cells or sperm, then mixes the material with salt water, along with a little bit of detergent. A typical human cell looks like a fried egg, and the nucleus of the cell resembles the yolk. The detergent pops the eggs and the yolks, and stands of DNA spill out in the salt water. The debris falls to the bottom, leaving tangles of DNA suspended in the liquid.

One of Smith's research associates, a woman named Cindi Pfannkoch, showed me what shattered DNA was like. Using a pipet, she drew a tiny amount of liquid from a tube and let a drop go on a sheet of wax, where it beaded up like a tiny jewel, the size of the dot over this "i." An ant could have drunk it in full.

"There are two hundred million fragments of human DNA in this drop," she said. "We call that a DNA library."

She opened a plastic bottle, revealing a white fluff. "Here's some dried DNA." She took up a pair of tweezers and dragged out some of the fluff. It was a wad of dried DNA from the thymus gland of a calf; the wad was about the size of a cotton ball, and it contained several million miles of DNA.

"In theory," Ham Smith said, "you could rebuild the entire calf from any bit of that fluff."

I placed some of the DNA on the ends of my fingers and rubbed them together. The stuff was sticky. It began to dissolve on my skin. "It's melting—like cotton candy," I said.

"Sure. That's the sugar in DNA," Smith said.

"Would it taste sweet?"

"No. DNA is an acid, and it's got salts in it. Actually, I've never tasted it."

Later, I got some dried calf DNA. I placed a bit of the fluff on my tongue. It melted into a gluey ooze that stuck to the roof of my mouth in a blob. The blob felt slippery on my tongue, and the taste of pure DNA appeared. It had a soft taste, unsweet, rather bland, with a touch of acid and a hint of salt. Perhaps like the earth's primordial sea. It faded away.

DNA from six donors who contributed their blood or semen was used for Celera's human-genome project. The donors included both men and women, and a variety of ethnic groups. Just one person, a man, supplied the DNA for First Assembly. Only Craig Venter and one other person at the company are said to know who the donors are. "I don't know who they are, but I wouldn't be surprised if one of them is Craig," Ham Smith remarked.

Craig Venter grew up in a working-class neighborhood on the east side of Millbrae, on the San Francisco peninsula. His family's house was near the railroad tracks. One of his favorite childhood activities, he says, was to play chicken on the tracks. In high school, he excelled in science and shop. He built two speed boats, and spent a lot of time surfing Half Moon Bay. He attended two junior colleges in a desultory way, but mostly he surfed, until he enlisted in the Navy. He had long blond hair and a crisp body then. He was a medical corpsman in Vietnam, and twice he was sentenced to the brig for disobeying orders.

Venter has a history of confrontation with government authorities. He told me that as an enlisted man in San Diego he was court-martialled for refusing a direct order given by an officer. "She happened to be a woman I was dating," Venter said. "We had a spat, and she ordered me to cut my hair. I refused." A friend of his, Ron Nadel, who was a doctor in Vietnam, recalls that one of Venter's blowups with authority involved "telling a superior officer to do something that was anatomically impossible." Venter worked for a year in the intensive-care ward at Da Nang hospital, where, he calculates, more than a thousand Vietnamese and American soldiers died during his shifts, many of them while the 1968 Tet offensive was going on. When he returned to the United States, Venter finished college and then earned a Ph.D. in physiology and pharmacology from the University of California at San Diego.

Venter is married to a molecular biologist, Claire Fraser, who is the president of The Institute for Genomic Research (TIGR, pronounced "Tiger"), in Rockville, a nonprofit institute that he and Fraser helped establish in 1992. In 1998, he endowed TIGR with half of his original stake in Celera—5 per cent of the company. The gift is currently worth about a hundred and fifty million dollars, and it will be used to analyze the genomes of microbes that cause malaria and cholera and other diseases.

A few years ago, Venter developed a hole in his intestine, due to diverticulitis. He collapsed after giving a speech, and nearly died. He is fine now, but he blames stress caused by his enemies for his burst intestine. Venter has enemies of the first water. They are brilliant, famous, articulate, and regularly angry. At times, Venter seems to thrive on his enemies' indignation with an indifferent grace, like a surfer shooting a tubular wave, letting himself be propelled through their cresting wrath. At other times, he seems baffled, and says he can't understand why they don't like him.

One of Venter's most venerable enemies is James Watson, who, with Francis Crick and Maurice Wilkins, won the Nobel Prize in Medicine in 1962 for discovering the shape of the DNA molecule—what they called the double helix. Watson helped found the Human Genome Project, and he was the first head of the N.I.H. genome program. I visited him in his office at the Cold Spring Harbor Laboratory, on Long Island. The office is panelled in blond oak and has a magnificent eastward view across Cold Spring Harbor. Watson is now in his seventies. He has a narrow face, lopsided teeth, a frizz of white hair, sharp, restless eyes, a squint, and a dreamy way of speaking in sentences that trail off. He put his hands on his head and squinted at me. "In 1953, with our first paper on DNA, we never saw the possibility . . ." he said. He looked away, up at the walls. "No chemist ever thought we could read the molecule." But a number of biologists began to think that reading the human genome might just be possible, and by the mid-1980s Watson had become convinced that the decryption of the genome was an important goal and should be pursued, even if it cost billions and took decades.

Watson appeared before Congress in May of 1987 and asked for an initial annual budget of thirty million dollars for the project. The original plan was to sequence the human genome by 2005, at a projected cost of about three billion dollars. The principal work of the project is now carried out by five major DNA-sequencing centers, as well as by a number of smaller centers around the world—all academic, nonprofit labs. The big centers include one at Baylor University in Texas, one at Washington University in St. Louis, the Whitehead Institute at M.I.T., the Joint Genome Institute of the Department of Energy, and the Sanger Centre, near Cambridge, England. The Wellcome Trust of Great Britain—

the largest nonprofit medical-research foundation in the world—
is funding the Sanger work, which is to sequence a third of the
human genome. One of the founding principles of the Human
Genome Project was the immediate release of all the human code
that was found, making it available free of charge and without any
restrictions on who could use it or what anyone could do with it.

In 1984, Craig Venter had begun working at the N.I.H.,
where he eventually developed an unorthodox strategy for decoding bits of genes. At the time, other scientists were painstakingly
reading the complete sequence of each gene they studied. This
process seemed frustratingly slow to Venter. He began isolating
what are called expressed sequence tags, or E.S.T.s, which are fragments of DNA at the ends of genes. When the E.S.T.s were isolated, they could be used to identify genes in a rough way. With
the help of a few sequencing machines, Venter identified bits of
thousands of human genes. This was a source of unease at the
N.I.H., because it was a kind of skimming rather than a complete
reading of genes. Venter published his method in 1991 in an article in *Science,* along with partial sequences from about three hundred and fifty human genes. The method was not received well by
many genomic scientists. It was fast, easy, and powerful, but it
didn't look elegant, and some scientists seemed threatened by it.
Venter claims that two of his colleagues, who are now heads of
public genome centers, asked him not to publish his method or
move forward with it for fear they would lose their funding for
genome sequencing.

The N.I.H. decided to apply for patents on the gene fragments
that Venter had identified. James Watson blew his stack over the
idea of anyone trying to patent bits of genes, and he got into a hostile situation with the director of the N.I.H., Bernadine Healy,
who defended the patenting effort. In July of 1991, during a
meeting in Washington called by Senator Pete Domenici, of New
Mexico, to review the genome program, Watson dissed Venter's
methods. "It isn't science," he said, adding that the machines
"could be run by monkeys."

It was a strange moment. The Senate hearing room was almost empty—few politicians were interested in genes then. But Craig Venter was sitting in the room. "Jim Watson was clearly referring to Craig as a monkey in front of a U.S. senator," another scientist who was there said to me. "He portrayed Craig as the village idiot of genomics." Venter seemed to almost thrash in his chair, stung by Watson's words. "Watson was the ideal father figure of genomics," Venter says. "And he was attacking me in the Senate, when I was relatively young and new in the field."

Today, James Watson insists that he wasn't comparing Craig Venter to a monkey. "It's the patenting of genes I was objecting to. That's why I used the word 'monkey'! I hate it!" he said to me. The patent office turned down the N.I.H.'s application, but a few years later, two genomics companies, Incyte and Human Genome Sciences, adopted the E.S.T. method for finding genes, and it became the foundation of their businesses—currently worth, combined, about seven billion dollars on the stock market. Incyte and Human Genome Sciences are Celera's main business competitors. Samuel Broder, the chief medical officer at Celera, who is a former director of the National Cancer Institute, said to me, heatedly, "None of the people who severely and acrimoniously criticized Craig for his E.S.T. method ever said they were personally sorry. They ostracized Craig and then went on to use his method with never an acknowledgment."

James Watson now says, "The E.S.T. method has proved immensely useful, and it should have been encouraged."

Venter was increasingly unhappy at the N.I.H. He had received a ten-million-dollar grant to sequence human DNA, and he asked for permission to use some of the money to do E.S.T. sequencing, but his request was denied by the genome project. Venter returned the grant money with what he says was a scathing letter to Watson. In addition, Claire Fraser had been denied tenure at the N.I.H. Her review committee (which was composed entirely of middle-aged men) explained to her that it could not evaluate her work independently of her husband's. At the time, Fraser and Venter had separate labs and separate research programs. Fraser considered suing the N.I.H. for sex discrimination.

Watson was forced to resign as head of the genome project in April of 1992, in part because of the dispute over patenting Craig Venter's work. That summer, Venter was approached by a venture capitalist named Wallace Steinberg, who wanted to set up a company that would use Venter's E.S.T. method to discover genes, create new drugs, and make money. "I didn't want to run a company, I wanted to keep doing basic research," Venter says. But Steinberg offered Venter a research budget of seventy million dollars over 10 years—a huge amount of money, then, for biotech. Venter, along with Claire Fraser and a number of colleagues, left the N.I.H. and founded TIGR, which is a nonprofit organization. At the same time, Steinberg established a for-profit company, Human Genome Sciences, to exploit and commercialize the work of TIGR, which was required to license its discoveries exclusively to its sister company. Thus Venter got millions of dollars for research, but he had to hand his discoveries over to Human Genome Sciences for commercial development. Venter had one foot in the world of pure science and one foot in a bucket of money.

By 1994, the Human Genome Project was mapping the genomes of model organisms, which included the fruit fly, the roundworm, yeast, and *E. coli* (the organism that lives in the human gut), but no genome of any organism had been completed, except virus genomes, which are relatively small. Venter and Hamilton O. Smith (who was then at the Johns Hopkins School of Medicine) proposed speeding things up by using a technique known as whole-genome shotgun sequencing. In shotgunning, the genome is broken into small, random, overlapping pieces, and each piece is sequenced, or read. Then the jumble of pieces is reassembled in a computer that compares each piece to every other piece and matches the overlaps, thus assembling the whole genome.

Venter and Smith applied for a grant from the N.I.H. to shotgun-sequence the genome of a disease-causing bacterium called *H. influenzae,* or H. flu for short. It causes fatal meningitis in children. They proposed to do it in just a year. H. flu has 1.8 million letters of code, which seemed massive then (though the human code is two thousand times as long). The review panel at the N.I.H. gave Venter's proposal a low score, essentially rejecting it. According to Venter, the panel claimed that an attempt to shotgun-sequence a whole microbe was excessively risky and perhaps impossible. He appealed. The appeals process dragged on, and he went about shotgunning H. flu anyway. Venter and the TIGR team had nearly finished sequencing the H. flu genome when, in early 1995, a letter arrived at TIGR saying that the appeals committee had denied the grant on the ground that the experiment wasn't feasible. Venter published the H. flu genome a few months later in *Science.* Whole-genome shotgunning had worked. This was the first completed genome of a free-living organism.

It seems quite possible that Venter's grant was denied because of politics. The review panel seems to have hated the idea of giving N.I.H. money to TIGR to make discoveries that would be turned over to a corporation, Human Genome Sciences. It turned down the grant, in spite of the fact that "all the smart people knew the method was straightforward and would work," Eric Lander, the head of the genome center at M.I.T. and one of the leaders of the public project, said to me.

Around this time, Wallace Steinberg died of a heart attack, and his death provided a catalyst for a split between TIGR and Human Genome Sciences, which was run by a former AIDS researcher, William Haseltine. Venter and Haseltine were widely known to dislike each other. Venter sold his stock in Human Genome Sciences because of the rift between them, and after Steinberg died the relationship between the two organizations was formally ended.

Late in 1977, TIGR was doing some DNA sequencing for the Human Genome Project, and Venter began going to some of the project's meetings. That was when he started calling the heads of the public project's DNA-sequencing centers the Liars' Club, claiming that their predictions about when they would finish a task and how much it would cost were false. This did not win Venter many friends. But he seemed to have a point.

Francis Collins, a distinguished medical geneticist from the University of Michigan, had become the head of the N.I.H. genome program shortly after James Watson resigned in 1992. In early January 1998, an internal budget projection from Collins's office somehow found its way to Watson (he seems to find out everything that's happening in molecular biology). This budget projection—it is not clear whether it was formal or was just an unofficial projection—was a document about eight pages long. It contained a graph marked "Confidential" indicating that Collins planned to spend only sixty million dollars per year on direct human-DNA sequencing through 2005. It also predicted that by that year—when the human genome was supposed to be completed—only 1.6 billion to 1.9 billion letters of human code would be sequenced; that is, slightly more than half of the human genome.

This upset Watson, and he decided to discuss it with Eric Lander. On January 17, Watson travelled to Rockefeller University, on the East Side of Manhattan, where Lander was giving the prestigious Harvey Lecture. The two men met after the lecture at the faculty club at Rockefeller. They were dressed in black tie and were somewhat inebriated. Traditionally among medical people, the Harvey Lecture is given and listened to under the influence.

The Rockefeller faculty club overlooks a lawn and sycamore trees and the traffic of York Avenue. Watson and Lander sat down with cognacs at a small table in a dim corner of the room, on the far side of a pool table, where they could talk without being overheard. Also present and drinking cognac was a biologist named Norton Zinder, who is one of Watson's best friends. Zinder, like Watson, is a founder of the Human Genome Project. One of the older men brought up the confidential budget document with Lander, and both of them began to press him about it. They felt that it provided evidence that Collins did not intend to spend more than sixty million dollars a year on human-DNA sequencing—nowhere near enough to get the job done, they felt.

Watson evidently felt that Lander had influence with Francis Collins, and he urged him to try to persuade Collins to spend more on direct sequencing of human DNA, and to twist Congress's arm for more money.

Norton Zinder was somewhat impaired with cocktails. "This thing is potchkeeing along, going nowhere!" he said, hammering the little table and waving his arms as he spoke. For him, the issue was simple: he had had a quadruple coronary bypass, and he had been receiving treatments for cancer, and now he was afraid he would not live to see the deciphering of the human genome. This was intolerable. The human genome had begun to seem like a vision of Canaan to Norton Zinder, and he thought he wouldn't make it there.

Eric Lander did not view things the way the older biologists did. In his opinion, the problem was organizational. The Human Genome Project was "too bloody complicated, with too many groups." He felt the real problem was a lack of focus. He wanted the project to create a small, élite group that would do the major sequencing of human DNA—shock cavalry that would lead a charge into the human genome. Implicitly, he thought its leader should be Eric Lander.

The three men downed their cognacs with a sense of frustration. "I had essentially given up seeing the human genome in my lifetime," Zinder says.

At about the same moment that Watson and his friends were lamenting the slowness of the public project, the Perkin-Elmer Corporation, which was a manufacturer of lab instruments, was secretly talking about a corporate reorganization. It controlled more than ninety per cent of the market for DNA-sequencing equipment, and it was developing the ABI Prism 3700. The Prism was then only a prototype sitting in pieces in a laboratory in Foster City, California, but already it looked as if it were going to be at least ten times faster than any other DNA-sequencing machine. Perkin-Elmer executives began to wonder just what it could do. One day Michael Hunkapillar, who was then the head of the company's instrument division, got out a pocket calculator and estimated that several hundred Prisms could whip through a molecule of human DNA in a few weeks, although only in a rough way. To fill in the gaps—places where the DNA code came out garbled or wasn't read properly by the machines—it would be necessary to sequence the molecule again and again. This is known as repeat sequencing, or manyfold coverage, and might take a few years. Hunkapillar persuaded the chief executive of Perkin-Elmer, Tony White, to restructure the business and create a genomics company.

In December 1997, executives from Perkin-Elmer began telephoning Venter to see if he'd be interested in running the new company. He blew them off at first, but in early February 1998, he went to California with a colleague, Mark Adams, to look at the prototype Prism. When they saw it, they immediately understood its significance. Before the end of that day, Venter, Adams, and Hunkapillar had laid out a plan for decoding the human genome. A month later, Norton Zinder, Watson's friend, flew to California to see the machine. "It was just a piece of equipment sitting on a table, but I said, 'That's it! We've got the genome!' he recalled. Zinder joined Celera as a member of its board of advisers, and received stock in the company, which has considerably enriched him. ("The chemists have been cleaning up," he said to me. "Now biologists have their hands on the money, too.") Zinder and Watson have maintained their friendship but have agreed not to speak about Celera with each other. They evidently fear that one or both of them could have a stroke arguing about Craig Venter.

At eleven o'clock in the morning on May 8, 1998, Craig Venter and Mike Hunkapillar walked into the office of Harold Varmus, who was then the director of the N.I.H., and announced the pending formation of a corporation, led by Venter, that was going to decode the human genome. (Celera did not yet have a name.) They proposed to Varmus that the company and the public project collaborate, sharing their data and—this point is enormously important to scientists—sharing the publication of the human genome, which meant sharing the credit and the glory for having done the work, including the unspoken possibility of a Nobel Prize. Varmus strongly suspected that this wasn't a sincere offer, and he told them that he needed time, particularly to check with Francis Collins. Later that same day, Venter and Hunkapillar drove to Dulles Airport, where they met Collins at the United Airlines Red Carpet Club, and again offered collaboration. Venter recalls that Collins seemed upset. Collins recalls that he merely asked Venter for time to consider the offer. Time was one thing Venter was not prepared to give.

Venter had alerted *The New York Times* to the story about the creation of the new company, and just an hour or so after the meeting with Collins he called the *Times* and told the paper it should run it. In the story, Venter announced that he would sequence the human genome by 2001—four years ahead of the public project— and he would do it, he claimed, for between a hundred and fifty and two hundred million dollars—less than a tenth of the projected cost of the public project. The *Times* reporter, Nicholas Wade, implied that the Human Genome Project might not meet its goals and might be superfluous.

Four days later, on May 12, Venter and Hunkapillar went to the Cold Spring Harbor Laboratory, where a meeting of the heads of the Human Genome Project was taking place. Venter got up and told them, in effect, that they could stop working, since he was going to sequence the human genome *tout de suite.* Later that week, sitting beside Varmus and Collins at a press conference, Venter looked out at a room full of reporters and suggested that biology and society would be better off if the Human Genome Project shifted gears and moved forward to do the genome of the . . . mouse.

It was a fart in church of magnitude nine. "The mouse is essential for interpreting the human genome," Venter tried to explain, but that didn't help. In the words of one head of a sequencing center who was at the Cold Spring Harbor meeting, "Craig has a certain lack of social skills. He goes into that meeting thinking everyone is going to thank him for doing the human genome himself. The thing blew up into a huge explosion." The head of another center recalled, "Craig came up to me afterward, and he said, 'Ha, ha, I'm going to do the human genome. You should go do the mouse.' I said to him, 'You bastard. You *bastard*,' and I almost slugged him."

They felt that Venter was trying to stake out the human genome for himself as a financial asset while at the same time stealing the scientific credit. They felt that he was belittling their work. Venter said that he would make the genome available to the public but would charge customers who wanted to see and work with Celera's analyzed data.

James Watson was furious. He did not like the idea of having to pay money to Craig Venter for anything. Watson did not attend Venter's presentation, but he appeared in the lobby afterward, where he repeatedly said to people, "He's Hitler. This should not be Munich." To Francis Collins he said, "Are you going to be Churchill or Chamberlain?"

Venter left the meeting soon afterward, and he and Watson have exchanged only chilly greetings since.

The British leaders of the public project—John Sulston, the director of Sanger Centre, and Michael Morgan, of the Wellcome Trust—reacted swiftly to Venter's announcement. They were in England, but they flew to the United States, and the next day arrived at Cold Spring Harbor, where they found things in disarray, if not in fibrillation, with scientists wondering if the Human Genome Project was about to die. To a standing ovation, Michael Morgan got up and read a Churchillian statement declaring that the Wellcome Trust would nearly double its funding for the public project, and would decode a full third of the human genome, and would challenge any "opportunistic" patents of the genome. "We were reacting, in part, to Craig's suggestion that we just close up shop and go home," Morgan says now.

Venter also announced that Celera would use the whole-genome shotgun method. The public project was using a more conventional method. John Sulston and Robert Waterston, the head of the sequencing center at Washington University, published a letter in *Science* asserting that Venter's method would be "woefully inadequate." Francis Collins was quoted in *USA Today* as saying that Celera was going to produce "the Cliffs Notes or the Mad Magazine version" of the human genome. Collins says now that his words were taken out of context, and he regrets the quote.

The company forged from Perkin-Elmer amid the turmoil was the P.E. Corporation, which holds the P.E. Biosystems Group, the unit that makes the Prism machines, and Celera Genomics. Michael Hunkapillar, who is now the president of P.E. Biosystems, believed that he could sell a lot of machines to everyone, including the Human Genome Project. There was a fat profit margin in the chemicals the machines use. The chemicals cost far more than the machine over the machine's lifetime. This was the razor-blade principle: if you put razors in people's hands, you will make money selling blades.

In August, Incyte Pharmaceuticals announced that it was starting a human-genome project of its own. In September, James Watson quietly went to some key members of Congress and persuaded them to spend more money on the public project. At the same time, the leaders of the project announced a radical new game plan: they would produce a "working draft" of the human genome by 2001—a year ahead of when Venter said he'd be done—and a finished, complete version by 2003. An epic race had begun.

A couple of months ago, Michael Morgan, of the Wellcome Trust, was talking to me about Venter and what had happened with the creation of Celera. "From the first press release, Craig saw the public program as something he wanted to denigrate," Morgan said. "This was our first sign that Celera was setting out to undermine the international effort. What is it that motivates Craig? I think he's motivated by the same things that drive other scientists—personal ego, a degree of altruism, a desire to push human knowledge forward—but there must be something else that drives the guy. I think Craig has a huge chip on his shoulder that makes him want to be loved. I actually thing Craig is desperate to win a Nobel Prize. He also wants to be very, very rich. There is a fundamental incompatibility there."

One day, I ran into a young player in the Human Genome Project. He believed in the worth and importance of the project, and said that he had turned down a job offer from Celera. He didn't have any illusions about human nature. He said, "Here's why everyone is so pissed at Craig. The whole project started when James Watson persuaded Congress to give him money for the human genome, and he turned around and gave it to his friends— they're the heads of centers today. It grew into a lot of money, and then the question was, Who was going to get the Nobel Prize? In the United States, there were seventeen centers in the project, and there was no quality control. It didn't matter how bad your data was, you just had to produce it, and people weren't being held accountable for the quality of their product. Then Celera appeared. Because of Celera, the N.I.H. was suddenly forced to consolidate its funding. The N.I.H. and Francis Collins began to dump more than eighty per cent of the money into just three centers—Baylor, Washington University, and M.I.T.—and they jacked everybody else. They had to do it, because they had to race Celera, and they couldn't control too many players. So all but three centers were cut drastically, and some of the labs closed down. Celera was not just threatening their funding but threatening their very lives and everything they had spent years building. It's kind of sad. Now those people hang around meetings, and the leaders treat them like 'If you're really nice, we'll give you a little piece of the mouse.' That's the reason so many of them are so angry at Celera. It's easier for them to go after Craig than to go after Francis Collins and the N.I.H."

At Celera's headquarters in Rockville, I was shown how human DNA was shotgunned into small pieces when it was sprayed through a hospital nebulizer that cost a dollar-fifty. The DNA fragments were then introduced into *E. coli* bacteria, and grown in glass dishes. The bacteria formed brown spots—clones—on the dishes. Each spot had a different fragment of human DNA growing in it. The dishes were carried to a room where three robots sat in glass chambers the size of small bedrooms. Each robot had an arm that moved back and forth rapidly over a dish. Little needles on the arms kept stabbing down and taking up the brown spots.

Craig Venter stood watching the robots move. The room smelled faintly like the contents of a human intestine. "This used to be done by hand. We've been picking fifty-five thousand clones a day," he said. (Later, Celera got that rate up to a hundred and twenty thousand clones a day.) All the DNA fragments would eventually wind up in the Prism sequencing machines, and what would be left, at the end, was a collection of up to twenty-two million random fragments of sequenced human DNA. Then the river of shattered DNA would come to the computer, and to a computer scientist named Eugene Myers, who with his team devised the First Assembly.

Gene Myers has dark hair and a chiselled, handsome face. He wears glasses and a green half-carat emerald in his left ear and brown Doc Martens shoes. He also has a ruby and a sapphire that he will wear in his ear, instead of the emerald, depending on his mood. He is sensitive to cold. On the hottest days of summer, Myers wears a yellow Patagonia fibrepile jacket, and he keeps a scarf wrapped around his neck. "My blood's thin," he explained to me. He says the scarf is a reference to the DNA of whatever organism he happens to be working on. When I first met Myers, in the hot summer of 1999, he was keeping himself warm in his fruit-fly scarf. It had a black-and-white zigzag pattern. This spring, Myers started wearing his human scarf, which has a green chenille weave of changing stripes. He intended his scarf to make a statement about the warfare between Celera and the public project. "I picked green for my human scarf because I've heard that green is a positive, healing color," he said. "I really want all this bickering to go away." His office is a cubicle in a sea of cubicles, most of which are stocked with Nerf guns, Stomp Rockets, and plastic Viking helmets. Occasionally, Myers puts the "Ride of the Valkyries" on a boom box, and in a loud voice he declares war. Nerf battles sweep through Celera whenever the tension rises. Myers fields a compound double-action Nerf Lock-N-Load Blaster equipped with a Hyper*Sight. "Last week we slaughtered the chromosome team," he said to me.

Myers used to be a professor of computer science at the University of Arizona in Tucson. He specializes in combinatorial algorithms. This involves the arrangements and patterns of objects. One day in 1995, he got a telephone call from a geneticist named James Weber, at the Marshfield Medical Research Foundation in Wisconsin. Weber said he felt that whole-genome shotgunning would work for organisms that have very long DNA molecules, such as humans. He wondered if Myers could help him with the math.

Jim Weber submitted a proposal to the N.I.H. for a grant—twelve million dollars—to support a pilot study of the shotgun approach on the human genome. This might speed up the project dramatically, he suggested. Weber was invited to speak to the annual meeting of the heads of the project, held in Bermuda.

Weber was nervous about it, and wanted Gene Myers to go with him to help explain the math. "Jim asked them to invite me, but they didn't," Myers says. So on February 26, 1996, Jim Weber went alone to the meeting in Bermuda and tried to make a case for shotgunning the human genome. He found himself facing a U-shaped table with about 40 people at it. "They trounced Jim," Myers said. "They said it wouldn't work. They said it would be full of holes. 'A Swiss-cheese genome'—that's the term we've often heard. The grant proposal was soundly rejected."

Jim Weber says that the Swiss-cheese analogy was not far off, but that "it would have been much better to get most of the human genome quickly, even with holes in it, so that people could start using the information to understand diseases and begin to find cures for them. It would have been better if the N.I.H. had funded a pilot study. Instead, Gene and his team went out and did it. That is a huge accomplishment."

Craig Venter was hanging around while I was talking with Myers. He came up to us and said, "They not only shot Gene down—they ridiculed him. They said he was a kook. We're going to prove that Gene was right, and we're going to prove that there's something fundamentally wrong with the system."

On September 9, 1999, Venter announced that Celera had completed the sequencing of the fruit fly's DNA, and had begun to run human DNA through its sequencing machines—there were now three hundred of them crammed into Building One in Rockville. The Command Center was up and running, and from then on Celera operated in high-speed mode. One day that fall, I talked with the company's information expert, a stocky man named Marshall Peterson. He took me to the computer room, in Building Two. To get into the room, Peterson punched in a security code and then placed his hand on a sensor, which read the unique pattern of his palm. There was a clack of bolts sliding back, and we pushed through the door.

A chill of cold air washed over us, and we entered a room filled with racks of computers that were wired together. "What you're looking at in this room is roughly the equivalent of America Online's network of servers," Peterson said. "We have fifty-five miles of fibre-optic cables running through this building." Workmen standing on ladders were installing many more cables in the ceiling. "The disk storage in this room is five times the size of the Library of Congress. We're getting more storage all the time. We need it."

He took me to the Command Center, where a couple of people were hanging around consoles. Some of the consoles had not had equipment installed in them yet. A big screen on the wall showed CNN Headline News. "I've got a full-time hacker working for me to prevent security breaches," Peterson said. "We're getting feelers over the Internet all the time—people trying to break into our system." Celera would be dealing with potentially valuable information about the genes of all kinds of organisms. Peterson thought that some of what he called feelers—subtle hacks and unfriendly probes—had been emanating from Celera's competitors. He said he could never prove it, though. Lately, the probes had been coming from computers in Japan. He thought it was American hackers co-opting the Japanese machines over the Internet.

By October 20, forty days after Celera started running human DNA through its machines, the company announced that it had sequenced 1.2 billion letters of human code. The letters came in small chunks from all over the genome. Six days later, Venter announced that Celera had filed provisional patent applications for six thousand five hundred human genes. The applications were for placeholder patents. The company hoped to figure out later which of the genes would be worth patenting in earnest.

A gene patent gives its holder the right to make commercial products and drugs derived from the gene for a period of 17 years. Pharmaceutical companies argue that patents are necessary, because without them businesses would never invest the hundreds of millions of dollars that are needed to develop a new drug and get it through the licensing process of the Food and Drug Administration. ("If you have a disease, you'd better hope someone patents the gene for it," Venter said to me.) On the other hand, parcelling out genes to various private companies could lead to what Francis Collins refers to as the "Balkanization of the human genome," a paralyzing situation that might limit researchers' access to genes.

Venter insists that Celera is an information company and that patenting genes is not its main goal. He has said that Celera will attempt to get patents on not more than about three hundred human genes. There is no question that Celera hopes to nail down some very valuable genes—billion-dollar genes, perhaps.

Celera's stock has drifted since the summer, but around Halloween, as investors began to realize that the company was cranking out the human genome—and filing large numbers of placeholder patents—it jumped up to forty dollars a share. (The prices here are pre split prices. Adjusted for today's prices, the stock moved up to twenty dollars.) On December 2, the Human Genome Project announced that it had deciphered most of the code on chromosome No. 22, the second-shortest chromosome in the human genome. This made the reading of the whole genome seem more imminent, and Celera's stock began a spectacular rise. It shot up that day by nine points, to close at over seventy dollars. Then, after the market's close on Thursday, December 16, Jeff Fischer, a cofounder of the Web site called The Motley Fool, announced that he was buying shares of Celera for his own portfolio. It is called the Rule Breaker Portfolio, and it has famously delivered wealth— Fischer bought AOL very early, for example. On that Friday morning, a great number of people tried to buy Celera, and they drove the stock up twenty points. It was on its way to the pre-split equivalent of more than five hundred dollars a share. That past summer, it had been trading at fourteen.

I went to visit Celera on Tuesday of the following week, and that morning the company's stock could not open for trading. Everyone wanted to buy it, and nobody wanted to sell it. While the stock was halted—at a hundred and one dollars a share—I wandered around. There was a feeling of paralysis in the air, and I sensed that not much work was getting done that day, except by the machines. Employees were checking the quote on the Internet and wondering what their net worth would be when the stock opened. The lobby now sported fish-eye security cameras. The walls smelled of fresh paint, and the floors had a new purple carpet with a pattern that resembled worms. They were meant to look like fragments of DNA.

I found Hamilton O. Smith in his lab, puttering around with human DNA in tiny test tubes, but his heart was not in the job. He was tired. He explained that he was renovating an old house that he and his wife had bought. He had stayed up all night ripping carpet out of the basement, because new carpets were due to arrive that morning. He had driven to work in his '83 Mercury Marquis. He owned thousands of shares of Celera.

Smith passed a computer, stopped, and brought up a quote.

Celera had finally opened for trading. It had gapped up—jumped instantly upward—by thirteen points. It was at a hundred and fourteen. Smith's net worth had gapped up by something on toward a million dollars. "Is there no end to this?" he muttered.

Craig Venter came into Smith's lab and asked him to lunch. In the elevator, Smith said to him, "I can't stand it, Craig. The bubble will break." They sat down beside each other in the cafeteria and ate cassoulet from bowls on trays.

"This defies common sense," Smith said. "It's really impossible to put a value on this company."

"That's what we've been telling the analysts," Venter said.

Later that day, I ended up in Claire Fraser's office at TIGR headquarters, a complex of semi-Mission-style buildings a couple of miles from Celera's offices and labs. Fraser is a tall, reserved woman with dark hair and brown eyes, and her voice has a faint New England accent. She grew up in Saugus, Massachusetts. In high school, she says, she was considered a science geek. "The only lower citizens were the nerdy guys in the audiovisual club. Of course, now they're probably in Hollywood." Her office has an Oriental rug on the floor and a table surrounded by Chippendale chairs. It was originally Venter's office. ("This is Craig's extravagant taste, not mine," she explained.) She wore an expensive-looking suit. Two poodles, Cricket and Marley, slept by a fireplace.

"Before genomics, every living organism was a black box," she said. "When you sequence a genome, it's like walking into a dark room and turning on a light. You see entirely new things everywhere."

Fraser placed a sheet of paper on the table. It contained an impossibly complicated diagram that looked like a design for an oil refinery. She explained that it was an analysis of the genome of cholera, a single-celled microbe that causes murderous diarrhea. TIGR scientists had finished sequencing the organism's DNA a few weeks earlier. Much of the picture, she said, was absolutely new to our knowledge of cholera. About a quarter of the genes of every microbe that had been decoded by TIGR were completely new to science, and were not obviously related to any other gene in any other microbe. To the intense surprise and wonder of the scientists, nature was turning out to be an uncharted sea of unknown genes. The code of life was far richer than anyone had imagined.

Fraser's eyes moved quickly over the diagram. "Yes . . . wow. . . . There may be important transporters here. . . . You see these transporters in other bacteria, and . . . I don't know . . . it looks like there could be potential for designing a new drug that could block them."

The phone rang. Fraser walked across her office, picked up the receiver, and said softly, "Craig? Hello. What? It closed at a hundred and twenty-five?" Pause. "I don't know how much it's worth—you're the one with the calculator."

Their net worth had jumped above a hundred and fifty million dollars that day.

Fraser drove home, and I followed her in my car. Their house is in the country outside Washington. It sits behind a security gate at the end of a long driveway. Venter arrived in a new Porsche. The car would do zero to sixty in five seconds, he said. In the vaulted front hall of the house there was a large stained-glass window showing branches of a willow tree, and there was a model of H.M.S. *Victory* in a glass case. A jumble of woodworking machines—a bandsaw, a table saw, a drill press—filled a shop attached to the garage. Venter has worked with wood since high school.

In the kitchen, Claire fixed dinner for the poodles, while Craig circled the room, talking. "We created close to two hundred millionaires in the company today. I think most of them had not a clue this would happen when they joined Celera. We have a secretary who became a millionaire today. She's married to a retired policeman. He went out looking to buy a farm." He popped a Bud Light and swigged it. "This could only happen in America. You've got to love this country." Claire fed the poodles.

There were no cooking tools in the kitchen that I could see. The counters were empty. The only food I noticed was a giant sack of dog food, sitting on top of an island counter, and two boxes of cold cereal—Quaker Oatmeal Squares and Total. In the guest bathroom, upstairs, there were no towels, and the walls were empty. The only decorative object in the bathroom was a cheap wicker basket piled with little soaps and shampoos they had picked up in hotels.

We went to a restaurant and ate steak. "We're in the Wild West of genomics," Venter said. "Celera is more than a scientific experiment; it's a business experiment. Our stock-market capitalization as of today is three and a half billion dollars. That's more than the projected cost of the Human Genome Project. I guess that's saying something. The combined market value of the Big Three genomics companies—Celera, Human Genome Sciences, and Incyte—was about twelve billion dollars at the end of today. This wasn't imaginable six months ago. The Old Guard doesn't have control of genomics anymore." He chewed steak, and looked at his wife. "What the hell are we going to do with all this money? I could play around with boats. . . ."

Claire started laughing. "My God, I couldn't live with you."

"The money's nice, but it's not the motivation," Venter said to me. "The motivation is sheer curiosity."

In December 1999, Celera and the Human Genome Project discussed whether it would be possible to collaborate. There was one formal meeting, and there were many points of difference. Meanwhile, Celera's stock seemed to go into escape velocity from the earth. In January, it soared over two hundred dollars a share. Celera filed to offer more shares to the public, and declared a two-for-one stock split. Shortly after the split, on February 25, the stock hit an all-time high of two hundred and seventy-six dollars a share (more than five hundred and fifty dollars, pre-split). Celera's stock-market value reached fourteen billion dollars, and Venter's worth surpassed seven hundred million dollars. It looked as if Venter could become a billionaire of biotechnology.

Then, on March 6, newspapers carried reports that the discussions between Celera and the public project had collapsed. The main point of disagreement, according to officials at the public project, was that Celera wanted to keep control of intellectual property in the human genome. Celera intended to license its analyzed database to pharmaceutical companies and nonprofit research institutions, for payment. Celera said that it would let anyone use the data, but that any other company would be forbidden from reselling the data. The Human Genome people insisted that the period of restriction on the data could be for no more than a year, and after that the data should be totally public. Celera argued that it didn't want its competitors to resell the information and profit from Celera's work. Celera's stock began to drop.

On March 14, President Clinton and Prime Minister Blair of Great Britain released a joint statement to the effect that all the genes in the human body "should be made freely available to scientists everywhere." The statement had been drafted with the help of Francis Collins and his staff, and had been in the works for a year. It was vague, but it looked like an Anglo-American smart bomb aimed at Celera, and it scared the daylights out of investors in biotechnology stocks, who feared that potentially lucrative patents on genes might be undermined by some new government policy.

On the day of the Clinton-Blair statement, Celera's stock went into a screaming nosedive. It dropped 57 dollars in a matter of hours, amid trading halts and order imbalances. The other genomic stocks crashed in sympathy with Celera, and this, in turn, dragged down the Nasdaq, which that day suffered the second-largest point loss in its history. Short-sellers—people who profit from the decline of a stock—encrusted Celera like locusts. As of this writing, the Nasdaq has not recovered. Venter's mother telephoned him afterward, and said to him, "Craig, you've managed to do overnight what Alan Greenspan has been trying to do for years."

"It's not every day you get attacked by the President and the Prime Minister," Venter said to me late that night on the telephone. "I'm expecting a call from the Pope any day now, asking me to recant the human genome." He sounded wired and exhausted. "I feel a little like Galileo. They offered to have a barbecue with him, right? Look, I'm not likening myself to Galileo in terms of genius, but it is clear that the human genome is the science event of our time. I am going to publish the genome, and that's what the threat to the public order is. If Celera was keeping the genome a secret, the way Incyte and Human Genome Sciences are, you wouldn't hear a peep out of the government. Our publishing the genome makes a mockery of the fifteen years and billions of dollars the public project has spent on it."

Venter seemed particularly upset with the British part of the public project. "In my opinion," he said, "the Wellcome Trust is now trying to justify how, as a private charity, it gave what I think was well over a billion dollars to the Sanger Centre to do just a third of the human genome, largely at the expense of the rest of British medical science. Clinton and Blair took forty billion dollars out of the biotechnology industry today—that's how much was lost by investors. It was money that would pay for cures for cancer, and it was taken off the table, all because some bastards at the Wellcome Trust are trying to cover up their losses."

I called Michael Morgan, at the Wellcome Trust, to see what he had to say about this. "In hindsight, it is easy to ascribe to us Machiavellian powers that the Prince would have been proud of," he said dryly. "As for the allegation that I'm a bastard, I can easily disprove it using the technology of the Human Genome Project."

The day after the Clinton-Blair statement and the crash in biotech stocks, a White House spokesman made a point of telling reporters that the Administration supported the patenting of genes.

On March 24, Venter and his colleagues published a substantially complete genome of the fruit fly—*Drosophila*—in *Science.* It was also published by Celera on a CD, which Venter had placed on the chairs of thirteen hundred fly researchers at a conference in Pittsburgh. Venter emphasized the fact that the fly genome had been a collaboration with a publicly funded project. In other words, he was suggesting there was no real reason that the Human Genome

Project couldn't collaborate with Celera, too. The fly project—known as the Berkeley Drosophila Genome Project—is headed by a fly geneticist named Gerald Rubin.

"One of the things I really like about Craig Venter is that he almost totally lacks tact," Rubin said to me. "If he thinks you are an idiot, he will say so. I find that way of dealing very enjoyable. Craig is like somebody who's using the wrong fork at a fancy dinner. He'll tell you what he thinks of the food, but he won't even think about what fork he's using. It was a great collaboration."

John Sulston, the head of the Sanger Centre, told the BBC that he felt Celera planned to "Hoover up all the public data, which we are producing, add some of their own, and sell it as a packaged product." He added, "The emerging truth is absolutely extraordinary. They really do intend to establish a complete monopoly position on the human genome for a period of at least five years," and he said, "It's something of a con job."

"Sulston essentially called us a fraud. It's like he's been bit by a rabid animal," Venter fumed.

"It's puzzling. To me, the whole fight defies rational analysis," Hamilton O. Smith said to me, shortly after his net worth had cratered in Celera's mudslide. "But the publicly funded labs are angry for reasons I can partly understand. We took it away from them. We took the big prize away from them, when they thought they would be the team that would do the whole human genome and go down in history. Pure and simple, they hate us."

On April 6, Venter announced that Celera had finished the sequencing phase of the human genome, and was moving on to First Assembly. Celera had produced some eighteen million fragments of the first genome, perhaps Craig Venter's. Soon afterward, on an unseasonably warm day, while the cherry trees were in full blossom, I visited Celera to see how the assembly was going. I found Gene Myers in his cubicle, looking chilled. He was bundled up in his yellow fibrepile jacket and his green human scarf. He and his team had started running chunks of human DNA code through the computers over the weekend. The first run had resulted in a mess—something was wrong with the software. They had done some tweaks, and they were running a few more chunks of code. It would take months to assemble the whole thing.

"Assembly is pretty boring," he said, somewhat apologetically.

Myers said that Celera would be using all of the Human Genome Project's human DNA code—which was published on the GenBank Web site—and would tear it into fragments and compare them with Celera's DNA code, and then the software that his team had written would try to assemble all the fragments into a whole human genome. At the same time, Celera was coolly telling the public project that its scientists could see Celera's data but only if they came to look at the data on Celera's computer. The collaboration had never come to pass.

Minutes later, one of Myers's people, a computer scientist named Knut Reinert, hurried in, and told him that the first assembled human-genome sequence had just come out of the computers. Myers put the "Ride of the Valkyries" on the boom box, and fifteen people tried to crowd into Reinert's cubicle.

Myers bent over Reinert's shoulder and said, "We got it! We got the first one! This is the first assembled human sequence we've gotten out of nature!"

What appeared on the screen was a mathematical diagram of a stretch of human DNA. It showed arrows going in various directions, connecting dots together. "The picture looks like a Super Bowl debriefing," one Celera programmer remarked.

They talked about it for a few minutes, and then everyone drifted back to work. That day, Celera's stock dropped another 20 per cent.

In early May, another company got into the business of the human genome. DoubleTwist, Inc., announced that it had teamed up with Sun Microsystems to compete with Celera. DoubleTwist and Sun were offering an analyzed database of the human genome to anyone for a fee, using the data from the Human Genome Project, not from Celera. The price was six hundred and fifty thousand dollars for a database that would be updated regularly.

At the same time, Celera's stock had gone down below a hundred dollars a share. Many investors had recently bought the secondary offering, paying 225 dollars a share for it. This brought on a slew of class-action lawsuits against Celera, filed by law firms specializing in shareholder suits. There were various claims, sparked by the fact that the secondary investors had lost 60 per cent of their money. These lawsuits will probably be consolidated, and Celera will either settle or fight them in court.

As for the science, knowledgeable observers believed that, in the end, Celera had actually spent about half a billion dollars to sequence the human genome—three hundred million more than Venter had originally predicted. Was it worth it? I asked many biologists about this, and most of them spoke the way scientists do when they believe that a great door has been opened, and light is shining deep into nature, suggesting the presence of rooms upon rooms that have never been seen before. There was also a clear sense that the door would not have been opened so soon if Craig Venter and Celera had not given it a swift kick.

"We can thank Venter in retrospect," James Watson said, leaning back and smiling and squinting at the ceiling. "I was worried he could do it, and that would stop public funding of the Human Genome Project. But if an earthquake suddenly rattled through Rockville and destroyed Celera's computers, it wouldn't make much difference." He stood up, and offered me the door.

Eric Lander, who professes to like Venter, said, "Having the human genome is like having a Landsat map of the earth, compared to a world where the map tapers off into the unknown, and says, 'There be dragons.' It's as different a view of human biology as a map of the earth in the fourteen-hundreds was compared to a view from space today." As for the war between Celera and the public project, he said, "At a certain level, it is just boys behaving badly. It happens to be the most important project in science of our time, and it has all the character of a schoolyard brawl."

Norton Zinder, Watson's friend, who had feared that he would die before he saw the human genome, said that he felt marvellous. "I made it. Now I've gotta stay alive for four more years, or I won't get all my options in Celera." Zinder, who is a vigorous-seeming older man, was sprawled in a chair in his office overlooking the East River, gesturing with both hands raised. He shifted gears and began to look into the future. "This is the beginning of the beginning," he said. "The human genome alone doesn't tell you crap. This is like Vesalius. Vesalius did the first human anatomy." Vesalius published his work in 1543, an anatomy based on his dissections of cadavers. "Before Vesalius," Zinder went on, "people didn't even know they had hearts and lungs. With the human genome, we finally know what's there, but we still have to figure out how it all works. Having the human genome is like having a copy of the Talmud but not knowing how to read Aramaic."

Family-friendly benefits such as flextime are highly touted by corporations, but low-wage workers aren't as readily permitted to use them as their higher-paid coworkers. This article by Betty Holcomb in *Ms.* magazine includes the first study to document how income and job level affect access to benefits, and interviews real people who found themselves on the outside looking in when it came to many important perks.

Betty Holcomb

FRIENDLY FOR WHOSE FAMILY?

ONE MIGHT ASSUME that Lynnell Minkins, a single mother of three, would be thrilled to work for Marriott International. Last year, Marriott made *Working Mother* magazine's list of the 100 best companies for working mothers, largely because it offers flexible work schedules, hot lines to help employees deal with child-care emergencies, and three on-site child-care centers. Minkins, a food server at the San Francisco Marriott, could use that sort of help. But it's not available to her. Instead, she never knows from week to week what her hours will be, making it hard to find and hold on to decent child care, let alone make plans. "How can I get doctor appointments if I don't know when I'll be working?" she asks. "A month ahead, the clinic says there are only these days. I take them, and then I have to work."

When her kids were younger, she relied on a neighbor, paying a flat rate to send them over whenever she had to work. But not that they're in school, she has to figure out how to get them there on days she has to be at work early. A simple schedule change could solve everything, but she hasn't asked for one. "I don't dare bring it up. I'm afraid I'll get written up." A write-up means getting disciplined, and too many write-ups can lead to losing her job.

The irony is that, at least officially, Marriott offers flextime to its approximately 135,000 U.S. employees. Yet the one time Minkins tried it, her supervisors constantly pressed her to fix the "problem," and in her annual performance review that year she was described as being "challenged" by time management. "I should have called them on it, but I let it go," she says. "People who work in these jobs, they need the money. So you don't tell anybody what's going on." Senior managers, says Minkins, don't seem to suffer the same scrutiny. "It doesn't look like their job is being challenged. The lower people, the people in the back of the house, they're having the problems."

So it goes for hundreds of thousands of lower-level workers at companies widely recognized for their "family-friendly" policies. In fact, the research conducted by the Families and Work Institute exclusively for this article shows that the workers who most need benefits such as child care and flexible hours are the least likely to get them.

Consider these facts from the study. Workers in low-wage jobs are:

- half as likely as managers and professionals to have flextime;
- less likely to have on-site child care;
- more likely to lose a day's pay when they must stay home to care for a sick child;
- three times less likely to get company-sponsored tax breaks to help pay for child care.

In addition, other studies show that workers in entry-level, low-paying, or low-status jobs are much less likely to be offered a paid maternity leave than managers are, and in the case of unpaid leave, they are less likely to get as much time off after having a baby.

"It's clear that more advantaged workers have more access to certain benefits," says Ellen Galinsky, president of the Families and Work Institute. Put another way, some families seem to count more than others. "You ask yourself if people really care about the family benefits of people who clean the toilets, who clean the office buildings after everyone else leaves," says Netsy Firestein, director of the Labor Project for Working Families in Berkeley, California. "Who's taking care of their kids? Often it's older children putting younger ones to bed, while the parents struggle to make wages and get health insurance paid."

The types of benefits currently offered are also skewed toward higher-paid workers. Child-care help, for example, comes most often in the form of company-sponsored tax breaks or "resource and referral" hot lines. Both are useless to workers like Minkins, who don't make enough to pay much in taxes and can't afford the licensed child care the hot line refers them to. "Most of it is as much as $100 a week just to watch my kids before and after school. Maybe I could afford $50, but not $100!" Minkins says. Her problem is far from unique. According to *The Wall Street Journal,* a huge 85 percent of Marriott's U.S. employees are hourly workers—meaning low-wage. Its "core hourly employees simply couldn't afford paid care, the cost of which can easily exceed 50 percent of gross income," reports the *Journal.*

The rare companies that offer on-site child care—about 5,000 of the nation's millions of employers—often do so only at head-quarters, where managers and executives work, and the fees may still be too high for the clerical and office support staff. Just as much of a problem is that many benefits are offered only at the discretion of supervisors—who expect lower-level workers to stick to unbending schedules.

"My boss told me I should put my son in a new day care, when I couldn't work overtime on short notice," says one mother in New Hampshire who works for Bell Atlantic. "It was hard enough to find this place. I don't want to switch him now that he's used to it, and I don't think it's any of their business to tell me where to put him." Her only recourse is to transfer jobs or else continue to get disciplined for "unexcused" absences. She put in for a transfer, but that could take months and is likely to mean a loss in pay.

Even winning a temporary accommodation can be difficult. Consider the case of Tracey Kullman, an office technician for a large communications company in Albany, New York. Last summer, her disabled son was accepted for a 14-week program for special-needs kids. The only glitch: she'd have to pick him up at 4:30 every afternoon, which meant leaving work a half hour early. She figured she could work it out, given that her employer has a flextime policy and frequently wins awards for its family-friendly culture, and her job is a fairly independent one.

Yet when she approached her boss with several proposals, including taking a shorter lunch or coming in earlier, "I was told, 'Absolutely not. If we let you do this, everyone will want to do it,'" Kullman recalls. In the end, she was docked a half-hour's pay for every day her son was in the program.

Perhaps the biggest irony behind family-friendly benefits is that the workers most likely to get them don't need the help. Last year, the Hyatt Regency San Diego touted the success of a job-sharing initiative. Six women out of a workforce of 800 were sharing three jobs, and each of the women said they could afford to stop working if they had to.

"I only wanted to work part-time or I wouldn't work at all," said Dana Mazis, one of the lucky six. "This allows me time to be with my children, to take part in their school activities, and just be there for them. It also allows me to keep my career on track."

That is, of course, something that nearly all working parents say they want. Survey after survey shows that parents are hungry for more time with their families. But not many hourly workers have hopes of getting that time.

Even more disturbing, the time bind is growing worse. Short-notice overtime, rotating shifts, and strict attendance policies are growing ever more common. Many workers like Lynnell Minkins and Tracey Kullman must choose between jeopardizing their paychecks or their children's safety—an unconscionable situation, especially at companies that wave the family-friendly banner. "Your ability to care for your family should not depend on the kindness of your employer or your own doggedness in trying to win some accommodation," says Ellen Bravo, codirector of 9to5, National Association of Working Women. "Everyone should have equal access to these policies once they are on the books."

It's not that corporate leaders haven't confronted the issue of equity. Most trumpet their efforts to make benefits universally available. In presentations, Marriott officials stress that family-friendly benefits are meant for everyone, from the most senior manager to the busboy in the company's restaurants. "We have a firm stake in the sand in seeing to it that our hourly employees are served well," says Donna Klein, vice president for diversity and workforce effectiveness, and chief architect of many of Marriott's family-friendly benefits. "We have master's-level social workers dedicated to Marriott callers 24 hours a day. We help with everything from finding child care, child-care subsidies, even immigration and housing issues."

But for Minkins, that's just a lot of talk if she can't afford the benefits. Meanwhile, Marriott has refused to contribute to a fund created by hotel workers' unions to help pay for care, saying they won't contribute to something that involves employees from other companies. If Marriott participated in the union/management effort, Minkins could receive a child-care subsidy based on need—just the opposite of the way most companies dole out benefits.

The central question is whether management thinks of lower-wage workers as important to their companies, and therefore deserving of benefits. This was the issue that a group of human resource executives from the nation's leading corporations found themselves asking at a conference on the family-friendly workplace in New York City back in April of 1995. Wining and dining at the luxurious Waldorf-Astoria, they began to talk about a problem emerging in the field. They'd broken ground by introducing flextime, part-time work with benefits, job-sharing, and on-site child care at their companies. And they were getting plenty of attention for their efforts. But now, in an attack of conscience, they turned their attention to the workers who made their beds, served their food, and cleared their tables while they set workplace policies. "What about the chambermaids?" asked Arlene Johnson, a leading researcher on work-family conflict who was chairing the plenary session. "How are we meeting their needs?"

J. Thomas Bouchard, a senior vice president of IBM, who had championed the growing visibility of family-friendly benefits a few minutes earlier, now sounded a more somber note. "I don't see how we can or will. Who's going to pay for it if we try to make these things universal?" In fact, he insisted, it was probably best not to even suggest that all workers might someday have access to child care and flexible schedules via their employers. "There's nothing worse than false hope," he insisted. Better to simply acknowledge that most companies don't want to add costly new benefits or change the way people work.

In the audience, many listeners nodded their heads. Most had struggled against the corporate grain to introduce new schedules and new benefits. "It is truly guerrilla warfare in a lot of companies," says Karol Rose, a managing director of DCC, a consulting firm for family benefits. Even the tiniest schedule change can set off jitters among managers, who are terrified of losing control of workers or being dressed down for doing so. "Many workers must live with a double message from their managers," says Rose. "On the one hand, they're told that flextime and job-sharing is O.K., and on the other, they're told they have to constantly produce more with less resources. They don't know what to do."

Not only that, but the impulse to change originates most often in human resource departments, because it's the personnel people who hear workers' problems. Yet human resource people often have very little real power. Most work/family conferences, including the one in New York City, have to run sessions on how to get high-level executives to support family-friendly policies.

It can be a tough sell, especially since many top executives have never struggled with conflicts between showing up at work and taking care of their children. The benefits that companies offer tend toward low-cost or no-cost to them. Employers get their own tax write-off for providing child-care tax breaks. Flextime usually costs nothing, while it boosts productivity. Telecommuting can reduce the need for office space and improve productivity as well.

The Hyatt Regency San Diego, for example, gets a big bang for its flextime buck. Neither Dana Mazis, one of the hotel's six flextimers, nor her job-sharing partner have health insurance through the company because they are only part-time employees. And they are far more productive than just one worker would be. "It's very beneficial to the hotel. When one is out on sales calls, the other can be in the office," says Rob Cameron, their supervisor. So, will Hyatt embark on a job-sharing program open to all employees? "We're just at the beginning stages of this. We'll have to see how things work out and what is in the interest of the hotel," Cameron says.

That's the way it is at many workplaces—workers taking the risks and no certain future for family-friendly programs. And in place of institutional change, workers wind up cutting individual deals, then holding their breath, hoping they won't hurt their careers or the chances of those who follow them. It is just as easy, of course, to fail as to succeed without institutional support. "Most programs are only as strong as the supervisors," says Ellen Galinsky of the Families and Work Institute. "If you don't train supervisors, don't show them that the company is really behind flexible time and leave programs, the programs can easily fail."

Finding solutions isn't easy. Many advocates of family-friendly benefits say we have to challenge the notion that work and family are separate spheres; the workplace has to bend to the demands of the home. But those are long-range goals. In the short term, advocates are trying to win over executives by making a business case for these benefits. They are trying to disprove the ideas of people like IBM's J. Thomas Bouchard that companies can't afford benefits for all. The data is most assuredly there. Studies have shown again and again that family-friendly policies help the bottom line. Xerox, for example, improved productivity in its call centers simply by letting workers devise their own schedules.

In the end, the question is really one of power and privilege. Who has the power to change things, on what terms, and for whom? For the moment, the most progressive innovations arise out of the goodwill and good vision of a few corporate leaders. But even they are hesitant to challenge the notion that family-benefit funds could be better spent. If you ask them, "If there isn't enough money to provide benefits for everyone, why not spend what is available on the people who need it most?" they look at you as though you were speaking a foreign language. The truth is that professional, skilled workers are the ones corporations are trying to keep, and they do it with expensive benefits packages, among other things. Nonprofessional staff is more easily replaced, they believe, and thus not worth the financial investment. At the moment most employers see no need for dramatic change. "The companies sure do like getting on the lists and getting publicity," says Paul Ruppert of WFD, one of the leading consulting firms on work-family conflict in the U.S. "But you have to wonder how much change they really want to make."

The most lasting victories have come through collective action. The 40-hour work week, paid vacations, antidiscrimination laws, and, recently, the Family and Medical Leave Act were won by feminists, organized labor, and progressives working together. At long last, the labor movement has begun to take up the mantle of family-friendliness.

"The unions are finally getting religion on this," says Donna Dolan, director of work-family issues for the Communications Workers of America. Dolan has worked since the early 1980s to win pacts that include paid leave for childbirth, time off to care for sick family members, and subsidies for child care. She and other union activists helped create the first big family-friendly pact in

1989, when NYNEX agreed to create a $6 million fund to help develop and pay for child care.

In recent years, Dolan has been heartened to see the AFL-CIO take up the cause in earnest. "When you hear John Sweeney [president of the AFL-CIO] on the stump on these issues, you know we're getting somewhere," she says. Indeed, a growing number of unions have bargained for and won funds to help pay for family-friendly benefits. And there is a move afoot to help push for a paid family leave, one that replicates the sort of parental leave that workers in all other industrialized countries already have.

It is this sort of victory that gives Lynnell Minkins hope. Minkins has worked for Marriott for three years, and the stress has worn her down. "I have stomach problems, and I'm sure it's the tension of all this," she says. But she's not about to go elsewhere. "We've been fighting for three long years to get Marriott to give us regular schedules and to do what's right for people's families, to do the things that the other hotels are doing," she says. "I'm not going to quit until we win that fight for everybody."

Everybody is in play in today's job market, and *Fortune's* Devin Leonard presents a long list of inducements being dangled in front of prospective executives that range from Porsches to rock-concert tickets. In a world where Internet CEOs have changed the traditional ground rules, this story dramatizes the relentless nature of headhunters and the difficulty management has in maintaining a company amid this ongoing hiring chaos.

Devin Leonard

THEY'RE COMING TO TAKE YOU AWAY

MAX MICHAELS is getting annoyed. For the past half-hour, the 36-year-old cofounder and CEO of Knowledge-Cube, a 10-month-old startup, has been trying to persuade a young banker to come to work for him. Michaels loves the guy's résumé: Harvard Business School and a stint as associate at a major Wall Street firm before taking his current position at a boutique investment bank. This is their second meeting, and Michaels is doing all he can to pull him in. But the kid keeps throwing this unreal number at him.

Michaels tells the banker about the generous salary he could expect at KnowledgeCube and the stock options that would make him fabulously wealthy. The handsome young banker leans forward, resting his perfectly chiseled chin on his clasped hands. He nods politely. Then he reminds Michaels that he is making more than $500,000 a year. He won't come to KnowledgeCube for less.

"I can't bring you in for that much," Michaels sputters. "It would be totally unfair to everybody else."

Michaels is sitting on a faded green sofa in his office overlooking the Rockefeller Center skating rink in Manhattan. The young banker is in a matching chair on the other side of the coffee table. Michaels picked up the furniture on the cheap from the previous tenant when KnowledgeCube moved in two months earlier. Soon, he hopes to throw it all in a Dumpster and remodel the place into KnowledgeCube's corporate headquarters, the hub of branches around the world where the company plans to provide space and financing to high-tech entrepreneurs in exchange for a sizable ownership stake.

Michaels is such a fast-talking, single-minded dealmaker that, like a character out of a David Mamet play, he can almost convince you that he's really creating "the next KKR or Kleiner Perkins." In his former life, Michaels was a McKinsey consultant and then a Morgan Stanley Dean Witter investment banker. Now, having raised $40 million in capital, he's running his own show. After just 10 months in operation, he has outposts up and running in Boston and Seattle. But he needs more bodies.

So he's spending most of his time trying to woo talent to KnowledgeCube. Yes, Max Michaels is a body snatcher. He is after your best employees. He probably has some of their résumés in his briefcase right now—the four executive search firms he has retained send him stacks of them. But that's not enough. Michaels will work any angle to find the employees he needs. He offered this *Fortune* reporter $7,000 a pop to refer names of people interviewed for this article. (Nice try, Max.) Many of his other tactics work. His newly hired managing director is a former McKinsey strategy consultant. His senior managing director is from Lucent. Sitting beside Michaels on one of the sticky green chairs is his latest catch, Raghu Ram, a technology investment banker from ING Barings who joined KnowledgeCube just before the Nasdaq plunged 355 points on April 14.

Now it's April 19 and Michaels isn't letting a market slide get in his way. "I don't understand," he tells the chiseled recruit. "You're young. If this came along when I was your age, I would have jumped on it."

Ram joins in the assault. The tall, balding Ram has been on his cell phone for the past hour talking excitedly to his friends and overseas clients about his new job. Now this arrogant pup might as well be mocking him. "I'm 40 years old, I have a five-year-old kid who is autistic, and I'm trading away $2 million a year to do this," Ram explodes.

Michaels presses the banker for a quick decision: "The value [of our options] has gone up a lot since you first came in. If I were you, I'd sign up now."

"What's your doomsday scenario?" the banker asks.

"What's yours?" Michaels shoots back. "Right now, you're just one of 20,000 investment bankers in [one Wall Street recruiter's] database. My scenario is better than your current scenario."

The banker says he has a plane to catch. Matt Bruck, a KnowledgeCube managing director, shows him to the door. Michaels stays behind in the room with Ram. He takes a sip of his Dean & DeLuca takeout coffee. He is starting to wonder if he is wasting his time. "My concern with this guy," says Michaels, "is I bring him in and I'll be having the same conversation every Friday about why he's not making as much money as everybody else." He winces at the thought.

Just then, Bruck sticks his head in. "He just asked me if I could get together over the weekend," Bruck says.

Michaels cocks an eyebrow and grins. He's not through with the banker yet.

Max Michaels' no-holds-barred recruiting approach is swiftly metastasizing through the business world. The reason is obvious: Recruiting smart, capable people is the single most important job in corporate America today. The most important, that is, after keeping smart, capable people out of the hands of other body snatchers.

Customers? People are still spending. Financing? Capital's plentiful. What companies need these days is talent. That, however, is in short supply. Start with the fact that in the past three decades the nation's economy has doubled while the birth rate has dropped by 24 percent. In April the national unemployment rate fell to 3.9 percent— dipping below 4 percent for the first time in 30 years. The most frightening shortage is of skilled employees, and companies are in an all-out war for them. On the frontlines are the recruiters. According to Hunt-Scanlon Advisors, a Stamford, Conn., firm that tracks the search industry, the number of corporate headhunters skyrocketed 45 percent over the past three years, to 9,500. But even with 3,000 more recruiters on the prowl, some industries are still pleading for résumés. The Information Technology Association of America predicts that 1.6 million new jobs involving computer, Internet, and telecommunications expertise will be created in the next 12 months—and more than half are likely to go unfilled. Whoever winds up with those empty cubicles loses bigtime.

What's made all of this completely ridiculous, of course, is the explosion of high-tech startups. Armed with venture capital dollars and business plans promising swift public stock offerings, they are sucking people out of the *Fortune* 500. "We open several searches a day now in the dot-com arena," boasts Jim Boone, a top executive at recruiting firm Korn/Ferry International.

This invasion has created nightmares for anybody trying to run a business. Your skin crawls every time a valued employee requests a closed-door meeting. Not another dot-com defector! You cringe when one of them answers the phone and starts speaking in hushed tones. Is it a headhunter call? Why won't they leave your people alone? Sounds paranoid. But sometimes the paranoids have it right. When New York recruiter Cynthia Remec surveyed Wall Street investment bankers this year about their interest in dotcoms, she found that more than half had already been approached by Internet companies.

Snatching a programmer out of IBM or an e-commerce expert from PricewaterhouseCoopers is no easy task. That's why Internet CEOs have radically altered the nature of corporate recruiting, transforming it from a genteel parlor game to a fast-paced, high-stakes competition fraught with intrigue and mind games. It's not simply a matter of tempting people with stock options and a chance to work in shorts. It's about putting a recruit at the center of the universe. Want some quality time with our CEO? He's available for drinks tonight. Need some help looking for a new home? The CEO will go house-hunting with you. Worried the company might blow to smithereens? No problem. We'll find you another position. Says Ramana Bodepudi, CEO of eDaycare, a Silicon Valley startup serving day-care providers: "I tell them, 'You can find another job within half an hour—especially with this Internet experience under your belt. Hey, I'll find you another job!'"

There may even be a car in the deal. "I got a call a couple of days ago where somebody offered me a Porsche if I took a job," says Barry Trout, a senior financial services manager at Andersen Consulting's Atlanta office. "I said, 'I'm not leaving.' He said, 'We'd still like you to help us with our business plan. Can you do it on evenings or weekends? We'll pay you a great salary. We'll even buy you the Porsche!'"

This scenario may sound ludicrous, but corporate America is not laughing. All you have to do is look at the measures it has taken to keep the body snatchers at bay. Prestigious investment banks went casual. Law firms around the country raised associate salaries overnight by as much as 50 percent in January. Consulting partnerships that can't offer employees stock formed internal investment funds so they could share some Internet wealth with their employees. These defensive measures, however, go only so far. Many big companies—the smart ones, that is—are adopting the same guerrilla tactics Internet startups have used against them. They recruit people at rock concerts. They hire them at blinding speed. And, most interesting, as Internet stocks plummeted this year, they swooped in to yank their former employees back from troubled startups. "We are encouraging our people to call people who might have left and tell them to come home," says Jeanie Mabie, a recruiting director for PricewaterhouseCoopers.

Yes, the April collapse of the Nasdaq did set the body snatchers back a little. But they aren't going to stop. Nobody is. Any company that thinks it can sit back and wait for talent is kidding itself, because what we're witnessing now is just the beginning. Barring a major catastrophe, the economy should grow by 2.4 percent a year, on average, through 2008, according to the U.S. Bureau of Labor Statistics. However, the annual growth rate of the U.S. labor force is stuck at 1.2 percent, and it isn't expected to change for eight years. "If you took all of the dot-coms that have started in the last 24 months and wiped them out, you'd still have a tremendous problem in this country," says Jac Fitzenz, chairman of the Saratoga Institute, a human resources think tank in Santa Clara, Calif. Which means that in this job market, where anyone with a decent résumé gets multiple job offers, the company that does the best recruiting wins.

It was a beautiful afternoon for golf in May last year, and Myles Owens, a senior business development executive at Compaq, was playing surprisingly well considering what was really on his mind: his waterlogged stock options. No matter where he was, somebody always reminded him of them, especially the head-hunters who had started calling just as the stock began to tank. Recruiters were circling Compaq like vultures. Owens was in line for a major promotion, so he wasn't in any hurry to leave. But his phone never stopped ringing.

He couldn't even get away from the pitches as he made his way around the back nine holes of the Washington Duke Inn golf course in Durham, N.C. One of the members of his party was Bill Glynn, a partner at Southeast Interactive Technology Funds, a local venture capital firm. Glynn was talking nonstop about the startups he was backing and their upside potential. Owens had only met Glynn that morning when he spoke at a conference that Southeast Interactive sponsored at nearby Duke University. But Glynn certainly had taken a shine to him. Finally, Owens let slip what was on his mind—Compaq's share price, which had tumbled from $49 in January to the mid-20s. "You know," he told Glynn, "I'd think about doing something like that if Compaq stock ever hits fifty again."

"Why wait?" Glynn asked.

"Why wait?" Owens replied. "Because I have a lot of stock options."

Glynn gave him a penetrating look. "We could put together a package that would address that," he said.

After they'd finished their round, Glynn maneuvered Owens into his BMW 740iL and drove him back to their hotel. On the way, Glynn pitched him for 15 minutes about becoming CEO of one of Southeast's startups.

Owens' head was spinning by the time he got out of the car. What he didn't know was that Glynn had orchestrated the whole thing. Having heard good things about Owens through the industry grapevine, Glynn invited him to speak at the conference and arranged their golf outing for the sole purpose of talking to him about a job. "It was completely crafted," Glynn admits. "Everybody is in play." Including Owens: He took the job as CEO of Web startup NxView Technologies five months later.

Venture capitalists like Glynn are the people setting the tone for the new style of recruiting. The bright young nerds who constantly pitch them ideas for the next big thing rarely arrive with a battle-tested CEO. Finding one is part of what they want from venture capitalists. "It's the key to the business," says Jordan Levy, co-founder of Seed Capital Partners in Buffalo, an early-stage VC fund. "Businesses will live and die based on your ability to attract the right talent for the job."

So venture capitalists, like heart surgeons, have to be ready to intervene with extraordinary measures. Levy once flew to Denver and showed up, unannounced, at the front door of a CEO candidate for one of his startups. It was the only way he could talk to the busy executive. Every time Levy tried to call his home, the man's wife hung up on him. Why? She didn't want to move to Buffalo. The impromptu visit also gave Levy a chance to sell the man's wife on relocating, and relocate they did.

When it comes to recruiting, VCs *never* relax; after all, the right touch at the right moment can seal a deal. In March, Susan Blum, an advertising executive at A&E Television Network, was riding the chair lift up a Lake Tahoe ski slope with her husband. They struck up a conversation with another skier, who turned out to be Scott Walcheck, general partner of Integrity Partners. Walcheck told them he was investing in interactive television. What a coincidence! Blum was considering a job at RespondTV, a San Francisco company in that very field. Perhaps the venture capitalist knew the company.

Walcheck reached over and shook her hand. "I sit on the board," he said. "That company rocks." And then he whispered in Blum's ear: "You're going to be rich!"

Blum was close to accepting the job. Her ski slope encounter clinched it.

Once venture capitalists win their perfect CEO, they expect that person to recruit just as aggressively as they do. With investors looking over his shoulder, Max Michaels knows the pressure is on. He needs 60 people ASAP, which is why he's not above resorting to hardball tactics—like massaging the facts.

On that April day when he interviews the young $500,000-a-year banker, Michaels' first appointment is with Ophira Segal, a 26-year-old executive recruiter at Magdalin Weiss, a New York City search firm. Michaels wants her on board—he needs another body snatcher. But it may not be easy. Segal is nervous. She sits with her legs crossed, her hands folded in her lap, reluctant to give up her $160,000 annual income one week after the Nasdaq spill. So Michaels offers to match her current pay with a $75,000 salary, a $25,000 bonus, and KnowledgeCube options worth $60,000 at the company's current valuation. He tells her they could be worth $6 million in ten years. "I only own mutual funds," Segal says. "What if my options turn out to be worthless?"

"Come on," Michaels says. "It's very unlikely all this will go down the drain. And what's your downside really? You are going to have a great company on your résumé and you will have learned a lot. That in itself is downside protection."

Segal also feels loyal to her superiors at Magdalin Weiss. But Michaels has an answer for that. "Maybe you can help them," he insists. "Maybe we'll retain them. So you'd be doing them a favor. As long as they make money, they don't care."

Later, Michaels interviews a clean-cut associate from a major Wall Street firm, who snuck out of his office for the interview. He's definitely interested, but he also has an offer from Warburg Pincus. "It's a really tough decision," he laments.

Michaels is glad to be of assistance. He paints a picture of Warburg Pincus as an old-economy mastodon mired in a tar pit of tradition and timidity. His startup is way cooler, and Michaels assures the associate that he won't be alone if he accepts an offer. The CEO says many other bright young winners are flocking to KnowledgeCube: the recruiter from Magdalin Weiss, the chiseled banker, a Ph.D. from Cal Tech. Trouble is, Michael hasn't hired any of them yet.

At the end of the day, Michaels interviews his final candidate. The guy's résumé includes stints at Bain & Co., Lehman Brothers, and the U.S. Air Force. But more recently, he has launched two failed startups. He is unemployed and a little too eager. Michaels has the upper hand.

"I don't know about you," Michaels scolds him. "You canceled a meeting on us. [KnowledgeCube Chairman] Richard [Berman] was pissed."

"Oh," says the startup veteran, laughing nervously. He is not sure if Michaels is toying with him. (The answer: He is, like a cat playing with a small furry animal.)

"Yeah, the chairman was pissed," Michaels says. "So I think we should make you an offer and you should accept before he comes back from vacation."

Pressure tactics? You bet. This is war. And like good generals, dot-com CEOs study up on the enemy. Startup heads who poach regularly from the same big companies get a tactical edge—a blueprint of the enemies' counteroffensives.

Last September, Larry Deaton, CEO of Technauts, an Internet

software startup in Cary, N.C., wanted to steal Steven Petriccione, a 39-year-old engineer, away from IBM. Having already lured two people from IBM, Deaton knew Big Blue doesn't give up without a struggle. So Deaton sat the engineer down in a booth at a local diner and warned him it wouldn't be easy. "You should expect a sizable counteroffer," he cautioned. "Don't let it turn your head. You're not joining me for the money."

Petriccione didn't give the words of warning much thought, but Deaton was absolutely right. Petriccione's managers offered him three escalating raises, starting at 10 percent and reaching 20 percent of his salary. One of them practically got down on his knees and begged him to stay. But Petriccione announced his resignation anyway. Four days later, he picked up his 10-year-old daughter, Leah, at school on the way home. The two of them had planned a camping trip in the Blue Ridge Mountains that weekend. But as they were packing up their sweaters and sleeping bags, Petriccione's cell phone rang. It was his boss at IBM. "Look, I gotta get this resolved before the weekend," he told Petriccione. "What's it going to take?"

Petriccione cut him off. He had a four-hour car trip ahead of him. But as he headed down Interstate 40 in his Honda Prelude, his cell phone rang again. "What can we do to keep you here?" his boss pleaded. "You've proven you can produce for IBM, and we don't want to let you go."

There was a part of Petriccione that wanted to cave in. It would have made things so much simpler. His wife thought he was crazy to go to a startup. After all, her husband had been with IBM for 16 years. But Deaton's coaching had paid off. "Listen, I gotta call you back," he told his boss. He took a few minutes to collect his thoughts as he drove on through the darkening hills. Then he grabbed his cell phone and called IBM. "Look," he said to his boss. "This just isn't going to work out."

Of course, after he moved to Technauts, Petriccione himself became a recruiter, luring one of his former IBM colleagues. Most startup chiefs expect that from their new recruits, and will pay for good leads—anything from Palm Pilots to cash to, yes, cars. Sitting in the parking lot of ArsDigita, a Cambridge, Mass., software company, is a new Ferrari. It's a prize for the first employee who refers ten new hires. "It's just a way of reminding people every day as they walk in this door, 'This is important,'" says Chairman Philip Greenspun. The pandering of dot-com CEOs knows no bounds in a talent tug of war. When Dave Margulius decided to leave his job as entrepreneur-in-residence at IVP, a Silicon Valley venture capital firm, Jeff Bezos, CEO of Amazon, flew him up to his Seattle headquarters for an interview. He sat Margulius down in front of a computer and booted up the company's Web site. As Bezos was explaining why he thought Amazon's auction site was better than eBay's, Margulius was intrigued by a $150 yo-yo that was for sale. "What do you think a $150 yo-yo could be like?" he wondered aloud.

"Let's find out," Bezos replied. He hit a few keys and bought the yo-yo for his guest. (It turned out to be a competition model used by very serious yo-yo enthusiasts.)

But Bezos, who didn't return calls for this story, was bested by Josh Silverman, CEO of Evite, an event-planning Web startup in San Francisco. Silverman invited Margulius to a disco bowling party with the Evite staff, and later took him to a Barenaked Ladies concert. "Between songs, he'd say, 'How do you improve double-click on a site?'" Margulius remembers. "We were having a business discussion among 30,000 drunken revelers."

It's hard to imagine Jack Welch or any other *Fortune* 500 CEO at a Barenaked Ladies concert, but maybe they should give it a try. Indeed, until the dot-com invasion collided with a tightening job market, attracting and retaining talent was hardly Topic A at most companies. Last year, Watson Wyatt, a human resources consulting firm, surveyed 551 large U.S. companies and found that 45 percent had no formal recruiting strategy. "Even more employers [54 percent] don't have a formal strategy for retaining employees once they have been successfully recruited," the firm concluded ominously.

Perhaps that's why some of the most highly publicized efforts by big companies to keep people from hopping to the Internet—going casual, throwing perks at junior firm members—seem more like acts of desperation than serious counteroffensives. You might call it retention by fruit plate. "When I first started working here three years ago, we got free bagels two days a week and free lunch on Fridays," says one Goldman associate. "Then they took away the free bagels and they took away free lunch right before they went public. Now it's all back, and they give us this big fruit plate every day. I think they are scared to death."

Elite consulting firms that have also been targeted by dot-coms deliver the same mixed messages. Clay Deutsch, a McKinsey director who heads the firm's recruiting efforts, downplays the fact that McKinsey plans to offer associates the chance to invest in exclusive venture capital and private equity deals. It's the first time in McKinsey's 74-year history that such perks will be lavished on junior employees. But the firm isn't panicking or anything. Says Deutsch: "We are still running a net (talent) surplus." That kind of bravado makes Tom Rodenhauser laugh. He tracks McKinsey and its competitors for his consulting newsletter, *The Rodenhauser Report*. "Realistically, some of the best and brightest have left," he says. "That's scaring the bejesus out of these people."

Some companies are so scared they aren't waiting for an act of God (or an even worse Nasdaq crash) to rescue them. They are coming up with their own body-snatching tactics. Nortel Networks has started sending recruiters to baseball games, bike races, and rock concerts. Its goal is to have recruiting booths this summer at every Jimmy Buffett show. Why? It turns out engineers are parrot heads. (As well as huge Barenaked Ladies fans!) Nortel is also throwing perks like free housecleaning or spa weekends to employees who refer new hires. Twenty-nine percent of the company's 8,000 external hires in this country last year were employee referrals. "This is a war," says Mark Minichiello, Nortel's director of North American recruiting. "You need to create the mindset that this is just as much a priority as delivering the next product."

Nortel's main competitor, Lucent, is also striking back. The company got tired of watching fast-moving startups snap up prime candidates. So, in January, the corporation started hosting quick-hire job fairs around the country. Recruiters meet job applicants who have been prescreened over the telephone or via the Web. The candidates are interviewed, drug-tested, and hired the same day if they meet Lucent's standards. Some 6,000 people recently went through the grueling 12-hour process in New Jersey. At the end of the day, 200 walked out with new jobs and T-shirts announcing their career change. "They literally walked out with a starting date," says Jim Baughman, Lucent's recruiting director.

Lucent is also trying to make sure that dot-coms don't seduce its star employees. Plenty have tried to woo Jacob Larsen, a 30-year-old director in Lucent's optical networking group. You can hardly blame them. He speaks four languages, got his MBA from Dartmouth, and entered Lucent's Global Leadership Development Program in 1977. Larsen's customers regularly drop hints that they'd like to hire him. Frankly, it gets tiresome. "It kind of screws up the business relationship," he says. "I'm trying to generate interest in breakthrough technology and they are interested in me personally."

Then again, it's always nice to get an offer. Larsen has gotten four serious ones, and he used them to evaluate his deal at Lucent. His conclusion: His situation at the *Fortune* 500 company is hard to beat. Lucent has assigned Larsen a career mentor, given him more stock options, and sent him off on a Caribbean vacation in recent months. "I have a personal friend who is on his sixth startup and is poor as a dog," Larsen says. "Meanwhile, I'm going to the Bahamas with my wife. So I'm at peace with my decision to stay at Lucent."

In this climate, any valued employee who shows a touch of wanderlust is likely to be accosted by a manager with a menu of financial treats. Disney gave certain managers the authority to award salary increases on the spot. "It's responsive to the dot-com speed," says William Wilkinson, Disney's senior HR vice president. Managers at FedEx, too, have the power to reward employees with instant raises and bonuses.

It was probably inevitable that some companies would seek revenge on the body snatchers. In May, Andersen Consulting sent a letter to nearly 3,000 of the firm's recently departed alumni telling them the door was open if they wanted to come back. "We actually started this before the recent Nasdaq roller coaster, but we couldn't be happier with the timing," gloats David Reed, Andersen's director of U.S. recruiting. "There are a lot of people out there whose options are underwater and whose IPO aspirations are dashed."

It's a big change for a giant consulting firm that once treated former employees as personae non gratae. But Andersen was hit hard by the body snatchers. Famously, its former CEO George Shaheen abandoned ship last fall to go to Webvan, an Internet grocer. In the May letter, Andersen boasts of changes: the newly created internal venture capital fund, the pre-IPO startups it is investing in and nurturing at its 22 Dot.Com Launch Centers, and the profits the firm hopes to share with employees. Come back before August 31, the letter promises, and get extra equity! Maybe Shaheen is on the mailing list.

Andersen sent a letter, PricewaterhouseCoopers directed its people to drag back defectors. Bob Hallman, a partner in the company's Falls Church, Va., management consulting division, didn't have to be told. In March he learned that Gregg Shaw, who had left his group ten months earlier to join an e-consulting startup, was fed up with his new colleagues. Hallman called immediately, hoping Shaw's old cell-phone number still worked. It did. He reached Shaw in Atlanta as he was driving home after a tiring day. "Gregg, I hear you might be interested in coming home," Hallman said.

"Well, I've been thinking about it actually," Shaw admitted. "Is it possible?"

"When do you want to start?" Hallman asked. Shaw got his old job back.

Hallman was so exhilarated by the experience that he is trying to steal another former group member from a rival consulting firm. "It just got my wheels spinning," Hallman says. "They raid us, so I have no qualms about raiding them."

In other words, corporate America is finally catching on—bodysnatching isn't just important, it can be a rush! Just ask KnowledgeCube's Max Michaels. He hired one of the people *Fortune* watched him interview. He's in serious talks with two others. And remember the $500,000 investment banker? Lately, he has been calling KnowledgeCube a lot. The other people at the company are prodding Michaels to hire the kid. But the CEO wants him to suffer a little. "That guy?" Michaels says, laughing. "I'm not even returning his telephone calls right now."

Hotels are wielding increasing power in the meeting contracts they offer to companies holding events. Melinda Ligos' story in *Successful Meetings* magazine features horror stories of unexpected fees, switched facilities, and disappearing rooms. But it also offers a survey of meeting planners and some expert advice on how some of the worst incidents could have been avoided altogether.

Melinda Ligos

KILLER CONTRACTS

LIKE A GOOD HORROR STORY? Here are a few that will make your blood curdle.

After a recent Chicago meeting, the hotel sent a meeting group a bill for more than $15,000 for items attendees didn't even use, like in-room videos. In North Carolina, the Tennessee Bar Association's room block was slashed in half against its will. In Orlando, a popular hotel moved a meeting group to a less desirable property without its consent. And in Austin, a pharmaceutical group was charged $2,000 for canceling a small meeting, even though the property promptly rebooked the space. Here's the stunner: All of these actions were perfectly legal.

Whether they're taking advantage of their position in a seller's market or simply becoming shrewder at doing business, hotels are adding new clauses to hotel contracts every day. Signing them can result in some pretty frightening penalties for planners: attrition fees for everything under the sun, iron-clad cancellation clauses, pay-in-full-before-the-meeting-even-starts stipulations, room rates that skyrocket into the future.

Nightmarish stuff. "I'm seeing a lot more hotels shift a lot more risk over to the meeting sponsor," says John Foster, an attorney with Foster, Jensen & Gulley, an Atlanta-based firm specializing in meeting contracts.

That seems to be an understatement. 69 percent of planners who responded to a recent *SM* survey said that most of the hotel contracts they've seen recently "are heavily slanted in the hotel's favor." One planner's take on the situation? "All the cannons are pointed to my head," says Bill Thomas, president of Excel Management Dynamics Inc., a consulting firm in Baldwinsville, New York. "I feel like if I don't perform like the contract says I should, I'll be financially ruined and sent to jail."

Screaming won't save you. But knowledge will. Below, a primer on how some hotels are raising planners' blood pressure with new contract twists, along with expert advice from planners, lawyers, and hoteliers themselves on how your group can avoid being haunted by the contract from hell.

FRIGHTENING FEES

The Horror Story: "We were gouged, plain and simple," says Erika Jordan, meetings manager for TSI, a Los Angeles–based meeting planning firm. That was Jordan's first reaction when she and her client, a pharmaceutical company, received a post-meeting bill demanding attrition penalties, fees a group must pay for not meeting its room block commitment, upwards of $15,000 for a meeting her firm had organized in a Chicago hotel last fall. Jordan's group had used 100 room nights, 20 percent fewer than it had set aside in the contract with the hotel. The group had expected to pay an attrition fee for the rooms not picked up, minus the agreed-upon 10 percent slippage rate (the organization can fall under its room block by this margin without penalty)—which would have amounted to a few thousand dollars—but the hotel insisted that Jordan pay penalties for much more than the room rates.

"They wanted us to pay attrition fees for meeting space, food and beverage pick-up, in-room movies that the missing attendees might have rented, telephone calls they might have made, and anything else they could think of," Jordan says. "Who knows if any of the attendees who didn't show up would have even ordered an in-room movie? [The bill] was ludicrous."

Maybe so, but attrition fees for items other than sleeping rooms have become commonplace in the past six months. Many properties are adding clauses that give groups free meeting space if they meet their room blocks, but make them pay for unused sleeping rooms *and* cough up a meeting room fee if they don't meet the block. Others have penalties tied to food and beverage and a host of ancillary areas from lost greens fees to anticipated gift shop purchases. The worst part? Sometimes the language in these clauses is so vague that planners have no idea what they'll pay for if they fall below their room blocks.

For example, many such clauses say a planner is responsible for paying a certain percentage of "anticipated gross revenues" or "total projected revenues" if the group doesn't meet a room block. That was the case with Jordan's meeting, and she now regrets not going over the clause with a fine-toothed comb. "I just assumed that 'anticipated gross revenues' meant 'sleeping room revenues,'" she says. "I never dreamed it could mean revenues from a telephone call that nobody even made."

Experts' Advice: Jordan's first error was not insisting on an attrition clause that allowed for more than a 10 percent room-block slippage. Even some hoteliers admit that 10 percent is pretty tight by industry standards. "We allow any group twenty percent attrition off their room block before we ever start to talk about penalties," says Kristy Sartorious, director of hotel sales for the Wyndham Anatole Hotel in Dallas.

"Eighty percent room pick-up is pretty standard," agrees

James M. Goldberg, an attorney at Goldberg & Associates, in Washington, D.C.

But the real problem with Jordan's penalty clause is the portion requiring fees based on "anticipated gross revenues."

"You're always going to get into an argument when you base something on such vague language," Goldberg says.

This is not to say a planner should never agree to pay penalties for anything but unused sleeping rooms if the meeting group fails to meet its room block. "It's perfectly legitimate for a hotel to consider all of its revenue sources [when writing an attrition clause]," says Steve Rudner, an attorney at O'Connor, Cavanagh, Anderson, Westover, Killingsworth & Beshears, a Phoenix-based law firm. For instance, Rudner says, a resort that has a golf course might lose a large chunk of its profits if a planner's group falls short.

But the key is to negotiate an exact dollar amount for attrition penalties, rather than leaving it open for the hotel to interpret. "Make it simple," says Goldberg. "Say, 'If I don't get my room block up to eighty percent, I'll pay you $3,500.'" Better yet, come up with a sliding scale for attrition fees: The fewer rooms you pick up, the more you have to pay, and vice versa.

"Spell it out in monetary terms so that everybody understands what is owed," agrees Christie Hicks, vice president of national sales for Hyatt Hotels Corporation, who says that Hyatt properties typically have attrition fees tied only to room pick-up, rather than other ancillary fees.

One other caveat: That exact dollar amount you specify for attrition penalties should be based on the hotel's lost profits, not lost revenues. "Planners need to understand profit percentages in the hotel business," says attorney Foster. A hotel's profit margin for food and beverage functions, for example, is these days about 20 to 25 percent. "So if you pay them for lost food and beverage revenues, they're actually making more money when your attendees don't show up," he says.

MYSTERY MEETING VENUE

The Horror Story: Three weeks before his scheduled meeting in Orlando, Excel Management Dynamics' Thomas got a call from the host hotel. It seems that Margaret Thatcher and Colin Powell were coming to town for a political powwow, and both wanted to stay—along with their entire entourages—at the same hotel where Thomas' meeting was booked, on the exact dates his group would be there.

Guess whose group got booted? "They put us up in one of their other facilities nearby," says Thomas. Besides causing logistical headaches, "[the second facility] was very substandard compared to where we were booked," he claims. Thomas was fuming, but he had absolutely no recourse: The contract he'd signed had an "alternative accommodations" clause: The hotel could move his group to another property of its choosing without his permission.

At least one hotel chain, Embassy Suites, has made this type of clause standard in contracts for its corporate-owned properties. "We need it for protection," says Jennifer Hoffman, brand manager for the hotel chain, who adds that the hotel chain "rarely" takes advantage of the clause. "It's usually used only when a group falls way short of its room block and another group wants to book a meeting at the same time."

Experts' Advice: "This one doesn't even get off the launching pad," says Goldberg. For one thing, he says, many such provisions offer no guarantees that the "alternative" hotel will be located nearby—let alone within the same city—as the hotel the planner has contracted with. "If I'm holding a meeting with a chain hotel in Washington D.C., I sure as heck don't want them telling me that they're moving me to their sister property in Alexandria, Virginia," Goldberg adds.

"It's not fair," says Elizabeth Sykes, director of meetings for the American Association of Neurological Surgeons in suburban Chicago. "Hotels make us sign clauses saying that we can't move our meeting from their hotel. Why should they be allowed to move me at *their* whim?"

It might be of some consolation to planners who sign such contracts that most state laws would hold a hotel liable for damages, such as transportation or the cost of reprinting collateral materials, for bumping a group to another hotel. "A nice resort in Scottsdale can't say, 'Ha, ha, ha, we're dumping you at the Motel 6 on the other side of town,'" Rudner says. Regardless, most meetings experts recommend that planners walk away from contracts with alternative accommodations clauses. "At the very least, adjust the clause to state that the hotel will pay you *x* amount if it moves you," Sykes says. "At least then you don't have to go to court to be compensated for damages."

GHOST OF ATTRITION PAST

The Horror Story: When the Women's International Bowling Congress signed a contract with the Hyatt Regency Buffalo in 1993 to use the property as its headquarters hotel for its 1996 Annual Meeting, no attrition clause was included. (At that time, such clauses were practically unheard of.) The meeting came and went, and the group picked up about 80 percent of its 4,735-room block.

Now, six years after the original contract was signed, Hyatt is suing the WIBC for more than $100,000 in room nights lost due to a less than 100 percent pick-up rate. Hyatt claims the group repeatedly assured the hotel that it would be responsible for the entire room block, even though an attrition clause wasn't in the contract, says Jonathan Howe, an attorney with Chicago-based Howe & Hutton, who is representing the hotel in the lawsuit pending in Buffalo's Federal District Court.

But the WIBC maintains that it clearly stated in both site inspections and negotiations that it would not be responsible for any rooms not used by the convention delegates or tournament bowlers, according to Foster, who is representing the WIBC in the case.

No matter what its outcome, legal experts say the case could set a dangerous precedent for meetings contracts.

Experts' Advice: This is a case wherein a hotel's omission of an attrition clause could actually hurt a planner, Foster says. While the WIBC can't go back in history and add an attrition clause to its contract, this case should be a lesson to planners: "Even if your intent is not to be responsible for a room block, that needs to be said in the contract so it's not left open for interpretation later on," Foster says. "A lot can happen in five years. Hotels change managers, and all that's left is what's in the contract. You'd better make damned sure it's not ambiguous."

TERRIFYING CANCELLATION CLAUSES

The Horror Story: It used to be that most meetings contracts had cancellation clauses that required a planner to pay no—or at least fewer—penalties if the group canceled a meeting long before its scheduled date. And many had clauses that stipulated a planner would owe nothing if the property was able to rebook the space. Welcome to 1999, where many contracts now require planners to pay stiff penalties—sometimes a full 100 percent of "adjusted gross revenues"—for canceling a meeting. For example, a chain hotel in Fort Lauderdale recently sent a planner a contract that required the group to pay "100 percent of total projected revenues" for canceling a meeting within 89 days of its scheduled date. Others force planners to ante up hefty sums even if they cancel months—or even years—in advance.

Shahira Hoffman, meetings and marketing manager for Media Cybernetics, a media software company in Silver Spring, Maryland, recently was socked with a $2,000 fee for canceling a small training session several months in advance of the meeting's date. "The contract had no dates in it" that would allow for lesser fees for early cancellation, she says. And, it had no clause stipulating that the hotel would not charge the group if it rebooked the space—which it did. "The whole thing really pissed me off," Hoffman says. "From now on, I'm going to read these contracts much more carefully."

Experts' Advice: "You shouldn't have to pay the same fee if you cancel a meeting ten months in advance or two days in advance," says Foster, and most of our experts agree.

But some hotels beg to differ. The Wyndham Anatole, for example, includes a cancellation clause that requires planners to pay for 100 percent of lost revenues for sleeping rooms and food and beverage functions if they cancel within a year of the scheduled meeting.

"That may sound stiff," says Sartorious, "but we're a convention hotel, and people book us five to seven years out. So if a group cancels, we would never be able to recoup that business."

Cancellation clauses should include a sliding scale that penalizes planners less the farther out they cancel a meeting, with few or no penalties for a cancellation more than a year out. And, as in the case of attrition fees, the penalties should be stipulated in an exact dollar amount; 80 percent of room block revenues, minus taxes, is a fair number.

Plus, Goldberg says, "All fees should be offset by whatever the hotel can recoup by reselling the rooms."

Another option: Try to negotiate a clause that would waive the fee if the planner promises to rebook the meeting within a certain period of time.

THE CASE OF THE DISAPPEARING ROOM BLOCK

The Horror Story: This March, hundreds of lawyers who are members of the Tennessee Bar Association (TBA) got a big surprise when they called the Grove Park Inn in Asheville, North Carolina, to book rooms for the association's June convention: They were told the group's room block was full.

"Initially, we were thrilled that so many people had already booked rooms for the convention," TBA President Pamela L. Reeves explained in a March letter to all members. But upon further investigation, the group found out that its room block had been cut in half without its permission. A source close to the negotiations accuses the hotel of reducing the block in order to accept a more lucrative piece of business. The resort, however, says the block was cut due to an "inadvertent, human error in room block management," according to general manager James S. France.

The forced room block reduction—which occurred just three months before the event—left the TBA fuming. "We have talked, cajoled, pleaded, threatened, and literally begged the Grove Park to restore our room block," Reeves said in the letter. But the resort stood firm: At one point, says a party to the negotiations, the hotel justified its actions by pointing to a clause in the contract that said the hotel could adjust a room block due to the group's poor "past history" of room block pickup, a provision that's become standard in many contracts. Grove officials allegedly held that since the association didn't pick up a full room block at a previous meeting in Tennessee, that was grounds for a reduction. But the association says that logic is faulty, because the Tennessee meeting was within driving distance to many members' homes, and the Asheville location is not.

The two parties resolved the situation in late March "after two of the most agonizing weeks of my life," says Reeves, by moving the entire group to the Pinehurst Resort & Country Club, another North Carolina property. And the Grove has agreed to pay an unspecified amount of damages to the association for costs associated with moving the group at such a late date.

Experts' Advice: Although the venue change undoubtedly angered some members and caused others to cancel, the situation could have been worse. The resort could have refused to settle, or the TBA might have had to cancel its meeting had Pinehurst not been available.

Other groups might not be so lucky. "We're starting to see

more clauses that permit a hotel to make adjustments to room blocks," says one of our legal experts, Rudner. Although the rationale is sound—some hotels have been burned too many times in the past by groups that ask them to hold blocks that are unrealistic—Rudner says he doesn't "think the clause is appropriate."

"If a [hotelier] is concerned about a group's history before they sign a contract, they shouldn't give that group the block in the first place," he says. The only cases where such a clause might be necessary, Rudner adds, are in situations where a meeting is booked five or more years in advance, and the group's history could change between the time of the booking and the actual event. If a hotel fears that is the case, he says, it might reserve the right to ask for an increase of deposit based on changing history. Or, the clause might require the planner to guarantee a full 100 percent of the block if the group's history changes significantly.

"But, the clause shouldn't give hoteliers the right to boot people," he adds.

PAY UP OR ELSE!

The Horror Story: Thomas, the meetings organizer from Excel Management Dynamics, recently had a group that signed a contract with a major chain property that had some unique deposit requirements. First, it asked him to cough up a $2,000 nonrefundable deposit. That part is pretty standard, although most hotels will refund deposits for extreme situations, such as earthquakes or work stoppages. But here's the sticky part: The clause stipulated that he pay 100 percent of the estimated room revenue, food and beverage revenue, and "other charges" a full 30 days before the meeting (30 days *before,* not *after*).

Other planners are reporting similar situations. One meetings manager says she recently received a contract from a resort in Miami asking for $20,000 up front—for a meeting that would likely cost $40,000 total. "They wanted fifty percent [of the total cost] three months before the meeting," she says. "I just bought a house and didn't have to pay that large a percentage up front!"

Another planner says he just negotiated a contract with a hotel in Key West, Florida, where he was required to pay for 100 percent of anticipated meeting costs within two weeks of signing the contract (the meeting was not for another four months). "They had me over a barrel, because it was the only place where I could hold the meeting," he says.

Experts' Advice: Paying for a meeting in full before it happens is commonplace in many countries, but this concept has only recently begun to catch on in the United States. Don't do it. "If you're having a corporate or association meeting, paying 100 percent up front is out of the question," says Howe. "The only way a hotel should ask you to do that is if you're planning a family reunion, a wedding, or some other, nonbusiness type of event that spreads the expenses out among several people."

Plus, Howe says, planners who pay in advance need to worry about the hotel going bankrupt or closing before the meeting date. "I'd insist the money go into an escrow account until the meeting date."

"Paying up front is too risky," agrees Joan Eisenstodt, president of Eisenstodt & Associates, a Washington, D.C.–based meeting planning firm. "If the service turns out to be bad, or something else goes wrong, it makes the client work too hard to recover the money."

Eisenstodt says the only groups that should be required to pay for a large amount of a meeting's costs beforehand are those that have bad credit or are notorious for not paying their bill on time. "Even then, there can be a compromise," she says. "The group should pay seventy-five percent of the entire estimated charges two to four weeks before the meeting; and the balance could be due thirty days after the final bill arrives."

ROOM RATE ROULETTE

The Horror Story: Stuart Carson is accustomed to signing hotel contracts for conventions four and five years out without agreeing upon a room rate for attendees. "What used to be standard was a clause in the contract stating that the hotel would increase its room rate no more than five percent a year between now and the event," says Carson, who plans meetings for an educational group based in the Midwest.

No more. Carson says he's recently seen hotel contracts for his group's convention in 2004 that up the room rate increase to 7 or even 8 percent per year. "I don't know what [hotels] are basing the increase on, but I think it's ludicrous," he says.

The new clause leaves Carson in a quandary: "If I wait a while, the market might soften, and hotels might rethink the increase," he says. "But if I wait too long, I might not have as much choice in properties."

Experts' Advice: Our legal eagles, too, are seeing contract clauses that have elevated per-year room rate increases to 8 percent. "Frankly, the word 'greed' comes to mind," says Goldberg. "Given the fact that the consumer price index last year increased by less than two percent, this is really, really out of whack."

Rework the provision to state that the room rates for the meeting will be the lower of the following numbers: an increase of no more than 8 percent on the previous year's rate, x percent of the rack rate, or, most importantly, no more than the consumer price index increase over that period of time. "By saying the lower of the three, you're really protected," he says.

Another option is to simply try to negotiate a reduced yearly percentage. Although the Wyndham Anatole typically includes a provision calling for no more than a 7 percent increase per year, Sartorious says that rate is often negotiable. "There's more wiggle room in this clause than there is in attrition and cancellation clauses," she says.

HOW WILL IT ALL END?

Most horror stories have gruesome endings. This one doesn't have to.

We'd like to give you a really happy ending by predicting that, as the economy changes and hotels are no longer in the catbird seat (recent figures from hospitality consulting firms indicate that occupancy rates in some areas are beginning to decline slightly), rapacious attrition fees, harsh cancellation clauses, and other penalties will magically disappear from hotel contracts. But that's not going to happen. "Attrition and cancellation fees are here to stay," says the Wyndham Anatole's Sartorious. "These contract clauses have nothing to do with being in a seller's market, and everything to do with our responsibility to our owners."

Because of new tax laws in the past few years. Sartorious says, "We're no longer tax write-offs or tax havens. We have to show a profit, and [such fees] are a way to ensure we can do it."

And we'd like to end this story on a *really* rosy note by saying that hotels across the board are most concerned with developing long-term relationships with planners, so some shrewd negotiating will convince them to waive some of these new penalties. But that's not likely. In fact, some meetings experts say the opposite is true. "Hotels will look you in the eye and tell you otherwise, but many don't care about long-term relationships," Foster says. "Most salespeople want to maximize their profit today, because eight months down the road, they'll be working somewhere else."

But none of this necessarily spells doom and gloom for planners. What it should do is put them on alert to read and negotiate meetings contracts much more carefully. "Reread a contract—fifty times if you have to—before signing it," advises Judy Johnson, director of meetings for E. Harden & Associates of Carrollton, Texas.

And if you see clauses that seem exceedingly unfair, by all means, plead your case to the hotelier. "Many hotels are perfectly willing for a planner to sign a contract with a clause that is unfairly skewed toward the hotel, but will change the clause if you ask them to," says Foster. "You have to be smart enough to point out what's wrong with it."

"When you sit down with a hotel and explain why you think a specific [clause] is unfair to your group, many are willing to rethink it," agrees Sykes of the American Association of Neurological Surgeons. The key, she says, is not to unilaterally pooh-pooh all attrition clauses, for example, but to be able to explain why your group needs a flat fee penalty rather than a penalty that requires paying a percentage of "anticipated gross revenues."

"As planners, we owe it to ourselves to perfect our knowledge of contracts so that we can make hotels—and each other—more accountable," Sykes says. "If we do this, we *will* find a common ground."

Maybe that's not the happy ending you were hoping for. But it's not the stuff of horror tales, either.

E-commerce is to the Information Revolution what the railroad was to the Industrial Revolution, and must therefore be placed in its historical context. That's what *The Atlantic Monthly's* Peter Drucker explains in this thought-provoking piece tracking a broad sweep of history that includes Eli Whitney's cotton gin and Machiavelli's *The Prince*. Since sheer greed will no longer be enough to keep modern "knowledge workers" at a company for very long, social recognition and social power must be injected into the equation.

Peter Drucker

BEYOND THE INFORMATION REVOLUTION

THE TRULY REVOLUTIONARY IMPACT of the Information Revolution is just beginning to be felt. But it is not "information" that fuels this impact. It is not "artificial intelligence." It is not the effect of computers and data processing on decision-making, policymaking, or strategy. It is something that practically no one foresaw or, indeed, even talked about ten or fifteen years ago: *e-commerce*—that is, the explosive emergence of the Internet as a major, perhaps eventually *the* major, worldwide distribution channel for goods, for services, and, surprisingly, for managerial and professional jobs. This is profoundly changing economies, markets, and industry structures; products and services and their flow; consumer segmentation, consumer values, and consumer behavior; jobs and labor markets. But the impact may be even greater on societies and politics and, above all, on the way we see the world and ourselves in it.

At the same time, new and unexpected industries will no

doubt emerge, and fast. One is already here: biotechnology. And another: fish farming. Within the next fifty years fish farming may change us from hunters and gatherers on the seas into "marine pastoralists"—just as a similar innovation some 10,000 years ago changed our ancestors from hunters and gatherers on the land into agriculturists and pastoralists.

It is likely that other new technologies will appear suddenly, leading to major new industries. What they may be is impossible even to guess at. But it is highly probable—indeed, nearly certain—that they will emerge, and fairly soon. And it is nearly certain that few of them—and few industries based on them—will come out of computer and information technology. Like biotechnology and fish farming, each will emerge from its own unique and unexpected technology.

Of course, these are only predictions. But they are made on the assumption that the Information Revolution will evolve as several earlier technology-based "revolutions" have evolved over the past 500 years, since Gutenberg's printing revolution, around 1455. In particular the assumption is that the Information Revolution will be like the Industrial Revolution of the late eighteenth and early nineteenth centuries. And that is indeed exactly how the Information Revolution has been during its first fifty years.

THE RAILROAD

The Information Revolution is now at the point at which the Industrial Revolution was in the early 1820s, about forty years after James Watt's improved steam engine (first installed in 1776) was first applied, in 1785, to an industrial operation—the spinning of cotton. And the steam engine was to the first Industrial Revolution what the computer has been to the Information Revolution—its trigger, but above all its symbol. Almost everybody today believes that nothing in economic history has ever moved as fast as, or had a greater impact than, the Information Revolution.

But the Industrial Revolution moved at least as fast in the same time span, and had probably an equal impact if not a greater one. In short order it mechanized the great majority of manufacturing processes, beginning with the production of the most important industrial commodity of the eighteenth and early nineteenth centuries: textiles. Moore's Law asserts that the price of the Information Revolution's basic element, the microchip, drops by 50 percent every 18 months. The same was true of the products whose manufacture was mechanized by the first Industrial Revolution. The price of cotton textiles fell by 90 percent in the 50 years spanning the start of the eighteenth century. The production of cotton textiles increased at least 150-fold in Britain alone in the same period. And although textiles were the most visible product of its early years, the Industrial Revolution mechanized the production of practically all other major goods, such as paper, glass, leather, and bricks. Its impact was by no means confined to consumer goods. The production of iron and ironware—for example, wire—became mechanized and steam-driven as fast as did that of textiles, with the same effects on cost, price, and output. By the end of the Napoleonic Wars the making of guns was steam-driven throughout Europe; cannons were made ten to twenty times as fast as before, and their cost dropped by more than two thirds. By that time Eli Whitney had similarly mechanized the manufacture of muskets in America and had created the first mass-production industry.

These 40 or 50 years gave rise to the factory and the "working class." Both were still so few in number in the mid-1820s, even in England, as to be statistically insignificant. But psychologically they had come to dominate (and soon would politically also). Before there were factories in America, Alexander Hamilton foresaw an industrialized country in his 1791 *Report on Manufactures*. A decade later, in 1803, a French economist, Jean-Baptiste Say, saw that the Industrial Revolution had changed economics by creating the "entrepreneur."

The social consequences went far beyond factory and working

class. As the historian Paul Johnson has pointed out, in *A History of the American People* (1997), it was the explosive growth of the steam-engine-based textile industry that revived slavery. Considered to be practically dead by the Founders of the American Republic, slavery roared back to life as the cotton gin—soon steam-driven—created a huge demand for low-cost labor and made breeding slaves America's most profitable industry for some decades.

The Industrial Revolution also had a great impact on the family. The nuclear family had long been the unit of production. On the farm and in the artisan's workshop husband, wife, and children worked together. The factory, almost for the first time in history, took worker and work out of the home and moved them into the workplace, leaving family members behind—whether spouses of adult factory workers or, especially in the early stages, parents of child factory workers.

Indeed, the "crisis of the family" did not begin after the Second World War. It began with the Industrial Revolution—and was in fact a stock concern of those who opposed the Industrial Revolution and the factory system. (The best description of the divorce of work and family, and of its effect on both, is probably Charles Dickens's 1854 novel *Hard Times*.)

But despite all these effects, the Industrial Revolution in its first half century only mechanized the production of goods that had been in existence all along. It tremendously increased output and tremendously decreased cost. It created both consumers and consumer products. But the products themselves had been around all along. And products made in the new factories differed from traditional products only in that they were uniform, with fewer defects than existed in products made by any but the top craftsmen of earlier periods.

There was only one important exception, one new product, in those first fifty years: the steamboat, first made practical by Robert Fulton in 1807. It had little impact until 30 or 40 years later. In fact, until almost the end of the nineteenth century more freight was carried on the world's oceans by sailing vessels than by steamships.

Then, in 1829, came the railroad, a product truly without precedent, and it forever changed economy, society, and politics.

In retrospect it is difficult to imagine why the invention of the railroad took so long. Rails to move carts had been around in coal mines for a very long time. What could be more obvious than to put a steam engine on a cart to drive it, rather than have it pushed by people or pulled by horses? But the railroad did not emerge from the cart in the mines. It was developed quite independently. And it was not intended to carry freight. On the contrary, for a long time it was seen only as a way to carry people. Railroads became freight carriers 30 years later, in America. (In fact, as late as the 1870s and 1880s the British engineers who were hired to build the railroads of newly Westernized Japan designed them to carry passengers—and to this day Japanese railroads are not equipped to carry freight.) But until the first railroad actually began to operate, it was virtually unanticipated.

Within five years, however, the Western world was engulfed by the biggest boom history had ever seen—the railroad boom. Punctuated by the most spectacular busts in economic history, the boom continued in Europe for 30 years, until the late 1850s, by which time most of today's major railroads had been built. In the United States it continued for another 30 years, and in outlying areas—Argentina, Brazil, Asian Russia, China—until the First World War.

The railroad was the truly revolutionary element of the Industrial Revolution, for not only did it create a new economic dimension but also it rapidly changed what I would call the *mental geography*. For the first time in history human beings had true mobility. For the first time the horizons of ordinary people expanded. Contemporaries immediately realized that a fundamental change in mentality had occurred. (A good account of this can be found in what is surely the best portrayal of the Industrial Revolution's society in transition, George Eliot's 1871 novel *Middle-*

march.) As the great French historian Fernand Braudel pointed out in his last major work, *The Identity of France* (1986), it was the railroad that made France into one nation and one culture. It had previously been a congeries of self-contained regions, held together only politically. And the role of the railroad in creating the American West is, of course, a commonplace in U.S. history.

ROUTINIZATION

Like the Industrial Revolution two centuries ago, the Information Revolution so far—that is, since the first computers, in the mid-1940s—has only transformed processes that were here all along. In fact, the real impact of the Information Revolution has not been in the form of "information" at all. Almost none of the effects of information envisaged forty years ago have actually happened. For instance, there has been practically no change in the way major decisions are made in business or government. But the Information Revolution has routinized traditional *processes* in an untold number of areas.

The software for tuning a piano converts a process that traditionally took three hours into one that takes 20 minutes. There is software for payrolls, for inventory control, for delivery schedules, and for all the other routine processes of a business. Drawing the inside arrangements of a major building (heating, water supply, sewerage, and so on) such as a prison or a hospital formerly took, say, 25 highly skilled draftsmen up to 50 days; now there is a program that enables one draftsman to do the job in a couple of days, at a tiny fraction of the cost. There is software to help people do their tax returns and software that teaches hospital residents how to take out a gall bladder. The people who now speculate in the stock market online do exactly what their predecessors in the 1920s did while spending hours each day in a brokerage office. The processes have not been changed at all. They have been routinized, step by step, with a tremendous saving in time and, often, in cost.

The psychological impact of the Information Revolution, like that of the Industrial Revolution, has been enormous. It has perhaps been greatest on the way in which young children learn. Beginning at age four (and often earlier), children now rapidly develop computer skills, soon surpassing their elders; computers are their toys and their learning tools. Fifty years hence we may well conclude that there was no "crisis of American education" in the closing years of the twentieth century—there was only a growing incongruence between the way twentieth-century schools taught and the way late-twentieth-century children learned. Something similar happened in the sixteenth-century university, a hundred years after the invention of the printing press and movable type.

But as to the way we work, the Information Revolution has so far simply routinized what was done all along. The only exception is the CD-ROM, invented around twenty years ago to present operas, university courses, a writer's oeuvre, in an entirely new way. Like the steamboat, the CD-ROM has not immediately caught on.

THE MEANING OF E-COMMERCE

E-commerce is to the Information Revolution what the railroad was to the Industrial Revolution—a totally new, totally unprecedented, totally unexpected development. And like the railroad 170 years ago, e-commerce is creating a new and distinct boom, rapidly changing the economy, society, and politics.

One example: A mid-sized company in America's industrial Midwest, founded in the 1920s and now run by the grandchildren of the founder, used to have some 60 percent of the market in inexpensive dinnerware for fast-food eateries, school and office cafeterias, and hospitals within a hundred-mile radius of its factory. China is heavy and breaks easily, so cheap china is traditionally sold within a small area. Almost overnight this company lost more than half of its market. One of its customers, a hospital cafeteria where someone went "surfing" on the Internet, discovered a European manufacturer that offered china of apparently better quality at a lower price and shipped cheaply by air. Within a few months the main customers in the area shifted to the European supplier. Few of them, it seems, realize—let alone care—that the stuff comes from Europe.

In the new mental geography created by the railroad, humanity mastered distance. In the mental geography of e-commerce, distance has been eliminated. There is only one economy and only one market.

One consequence of this is that every business must become globally competitive, even if it manufactures or sells only within a local or regional market. The competition is not local anymore—in fact, it knows no boundaries. Every company has to become transnational in the way it is run. Yet the traditional multinational may well become obsolete. It manufactures and distributes in a number of distinct geographies, in which it is a *local* company. But in e-commerce there are neither local companies nor distinct geographies. Where to manufacture, where to sell, and how to sell will remain important business decisions. But in another twenty years they may no longer determine what a company does, how it does it, and where it does it.

At the same time, it is not yet clear what kinds of goods and services will be bought and sold through e-commerce and what kinds will turn out to be unsuitable for it. This has been true whenever a new distribution channel has arisen. Why, for instance, did the railroad change both the mental and the economic geography of the West, whereas the steamboat—with its equal impact on world trade and passenger traffic—did neither? Why was there no "steamboat boom"?

Equally unclear has been the impact of more-recent changes in distribution channels—in the shift, for instance, from the local grocery store to the supermarket, from the individual supermarket to the supermarket chain, and from the supermarket chain to Wal-

Mart and other discount chains. It is already clear that the shift to e-commerce will be just as eclectic and unexpected.

Here are a few examples. Twenty-five years ago it was generally believed that within a few decades the printed word would be dispatched electronically to individual subscribers' computer screens. Subscribers would then either read text on their computer screens or download it and print it out. This was the assumption that underlay the CD-ROM. Thus any number of newspapers and magazines, by no means only in the United States, established themselves online; few, so far, have become gold mines. But anyone who twenty years ago predicted the business of Amazon.com and barnesandnoble.com—that is, that books would be sold on the Internet but delivered in their heavy, printed form—would have been laughed off the podium. Yet Amazon.com and barnesandnoble.com are in exactly that business, and they are in it worldwide. The first order for the U.S. edition of my most recent book, *Management Challenges for the 21st Century* (1999), came to Amazon.com, and it came from Argentina.

Another example: Ten years ago one of the world's leading automobile companies made a thorough study of the expected impact on automobile sales of the then emerging Internet. It concluded that the Internet would become a major distribution channel for used cars, but that customers would still want to see new cars, to touch them, to test-drive them. In actuality, at least so far, most used cars are still being bought not over the Internet but in a dealer's lot. However, as many as half of all new cars sold (excluding luxury cars) may now actually be "bought" over the Internet. Dealers only deliver cars that customers have chosen well before they enter the dealership. What does this mean for the future of the local automobile dealership, the twentieth century's most profitable small business?

Another example: Traders in the American stock-market boom of 1998 and 1999 increasingly buy and sell online. But investors seem to be shifting away from buying electronically. The major U.S. investment vehicle is mutual funds. And whereas almost half of all mutual funds a few years ago were bought electronically, it is estimated that the figure will drop to 35 percent next year and to 20 percent by 2005. This is the opposite of what "everybody expected" 10 or 15 years ago.

The fastest-growing e-commerce in the United States is in an area where there was no "commerce" until now—in jobs for professionals and managers. Almost half of the world's largest companies now recruit through Web sites, and some two and a half million managerial and professional people (two thirds of them not even engineers or computer professionals) have their résumés on the Internet and solicit job offers over it. The result is a completely new labor market.

This illustrates another important effect of e-commerce. New distribution channels change who the customers are. They change not only *how* customers buy but also *what* they buy. They change consumer behavior, savings patterns, industry structure—in short, the entire economy. This is what is now happening, and not only in the United States but increasingly in the rest of the developed world, and in a good many emerging countries, including mainland China.

LUTHER, MACHIAVELLI, AND THE SALMON

The railroad made the Industrial Revolution accomplished fact. What had been revolution became establishment. And the boom it triggered lasted almost a hundred years. The technology of the steam engine did not end with the railroad. It led in the 1880s and 1890s to the steam turbine, and in the 1920s and 1930s to the last magnificent American steam locomotives, so beloved by railroad buffs. But the technology centered on the steam engine and in manufacturing operations ceased to be central. Instead the dynamics of the technology shifted to totally new industries that emerged almost immediately after the railroad was invented, not one of which had anything to do with steam or steam engines. The electric telegraph and photography were first, in the 1830s, followed soon thereafter by optics and farm equipment. The new and different fertilizer industry, which began in the late 1830s, in short order transformed agriculture. Public health became a major and central growth industry, with quarantine, vaccination, the supply of pure water, and sewers, which for the first time in history made the city a more healthful habitat than the countryside. At the same time came the first anesthetics.

With these major new technologies came major new social institutions: the modern postal service, the daily paper, investment banking, and commercial banking, to name just a few. Not one of them had much to do with the steam engine or with the technology of the Industrial Revolution in general. It was these new industries and institutions that by 1850 had come to dominate the industrial and economic landscape of the developed countries.

This is very similar to what happened in the printing revolution—the first of the technological revolutions that created the modern world. In the 50 years after 1455, when Gutenberg had perfected the printing press and movable type he had been working on for years, the printing revolution swept Europe and completely changed its economy and its psychology. But the books printed during the first 50 years, the ones called incunabula, contained largely the same texts that monks, in their scriptoria, had for centuries laboriously copied by hand: religious tracts and whatever remained of the writings of antiquity. Some 7,000 titles were published in those first 50 years, in 35,000 editions. At least 6,700 of these were traditional titles. In other words, in its first 50 years printing made available—and increasingly cheap—traditional information and communication products. But then, some 60 years after Gutenberg, came Luther's German Bible—thousands and thousands of copies sold almost immediately at an unbelievably low price. With Luther's Bible the new printing technology ushered in a new society. It ushered in Protestantism, which conquered half of Europe and, within another 20 years, forced the Catholic Church to reform itself in the other half. Luther used the new medium of print deliberately to restore religion to the center of individual life and of society. And this unleashed a century and a half of religious reform, religious revolt, religious wars.

At the very same time, however, that Luther used print with the avowed intention of restoring Christianity, Machiavelli wrote and published *The Prince* (1513), the first Western book in more than a thousand years that contained not one biblical quotation and no reference to the writers of antiquity. In no time at all *The Prince* became the "other best seller" of the sixteenth century, and its most notorious but also most influential book. In short order there was a wealth of purely secular works, what we today call literature: novels and books in science, history, politics, and, soon, economics. It was not long before the first purely secular art form arose, in England—the modern theater. Brand-new social institutions also arose: the Jesuit order, the Spanish infantry, the first modern navy, and, finally, the sovereign national state. In other words, the printing revolution followed the same trajectory as did the Industrial Revolution, which began 300 years later, and as does the Information Revolution today.

What the new industries and institutions will be, no one can say yet. No one in the 1520s anticipated secular literature, let alone the secular theater. No one in the 1820s anticipated the electric telegraph, or public health, or photography.

The one thing (to say it again) that is highly probable, if not nearly certain, is that the next 20 years will see the emergence of a number of new industries. At the same time, it is nearly certain that few of them will come out of information technology, the computer, data processing, or the Internet. This is indicated by all historical precedents. But it is true also of the new industries that are already rapidly emerging. Biotechnology, as mentioned, is already here. So is fish farming.

Twenty-five years ago salmon was a delicacy. The typical convention dinner gave a choice between chicken and beef. Today salmon is a commodity, and is the other choice on the convention menu. Most salmon today is not caught at sea or in a river but grown on a fish farm. The same is increasingly true of trout. Soon, apparently, it will be true of a number of other fish. Flounder, for instance, which is to seafood what pork is to meat, is just going into oceanic mass production. This will no doubt lead to the genetic development of new and different fish, just as the domestication of sheep, cows, and chickens led to the development of new breeds among them.

But probably a dozen or so technologies are at the stage where biotechnology was 25 years ago—that is, ready to emerge.

There is also a *service* waiting to be born: insurance against the risks of foreign-exchange exposure. Now that every business is part of the global economy, such insurance is as badly needed as was insurance against physical risks (fire, flood) in the early stages of the Industrial Revolution, when traditional insurance emerged. All the knowledge needed for foreign-exchange insurance is available; only the institution itself is still lacking.

The next two or three decades are likely to see even greater technological change than has occurred in the decades since the emergence of the computer, and also even greater change in industry structures, in the economic landscape, and probably in the social landscape as well.

THE GENTLEMAN VERSUS THE TECHNOLOGIST

The new industries that emerged after the railroad owed little technologically to the steam engine or to the Industrial Revolution in general. They were not its "children after the flesh"—but they were its "children after the spirit." They were possible only because of the mind-set that the Industrial Revolution had created and the skills it had developed. This was a mind-set that accepted—indeed, eagerly welcomed—invention and innovation.

It was a mind-set that accepted, and eagerly welcomed, new products and new services.

It also created the social values that made possible the new industries. Above all, it created the "technologist." Social and financial success long eluded the first major American technologist, Eli Whitney, whose cotton gin, in 1793, was as central to the triumph of the Industrial Revolution as was the steam engine. But a generation later the technologist—still self-taught—had become the American folk hero and was both socially accepted and financially rewarded. Samuel Morse, the inventor of the telegraph, may have been the first example; Thomas Edison became the most prominent. In Europe the "businessman" long remained a social inferior, but the university-trained engineer had by 1830 or 1840 become a respected "professional."

By the 1850s England was losing its predominance and beginning to be overtaken as an industrial economy, first by the United States and then by Germany. It is generally accepted that neither economics nor technology was the major reason. The main cause was social. Economically, and especially financially, England remained the great power until the First World War. Technologically it held its own throughout the nineteenth century. Synthetic dyestuffs, the first products of the modern chemical industry, were invented in England, and so was the steam turbine. But England did not accept the technologist socially. He never became a "gentleman." The English built first-rate engineering schools in India but almost none at home. No other country so honored the "scientist"—and, indeed, Britain retained leadership in physics throughout the nineteenth century, from James Clerk Maxwell and Michael Faraday all the way to Ernest Rutherford. But the technologist remained a "tradesman." (Dickens, for instance, showed open contempt for the upstart ironmaster in his 1853 novel *Bleak House.*)

Nor did England develop the venture capitalist, who has the means and the mentality to finance the unexpected and unproved. A French invention, first portrayed in Balzac's monumental *La Comédie humaine,* in the 1840s, the venture capitalist was institutionalized in the United States by J. P. Morgan and, simultaneously, in Germany and Japan by the universal bank. But England, although it invented and developed the commercial bank to finance trade, had no institution to finance industry until two German refugees, S. G. Warburg and Henry Grunfeld, started an entrepreneurial bank in London, just before the Second World War.

BRIBING THE KNOWLEDGE WORKER

What might be needed to prevent the United States from becoming the England of the twenty-first century? I am convinced that a drastic change in the social mind-set is required—just as leadership in the industrial economy after the railroad required the drastic change from "tradesman" to "technologist" or "engineer."

What we call the Information Revolution is actually a Knowledge Revolution. What has made it possible to routinize processes is not machinery; the computer is only the trigger. Software is the reorganization of traditional work, based on centuries of experience, through the application of knowledge and especially of systematic, logical analysis. The key is not electronics; it is cognitive science. This means that the key to maintaining leadership in the economy and the technology that are about to emerge is likely to be the social position of knowledge professionals and social acceptance of their values. For them to remain traditional "employees" and be treated as such would be tantamount to England's treating its technologists as tradesmen—and likely to have similar consequences.

Today, however, we are trying to straddle the fence—to maintain the traditional mind-set, in which capital is the key resource and the financier is the boss, while bribing knowledge workers to be content to remain employees by giving them bonuses and stock options. But this, if it can work at all, can work only as long as the emerging industries enjoy a stock-market boom, as the Internet companies have been doing. The next major industries are likely to behave far more like traditional industries—that is, to grow slowly, painfully, laboriously.

The early industries of the Industrial Revolution—cotton textiles, iron, the railroads—were boom industries that created millionaires overnight, like Balzac's venture bankers and like Dickens's ironmaster, who in a few years grew from a lowly domestic servant into a "captain of industry." The industries that emerged after 1830 also created millionaires. But they took 20 years to do so, and it was 20 years of hard work, of struggle, of disappointments and failures, of thrift. This is likely to be true of the industries that will emerge from now on. It is already true of biotechnology.

Bribing the knowledge workers on whom these industries depend will therefore simply not work. The key knowledge workers in these businesses will surely continue to expect to share financially in the fruits of their labor. But the financial fruits are likely to take much longer to ripen, if they ripen at all. And then, probably within 10 years or so, running a business with (short-term) "shareholder value" as its first—if not its only—goal and justification will have become counterproductive. Increasingly, performance in these new knowledge-based industries will come to depend on running the institution so as to attract, hold, and motivate knowledge workers. When this can no longer be done by satisfying knowledge workers' greed, as we are now trying to do it, it will have to be done by satisfying their values, and by giving them social recognition and social power. It will have to be done by turning them from subordinates into fellow executives, and from employees, however well paid, into partners.

Talk about haves and have-nots. Amid dot-com opulence, Silicon Valley also has one of the nation's fastest-growing homeless populations. Jeff Goodell's story in *Rolling Stone* talks to everyday working people about the financial stress of trying to make ends meet in a costly region populated by millionaires. He examines the lack of opportunity for minorities and raises the issue of whether the nation's entire work force will experience the same divisions along class lines.

Jeff Goodell

DOWN AND OUT IN SILICON VALLEY

AS THE SUN GOES DOWN over Silicon Valley, Thad Wingate vibrates with mad energy. It's the end of his workday as a driver for Guaranteed Express, a local courier service. He seems to have absorbed all the tension and stress and speed that are channeled through the highways of Silicon Valley, and now, as darkness falls, he radiates it back like heat off a rock. He's six feet six, wire thin, and his wraparound sunglasses are permanently glued over his eyes. Every day he logs roughly 400 miles, delivering business plans to high-tech execs and diapers to rich housewives and T-bone steaks to busy hotels. He takes home about $2,400 a month—a decent salary, you'd think. But home, for the moment, is the Emergency Housing Consortium's James F. Boccardo Regional Reception Center in San Jose: a homeless shelter.

Several years ago, Wingate's six-week-old daughter died in his arms, a victim of sudden infant death syndrome. He was overcome with grief. His marriage unraveled, he lost his job at a testing lab and started doing an eight ball of crank a day. He spent a few months in jail, got clean and now is trying to reassemble his life—not an easy task in the hard-charging world of Silicon Valley.

Inside the shelter's main room, where about 125 beds are arranged in rows, the air is stale and sweaty. Wingate picks up a "fresh" bedroll from a pile near the front door—a scratchy wool blanket, a threadbare sheet. "My big dream right now," he says, holding the bedroll as if it were a dead animal, "is to sleep on my own sheets again."

As in most shelters, the crowd includes ex-cons, recovering alcoholics and the mentally ill. But there's also a surprising number of working people: a male nurse still in his green scrubs, a Puerto Rican woman in a McDonald's uniform, a middle-aged trucker. Many of them are wearing faded T-shirts with high-tech logos: APPLE, ORACLE, SUN MICROSYSTEMS. Like Air Jordans in the South Bronx, these T-shirts are status items in the shelter, links to the better world that these people are living right in the middle of but cannot touch.

In Silicon Valley, it's hard not to feel lucky. The sky is Netscape blue, the hills are dotted with oaks and horses, the Fry's Electronics stores are stocked with every gizmo a geek could want. And, of course, money is gushing down El Camino Real, the Valley's main drag, like water through a broken dam. According to recent data compiled by the *San Jose Mercury News,* 65,000 Santa Clara County residents—roughly one in nine—are worth more than $1 million apiece, not including the values of their homes. There are several hundred residents worth $25 million or more and at least thirteen billionaires in the Valley worth more than $45 billion combined. There's no sign that this is going to slow down anytime soon: In 1997, $1.1 billion in venture capital was invested in Bay-area companies; in just the first six months of 1999, the number was $2.6 billion. John Doerr, a pioneering venture capitalist with Kleiner Perkins Caufield & Byers, in Menlo Park, has often called Silicon Valley "the largest legal creation of wealth in the history of the planet."

The wealth machine hasn't only created millionaires. Between January 1995 and June 1998, Silicon Valley created 171,000 new jobs. The average annual wage in the region is $48,000, the highest in the country and $18,000 above the national average. For people with decent technical skills, jobs that pay $75,000 a year are a dime a dozen.

But the new economy has not been so generous to people without technical skills or college degrees. Between 1991 and 1997, the median income for the lowest 20 percent of households in the Valley increased by just 5 percent. Meanwhile, the cost of living has skyrocketed, surpassing Manhattan and Boston and Los Angeles. It is now the highest in the country—37 percent above the national average. The median price for a home is $410,000, more than twice the average for the rest of the country. Studio apartments in bad neighborhoods rent for $1,000 a month; a decent one-bedroom goes for $1,500. The price for a gallon of regular gas hovered around $1.80 for most of the summer, some 50 cents above what much of the rest of the country paid. This January, after a federal rent-assistance program reopened in the area, 19,000 people applied in the first week alone. "If you have a family and you're not making $75,000 a year," says Brian Reed, a case manager at the EHC shelter, "a decent life is an unattainable goal."

Wingate is finding it almost impossible to locate a place to live. "I could leave the area, of course, but then when would I see my son?" he asks. "As soon as a landlord hears you're living in a shelter, they don't want to rent to you. They all have 50 people calling for every vacancy—none of them want to rent to someone like me."

Not surprisingly, lots of people are finding it increasingly difficult to keep up with life in the Silicon Valley fast lane. In 1995 (the last year for which figures are available), 13 percent of children in Santa Clara County were living below the poverty line. That amounts to more than 55,000 kids. The high school dropout rate has steadily increased during the last six years. Domestic abuse is up, road rage is epidemic, and AA meetings around the

Valley are packed with people who wonder why they are working so hard and getting nowhere. Second Harvest, the Valley's largest food bank, served 19.3 million pounds of food in 1997; this year, the agency is on target to do the same. Sixty-one percent of that food will be consumed by working families. The wait for housing through the EHC family shelter is more than a year long.

The brutality of the Silicon Valley economy is apparent not just to newcomers who arrive here to seek their fortune but also to anyone who is so unwise as to choose a field of work for love, not money. Schoolteachers, cops, construction workers, nurses, even doctors and lawyers—as the tide of wealth rises around them, many are finding it harder to stay afloat. Despite the utopian rhetoric of Silicon Valley boosters like T. J. Rodgers, the CEO of Cypress Semiconductor, who promotes the Valley as a meritocracy where anyone, "regardless of race, color, or creed," can succeed, it's clear that Silicon Valley is developing into a two-tier society: those who have caught the technological wave and those who are being left behind. This is not simply a phenomenon of class or race or age or the distribution of wealth—although those are all important factors. It's really about the Darwinian nature of unfettered capitalism when it's operating at warp speed.

And while the divide between the haves and have-nots may be more extreme in Silicon Valley than in other parts of the country right now, that won't last long. "Silicon Valley-style economics are what we can look forward to everywhere," says Robert H. Frank, an economist at Cornell University who has long studied the increasing gap between the rich and poor. "In this new economy, either you have a lottery ticket or you don't. And the people who don't are not happy about it."

Even some of the people who do have lottery tickets aren't happy about it. Bob Metcalfe, an Internet pioneer and co-founder of 3Com, lived in the Valley for 22 years until he dropped his kids off at school one day and saw all the other kids being dropped off by "blond au pairs in BMWs." A few months later, he and his wife sold their house in Woodside and moved to Maine. "I want my kids to grow up in a place that's not so dominated by envy and greed," Metcalfe says. Eric Schmidt, a longtime Valley booster and the CEO of Novell, one of the largest software companies in the region, agrees that something has been lost. "The Valley used to be a profoundly democratic place," he says. "It was all about hot tubs and topless weddings on Mount Tamalpais. Now that's gone. It's all about deals and pushing change. It's all about money."

The Emergency Housing Consortium estimates that about 35 percent of the people who stay at the shelter have full-time jobs. When the center opened in 1997, says EHC communications manager Maury Kendall, "we knew the demand for our services would be high. But what we didn't anticipate was the number of families that would come to us—that's where the screaming demand has been." EHC got started in the early eighties with the help of a $50,000 gift of Apple stock from Apple cofounder Steve Wozniak. Since then, the high-tech industry has been intermittently supportive: Adobe Systems donated a courtyard, Apple and Silicon Graphics send over a group of employees once in a while to help serve dinner, Cisco Systems has plans to develop an educational-outreach program there. "We're grateful for all the help we've received," says Barry Del Buono, a former diocesan priest who is now EHC's executive director, "but given the amount of money in the Valley, there's much more that could be done."

At times, the EHC shelter feels like little more than a dumping ground for the digital revolution's wounded and maimed. One afternoon, a woman named Natalie holds out her arms to show me two faint scars on the inside of both wrists. "A razor blade?" I ask, thinking she had slashed her wrists. "No, a keyboard," she says. She worked as a customer-service rep for a local telephone company for seven years, until all the pounding caused carpal tunnel syndrome so severe that she needed surgery—and was promptly fired from her job. "Now I can't use a keyboard," she says angrily. "Where do you think that leaves me in this valley?"

One night, I wander out to the front desk at 3 A.M. and meet an animated woman named Melondy Spears James. She and her four kids moved to the Valley a few years ago from Richmond, California, because she had heard there were lots of good jobs here and she wanted to get off welfare. Almost immediately, she found a temp job at an IBM chip-manufacturing plant in San Jose, where she made more than $10 an hour. Twelve hours a day, four days a week, she stood in front of a slicing machine, cutting silicon wafers into thin chips. It was brutal, monotonous work. On a good night, she made 190 cuts. Before long she had to wear a back brace to work and a wrap around one leg to keep it from throbbing. Still, it was worth it because she thought she'd soon be hired permanently, with benefits and vacation time. "Then they decided to send my job down to Guadalajara," she says coolly. "So that was the end of that." Now she's applying for a job at the Mervyn's distribution center while working two nights a week at the shelter.

At 7 A.M. I watch Kevin Landsdown straighten up his semiprivate cubicle. Landsdown, a tall, soft-spoken man, lives a double life: From nine to five he works at the tree-lined Hewlett-Packard campus in the heart of the Valley, where he helps manage the distribution of new HP products. At night he returns to the shelter, where he's been living for the past few months. I tell him that most people won't understand how a man with a college degree and a good job can end up in a shelter. "Then those people," he notes, "have never lived in Silicon Valley."

James and Landsdown, like many of the residents of the shelter during my stay this past summer, are black. This is not a coincidence. The fact that blacks and Hispanics are not sharing equally in the Valley's economic boom is obvious to anyone who spends any time here. Explanations range from generally poor education among blacks and Hispanics to subtle yet pervasive racism. Landsdown, who grew up on the South Side of Chicago and has worked in Silicon Valley since the mid 1980s, says, "Yes, there are a lot of people of color working here, but most of them are Asians and Indians—people the white man has no grudge against." He believes that "black people are different. When I worked at Silicon

Graphics a few years ago, an engineer called me a gorilla. At Amdahl, people called me a nigger—not once but five times."

Ugly stuff—but is it any worse than what goes on every day in offices all across America? Last year the *San Francisco Chronicle* examined the employment records for 33 leading Silicon Valley corporations and determined that the staffs at these companies were about 4 percent black and 7 percent Latino. Compare this with the fact that blacks make up 8 percent of the labor force in the Bay area, while Hispanics make up 14 percent. Clearly, there's a problem. "Everyone here wants to believe the Valley is a perfect place and they are living a perfect life," says one veteran Silicon Valley real estate agent. "Racism obviously exists, but no one is allowed to talk about it, because to talk about it would be to admit that life here is not some twenty-first-century utopia."

One of the last agricultural areas remaining in the Valley was North First Street, which runs from downtown San Jose out toward the foot of the San Francisco Bay. Today, thanks to San Jose's new light-rail service, dozens of high-tech companies have sprung up here, including a sprawling new Cisco Systems campus. A single open field is left, and in that field an old white ranch house sits abandoned, surrounded by a chain-link fence—in the Valley, this is a sure sign that the bulldozers are coming. A quiet side street runs in front of the house, and on a recent Sunday afternoon, four dilapidated motor homes are parked there. They look like four Conestoga wagons circled against Indian attack. Sitting in a lawn chair outside one of them is a middle-aged woman with bright blue eyes and dark hair. Her name is Lu Elaine Johnson, and she's a student at a nearby chiropractic college. "I live in here because I can't afford an apartment," she tells me. She says that the people in the other trailers are also students and that a few blocks away I can find another street where a half-dozen motor homes are illicitly camped out. "We're the wandering homeless," she says. I ask her about the fenced-off field across the street. She explains, accurately, that open land in this area routinely sells for a million dollars or more per acre. "Where does all this money come from? Is there some printing press up in the hills that I don't know about?"

Many are asking the same question. Although the class divide in the Valley has never been greater, geographically the gap is shrinking every day. In the adjacent towns of Los Altos and Mountain View, the increasingly uncomfortable juxtaposition of two vastly different worlds is palpable. One night, as I ride along with officer Thomas Joy of the Los Altos Police Department, we come upon the home of John Warnock, the CEO of Adobe Systems. It's an enormous old mansion, the grounds shrouded by hundred-year-old oak trees. Joy, who recently worked a security detail at the house when Warnock hosted a Democratic Party fund-raising dinner, shines his spotlight at the rear of the house. He gushes, "There's a huge guest house out there and a bandstand and a picnic area. It's stunning." We cruise quietly past row after row of sprawling mansions on the lots of what were formerly modest middle-class houses. "This is all Silicon Valley money," Joy says. Then he adds, "Now let's look at the other side."

We drive for about 90 seconds, cross El Camino Real and enter the town of Mountain View. Immediately, everything changes. Flimsy four-story apartment buildings press against the street. Teenage girls are hanging out on the corner, stop signs are scrawled with gang graffiti. "I responded to a call here a few weeks ago—some domestic trouble," Joy says, pointing to a white-stucco apartment building. "I walked in the front door, and the floors were covered with mattresses. There must have been nine or ten people crashed out there. Not junkies, either. Guys looking for work. Day laborers, mostly."

In New York or Washington, D.C., the rich and poor have always lived in close proximity. Not in Silicon Valley. One of the secrets of the Valley's success is that until recently, it was a balmy paradise of the middle class. I grew up there in the 1970s, during the Cold War, when the Valley's economy was tied to government spending, not Wall Street. Many of the men in the tract-house neighborhood where I lived worked in the defense industry, building missiles and satellites. But there were also teachers, carpenters, auto repairmen, salesmen. No one was appreciably richer than anyone else. There were always the Hispanic families who had lost their jobs when the canneries went out, but the gap between us and them was not so profound. There were no millionaires, no IPOs. Indeed, had the Valley been rich, the whole PC revolution might never have ignited. "I decided to build my first computer," Steve Wozniak once told me, "because I couldn't afford to go out and buy one." Of course, computers cost tens of thousands of dollars in those days, but the point remains. If it weren't for the struggling middle class—Woz is the son of a mid-level Lockheed engineer, while Steve Jobs, whose adoptive father was a machinist, came from even humbler roots—there might be no Macintosh, no Yahoo!, no Internet.

Thanks to the boom, however, and the skyrocketing housing prices, there is no such thing as a middle class in the Valley anymore—there's rich and poor, and very little in between. "One hundred thousand dollars a year gets you nothing," says Dan Hingle, 35, a quality-assurance engineer at a start-up called Inter-Niche Technologies. Hingle grew up in the Valley and now, despite his $50,000 annual salary, lives in a trailer park. "With $200,000, you can begin to approach a middle-class life. How many people have jobs that pay $200,000? Not many. So people move out of the area, to where they can afford to buy a house, and commute an hour or two to work every day. That's fine, but then you're spending three or four hours on the road, and it's real easy to start hating life."

Many affluent communities, like Aspen or Nantucket, are facing a crisis: The people needed to run the essential services can't afford to live there. In Silicon Valley, the problem is multiplied a thousandfold. "Silicon Valley is in danger of collapsing under the weight of its own prosperity," wrote Todd Dwyer, a high school economics teacher with a $35,000 salary, in a recent letter to the *San Jose Mercury News.*

Officer Joy is a case in point. Although he works in Los Altos, he lives in Sonora, a three-hour drive away, in the foothills of the

Sierra Nevada. He drives in to Los Altos once a week, stays on his mother's couch for four days, then drives home to his family. This kind of grueling commute is not unusual. In Los Altos, police officers start at around $40,00 a year—on that, it'd be tough to afford a doghouse in town. Ideally, cops who live where they work are better cops—they know the community better, are less like a mercenary force. Of the 33 officers who patrol Los Altos, though, only one lives there; in nearby Los Gatos, 42 out of 45 live out of town; none of the 95 officers in Palo Alto is a local resident. Lt. Robert Brennan of the Palo Alto Police Department says, "It's a big problem in the whole Valley"—and not only for cops.

Two years ago, Jennifer Jolliff was offered a job teaching in a Los Gatos public school. The salary was $29,000, well above what she was making in a small town in central California. So she took the job, moved north and began searching for an apartment. "I always thought it was very important for a teacher to live in the community they teach—you can vote on local issues, get to know the families of your students," Jolliff says. In Los Gatos, an upscale Silicon Valley enclave, Jolliff discovered that her $2,100 monthly check didn't go very far. "I ended up living in a mobile home under an overpass for the next two years," she says. She eventually moved to a house in the Santa Cruz Mountains, and now, like almost everyone else, she commutes.

Los Angeles still leads the nation for the worst commute, but the Valley is closing in fast. It used to be proud of its gorgeous freeways, such as Highway 280, which swoops through the foothills between San Francisco and Los Altos; but the area's newest freeways, like Highway 87, are surrounded by high sound barriers, just like in L.A. Not surprisingly, violence on the highways is increasingly common. In September, a gunman poked his head out through the sunroof of his red sports car and opened fire with a semiautomatic, killing one person and wounding another. A few months earlier, a 20-year-old woman accidentally cut off another car in traffic. Its driver pulled up beside her and shot her.

*   *   *

If you dream of dot-com millions, the pain of life in the Valley is irrelevant. This is the place to meet like-minded Type A marketeers, hammer out a business plan, and roll the IPO dice. And you don't have to be Yahoo!'s Jerry Yang to hit it big. Two years ago, Samantha Jordan, 25, was cleaning horse barns in Michigan. "I thought computers were for geeks and wasn't interested in them in the slightest," she says. Bored with life in Michigan, she moved out to California, intending to get a job teaching horseback riding at a stable in the Bay area; instead she took a job in tech support— the bottom rung of the high-tech hierarchy—at Excite@Home. Today, thanks to her stock options, she owns a half-million-dollar house and drives a nice convertible.

But stories like this, which reinforce our dreams that we, too, might get lucky someday, are the exception not the rule. In fact, the majority of start-ups in the Valley fail; for those that do succeed, about 85 percent of the stock is owned by the company founders and venture capitalists, leaving only 15 percent to be split among the employees. At powerhouse companies like Cisco Systems and Microsoft, or overnight sensations like eBay and Yahoo!, the critical mass of wealth is so great that even lowly cubicle jockeys can get rich. Most companies, however, are not eBay or Cisco, and the majority of young high-tech workers in the Valley are 50K-a-year wage slaves who don't have stock options or whose stock options are worth little or nothing.

Still, everyone knows that stock options are the only way most worker bees are going to get ahead in the Valley. "It's becoming more and more like a casino," says Michael Neff, a senior Web designer who has been through three start-ups. He now works at a pre-IPO start-up called PublishOne, which is involved in digital-rights management. "So much of what makes a company succeed or fail is beyond your control. All you can do is believe in the people you're working with and hope you get lucky." Most people can go through the start-up craziness once, maybe twice. After that, if they haven't hit the jackpot, they're usually too old (which, in the Valley, means midthirties) and bitter to try it again.

God forbid you have a life: a spouse, a kid, even a dog. To work at a start-up, you have to toss them overboard, at least temporarily. For a single mother like Martha Hoffman, 42, that's out of the question. Hoffman, a smart, bouncy, career-minded woman with a 12-year-old daughter, has worked for the last 13 years at Panasonic. As a network-systems operator, she makes $46,000 a year. She lives in a mobile home that looks like something you'd find up-hollow in West Virginia, not in Silicon Valley: rusty metal siding; plywood steps up to the front door, where her dog, Charlie, is tied up and howling; her 11-year-old Nissan Pathfinder, with 154,000 miles, is parked nearby. "I'd love to go to work for a start-up," Hoffman says wistfully. "But that means working 12-hour days and on weekends and for very little salary. What am I supposed to say to my daughter—'I'll see you in two years'? No thanks."

In a way, people like Hoffman have the worst of it here: She has the skills and the technical know-how and the savvy to roll the dice at a start-up, but life circumstances won't allow it. So she commutes an hour a day to her corporate job, juggles her daughter's soccer schedule, shops, cooks, and worries about the $1,000 she recently invested in stock on eTrade. Meanwhile, Mercedes-Benzes zoom around her, and every time she opens the newspaper, she reads about another IPO multimillionaire. "I sometimes think, 'Why not me? What did they do to deserve it? Are they somehow a better person than me? Did they work harder?' I don't think so. They're just luckier," Hoffman says. "OK, that's fine, I can handle that. But to have to have your nose rubbed in it every day—it can get to you."

The obvious response to this, of course, is that if you don't like having your nose rubbed in other people's money, then leave. Some do, but for many with families, it's not so easy.

Ten years ago, Luis Estrada, 25, came to Silicon Valley from Zacatecas, Mexico. "Like everyone else," he says, "I wanted a better life." Estrada is a tall man with a gentle voice and large, rough hands. He went to a local high school, speaks excellent English and knew that if he wanted to get anywhere in America, he needed to go to college. But his family had no money for that, so he decided to get a job and save some money. He got hired five years ago as a maintenance worker at Flextronics International, a high-tech manufacturing firm. "When I started, there were about ten people there, and they were all driving jalopies," says Estrada. "Now the parking lot is full of BMWs."

Estrada's is a typical Silicon Valley story—but, of course, he didn't get any stock and therefore didn't share in that wealth. Now he's married and has an eight-month-old son, and, in order to make ends meet, he works two jobs: 40 to 50 hours a week at Flextronics, then evenings and weekends planting trees and doing yard work for the local elite. He knows that he's never going to get ahead in the Valley this way and that what he really needs to do is go back to school and learn about computers. "I don't want to do this the rest of my life," he says, pounding a stake in the ground next to a crab-apple tree in a new housing development in south San Jose. "But I don't see how it's going to change. I have to work 70 hours a week to pay the rent and provide for my child, and that doesn't leave me a lot of time for studying."

I ask him if he ever dreams of becoming a millionaire.

At first he does not understand the question. I repeat it. He chuckles. "You kidding?"

As soon as you take the Silver Creek Road exit off the freeway, the signs begin: ENCHANTMENT, JASMINE, SILVERCREST, TUSCAN HILLS, BEL AIRE, SUPER-LOANS.COM, THE GOOD LIFE STRAIGHT AHEAD. Drive along for a mile or so, up a grassy hillside at the south end of the Valley—two years ago, there was nothing but farmland and coyotes here—and the road crests at a plateau that's littered with brand-new million-dollar homes. A million-dollar home is no big deal here, but still, this place is nice. Many of the homes have views of Silicon Valley, which looks like a giant computer chip in the haze below. Most of the new residents are midlevel engineers at Cisco or Hewlett-Packard, people who've had some luck but not enough to get a spread in Woodside, where the venture capitalists and CEOs hang out.

Liliana and Peter Townshend live in one of the newest houses in the development—"a 3,500-square-foot, side-loading Spanish Provence," Liliana calls it. Red-tile roof, green shutters. Very nice. And very new. The house was finished only a couple of months ago, and the lot it's on is still mostly bare dirt—there's a big pile of sand in the driveway, a few pink poppies waving in the wind, a pair of small Prairie Fire crab-apple trees staked near the sidewalk. It feels like the frontier.

Liliana, 27, is Hispanic. Her parents were both born in Mexico and then moved to California, where her father picked apples. She grew up in a poor section of L.A., the sixth of seven kids, attended UC Berkeley and then law school at the University of Illinois. Now she's starting her own e-commerce business, Tuzona.com, which sells electronics and computer equipment to Spanish-speaking people all over the world. Her husband, Peter, 28, grew up in West L.A., the son of a UCLA physics professor. He got a law degree from Berkeley's Boalt Hall and is now a venture-capital lawyer at Heller Ehrman White & McAuliffe, one of the top law firms in the Valley. If anyone has crossed over the digital divide, it's the Townshends.

But when you step inside their house, you notice something odd: There's no furniture. There's a black leather couch in the den that they picked up at a yard sale; the dining room is completely empty; the living room has a couple of chairs and a simple coffee table; in the kitchen, they eat off an old wooden table that belonged to Peter's grandmother. Their only indulgences are electronic: a big-screen Mitsubishi in the TV room upstairs and a Sony Wega 32-inch flat-screen TV downstairs. And there are two cats, Jimmy and Sierra. Otherwise, the house is empty.

This is how the rich poor people or the poor rich people—the people who are straddling the line between those who have made it and those who have not—live in Silicon Valley. Peter makes $120,000 a year at his law firm; Liliana, at the moment, makes zip. They have a $3,600-a-month house payment, plus a second mortgage (to Peter's parents) for $90,000. Liliana still owes $60,000 in student loans, and they have $18,000 of debt on their credit cards. In his 401K plan, Peter has a whopping $6,000. Liliana shops for food at Costco: when she's down in L.A. visiting her family, she loads her Ford Explorer up with food for the drive home, because groceries are cheaper down there. "I feel like the poorest of the poor in Silicon Valley," Liliana says.

And yet she will sometimes say to Peter, as she did the other night after she saw a BMW commercial on TV: "Why don't you buy me a BMW? I've always wanted a BMW, and they're only $40,000." Or she'll see an ad for a Toyota and think, "Why don't we buy a couple of them? They're only $20,000 each." She says things like this because, like anyone who travels at the edge of the big money in the Valley, she and her husband are constantly bombarded with unreal numbers: Bill Gates is worth $90 billion, Amazon's Jeff Bezos is worth $7.8 billion, Jerry Yang is worth $3.7 billion (poor Jerry!). "The other day I walked into my office and there was $2 million worth of personal checks from clients sitting on my chair," says Peter. "When money like that is flying all around you, you lose perspective."

The Townshends, of course, are trying to get their share. They bought this house in November 1998, before it was even built, for $720,000, because they knew real estate is appreciating like crazy in the Valley. In September 1999, Peter guesses he could sell it for $920,000. If Liliana can get investors interested in Tuzona.com, maybe that will take off. Or if not, maybe Peter will make the leap to become an in-house lawyer for one of the start-ups he counsels every day. He already passed up that chance a couple of years ago, with a strange company that was going to auction stuff on the Web. "I thought it was a really dumb idea," he says. Peter drafted the initial documents for the company, then turned the work over to a junior associate at another firm. That junior associate ended up joining the company, which was named eBay, and now, just a year after it went public, that junior associate is worth $25 million, while the founder of the company, Pierre Omidyar, is worth $4.9 billion. How does it feel to have missed out on the start-up of the decade? Peter shrugs: "You can't take it seriously."

And yet it's clear that Peter does take it seriously. He and Liliana both want to hit escape velocity—that blissful state when you have enough money to escape the humdrum cares of daily life, like mortgages and jobs and worries about where your kids will go to school—before the Internet bubble bursts. Like many others who live on the edge in the Valley, Liliana and Peter have made the calculation that if they can score now, whatever pains they've suffered will be worth it. So Peter regularly works 12- to 15-hour days, five days a week. He's already been hospitalized twice for exhaustion. Liliana, who works equally hard, often wakes up at 3 A.M. sobbing, afraid that Tuzona.com won't fly and that all the money— about $25,000 so far—they've poured into it will be wasted. Peter's back aches, his neck aches, his belly hangs a little farther over his belt than he'd like, and his eyes have that permanent glaze of a person who has been pulling all-nighters so long that he can no longer tell whether the sun is going up or coming down. He misses his family. "I can count on my fingers the number of times I'll get to see my mother and father before they die," he says. Liliana complains that their marriage is suffering; they fight more than they should because they never see each other, or because when he comes home at night, she's sometimes too busy to fix him dinner. "But we're going to make it," Liliana says. "Nothing is going to stop us."

The brutality of the Silicon Valley economy is becoming increasingly difficult to ignore. "Die yuppie scum" can be found scrawled on walls in San Francisco, and local newspapers like the *San Jose Mercury News* have tempered their boosterish spirit and started to examine the costs of explosive prosperity. At a recent fund-raiser at the home of Novell CEO Eric Schmidt, President Clinton challenged a group of high-tech execs not to forget those left behind. "This is something you should all ponder," he warned the crowd. "Not everyone is participating in this economic growth."

According to the Silicon Valley Manufacturing Group, the advocacy arm of 150 of the Valley's major employers, the hardships of life in the area will only get worse in the future. By 2010, the Valley's population is projected to grow by 176,000 to 2.6 million, putting more strain on the region's infrastructure— roads, housing, schools, hospitals. "It is absolutely critical that we face these problems head-on," says Carl Guardino, president of the group. "Otherwise the Valley will cease to function as we know it."

Of course efforts to resolve the inequities in the new economy are motivated by enlightened self-interest not moral outrage. There's no such thing as moral outrage in Silicon Valley: There are only various degrees of problem solving. At its worst, this leads to the common assertion that, "Yes, the Valley has a problem, but I'm too busy to worry about it." At its best, it leads to a faith in the elitist idea that smart people should find a way to help the less-smart people help themselves. Recently, there has been an increased interest in applying venture-capital ideas to philanthropic causes. The Entrepreneurs' Foundation, for example, created by longtime venture capitalist Gib Myers, provides start-up funding to non-profit organizations. It's a good idea, except that it treats the human condition like a vast e-commerce site, where all our problems can be charted out on a white board, with arrows and stars and efficiency charts, and nobody actually has to get down in the trenches and get his hands dirty.

Maybe they don't have to. The brainpower of Silicon Valley should not be underestimated. And perhaps the benefits of our turbocharged economy—a low unemployment rate, a soaring Dow, new technology that is speeding information along and saving lives—outweigh the drawbacks. Maybe the ugly truth about the new economy is that for some to succeed, others must be left behind.

So far, the losers have gone quietly. But as I drive down Silver Creek Road one afternoon, past a group of Mexican laborers in the front yard of another million-dollar mansion, I'm reminded of my visit a few days earlier with Donald Howard, a broad-shouldered, blue-eyed construction worker. Howard has a ghoulish skeleton brandishing a shotgun tattooed on one bicep and women entwined in roses tattooed on the other. When I met him, he was building retaining walls in a yard across the street from the house where John Steinbeck once lived. It's a fitting irony that Steinbeck wrote *The Grapes of Wrath*, his powerful novel about migrant workers during the 1930s, in this small house perched on the edge of the new world. Howard tells me he makes $16 an hour: no union, no benefits. It's enough to allow him to rent a bedroom in a nice condo in Santa Clara, to keep his 1986 Cadillac running and to keep up with child-support payments. But that's about it.

I ask Howard whether he feels any anger about the fact that so many people are getting rich and he's not. "Not really," he shrugs. Howard believes that as long as the economy keeps going strong, no one's going to complain too loudly. "But if the bubble bursts," he says, leaning on his shovel, "maybe people will feel differently. They might start to think about what's fair and what's not fair. So far we haven't had any situations like they have in South America, where the poor people kidnap the children of rich people and hold them for ransom. But you know," he says gently, looking out over a smoggy view of the Valley, "that's what happens in a place where things get too far out of balance." He says this not as a threat but as a simple statement of fact.

Can't live without Fido? Have plenty of money? Canine cloning may be the answer. Just deposit a tissue sample from your pet and science will do the rest—for $250,000. Charles Graeber of *Wired* magazine takes you deep inside this bizarre world fraught with ethical doubts that brings science and animal lovers together. The process may be destined to become a multi-billion-dollar business.

Charles Graeber

HOW MUCH IS THAT DOGGY IN THE VITRO?

IN COLLEGE STATION, deep within the cinder-block bowels of a lab on the campus of Texas A&M University, Madeline the dog waits patiently on a metal table while a veterinary surgeon pulls green sterile scrubs over his pointy cowboy boots. Yesterday, Madeline's blood test revealed the telltale hormonal spike that signals ovulation. It's her turn.

The bathroom-sized preop room is crowded with onlookers, doctors, and nurses. One whispers soothingly in Madeline's ear while another shaves her leg, sucking the fuzz with a Dustbuster. She's a sweet little beagle, and the drugs make her sweeter. Buprenorphine to anesthetize, acepromazine to tranquilize, glycopyrolate to stop her drooling: She looks on passively as the surgeon measures a tracheal tube against her chest.

Deep doggy-sleep overwhelms Madeline in seconds. The tube is in now, her jaws tied around it with a bow of cheesecloth, and the surgeon presses down on her body until she pees into a metal bowl. A man in a surgical mask stabs in from a corner with a Sony digicam for the shot: On his tiny screen, a nurse squeezes an oxygen balloon, and Madeline's body inflates in rigid synchronization.

Under the lights, the nurses have abstracted Madeline's freckled belly to a square of shaved flesh framed by green cloth. The surgeon scalpels a thin red line through the square and stretches the incision with a retractor, O-ing a portal into her belly. Then, as if reaching into a pumpkin with its lid cut free, he pulls out the beagle's uterus and ovaries. Somewhere within his gloved fist are six microscopic dog eggs. For the moment, they are Madeline's.

Madeline is having her eggs harvested, a procedure that's only recently been perfected in dogs. The process is common for humans—the first step in making test-tube babies—but Madeline's surgery is special: The eggs will be used to try to make a clone.

Madeline and 60 other bitches are serving as doggy hens, egg machines that supply the raw materials for the world's only canine-cloning project, a joint venture between A&M and California-based Bio-Arts and Research Corporation (BARC). The $2.3 million effort, called Missyplicity, is privately funded by an anonymous Bay Area billionaire who wants to make an exact copy of his mutt, Missy.

Veterinary researcher Mark Westhusin leads the four-person team of scientists charged with carrying out the science behind Missy's cloning. For the past three years, Westhusin and his colleagues have been laboring at the frontier of canine reproductive biology. Before they could even dream of supplying their anonymous patron with his cloned puppy, techniques like this egg harvest had to be developed. In the process, surgeries like Madeline's have been repeated scores of times on dozens of lab dogs.

After Madeline's eggs are collected, they'll be retrofitted with Missy's DNA, cultured in vitro, and—if the embryo is viable—surgically implanted into another dog's oviduct for gestation. Right now, five Missyplicity dogs like Madeline are pregnant with potential Missy clones. None of their embryos have developed enough to have a perceptible heartbeat, but Westhusin is confident that this pregnancy—or another one soon—will stick. If everything goes perfectly today, Missy 2 will be born in 63 days.

Three years ago, Dolly the sheep was front-page news. Missyplicity was announced soon after, and sounded to many people like a biotech hoax—or, worse, a conspicuous waste of time and money at the expense of lab dogs like Madeline. But despite its cutesy aspects, Missyplicity is important. It brings the reality of cloning closer to home: Dolly was a scientific first, but she's hardly man's best friend. In Dolly's wake President Clinton signed a bill prohibiting the use of federal funds in human-cloning experiments. Four states took the clone ban one step further and made human cloning illegal regardless of who pays for it. The message seemed to be that cloning vegetables, or lab and farm animals is acceptable, but when cloning gets personal, it's illegal. Missy isn't human, but she's no farm animal either. A pet occupies a psychic middle ground. Even if Missy is never successfully cloned—and there's no guarantee that she will be—the very fact that people are trying is an implicit challenge to our legal and ethical comfort zones.

The man with the camera is Lou Hawthorne, an ectomorph with a full head of salt-and-pepper curls and a mischievous streak. A goateed sci-fi fanatic turned college hippie, then techie, and now Bay Area entrepreneur, he lives in Marin County and makes time every day for an hour of yoga. As president of BARC and middleman between Missy's billionaire owner and the Texas A&M cloning team, Hawthorne cuts the checks and manages Missyplicity's PR. Right now, he's shooting a documentary. He's having fun, too; there's a big grin beneath his surgical mask.

Since December 1997, Hawthorne has flown to observe Missyplicity about a dozen times. He's stayed at all the finest hotels and worn out the menus in all the best restaurants between College Station and Houston. But his latest trip is different. This time, Hawthorne is so sure of Missyplicity's success that he's arrived for something even bigger than the world's first dog-cloning project.

He's here to launch the world's first dog-cloning company, a gene bank called Genetic Savings & Clone.

A three-way partnership among the scientists, Hawthorne, and the wealthy client, GSC is opening the door to a clone-on-demand future. As little as a thousand dollars puts your doggy's DNA on ice. If today's surgery on Madeline yields a Missy clone, all you'll need to clone your own Fido this year will be the firm's URL (www.savingsandclone.com) and $250,000.

There's no way to predict the demand for cloned puppies, of course, but it's likely to be high. Remember how you cried when you buried your childhood pet in the backyard? Hawthorne can, and right now he has 200 potential clients lined up who never want to endure that loss again. In Hawthorne's vision of the future, people will pass a clone of their beloved family pooch down to their grandchildren. Statistically speaking, a dog lives in every other American household: No wonder Hawthorne wears a grin.

To make Madeline's egg into Missy's clone, Madeline's DNA must be replaced with Missy's in another lab across campus. It's a two-minute drive to the Reproductive Sciences Laboratory, long enough to kill an unheated oocyte, so Madeline's eggs are tucked into a warmed lunch box for the ride.

The RSL is a square gray building. Hawthorne leads me to Westhusin's office to show me the single photograph hanging there. "She's very photogenic, don't you think?" he asks.

The portrait is of Missy, and she *is* photogenic, a healthy-looking cutie with the pointy ears and snout of a collie and the robust bushiness of a Siberian husky. "We thought Mark should know what he's working toward," Hawthorne says waggishly. "You know, so he won't get it wrong." Hunkered behind a desk littered with grant proposals, Westhusin offers us a resigned smile.

We're here to watch Westhusin insert Missy's DNA into Madeline's eggs. Technically, this is the moment of creation for Missy's clone, and Hawthorne wants to film it. Westhusin dutifully dons a photogenic white lab coat before placing Madeline's fresh ova inside the micromanipulator, a powerful, $60,000 microscope equipped with two hair-thin microsurgical instruments and paid for by Missy's mysterious owner.

In theory, making a clone is easy: It's only a slight variation on standard sexual reproduction. You take an egg, remove its DNA, replace it with DNA from another cell, and—violà!—you have a fertilized clone egg that will then split and develop according to those new blueprints.

But in practice many complications arise. Though all the cells of a living creature contain a full set of genetic instructions (in the form of DNA), they don't perform the same functions. A liver is not a nose. A slew of failed frog-cloning experiments in the '60s convinced most scientists that cloning an entire animal from a differentiated body cell—a nasal cell, for example—would at best result in a giant nose. If you wanted to reproduce the entire animal, you'd have to use undifferentiated cells. For 40 years the only source of such cells was fertilized embryos. Scientists could make multiple copies of the unborn—Tetra, the first rhesus monkey clone, was recently created using this technology—but they couldn't produce a clone from an adult animal.

That changed on February 23, 1997, when a team of Scottish researchers trotted out Dolly, a seven-month-old Finn Dorset lamb that was cloned from the mammary cell of an adult ewe. Dolly's creators had cloned an adult by starving the cell—thus apparently tricking it back into an undifferentiated state before placing it inside another sheep's egg.

In attempting to clone Missy, Westhusin's team follows the same protocol used to create Dolly, a process known as somatic cell nuclear transfer. But before the Dolly protocol could even be applied, there was a set of species-specific problems that needed to be solved. For example, dogs have a bursa, or pouch, encasing their ovaries that makes egg harvesting difficult. Sheep don't. And while sheep ovulate regularly—once every 19 days—dogs release ova randomly, once every 6 to 12 months. In undertaking this cloning project, Team Missyplicity had to amass an understanding of canine biology far more comprehensive than dog breeders or vets have ever possessed.

At this point, Missyplicity scientists have overcome most of the problems, but they're still playing a numbers game that's very hard to win. Egg harvesting, tissue culture, enucleation, renucleation, embryo culture, gestation, birth: Even with the full knowledge of a species' reproductive biology, a clone team needs to make a lot of mistakes before nailing the whole sequence perfectly, which means burning through a lot of eggs. The tally was at 277 before Dolly was born. So far, Missyplicity has renucleated only 77 eggs, plus Madeline's 6 today.

In the RSL micromanipulation room, Westhusin motions Hawthorne's camera toward the scope's cathode-ray tube. The ovum filling the screen resembles a big, fuzzy zero—with Madeline's coiled DNA floating inside the nucleus. Taeyoung Shin, one of Westhusin's postdoctoral students, works a joystick on the scope, and a miniature tool slides into view: a glass pipette, with a blunt mouth only 20 micrometers wide. Shin hits the trigger, and the pipette attaches to the egg like a vacuum hose sucking on a beach ball.

"Now, watch here," Westhusin says to the camera. "It's not as easy as it looks."

Another pipette slides into view on the micromanipulator screen, this one thinner—and sharp. In a single, fluid motion, the sharp pipette pierces the egg, sucks in the nucleus, and pulls out.

"OK," Westhusin says. "Got it."

Click, click: The entire process has taken about five seconds. Genetically speaking, Madeline's egg is vacant. Now it must be retrofitted with Missy's DNA. Hawthorne sets up his camera for the next shot.

One of Westhusin's graduate students pulls a plate of Missy's body cells from a jug of liquid nitrogen, then incubates them back to body temperature under a sterile vacuum hood before Westhusin adds them to the micromanipulator dish. Onscreen, Missy's body cells are tiny and pale next to the giant egg, like moons around Jupiter.

Westhusin points to a small, round cell. "C'mon Shin, you know we're only giving you two more months," he jokes. "We want a dog. *I* want a dog."

Shin sucks the cell into his pipette, pokes into Madeline's empty egg, and injects. Click, click: done. Loaded with its new nuclear cargo, the egg spins free. It's genetically identical to the fertilized egg that divided and developed into Missy.

Westhusin claps his hands like a director cutting a scene. "OK, Shin," he says. "Great. Are we ready to fuse?"

Right now, Missy's body cell and Madeline's egg cell both have their own membrane. To combine them into a single cell within a single membrane, the final step of today's procedure will be to fuse the cells together with an electric pulse that sends charged ions busting through the cell walls. Afterward the cells should heal into a single whole, like a graft.

The procedure is cutting-edge, but the equipment—a BTX Electro Cell Manipulator—looks like vintage Radio Shack. It's a squat box, resembling a car battery. LCDs show amps and volts. There's a toggle switch marked POWER and an assortment of knobs and dials. The BTX is the perfect lab gizmo—the B-movie bolt of lightning.

Two wires, positive and negative, protrude from the BTX box. Westhusin attaches them with alligator clips to the dish containing the new Missy egg and turns the dials to their proper settings. It's a tasty image, but as Hawthorne pans over for a shot, Shin reflexively pushes out his hand, blocking the camera. "It's secret," he says. "You cannot take a picture." The exact power settings are owned by the project, and they're potentially valuable—patentable. Filming the BTX numbers crosses a line. Hawthorne pushes in for a tight shot of the machine's console anyway.

"Really, really," Shin says. "It's secret—you cannot film."

"Well, I'm paying for it," Hawthorne says. Shin, confused, turns to Westhusin.

But Westhusin has turned away. He gives the machine a final tweak and steps back to check his work: Everything's right. He flips the switch, sparking the BTX to life. Electricity surges through the renucleated cell, and another potential Missy is created.

"I just decided," Hawthorne announces excitedly. "In the documentary, we're definitely cutting to Gene Wilder in *Young Frankenstein:* 'It's aliiiiiive!'"

Missyplicity was born in the mind of a dog lover and successful Bay Area businessman who saw the Dolly headlines in 1997. Mr. E, as we'll call him, counted his spayed bitch, Missy, as one of his greatest joys. But she also wasn't getting any younger, a fact no man—not even a rich one—can change.

What followed was a whim, the sort of wild idea that strikes you as funny in the shower but evaporates by the time you've toweled off. But Mr. E—who declined to be interviewed, even with his anonymity protected—had kibble to burn and, more important, a friend who offered to turn his whim into reality: Lou Hawthorne.

Hawthorne is a professional dabbler—and by his own description, a successful if unsettled one. He has produced interactive multimedia projects for Apple, USWest, and Tandem, as well as a documentary on the ill-fated Biosphere 2. Six months before spearheading the Missyplicity project, Hawthorne was in India chronicling his motorcycle pilgrimage across the subcontinent for a Web site called Hell's Buddhas.

Four months later, armed with Mr. E's checkbook, Hawthorne attended the Transgenic Animals in Agriculture conference in Tahoe City, California, where he met Mark Westhusin. An associate professor at Texas A&M, Westhusin managed a 20-person, multimillion-dollar lab. Before that, Westhusin had worked for five years at Granada BioSciences, developing cattle-embryo cloning techniques. Hawthorne told him he wanted to clone a dog.

At scientific confabs, especially those dealing with new fields like cloning, it's not uncommon to encounter the odd civilian with big ideas but shallow pockets. After meeting Hawthorne, Westhusin wasn't sure what to think. "I listened to him," he remembers. "I told him that trying it would cost money—a lot of money. Millions. That this was fine with him really shocked me."

Westhusin returned to Texas to start building a Missyplicity team. He approached his mentor, Duane Kraemer—a Texas A&M biology professor and an internationally known embryo-transfer specialist—as well as Bob Burghardt, another Aggie faculty member and an expert in isolating, propagating, and characterizing cells for use in nuclear transfer. Lisa Howe, an A&M veterinary surgeon knowledgeable in tissue-collection protocols, was also recruited. Within nine months, the team was on its way to producing a canine clone, and Missy was flown to Texas to have cells harvested from her belly and lips. At mealtime she was brought to a College Station deli and, to Westhusin's amusement, hand-fed broccoli from the salad bar.

Lou Hawthorne and Mark Westhusin make a particularly odd couple. Westhusin has an easy familiarity with guns, cows, and football. With his flannel shirt tucked into neat blue jeans, he looks like a country boy. By contrast, Hawthorne, in silk shirt and supermarket tube socks, looks like an Ivy League yoga geek on a Texas vacation. When I ate dinner with them, Westhusin had cleaned his plate and checked his watch before Hawthorne had even decided on a suitable Sonoma red.

"We butt heads," Westhusin says, "but we've figured out how to work together. He pisses me off, and I pretty much tell him. And I piss him off, and he tells me."

The BBC broke the Missyplicity story in August 1998, well before the cloning experiments had actually started. "They told me they wanted to talk about cloning in general," Westhusin remembers. He agreed on the condition that they not address Missyplicity. "They had this smart-ass reporter who got me on camera and kept asking 'Isn't it true that you just accepted $2.3 million to clone an individual's dog?' *Gotcha* stuff. I just said 'Nope. Told ya. Not going to talk about that.' But you end up looking guilty anyway."

The story was picked up worldwide, but since the Missyplicity scientists weren't talking, dog cloning was cast as a believe-it-or-not footnote to Dolly. The phone on Texas A&M president Ray Bowen's desk began ringing nonstop. It was the first time he had heard of the project—which was not unusual, as scientific research at A&M is controlled by a separate bureaucracy. Reacting to the bad publicity, Bowen's first impulse was to pull the plug. Cooler heads prevailed, and today Texas A&M stands fully behind the project. But Westhusin still gets the occasional raised eyebrow from fellow researchers who question whether cloning a rich man's dog is serious science.

"We always knew this would be controversial," Westhusin says. "People say, 'This project is so compromised—why would you take this money, why would you get involved in this kind of thing?' You might as well ask if science is for sale. And the answer is yes—yes, it is for sale. We try to sell it every day to NIH and to private industry. As a scientist, you have to weigh what you learn against what the final product is."

Westhusin says he spends much of his time focused on money—raising it, spending it, and then filling out the paperwork. Beakers and test tubes are the small stuff: Micromanipulators cost real money, cryopreservation costs real money. Mistakes—the inevitable by-product of trial and error, the fallen soufflés of scientific knowledge—cost money.

With Mr. E's dollars, the Missyplicity scientists started to learn volumes about dog physiology and, as the e-mail flooded in, almost as much about dog lovers.

First came flames: "This project really stinks. It makes me feel sick. What's wrong with good, old-fashioned breeding? If you make copies, nothing will ever be better."

In response, Hawthorne created a PR-minded Web site (www.missyplicity.com). Gradually, the mailbag began filling with a different sort of message.

"My dog died, and I hope that someday he might be clonable. How should I go about preserving what is left of my lovely, perfect creature? His body is in the freezer."

"Personally, I say to hell with 'ethics' that tell us that we cannot preserve those we hold dear. The purpose of religion, in my opinion, is to celebrate life, not death."

"I am interested in cloning my cat, George. How much would it cost?"

The deluge stunned the scientists, especially Westhusin. "Three years ago, I'd have never guessed people were this crazy about pets," he says. "But there are a lot of people out there who think that what we're doing down here is the greatest thing since sliced bread."

Suddenly, without advertising, this quiet enterprise was getting hundreds of requests from pet lovers and potential customers. The Missyplicity team realized that they had their hands on more than just a privately funded research project: Suddenly, they had what looked like a very lucrative startup.

By the time you read this, Genetic Savings & Clone, a "companion-animal DNA storage bank," will be open for business. During my stay in College Station, Hawthorne proudly shows me GSC's 32-page business plan. To open an account, you deposit a tissue sample (preferably, the dog is alive, but a week-old corpse will do). Processing fees range from $1,000 to $3,000, plus $100 per year for cryogenic storage. Six months after Missy's clone is born, Hawthorne claims, the canine-cloning service will be available to the public for about $250,000 per cloned pup—onetenth the total cost of Missyplicity—and the prices should drop 50 percent every year.

As Hawthorne's plan points out, Americans own and care for 50 million dogs: "Most are beloved members of a family, with one critical difference from the other family members—on average, they live one-seventh as long." If GSC cryo-stores tissue from onetenth of 1 percent of them, that's an annual gross of $50 million. If GSC also serves one-fifth of 1 percent of the 5 million dogs Hawthorne estimates die each year, his company will be handling 10,000 dead dogs—another $27.5 million. (The partners— Hawthorne, the Missyplicity scientists, and Mr. E—have equity; the prospect of an IPO is mentioned as an encitingly viable possibility.)

Hawthorne figures his customers will find him on the Web. Let's say a prospective client—in the business plan, Hawthorne calls him Joe—wants to bank his dog's genes. Joe logs on to the GSC Web site, where he finds grief-counseling resources and a list of GSC-registered veterinarians. Later, Joe's vet logs on and schedules surgery, choosing from one of four levels of expediency—from "standard" to "emergency"—depending on whether the dog is healthy, sick, or dead. GSC ships the vet its trademarked BioBox, which contains the needed reagents and Tupperware, plus an instructional videotape that gives a step-by-step explanation of the procedure.

On the scheduled day, Joe's vet takes tissue samples from Joe's dog—Rocket, in the business plan—and FedExes them to Texas, where they're cultured for a month in a hormonal medium, checked for DNA viability, and cryo-stored in liquid nitrogen at minus 320 degrees Fahrenheit. Rocket's DNA has now been banked. If Joe later decides to clone his dog, he'll first have to click through several legal contracts. A cloned dog is not a resurrected dog—Rocket 2 won't actually be Rocket, she will be Rocket's identical twin, born well after the original. Rocket 2 will share Rocket's DNA, but the scientific jury is still out as to whether they'll necessarily look or act exactly the same. He doesn't want to get sued when Joe discovers that Rocket 2 can't remember his master's voice.

The GSC storage site eventually will have a constantly updated feed—"perhaps cameras trained on the dials and gauges of the liquid-nitrogen controls," Hawthorne says—so Joe can visit Rocket's DNA cylinder as if it were her "gravestone." The virtual DNA "visitation area" will be accompanied by a picture of the deceased and a few paragraphs of canine epitaph. It's a comfort for the grieving dog owner, but keeping the memory of the pooch alive is also good marketing. After cutting that $100 storage check each year, Joe might want to see where his money goes.

The Web interface also transforms what is essentially a giant refrigerator into what Hawthorne calls a "DNA marketplace for famous animals, such as Missy." GSC would take a brokerage fee for any transactions between owner and buyer and perform the actual cloning.

To really understand GSC's revenue potential, consider the cattle-cloning business, Westhusin's former livelihood. The cattle industry is a $36 billion-a-year enterprise that already traffics in embryo clones, so it's easy to see how highly the beef boys might value a service that lets them store and reproduce infinite genetic copies of their prize bulls—especially if the service is linked with Texas A&M, an aggie institution with a sterling reputation. And Hawthorne says pet dogs aren't the only critters on GSC's radar screen. There are racehorses, racing dogs, cats, and endangered species to think about. GSC's business plan leaves you with the impression that nothing, short of a total failure to clone, stands between the company and world domination. But, of course, as Hawthorne and Westhusin both know, there are pitfalls in the way.

At this point, competition seems to be the least of them, though four other doggy-gene banks are vying for market share: Canine Cryobank, perPETuate, Lazaron, and Clonaid. None of them has the backing of either universities or billionaires. None even has more than a dozen dogs in cold storage. All four are apparently banking on Missyplicity's success: Without the lure of a clone, cryopreservation is a pointless business.

The embryonic canine-cloning industry's real challenge, however, is not cloning a dog—that will happen, sooner or later—it's putting a smiley face on the process of cloning a dog. To that end, Hawthorne has chosen a beautiful bright Wednesday morning to take me to visit the vivisection facility. The kennels lie unmarked at the far end of a dirt road, past fields of frolicking lab bison and NO TRESPASSING signs. They aren't much to look at: several dozen thin, gray sheds arranged in rows like tobacco barns. On one side are the Missyplicity dogs; on the other, the 150 used by Texas A&M for experimental research and teaching.

Only the Missyplicity dogs are visible, romping in a newly constructed yard of fenced gravel. Hawthorne and I put on gray jumpsuits and stroll like shepherds through the surging brown sea of yipping, floppy-eared canines. These are Madeline's sisters, the egg donors and surrogate mothers for Missy's cloned embryo. Except for the telltale squares of pale fur growing over the subdermal microchips used to identify them, they look like any other pack of pups.

"Look at them all," Hawthorne says triumphantly. "Don't they just look—*happy?*"

One doesn't usually associate the words *lab animal* and *happy*, but resolving this paradox is critical to Hawthorne's conscience—and to his business. This is the paradox of GSC itself. These 61 dogs are being used solely for the Missy clone. To clone other pets, GSC will need hundreds of lab dogs to supply the clone eggs. The Madeline egg that I saw renucleated was a dud, and ended up, like thousands of others will ultimately end up, in a biohazard trash bin. Hawthorne may not have much market competition, but he can count on plenty of ethical opposition from the same dog lovers he's counting on to patronize his cloning business.

Michael W. Fox, a senior bioethicist at the US Humane Society, finds the idea of dog cloning abhorrent. "Dog cloning is a sentimental self-indulgence for those who can afford it," he says. "Those dogs in the Missyplicity dog colony are hormonally manipulated to ovulate faster than normal. Eventually that's going to wear them down to the point that they'll develop diseases earlier and start dying sooner. We've only recently gotten down from the trees, and we're already playing God. We need to think about our responsibilities to animals."

Hawthorne maintains that such thoughts are never far from his mind—or Mr. E's wallet. On my first night in Texas, Hawthorne had given me his card. Predictably, it was whimsical and highly designed, with a photo of Missy at one of its corners. But he was quick to point out the Photoshopped darkness beneath her. "That," he said solemnly, "is the long shadow of biotechnology."

In April 1998, Hawthorne tried to remove that shadow by writing a letter to People for the Ethical Treatment of Animals. ("To whom it may concern: I'm coordinating a multimillion-dollar canine-cloning project.") Each Missyplicity surgery carries the risk of death. Still, he wanted the animal-rights group to understand that he was "designing this project to a very high bioethical standard, involving not just the physical well-being of all animals involved, but also their psychological well-being." PETA responded two weeks later: It hoped his letter was a joke.

Selling PETA on a lab dog–based clone project was a losing proposition, but the rebuke still stung. Hawthorne is an animal lover—in the late '80s he even volunteered for PETA. He considers himself spiritual and, his new biotech business notwithstanding, philosophically opposed to vivisection. To balance his business with his Buddhist conscience, Hawthorne has come up with a kind of karmic spreadsheet, a ledger tallying Missyplicity's ethical red and black.

Central to it is the Missyplicity Code of Bioethics, a binding contract between the project and the scientists that ensures, among other things, preferential treatment for all the dogs in the cloning colony.

"As a precedent it's a big deal," Hawthorne explains as several confused beagles hump his leg. "I wouldn't have even considered a cloning project if I didn't feel that we could commit to seeing it through in a humane manner. This dog colony could have been an ethical disaster."

Ethics don't come cheap, but Mr. E's money covered the cost of that too, buying the canine equivalent of a luxury condo complex. It comes staffed with a dog trainer named Jessica Harrison, who gives out treats.

Westhusin and Hawthorne haven't always seen eye-to-eye on the necessity of pampering experimental dogs. "Initially," Hawthorne says, "I think Mark considered animal-rights folks all the same and all trouble—well-meaning, but fundamentally deluded. But this dog colony is pretty obviously a cool thing. I've even noticed that Mark sort of shifts gears mentally when he's around the colony: He slips into the persona of Dog Owner rather than Scientist."

If Hawthorne's dogs could consider, they might consider themselves fortunate indeed. Like their yelping brethren in the sheds, the Missyplicity dogs were bred for experimentation. But unlike the regular lab dogs, which live out their lives inside cages, the Missyplicity dogs have names and an hour of daily exercise. Here on the gravel, they gallop around their jumpsuited obedience trainer, who housebreaks them for home adoption after their eight-month stay.

"Ours are the lucky ones," Hawthorne says, scratching a beagle's tattooed ear. "Sometimes, walking through here, I feel like Schindler."

Genetic Savings & Clone does have a Spielbergian air about it, albeit less *Schindler's List* than *Jurassic Park*. Hawthorne is hoping that his own movie, the Missyplicity documentary, will be picked up by HBO, driving people to the GSC Web site. He has the cloning biz all planned out, from the science to the PR, from the design of the BioBox right down to the logo that goes on top of it. But there's something obviously missing from the plan: GSC's address.

That's why, five days after Madeline's surgery, I find myself cruising in the Corinthian-leather confines of Westhusin's cherried-out Chevy Surburban. Westhusin and Hawthorne are looking for a suitable office to house GSC's reception area, cryotanks, hot room, and computers. Steve Pittman is the real estate agent. He'll find them an office, he tells them. He has, after all, "the equivalent of a Ph.D. in real estate."

Like urban sprawl zones all over the country, College Station is a blur of Applebee's and Taco Bells and minimalls named for the trees plowed under. We've been driving past them all morning.

"Uh, you'll want to hang a right here, Mark," Pittman drawls. Westhusin squints intensely at the oncoming traffic and wheels the SUV into another strip mall. He's out the door, ready to examine the structure, before the engine starts to tick. In the backseat, Hawthorne readies his digicam.

Hawthorne and Westhusin lean against the tinted windows, peering in at the drop ceiling. Around us, cattle ranchers in pickups hunt for parking spaces. "I don't know," Hawthorne says. "It's going to be hard to put Genetic Savings & Clone between a Solar Tan and a Yogurt Plus. It just seems wrong."

Westhusin steps back and surveys the masonry. "Well, it's expensive," he says, swaggering up next to Hawthorne. He's thinking about GSC's bottom line. The two men stare at the brickwork in silence.

Hawthorne had told me earlier that, in the beginning—when GSC was just another idea—he had discovered that video documentaries and bioethics weren't his only concerns that Westhusin found irrelevant; the researcher also had no taste for making money. "Sure," Hawthorne had said, "he knew on some level that he *should* want to make money—but he didn't want to." Hawthorne smiled knowingly. "Now he's a convert."

Back in the car, Pittman is reassessing their needs. What sort of traffic does a cloning business create? What does a gene bank look like? What sorts of zoning, parking, and toilets does it need? Even with his real estate qualifications, Pittman has no reference: GSC breaks the mold.

"Uh, I hear ya on the high-speed Internet wires," he says. "Think y'all are gonna need a loading dock?"

"Probably," Westhusin says. "We might have some freight."

"Ah, okay. A loading dock or a dolly dock?" Pittman's wondering whether they need a ramp, but the unintended Dolly association sends secret smiles through the car.

The smiles fade fast as we pull into the next driveway—a series of corporate office spaces with a shared elevator. As Pittman fumbles for the key, we stare at our feet, trying to imagine the future GSC with this public, industrial-carpeted setting. Down the hall, a door opens. Then another—neighbors uneasily eyeballing the prospective tenants. We are, it must be said, an eclectic bunch for College Station: Hawthorne, overdressed in a suit and holding a camcorder, Westhusin in his rugged flannel, Pittman, and me. What sort of business could we possibly be in?

Hawthorne's starting to get nervous. He finds Texas hard to take on a good day, but this is too weird—he needs a reality check. In desperation, he turns to the only other non-Texas, non-Ph.D. in the hall: me.

"What do *you* think?" he asks.

"I don't know," I say. Pittman can sense our displeasure: His ears prick up.

"No, really," Hawthorne says. "Serious. I'm asking."

"Well," I say, "this just doesn't seem like the sort of place where, you know, folks will want to schlepp their frozen, rotting dogs."

Pittman's eyes go wide.

Back in the passenger seat, he nods to himself, reassessing. "Okay," he says finally. "I'm getting a better sense of what y'all need." He cranes around from his seat. "What I'm thinking is that you guys need a place which is—well, I don't want to say *secret,* but . . ."

"Well, how about *private?*" Hawthorne volunteers.

"Okay," Pittman agrees. "*Private.* Y'all need a location that offers . . . privacy."

About 10 miles down the road from the university, where the urban sprawl has finally trickled to an end, we hit Main Street, Bryan, Texas. It's a big-shouldered, windblown main drag, with abandoned storefronts reminiscent of Steinbeck's Salinas. And there, on a corner across from a Western hat shop, is Hawthorne's dream location: an abandoned, old-timey bank—the real thing— a big federal building with columns and everything. It's earnest as hell, the sort of stone strongbox they used to build when knocking over a bank wasn't just a turn of phrase.

Hawthorne is thrilled. He prances on the pavement, filming the building. He loves the blond concrete facade; he loves the idea of buying a real bank, just as he loves the cute names—Missyplic- ity and BARC and Genetic Savings & Clone.

Westhusin, meanwhile, just hangs back, hands on his hips. He couldn't care less about the facade. In his lab back on campus, Westhusin shares a can of Lysol and a single, squalid toilet with another professor and a half-dozen grad students. What West- husin cares about are tools. He wants ventilation, a loading dock, enough electrical juice to freeze nitrogen.

Hawthorne cares about tools, too, but his have to do with PR and the media. He's already turned down story requests from *The*

New York Times Magazine, The Tonight Show, Dateline NBC, Prime-time Live, The Roseanne Barr Show, and *The Oprah Winfrey Show.* I'm the first, but there will be others, writers and TV people who come to see the clone business with the cute name. And they'll want to see his gene bank. Maybe *this* bank. He knows the future that causes apprehension is the one in which biotech is a blank door in the minimall, symbolized by a little sign that reads CLONATEK or some other hybrid name—words and images mashed monstrously together.

But a bank. You can trust a bank. It's sacred: There's something cathedral-like about its grandiose appearance, something solid about Main Street. The answer to GSC's real estate quandary had been hiding in plain sight. A gene bank stores something more important than money. Hawthorne sees this, and he knows the public will too.

"What does Mark think?" asks Hawthorne.

Westhusin isn't sure. The implications of putting a gene bank in a real bank—like much of what he's taken on with Missyplicity—well, it's just not his department.

Westhusin told me that, when he first met Hawthorne and Mr. E, "the way they thought and saw the world" struck him as "rather silly." He still remembers when they started the project, after the contracts were signed and they flew Missy out on a Learjet. Westhusin was just trying to get things done: Sneak the dog into surgery and get her out of there—in secret. But Hawthorne wanted Westhusin—a scientist!—to organize a band of Texas A&M cadets, wanted them lined up in full uniform on the road from the airport, holding banners that said WELCOME, MISSY! Right there, in front of everybody. "I'm like, this is nuts!" he remembers.

At first he felt that way about the Missyplicity Code of Bioethics, and Hawthorne's video, too, but he's gradually come around to a different viewpoint. The way Westhusin sees it now, cloning is no longer only for scientists: Ready or not, the future is here, and he owns a piece of it.

On the sidewalk, Hawthorne's got his digicam in Westhusin's

face, fishing for a reaction. "Hey," he says, "find out if we can put a sign out front."

"A sign?" Westhusin squints up at the bank's facade. "You want a sign?"

"Yeah. You know, like a bank."

Westhusin shuffles over to Pittman and stuffs his hands in his pockets. "Whatcha think, Steve?" he asks. "Think they'd let us put a sign out front?"

Pittman looks at the two men and scratches his head. "Yeah, well, I'll talk to the guy," he says, walking back to the Chevy. "I betcha we can work something out."

PERMISSIONS ACKNOWLEDGMENTS